I0131560

Digital Java EE 7 Web Application Development

Develop Java enterprise applications to meet the emerging digital standards using Java EE 7

Peter Pilgrim

[PACKT] open source*

PUBLISHING   community experience distilled

BIRMINGHAM - MUMBAI

Digital Java EE 7 Web Application Development

Copyright © 2015 Packt Publishing

All rights reserved. No part of this book may be reproduced, stored in a retrieval system, or transmitted in any form or by any means, without the prior written permission of the publisher, except in the case of brief quotations embedded in critical articles or reviews.

Every effort has been made in the preparation of this book to ensure the accuracy of the information presented. However, the information contained in this book is sold without warranty, either express or implied. Neither the author, nor Packt Publishing, and its dealers and distributors will be held liable for any damages caused or alleged to be caused directly or indirectly by this book.

Packt Publishing has endeavored to provide trademark information about all of the companies and products mentioned in this book by the appropriate use of capitals. However, Packt Publishing cannot guarantee the accuracy of this information.

First published: September 2015

Production reference: 1240915

Published by Packt Publishing Ltd.
Livery Place
35 Livery Street
Birmingham B3 2PB, UK.

ISBN 978-1-78217-664-0

www.packtpub.com

Credits

Author
Peter Pilgrim

Reviewers
Cedric Gatay

Sandeep Nair

Commissioning Editor
Kevin Colaco

Acquisition Editor
Kevin Colaco

Content Development Editor
Anish Sukumaran

Technical Editor
Bharat Patil

Copy Editor
Tasneem Fatehi

Project Coordinator
Mary Alex

Proofreader
Safis Editing

Indexer
Mariammal Chettiyar

Production Coordinator
Nilesh R. Mohite

Cover Work
Nilesh R. Mohite

About the Author

Peter Pilgrim is a professional software developer, designer, and architect. He is an independent contractor living in Milton Keynes, England. Peter is the director and owner of Pilgrim Engineering Architecture Technology Ltd. In the Java community, he is a well-known specialist in the Java Enterprise Edition (Java EE) technology, focused on the server-side and agile digital transformation for blue-chip industry clients and financial services, which include many of London's top-tier investment banks. Peter has had recent real-world experience of working in the GOV.UK project in London by helping his clients to expand their digital by default services to the UK citizens. He, therefore, absorbed experiences from the frontend and backend software development for large consumer bases. Peter is the 91st Oracle Java Champion (February 2007).

Acknowledgment

The result of this book is like the happy delivery of a second newborn baby, because it almost did not make it to birth. Just like the famous 1970's rock song with the title *Nobody's Fault but Mine*, by the mega influential stadium rock band Led Zeppelin (https://en.wikipedia.org/wiki/Nobody%27s_Fault_but_Mine), let me say that this book was my responsibility, and so the delays were all mine. I had Java EE 7 instead of a Bible in my hand to keep me going.

As I finish the last section of this book inside a wonderful villa, Alhaurin el Grande, in sunny Andalucia in Southern Spain, I realize that there are so many people at Packt Publishing to thank for getting me over the finish line. Without these folks, my spectacular and bumbling efforts at writing copy and technical content would be nothing at all. Thanks to Kevin Colaco, Anish Sukumaran, Akshay Nair, Larissa Pinto, Silva Sundaran, Cedric Gatay, Sandeep Nair, Bala Subramanian, and Richard Kennard.

There were countless Java people in the 20 months of this project who provided advice and good suggestions for this second book. I can only mention selected people by name in a random order of importance: Chris Phelps, David Blevins, Roberto Cortez, Beverley Pereira, Josh Juneau, Daniel Byrant, Carl Dea, Alex Heusingfeld, Kazuyoshi Kamitsukasa, David Heffelfinger (a fellow Packt Publishing author), Aslak Knutsen (Red Hat and Arquillian), Yoshio Terado, Todd Costella, Ixchel Ruiz, and Andres Almiray. I want to especially thank Heather Vancura of the Java Community Process and Oracle for organizing the book signings at JavaOne 2015 (*Digital Java EE 7*) and Devoxx UK 2014 (*Java EE 7 Developer Handbook*).

I would like to thank my parents, June and Carl, for giving me the belief and will to carry on.

Finally, I would like to especially thank my endearing partner in life, Ms. Terry Neason. She put up with my constant procrastination about life, work, and the universe. She also provided love, wisdom, emotional support, and everything else when I most needed it.

About the Reviewers

Cedric Gatay has an engineering degree in computer science. He likes well-crafted and unit-tested code. He is an independent contractor located in Tours, France. He is the cofounder of the Code-Troopers software development team (`http://www.code-troopers.com`).

He has a very good understanding of the Java languages. He gives courses at engineering schools and talks at Java Users Groups.

He has been using Java EE technologies in various software projects since 2006. He is also the founder of a collaborative blog for developers called Bloggure, which can be found at `http://www.bloggure.info`.

Sandeep Nair has been working for Liferay for more than seven years and has more than nine years of experience in Java and Java EE technologies overall. He has executed projects using Liferay in various domains such as the construction, financial, and medical fields, providing solutions such as collaboration, enterprise content management, and web content management systems.

He has created a free and open source Google Chartlet plugin for Liferay, which has been downloaded and used by people across 90 countries as per SourceForge statistics. Besides developing, consulting, and implementing solutions, he has also been involved in giving training in Liferay in other countries. Before he jumped into Liferay, he had experience in the Java and Java EE platforms and has worked in EJB, Spring, Struts, Hibernate, and Servicemix. He also has experience in using JitterBit, which is an ETL tool.

He has authored *Liferay Beginner's Guide* and *Liferay Portal 6 Starter* both by Packt Publishing.

He has also reviewed *Liferay 6.2 User Interface Development*, *Packt Publishing*. When he is not coding, he loves to read books and write blogs.

> I would like to thank Mary Alex, who was the coordinator for this book. It was a pleasure working with her.

www.PacktPub.com

Support files, eBooks, discount offers, and more

For support files and downloads related to your book, please visit www.PacktPub.com.

Did you know that Packt offers eBook versions of every book published, with PDF and ePub files available? You can upgrade to the eBook version at www.PacktPub.com and as a print book customer, you are entitled to a discount on the eBook copy. Get in touch with us at service@packtpub.com for more details.

At www.PacktPub.com, you can also read a collection of free technical articles, sign up for a range of free newsletters and receive exclusive discounts and offers on Packt books and eBooks.

https://www2.packtpub.com/books/subscription/packtlib

Do you need instant solutions to your IT questions? PacktLib is Packt's online digital book library. Here, you can search, access, and read Packt's entire library of books.

Why subscribe?

- Fully searchable across every book published by Packt
- Copy and paste, print, and bookmark content
- On demand and accessible via a web browser

Free access for Packt account holders

If you have an account with Packt at www.PacktPub.com, you can use this to access PacktLib today and view 9 entirely free books. Simply use your login credentials for immediate access.

For my dear Terry

Thank you forever for your witty Scottish humor, indefatigable rock of common sense, undying love and wonderful affection.

For my family

"Look up, the sun it's just a cloud away. You're so afraid to cry, but your heart be feeling dry. It's time to change."

Rihanna, Singer, Model and Actress

For the world at large

"If you hire great people and you don't mess them up with a lot of analysis, conversation and speculation and nonsense, if you just get out of their way and shut up, they give you the performance that has made them the great performer that they are. That's the whole secret."

Woody Allen, Film Director

Table of Contents

Preface	**ix**
Chapter 1: Digital Java EE 7	**1**
Working in the digital domain	**2**
Digital Java developer requirements	**2**
Java in the picture	**3**
The impressive growth of JavaScript	**7**
The JavaScript module pattern	8
JavaScript advanced libraries	9
Information architecture and user experience	**11**
Java EE 7 architecture	**13**
Standard platform components and API	14
Xentracker JavaServer Faces	**16**
Application servers	**21**
Summary	**22**
Exercises	**23**
Chapter 2: JavaServer Faces Lifecycle	**25**
Introduction to JSF	**25**
JSF 1.0 and 2.0 history	27
Key JSF 2.2 features	27
Why choose JSF over alternatives?	28
The MVC design pattern	**29**
MVC in JSF	30
Facelets	**31**
The request processing lifecycle	**31**
The execute and render lifecycle	33
Restore View	33
Apply Request Values	34
Process Validations	35
Update Model Values	35

Invoke Application	35
Render Response	36
Event handling	36
A basic JSF example	**36**
A web deployment descriptor	39
JSF XML namespaces	40
A Composition example	**41**
JSF serving resources	44
Expression language	**46**
Immediate and deferred expressions	46
Value expressions	47
Map expressions	49
List expressions	49
Resolving the initial term	50
Method expressions	51
Parameterized method expressions	51
Arithmetic expressions	52
Page navigation	**53**
The navigation rules	53
Wildcards	55
Conditional navigation	56
Static navigation	57
Summary	**58**
Exercises	**58**
Chapter 3: Building JSF Forms	**61**
Create, Retrieve, Update, and Delete	**62**
A basic create entity JSF form	63
The JSF HTML output label	67
The JSF HTML input text	68
The JSF HTML select one menu	68
The JSF HTML select Boolean checkbox	69
The JSF HTML command button	70
The backing bean controller	71
Data service	74
JSF custom tags	**77**
The HTML render kit custom tags	77
The core JSF custom tags	79
The template composition custom tags	81
Common attributes	82
Displaying a list collection of objects	**82**
Enhanced date time entry	85
Editing data	**91**
Removing data	**97**

JSF and CDI scopes	**101**
Bean scopes	102
Summary	**103**
Exercises	**104**
Chapter 4: JSF Validation and AJAX	**107**
Validation methods	**107**
Server-side validation	108
Client-side validation	108
Faces messages	**109**
Validation	**111**
Constraining form content with Bean Validation	111
Validating user input with JSF	117
Customizing JSF validation	122
Custom validation methods	125
Defining custom validators	127
Validating groups of properties	130
Converters	136
Validating immediately with AJAX	142
Validating groups of input fields	146
AJAX custom tag in depth	149
A partial JSF lifecycle	**150**
Handling views	**151**
Invoking controller methods	151
Parameterized method invocations	151
Passing parameters to the controller	154
Invoking an action event listener	156
Redirection pages	157
Debugging the JSF content	158
Summary	**159**
Exercises	**160**
Chapter 5: Conversations and Journeys	**163**
Digital e-commerce applications	**165**
Conversational scope	**165**
Conversation timeout and serialization	167
The conversation scope controller	**168**
The Entity-Control-Boundary design pattern	170
The customer journey	170
Entity classes	173
Data service	175
Page views	**176**
An initial page view	177

Getting started page view   180
Contact details page view   181
Your rate page view   183
    HTML5 friendly support   184
    Using AJAX for a partial update   185
    Binding components   185
    Updating areas with AJAX partial updates   189
The address page view   193
The confirmation page view   194
The completion page view   197
Utility classes   198
Composite custom components   **200**
Components with XHTML   201
Composite components and custom components   206
Composite component with self-generating tag   208
Summary   **212**
Exercises   **212**
Chapter 6: JSF Flows and Finesse   **215**
What is Faces Flow?   **216**
Flow definitions and lifecycle   **216**
Simple Implicit Faces Flows   **217**
Implicit navigation   218
A Flow scoped bean   219
Facelet views   220
Handling view expired   **226**
A comparison with conversational scoped beans   227
Capturing the lifecycle of flow scoped beans   228
Declarative and nested flows   **228**
The flow node terminology   228
An XML flow definition description file   229
    A flow definition tag   230
    A mandatory flow return tag   230
    A view page tag   231
    An optional start page tag   231
    Switch, conditional, and case tags   231
A nested flow example   232
    XML flow definitions   234
    Flow beans   238
    Page views   240
A real-world example   **244**
Ensure the application populates the database   245
Securing page views and flows   247

Resource Library Contracts   **253**
  Static Resource Library Contract references   255
  Dynamic Resource Library Contract references   256
Advice for flows   **258**
Summary   **259**
Exercises   **259**

Chapter 7: Progressive JavaScript Frameworks and Modules   **261**
  JavaScript essentials   **262**
    Creating objects   262
      The console log   263
    Writing JavaScript object constructors   264
    The JavaScript property notations   265
    Dealing with a null and undefined reference pointer   266
    The JavaScript truth   267
    Runtime type information   268
    The JavaScript functions   268
  Introducing the jQuery framework   **270**
    Including jQuery in a JSF application   270
    jQuery ready function callbacks   271
    Acting on the jQuery selectors   272
      Manipulating the DOM elements   274
      Animation   275
  The RequireJS framework   **278**
    A RequireJS configuration   280
    An application module   282
    Defining modules   283
  UnderscoreJS   **285**
    The for-each operations   286
    The filter operations   287
    The map operations   288
    The flatten operations   288
    The reduction operations   290
  GruntJS   **290**
  Summary   **294**
  Exercises   **294**

Chapter 8: AngularJS and Java RESTful Services   **299**
  Single-page applications   **300**
  The caseworker application   **301**
  AngularJS   **302**
    How does AngularJS work?   304

Caseworker overview   **308**
  Caseworker main view   308
Project organization   **314**
Application main controller   **316**
New case record controller   **321**
  The case record modal view template   324
New task record controller   **327**
  The task modal view template   329
State change   **330**
  The template view code   332
  Toggling the task display state   334
Server-side Java   **335**
  Entity objects   335
  RESTful communication   337
    Retrieval of case records   337
    Creating a case record   340
    Updating a case record   341
    Creating a task record   342
    Updating a task record   344
    Deleting a task record   345
  WebSocket communication   346
    AngularJS client side   346
    Server-side WebSocket endpoints   348
Consider your design requirements   **350**
  Array collection of single-page applications   350
  Hierarchical collection of single-page applications   351
Summary   **351**
Exercises   **352**
Chapter 9: Java EE MVC Framework   **355**
Java EE 8 MVC   **356**
MVC controllers   **357**
  MVC page views and templates   360
  MVC models   363
  Response and redirects   364
    Reconfiguring the view root   366
Handlebars Java   **366**
  A compiled-inline template servlet   367
  Template expressions in Handlebars   368
  The welcome controller   370
  The custom view engine   372
  The product controller   374
    Block expressions   376

The retrieve and edit operations	378
The JAX-RS global validation	382
An MVC binding result validation	384
Design considerations	**387**
Majority server-side templating	388
Majority client-side templating	388
Shared templating	389
Summary	**389**
Exercises	**390**
Appendix A: JSF with HTML5, Resources, and Faces Flows	**391**
An HTML5 friendly markup	**391**
The pass-through attributes	391
The pass-through elements	393
Resource identifiers	**394**
Resource Library Contracts	**395**
A Faces servlet	**396**
Reconfiguration of the resource paths	397
A JSF-specific configuration	398
Internationalization	**399**
Resource bundles	399
Message bundles	401
A browser configured locale	401
An application controlled locale	402
An individual page controlled locale	402
A web deployment descriptor	**402**
Programmatic Faces Flows	**403**
View types	403
The Faces Flows programmatic interface	**404**
ViewNode	406
ReturnNode	407
MethodCall	408
FlowCall	408
SwitchNode	410
NavigationCase node	411
Builder types	412
Appendix B: From Request to Response	**413**
HTTP	**413**
An HTTP request	414
An HTTP response	414

Java Enterprise Architectures   **415**
Standard Java EE web architecture   415
Extended architectures   417
Containerless systems   419
Microservices   421
To be full stack or not   **423**
Appendix C: Agile Performance – Working inside Digital Teams   **425**
Digital teams and adaptation   **425**
Roles   **427**
The development perspective   427
A Java engineer   427
An interface developer engineer   427
Quality assurance tester   428
Software in developer test   428
The design perspective   428
A creative designer   429
A usability experience engineer   429
A content strategist   430
The architectural perspective   430
A data scientist   430
A technical architect   431
The management perspective   432
A business analyst and liaison officer   432
A project manager/scrum master   432
A digital development manager   433
Software quality   **433**
Class versus form   **434**
Appendix D: Curated References   **437**
Service delivery   **437**
Agile and leadership   **438**
Architecture   **439**
User interface   **439**
Java EE and JVM technology   **441**
Index   **445**

Preface

This is a book about the Java EE 7 platform and web digital development, and it is a continuation of the first book *Java EE 7 Developer Handbook*. The entire focus of this tome is the space and software architecture between the frontend technologies and business logic tier. While there was a lack of printing space and working balance between life and time for this subject in my first book, in this book *Digital Java EE 7*, there is plenty of effort and determination to write exclusively about the Java *presentation tier*. This book was written for the developers who want to become superior and adept at building a web application on JVM with the standard Java EE 7 platform.

This book mostly covers the presentation tier from the Java standard's point of view. Therefore, there are entire chapters dedicated to JavaServer Faces as it is the most important and oldest dedicated web framework on the Java EE 7 platform. Even though the technology has been around since 2004, there are commercial organizations and businesses around the world that rely on JSF. They range from blue-chip companies to well-respected investment banks. Yet, with the Java EE 7 release, JSF 2.2 has several key features that web developers will enjoy and find incredibly helpful such as the HTML5 friendly markup support and Faces Flow.

As a reader, it is my hope that you will become enlightened on the path to build software that enables you to stride up the mountainous paths of the contemporary Java web technology and that you will gain the qualification of an accomplished master (or mistress) in your mind.

So, starting with JSF, we will learn about the framework with a thorough introduction to its concepts. We will progress to the building of the JSF input forms and learn how to validate their input in several ways. The most important task of developing Create Retrieve Update and Delete (CRUD) for JSF web applications will hit the nail squarely on the head. Afterwards, we will add more style and finesse to the JSF applications. On the way, we will write applications that validate with AJAX for an immediate effect. We will continue our adventure into the elegant world of conversational scope backing bean controllers. We will find that these are handy little things that we will map together and capture our stakeholders' customer journeys. Finally, we will learn about Faces Flows, which are a standout addition in JSF 2.2.

No Java web technology book would be complete without telling the reader about the JavaScript programming language and emerging technologies. Many senior Java engineers would agree that Java on the Web has — to some degree — conceded ground on the presentation tier to the JavaScript client-side frameworks. Building REST/ UI frontend applications are now so common that it is difficult for the so-called digital Java engineer to ignore the influence of jQuery, RequireJS, and others. There are several known JavaScript frameworks out there in the wild. In this book, we will cover AngularJS. We will step into the middle of that blustery windy bridge in between the two major landscapes of Java, JVM, and JavaScript. I can't promise you that it will not be scary, but you might find yourself pleasantly surprised by the way that you will stand comfortably and negotiate the ledges and handholds between both the JAX-RS services and AngularJS controllers.

At the far end of this book, we have a special just-in-time release for you. We dedicate an entire single chapter to the upcoming Java EE 8 Model-View-Controller, which may become an alternative sizzling emerald in the way we build future REST/UI applications. Beyond this book's finish line, we have put together three essential appendices that I hope will act as excellent reference material.

At the end of each chapter, we have dedicated a special section to educational exercises, which I hope you find relevant and decent, and you have fun learning while your thought processes are being conveniently stretched. This was written for you, the Java web developer on a mission to innovate. Enjoy!

You can find my blog at `http://www.xenonique.co.uk/blog/`. You can follow me on Twitter at `@peter_pilgrim`.

The source code for this book is available on GitHub at `https://github.com/peterpilgrim/digital-javaee7`.

What this book covers

Chapter 1, *Digital Java EE 7*, introduces the topic of the enterprise Java platform with a perspective to web technology. We will see a brief JSF example, study the JavaScript module pattern, and examine the Java EE modern web architecture.

Chapter 2, *JavaServer Faces Lifecycle*, starts with the essential elements of the JSF framework. We will learn about the JSF phases and the lifecycle, custom tags, common attributes, and expression language.

Chapter 3, *Building JSF Forms*, gets us started with how to build the JSF Create-Update-Retrieve-Delete application forms. We will build the forms in a modern web method with JSF custom tags around the Bootstrap HTML5 framework.

Chapter 4, *JSF Validation and AJAX*, dives deep into the validation of the customer's data from the input form. We will study the various ways of checking the data from the backend and the persistence layer to the frontend with client-side AJAX.

Chapter 5, *Conversations and Journeys*, expands our JSF knowledge into the conversational scoped beans. We will learn how to map a digital customer's journey to a controller and apply other CDI scopes to our work.

Chapter 6, *Faces Flows with Finesse*, covers the JSF 2.2 release key highlight of the flow scope bean. We will grasp the differences between the Faces Flows and conversational scope beans, and along the way, add user-friendly features to our application.

Chapter 7, *Progressive JavaScript Frameworks and Modules*, provides you with a quick overview of modern JavaScript programming from a Java engineer's point of view. We will get up to speed with jQuery and other relevant frameworks such as RequireJS and UnderscoreJS.

Chapter 8, *AngularJS and Java RESTful Services*, builds on our new JavaScript knowledge. We will approach the writing of single page architecture applications with the popular AngularJS framework. We will also gain experience of writing the JAX-RS service endpoints.

Chapter 9, *Java EE MVC Framework*, takes a look under the hood of the upcoming Java EE 8 Model-View-Controller framework. We will utilize the port of the Handlebars templating framework in Java.

Appendix A, *JSF with HTML5, Resources, and Faces Flows*, provides references for using HTML5 support in JSF, Resource Library Contracts, and programmatic Faces Flows. It also includes important information on internationalization with the message and resource bundles.

Appendix B, From Request to Response, provides intense reference material on the architecture of the modern Java enterprise application. It answers the question about what happens when a web request is received and eventually when a response is sent back to the client.

Appendix C, Agile Performance – Working inside Digital Teams, covers the gamut of personalities and the variety of roles in modern digital and agile software development teams.

Appendix D, Curated References, is a set of specially selected bibliographic references, resources and links for further study.

What you need for this book

For this book, you will need the following list of software on a laptop or desktop PC:

- Java SE 8 (Java Development Kit) http://java.oracle.com/
- GlassFish 4.1 (https://glassfish.java.net/)
- A decent Java Editor or IDE for coding, such as IntelliJ 14 or better (https://www.jetbrains.com/idea/), Eclipse Kepler or better (http://www.eclipse.org/kepler/), or NetBeans 8.1 or better (https://netbeans.org/)
- Gradle 2.6 or better for building the software, which is a part of this book (http://gradle.org/)
- Chrome Web Browser with Developer Tools (https://developer.chrome.com/devtools)
- Firefox Developer Tools (https://developer.mozilla.org/en/docs/Tools)
- Chris Pederick's Web Developer and User Agent Switcher extensions (http://chrispederick.com/work/web-developer/)

Who this book is for

You should be a Java developer with a good command over the programming language. You should already know about classes, inheritance, and Java Collections. Therefore, this book is pitched at intermediate Java developers. You may have 1-2 years of experience in Java SE core development. You should have an understanding of the core Java EE platform, although an in-depth knowledge is not strictly required. You should be comfortable with Java persistence, Java servlets, and deployment of the WAR files to an application server such as GlassFish or WildFly or an equivalent server.

This book is aimed at people who want to learn JavaServer Faces or update their existing knowledge. You may or may not have experience in JavaScript programming; however, there is a dedicated start up topic in this book. This is mostly a Java EE web development book but covering AngularJS requires you to learn or reapply JavaScript coding skills.

Whether you come from a digital environment such as an agency or software house or have just stared a professional job with web development in mind, you will find this book a great help if you have to work with other staff members in your team. You will see industry terms, but I have kept the mentioning of them to a minimum so that you can focus on the technology at hand and achieve your learning goals. However, experts may recognize certain industry ideas creeping into the questions at the end of every of chapter.

Conventions

In this book, you will find a number of styles of text that distinguish between different kinds of information. Here are some examples of these styles, and an explanation of their meaning.

Code words in text, database table names, folder names, filenames, file extensions, pathnames, dummy URLs, user input, and Twitter handles are shown as follows: "We can include other contexts through the use of the `include` directive."

A block of code is set as follows:

```
[default]
exten => s,1,Dial(Zap/1|30)
exten => s,2,Voicemail(u100)
exten => s,102,Voicemail(b100)
exten => i,1,Voicemail(s0)
```

When we wish to draw your attention to a particular part of a code block, the relevant lines or items are set in bold:

```
[default]
exten => s,1,Dial(Zap/1|30)
exten => s,2,Voicemail(u100)
exten => s,102,Voicemail(b100)
exten => i,1,Voicemail(s0)
```

Any command-line input or output is written as follows:

```
# cp /usr/src/asterisk-addons/configs/cdr_mysql.conf.sample
    /etc/asterisk/cdr_mysql.conf
```

New terms and **important words** are shown in bold. Words that you see on the screen, in menus or dialog boxes for example, appear in the text like this: "clicking the **Next** button moves you to the next screen".

> Warnings or important notes appear in a box like this.

> Tips and tricks appear like this.

Reader feedback

Feedback from our readers is always welcome. Let us know what you think about this book—what you liked or may have disliked. Reader feedback is important for us to develop titles that you really get the most out of.

To send us general feedback, simply send an e-mail to feedback@packtpub.com, and mention the book title via the subject of your message.

If there is a topic that you have expertise in and you are interested in either writing or contributing to a book, see our author guide on www.packtpub.com/authors.

Customer support

Now that you are the proud owner of a Packt book, we have a number of things to help you to get the most from your purchase.

Downloading the example code

You can download the example code files for all Packt books you have purchased from your account at http://www.packtpub.com. If you purchased this book elsewhere, you can visit http://www.packtpub.com/support and register to have the files e-mailed directly to you.

Errata

Although we have taken every care to ensure the accuracy of our content, mistakes do happen. If you find a mistake in one of our books—maybe a mistake in the text or the code—we would be grateful if you would report this to us. By doing so, you can save other readers from frustration and help us improve subsequent versions of this book. If you find any errata, please report them by visiting http://www.packtpub.com/submit-errata, selecting your book, clicking on the **errata submission form** link, and entering the details of your errata. Once your errata are verified, your submission will be accepted and the errata will be uploaded on our website, or added to any list of existing errata, under the Errata section of that title. Any existing errata can be viewed by selecting your title from http://www.packtpub.com/support.

Piracy

Piracy of copyright material on the Internet is an ongoing problem across all media. At Packt, we take the protection of our copyright and licenses very seriously. If you come across any illegal copies of our works, in any form, on the Internet, please provide us with the location address or website name immediately so that we can pursue a remedy.

Please contact us at copyright@packtpub.com with a link to the suspected pirated material.

We appreciate your help in protecting our authors, and our ability to bring you valuable content.

Questions

You can contact us at questions@packtpub.com if you are having a problem with any aspect of the book, and we will do our best to address it.

1
Digital Java EE 7

"Nobody is madder than me about the fact that the website isn't working"

President Barack Obama, 21st October 2013 in a Rose Garden speech

Digital adaptation is a sign of the times for the software developers who are involved with contemporary web design. The phrase Digital Transformation is yet another buzzword pandered around by business executives. Enterprise Java developers do not have to be afraid of this new digital world, because we are involved in building the most exciting software on this planet. We are building software for users, customers, and people. Replace the word *Digital* with *User Experience* and you will instantly get what all the fuss is about.

So let's remove the marketing terms once and for all. Digital transformation takes a non-online business process and produces the equivalent online version. Of course, a ponderous ugly caterpillar does not suddenly morph into a beautiful Red Admiral butterfly overnight, without life experience and genetics. It takes the considerable skills of developers, designers, and architects to adapt, transform, and apply the business requirements to technology. In recent times, the software profession has recognized the validity of users and their experiences. Essentially, we have matured.

This book is about developers who can mature and want to mature. These are the developers who can embrace Java technologies and are sympathetic to the relevant web technologies.

In this chapter, we will start our developer's journey with the requirements of the web developer, engineers at the so-called front-end, and the digital and creative industry. We will survey the enterprise Java platform and ask the question, where does Java fit in? We will look at the growth of JavaScript. We will learn about the Java EE 7 modern web architecture. To conclude, we will finish with a simple JavaServer Faces example.

Working in the digital domain

Working in a digital domain requires the business to move beyond legacy and institutionalized thinking. It is no longer acceptable to slap together some HTML, a few links to press releases, and some white papers, bundle together some poorly written JavaScript code, and call it your web site. That strategy was suitable, once upon a time. Nowadays, private and public corporations, and even the government, plan web technology for the long-tail in business by focusing on high usability and content (`https://en.wikipedia.org/wiki/Long_tail`). If your web technology is hard to use, then you will not make any money and no citizen will use your online service.

Digital Java developer requirements

As a digital developer, you definitely need powerful development machines, capable of running several of the applications simultaneously. You need to be strong and assertive, and insist on your experience being the best that can be. You are responsible for your own learning. A digital developer should not be hamstrung with a laptop that is fit for the sales and marketing division.

Your workhorse must be able to physically handle the demands for every single tool in the following list:

Items	Explanation
Java SE 8 (or, at least, Java SE 7)	Java SE 8 was released on March 18th, 2014 and it provides Lambdas, where functions are first class citizens. Java 7 is an acceptable alternative for the short term and for a cautious business IT director.
Java EE 7	GlassFish 4.1 application server is the reference implementation for Java EE 7, but there is a lack of professional support. Alternatively, the IT directors may consider Red Hat JBoss WildFly 9 that does have Service Level Agreements.
Integrated Development Environment	IDE like IntelliJ IDEA 14, Eclipse Kepler 4.3, or NetBeans 8
Adobe Creative Suite	Adobe Photoshop CC (and sometimes Adobe Illustrator) are the de facto graphics work inside the creative digital media industry.
Cucumber or Selenium	Cucumber is a behavior-driven development for testing the features of a web application. It is written against Ruby programming and thus, requires that environment and the tool chain.

Items	Explanation
A suite of modern web browsers	Mozilla Firefox, Google Chrome, and Internet Explorer 10 and the de facto web browsers that support HTML5 and the latest W3C standard. Required Windows 10 recently launched with Edge.
Developer plug-in for web browsers	It really helps to have a JavaScript debugger, HTML, and a CSS element inspector in your tool set. Plug-ins such as Chrome developer tool ease digital engineering.
Text editor	A lightweight text editor to handle small-scale work is often very useful for editing the JavaScript, Puppet (or Chef) scripts, as well as HTML and CSS files.

By just examining this table of software, it is no wonder that the average business-supplied company laptop is so ill-equipped to handle this development.

Digital engineers are smart, professional engineers

I personally have a 2012 MacBook Pro Retina edition with 16 GB of RAM, 512 GB static hard disk drive as my main machine. Some of my clients have supplied me with badly configured machines. One particular client in finance gave me a Dell Latitude with only 4 GB RAM, running Windows 7 Professional. This developer machine was so poor in performance that I had to complain many times. Inform the decision makers in your business that digital workers need adequate development machines, fit for the purpose of engineering and designing great user experiences.

Let's switch from creativity and design to the Java platform.

Java in the picture

The Java platform is in widespread use today. It was the first commercial language featuring JVM and byte-code with garbage collection, sandbox security, and networking capability to be adopted by business. Java's greatest strength is that businesses trust this platform to power enterprise applications in server-side computing. Since 1995, this strength in depth has grown to such a level that the platform is seen as very mature and mainstream. The disadvantage of being part of the main herd is that innovation takes a while to happen; as the steward of the platform, earlier Sun Microsystems and now Oracle Corporation, always guarantee backward compatibility and the maintenance of standards through the Java Community Process.

The JVM is the crown jewel of the platform. Java is the mother programming language that runs on the JVM. Other languages such as Scala, Groovy, and Clojure also run the JVM. These alternative JVM languages are popular, because they introduced many functional programming ideas to the mainstream developers. Functional programming primitives such as closures and comprehensions and languages such as Scala demonstrated a pure object-oriented model and mix-ins. These languages benefited from an easy interaction tool called **REPL**.

> In fact, Java SE 9 will most likely have **Read-Evaluate-Print-Loop** (REPL). Keep an eye on the progression of the official OpenJDK project Kulla at `http://openjdk.java.net/projects/kulla/`.

Released in 2014, Java SE 8 features functional interfaces, otherwise known as Lambdas, which bring the benefits of closures and functional blocks to the main JVM language on the platform.

Whatever programming language you choose to develop your next enterprise application, Java or Scala or otherwise, I think you can bet on the JVM being around for a long time, at least for the next decade or so. The PermGen issue finally ended in Java SE 8, because there is no permanent generation in there. Before Java SE 8, PermGen was the source of many memory leaks (slow and steady memory hogs). This was also the dedicated space where the JVM would load classes into a piece of memory such as the Java Runtime (such as `java.lang.String`, `java.lang.System`, or `java.util.collection.ConcurrentHashMap`). However, classes were rarely unloaded or compacted in size, especially during a very long execution of a JVM. If you are running websites 24/7 over a number of days or even weeks at a time with some degree of user interaction, then there is a good chance that your applications (and their application server) could run out of memory (`java.lang.OutOfMemoryError: PermGen space`). The permanent generation was the storage area reserved for internal representation of Java classes in releases before JDK 8. For long running application servers and JVM processes, it was possible for references to metadata and classes to remain in permanent generation memory even after if WAR/EAR applications were undeployed and uninstalled. In Java SE 8, the reserved allocation of memory for the Java classes is adaptive. The JVM can now gracefully manage its own memory allocations and represents at least 10 percent efficiency improvement as compared to the previous versions.

In Java SE 8, we have a Garbage First Garbage collector known as G1, which is a parallel collector. Java SE 8 also includes new byte codes to improve the efficiency of dynamic languages such as JRuby and Clojure. The InvokeDynamic byte code from JDK 7 and the Method Handle API were particularly instrumented for the Nashorn, an implementation of JavaScript (ECMAScript Edition 6).

[
As of April 2015, Oracle stopped releasing updates to Java SE 7 to its public download sites. Please pass on this information to your CTO!
]

There is no doubt that the Java platform will continually serve digital engineers as a back-end technology. It may even occur to businesses to take advantage of the client-side technology in Java SE 8 that is now delivered with the platform. JavaFX is an interesting solution, but outside the scope of this book.

We should introduce some code now. The following is a Lambda function for Java SE 8:

```java
public interface PaymentIssuer {
  public void allocate( int id );
}


@ApplicationScoped
public class CreditCardTicketTracker() {
  // Rely on CDI product factory to inject the correct type
  @Inject PaymentIssuer issuer;

  public void processTickets( List<Ticket> ticketBatch ) {
  final LocalDate dt = LocalDate.now().plusDays(2)
    ticketBatch.stream()
      .filter(
        t -> t.isAvailable()  &&
        t -> t.paymentType == PaymentType.CreditCard &&
        dt.isBefore(DateUtils.asLocalDate(
      t.getConcertDate()))))
        .map(t -> t.getAllocation().allocateToTicket(t))
        .forEach(allocation -> issuer.allocate(allocation));
  }
}
```

If this code looks very strange to you, then you are probably not yet familiar with Lambda expressions. We have a **Context and Dependency Injection (CDI)** bean, which is application scoped, called `CreditCardTicketTracker`. It has a method called `processTickets()` that accepts a list collection of Ticket objects. The exact type of Ticket is unimportant. What is important, however, is the `PaymentIssuer` type that the CDI injects into a **Plain Old Java Object (POJO)**. The method `processTickets()` invokes the stream API of the Java SE 8 collection. Essentially, invoking the method `parallelStream()` causes processing on each element in the Java collection with multiple threads working in a concurrent operation. The Lambda expressions are on the `filter()`, `map()`, and the `forEach()` methods of the updated Collection API.

Moreover, the code reads close enough to written English. Let me now explain the method `processTickets()`. An outside component is sending batches of concert tickets for processing to our component `CreditCardTicketTracker`. For each ticket in the batch, we filter only those tickets that are marked as available, which have already been paid for using a credit card, and where the concert date is two or more days after the current date. By the way, we take advantage of `java.time.LocalDate`, which is new in Java SE 8.

So, very briefly, a Lambda expression is an anonymous method and the syntax follows this format:

```
( [[Type1] param1 [,  [Type2] param2 ....]] ) -> {
  /*
   * Do something here and return a result type
   * including void
   */
}
```

A lambda expression can be parameterless; therefore, the Java compiler can infer that an expression can be substituted for the `java.lang.Runnable` type. If there are parameters, the compiler can infer the types of the arguments given enough information. Therefore, the Type1 and Type2 declarations are optional. A Lambda must return a single instance of a type or it may be void, which means the curly braces may be left off.

Lambda expressions are concise, timesaving, and allow functions to be passed to the libraries. For more information, consult the excellent Java Tutorial for Java SE 8 on Oracle's website (`http://docs.oracle.com/javase/tutorial/java/index.html`). As we have seen in the previous example, your application could use the parallel stream facility in the collection to achieve concurrency.

One immediate use of the Lambda expressions is to replace the inner classes that call the managed thread services, `javax.enterprise.concurrent.ManagedExecutorService` in Java EE 7. We know that Java has multiple-thread support, networking, and security. Let us turn our attention to the client side.

The impressive growth of JavaScript

Over the past decade, digital engineers have adopted a healthy respect for JavaScript as a programming language. Despite its many shortcomings, developers have learned to write modular applications that truly exploit the functionality of this programming language, which executes inside web browsers and servers universally. The framework that eventually changed the game was something called jQuery. It was then written by John Resig in order to simplify the client-side scripting of HTML in JavaScript. Released in 2006, it is the most popular framework in the JavaScript library today.

The greatest innovation in jQuery was the selector engine called Sizzle that allowed JavaScript programming to filter out the DOM elements by declarations, allow traversal, and perform algorithm through a type of collection comprehension. It introduced a new direction for JavaScript development.

It is not just jQuery that has been driving JavaScript. In truth, the progress can be tracked back to the re-discovery of AJAX techniques and the emergence of several competing frameworks such **Script.aculo.us** and **Prototype**.

The following is an example of a JavaScript code that uses jQuery:

```
var xenonique = xenonique || {}

xenonique.Main = function($) {
    // Specifies the page marker ID
    var siteNavigationMarker = '#navigationMarker';

    var init = function() {
      $(document).ready( function() {
        $('#scrollToTheTopArrow').click( function() {
        $('html, body').animate({
              scrollTop: 0
          }, 750);
        })
      })
    }

    var oPublic = {
       init: init,
        siteNavigationMarker: siteNavigationMarker,
    };

    return oPublic;
}(jQuery);
```

Please do not worry if you are struggling to understand the preceding code and certainly do not run away from this piece of JavaScript. The code shows the modern idiom of developing JavaScript in a good, reliable, and maintainable way without using global variables. It perfectly illustrates the module technique of keeping the JavaScript variables and function methods inside an enclosing scope. Scope is the most important item to understand in JavaScript programming.

The preceding JavaScript code creates a namespace called **xenonique**, which exists in its own scope. We make use of the `Module Pattern` to create a module called `Main`, which depends on jQuery. There is a method defined called `init()`, which executes a jQuery selector with an anonymous function. Whenever the user clicks on the HTML element with the ID `#scrollToTheArrow`, the web page scrolls the top automatically in 750 milliseconds.

The JavaScript module pattern

The critical technique in this code, as elaborated by Douglas Crockford in his seminal book, *JavaScript: The Good Parts*, is to create a module that acts like a singleton object. The module is invoked by the interpreter immediately because of the parameter argument statement at the end of the declaration, which relies on a jQuery instance.

Let's simplify the module for effect:

```
var xenonique = xenonique || {}

xenonique.Main = function($) {
    /* ...a */
    return oPublic;
}(jQuery);
```

The module `xenonique.Main` in the preceding code is actually a JavaScript closure, which has its own scope. Thus, the module pattern simulates the private and public members and functions. The return value of the closure is an object that defines the publicly accessible properties and methods. In the module, the `init()` method and the `siteNavigationMarker` property are publicly accessible to other JavaScript variables. Closure is preserved in the return object with the JavaScript execution context and, therefore, all private and public methods will exist throughout the lifetime of the application.

JavaScript advanced libraries

For some engineers, writing custom JavaScript, even around a jQuery selector, is too detailed and low-level. AngularJS is an example of a JavaScript framework that takes the evolution of client-side programming further along its trajectory. AngularJS notably features two-way data binding of the DOM elements declaratively to each other or to the JavaScript module code. The creators of AngularJS intended to bring the **Model-View-Controller** (**MVC**) design pattern and the separation of concerns to web application development, as well as inspire behavior driven-design through a built-in testing framework.

AngularJS (`http://angularjs.org/`) is one of the highlights of the new modern movement in JavaScript. Whilst there is a JavaScript library being invented every week, it seems, the standouts in the professional development life also include GruntJS, Node.js, RequireJS, and UnderscoreJS.

GruntJS (`http://gruntjs.com/`) is particularly interesting, as it works like Make in C or C++ and Maven or Gradle in the Java space. Grunt is a JavaScript task management system and it can build applications, execute unit tests, compile Sass and LESS files to CSS, and perform other duties with the resources. It can also invoke utilities that will compress JavaScript using a process called minification, and optimize them into ugly (hard-to-reverse-engineer) files for both speed and some degree of security.

> Sass (`http://sass-lang.com/`) and LESS (`http://lesscss.org/`) are CSS preprocessors used by designers and developers. These tools transform reusable common-style configurations into specific device and site style sheets.

For a new digital engineer, I think you will, perhaps, find this discussion overwhelming. So I will summarize it in the following table:

JavaScript Item	Description
jQuery	The most important open source JavaScript library for manipulating the DOM and for selecting elements by ID and name. It has a very popular plugin architecture with many products on offer. `http://jquery.org/`
jQuery UI	This is a popular plugin that extends the standard jQuery, and adds additional animations, customizable themes, and UI components including a date calendar picker. `http://jqueryui.org/`

JavaScript Item	Description
RequireJS	A dependency management framework of a JavaScript file and modules loader. This framework has the ability to optimize bundles of modules for larger applications, especially through Asynchronous Module Definition API. `http://requirejs.org/`
Nashorn	A JavaScript runtime engine built by Oracle and shipped as standard with Java SE 8. Nashorn runs on the JVM, it is open source, and a part of the OpenJDK project. `http://openjdk.java.net/projects/nashorn/`
Dojo Toolkit and microkernel architecture	A refactored JavaScript modular framework and toolkit full of widget components. It makes use of AMD for fast download speed and the efficiency of modules to only load what is necessary for the client-side application. Dojo Toolkit has useful graphs and visualization components. `http://dojotoolkit.org/`
Ember JS	Ember is a framework for building client-side web applications. It uses JavaScript for invoking the templates to generate page content. Ember is aimed at the mobile developers who want to compete with native applications. The framework makes use of the Handlebars templating library. `http://emberjs.com/`
Handlebars JS	Handlebar is a JavaScript templating library for client-side web applications. The templates, on first examination, resemble HTML with the addition of the expressions tokens. Those familiar with AngularJS will see that the expressions are very similar in syntax. `http://www.handlebarsjs.com/`
Underscore JS	This is a JavaScript developer library that brings functional programming ideas and constructs into the language through an API. It has over 80 library helpers that include methods like select, map, flatMap, filter, reduce, forEach, and invoke. `http://underscorejs.org/`
Backbone JS	A JavaScript Framework that adds a modeling aspect to the client-side applications. It provides models with key-value binding to DOM and custom application events. Models and collections can be saved to the server. Backbone also provides views with declarative data binding. In many ways, this framework is seen as a viable competitor to AngularJS. `http://backbonejs.org/`

JavaScript Item	Description
Angular JS	AngularJS is a JavaScript framework that provides two-way data binding between the DOM elements and custom JavaScript module code. It has a Model-View-Controller architecture and also provides support for custom HTML components through a feature called directives. Angular JS is also strongly supported by the developers who currently work at Google, and therefore, it is a famous JavaScript framework. Its strength lies in single-page web applications and declarative programming. `http://angularjs.org/`

As you can see, there are a lot of challenges to face if you happen to work with front-end (interface developer) engineers versed in many of the above technologies. An enterprise Java or server-side engineer has to be aware of other peoples' skill sets. (See the worker roles in *Appendix C, Agile Performance – Working inside Digital Teams*).

Information architecture and user experience

The digital worker is confronted today by multiple inputs and customer design requirements. One of those is the so-called **Information Architecture (IA)**.This is essentially about the static structure of a website, and describes the flow in order to obtain the best customer-user experience. Information architecture models the shared visual and contextual data that a customer can see in a web page, application, and environment.

Most Java engineers might have seen IA diagrams being passed around among the designers and business analysts during business team discussions. It would be an error to simply gloss over or ignore these discussions, which is why a digital developer ought to have some awareness about how, why, and where is the IA applied. It looks a bit like the visualization of a site map. The following is an example of an information architecture diagram for an e-commerce application:

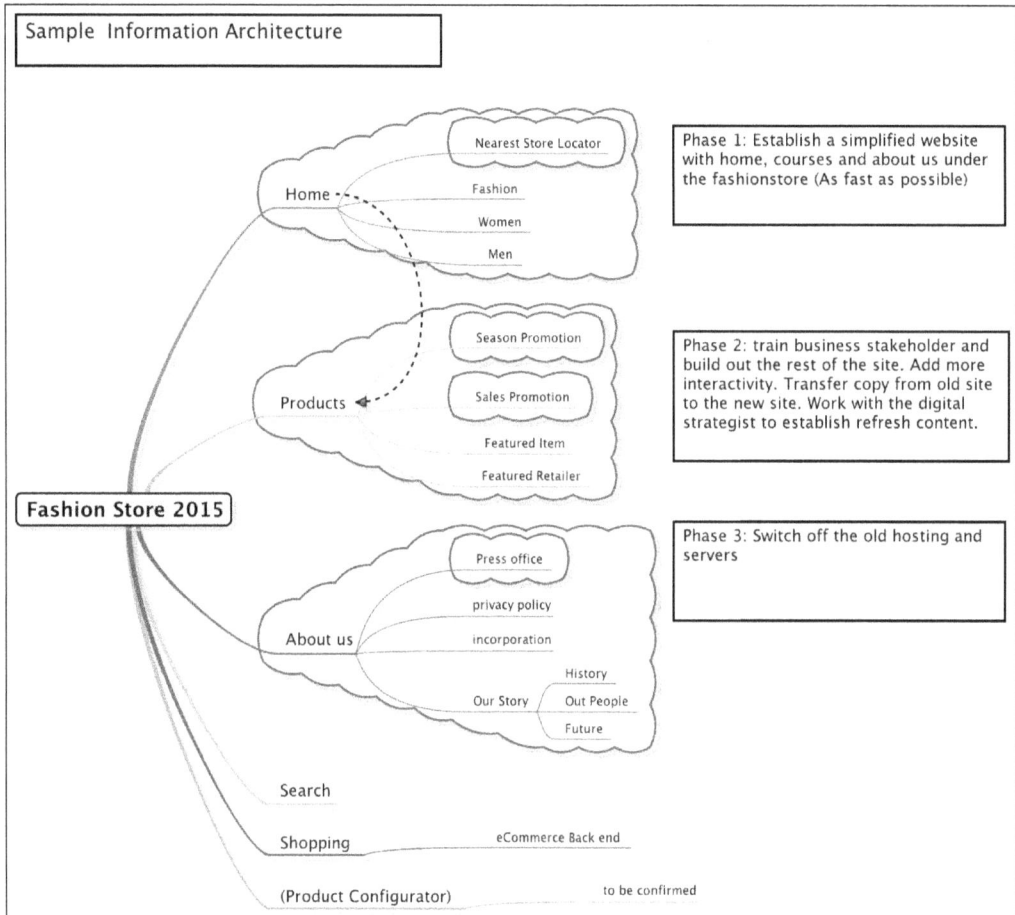

Basic information architecture for fashion store web site

The preceding diagram describes the IA for a potential fashion store web application. It might be considered too simplistic for this book. This diagram, however, is a work in progress for a pitch, a sales meeting in order to win the contract to develop and build the web application. Architecture is based on three components that are vital for the customer: the initial welcome page, the access to the catalogue and product, and content about the corporation. For this particular customer, the diagram reflects their concerns for the featured fashion items, brands, and promotions. The IA will evolve over time through further interactions with the customer. If we win the pitch to develop the fashion store application, potentially, it might be the searchability of the site that requires deeper investigation.

Information architecture helps the designers and developers along with the business stakeholder to understand the structure of the website through a shared language that consolidates the knowledge and purpose of the domain. A website owner and the business can view the IA as a breakdown of the content. They can comprehend how the site is built.

Information architecture can also be about kinesthetic reactions to the content (how someone feels inside). In the future, this would be important for wearable computers, because the user may not be looking at a screen for sensations and notifications. Interactions may be through sound or even through a smell or taste. These modeling techniques and an ability to write in a manner that has an emotional impact are embraced in a new and recent job title: the content strategist.

Writing and building a professional website or enterprise application has grown from its infancy. The developers now must be approachable, adaptable, and sophisticated. Approachable means the ability to work in harmony with others and as a team. Adaptable means being fearless in the face of constant challenges and changes; sophisticated means being able to cope with the stress and handling it gracefully.

Let's move on to understanding the technical aspect of the enterprise Java platform.

Java EE 7 architecture

Java EE is an open standard, an enterprise platform, and a specification for applications that execute on a server. For the digital worker, Java EE provides many services for building web applications including Servlets, JavaServer Faces, Facelets, Context and Dependency Injection, Java Message Services, WebSocket, and crucial Java for RESTful services.

Java EE 7 was announced and released in June 2013, and the overreaching theme was better HTML5 support and increased productivity. Currently, it looks like the future Java EE 8 specification might add support for the administrative configuration of services and application aspects through declarative annotations (extension of JSR 220).

Standard platform components and API

Java EE architecture is a container and layer-based architecture. At the crux of the design is an application server and an increasingly cloud-based solution, although this is yet to be standardized in the specification.

In the non-cloud-based Java EE, we can think of Java EE as four separate containers: the first one is the EJB container for life cycle management of Enterprise Java Beans and the second container is the Web container for life cycle management of the Java Servlets and Managed Beans. The third container is called the Application Client container, which manages the lifecycle of the client-side components. Finally, the fourth container is reserved for Java Applets and their life cycles.

Most of the time, digital engineers are concerned about the EJB, web, and the managed CDI bean containers.

> If you are interested in a full description of the architecture, please refer to my first book, *The Java EE 7 Developer Handbook* by *Packt Publishing*. You can consider it as a sister book to this one.

According to the Java EE 7 specification, there are two official implementation profiles: the full and the web profile. A fully conformant Java EE product such as Glassfish or JBoss WildFly application server implements the full profile, which means it has all containers: EJB, CDI, and web. A server like Apache Tomcat, which builds against the Java EE 7 web profile, implements only the web container. A server like Tom EE that extends the Apache Tomcat implements the web container, and may add extra facilities like CDI, EJB, and even JMS and JAX-RS.

The following diagram illustrates the full profile Java EE 7 architecture as an enterprise solution. The Java EE platform is an abstraction of the hardware, disk storage, networking, and the machine code. Java EE relies on the presence of a Java Virtual Machine for operation. There are versions of JVM that have been ported to hardware chips like Intel, ARM, AMD, Sparc, FreeScale, and others as well as to operating systems including Windows, Mac OS, Linux, Solaris, and even Raspberry Pi.

Therefore, Java and the other alternative languages can execute seamlessly on this chip architecture, and this applies to the enterprise applications. The Java EE provides additional standard API to the standard core Java SE. Let's take a brief look at some of the Java EE features.

Java EE 7 takes advantage of the **New Input Output** (**NIO**) feature in the Java SE edition to allow Java Servlets 3.1 to handle asynchronous communication.

JavaServer Faces 2.2 is now enhanced with tighter CDI integration, improved life cycle events, and a new queue control for AJAX requests. For the digital engineer, there is sensible HTML5 support, resource library contracts, faces flows, and stateless views.

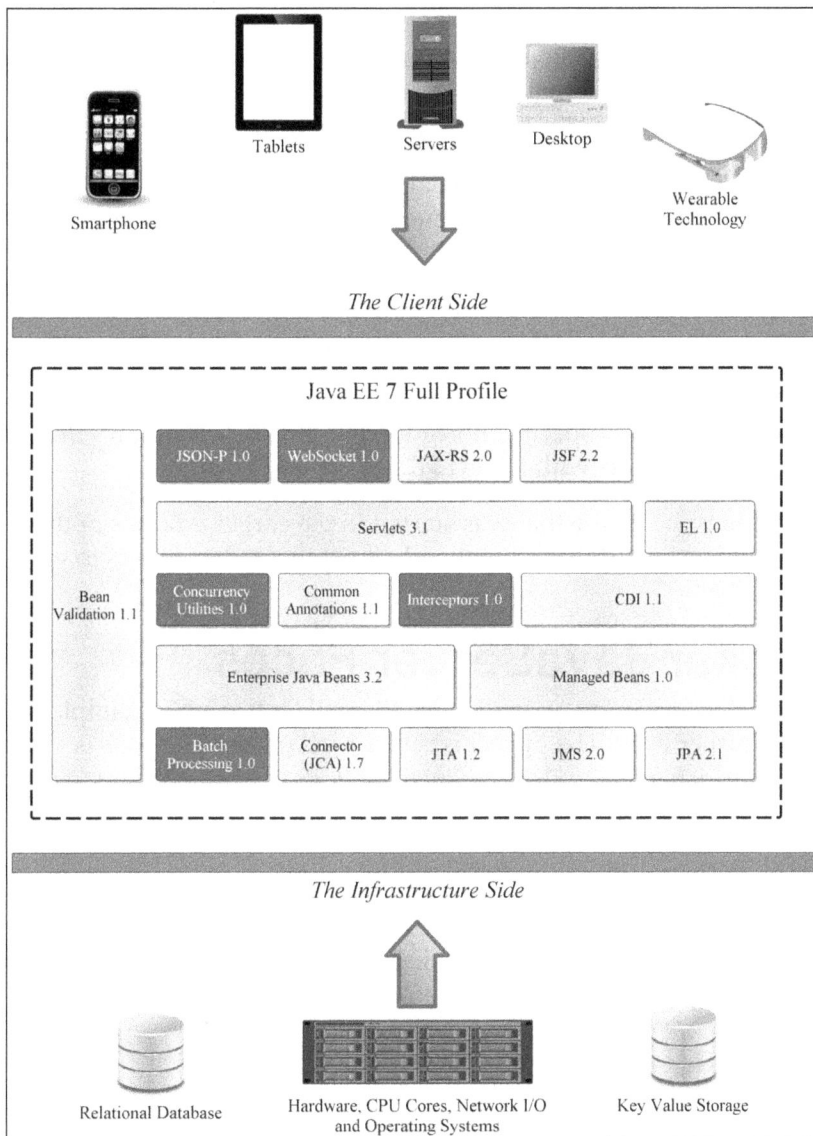

An illustration of the Java EE 7 full platform and JSR specifications

Expression Language 3.0 is not truly a new specification, but it is a broken-out specification from Servlets, JavaServer Pages, and JavaServer Faces. Developers can access the expression evaluator and invoke processing on custom expressions like, say, their own custom tag libraries or server-side business logic.

Perhaps, the most important change in Java EE 7 is the strengthening of the CDI in order to improve type-safety and the easier development of CDI extensions. CDI, Interceptors, and Common Annotations improve the type-safe dependency injection and the observation of life cycle events inside the CDI container. These three specifications together ensure that extensions, which address crosscutting concerns and can be applied to any component, can be written. Developers can now write portable CDI extensions to extend the platform in a standard way.

RESTful Services (JAX-RS) has three crucial enhancements: the addition of client-side API to invoke a REST endpoint, asynchronous I/O support for the client and server endpoints, and hypermedia linking.

Bean validation is a constraint validation solution for domain and value object. It now supports method-level validation and also has better integration with the rest of the Java EE platform.

WebSocket API 1.0 is a new specification added to Java EE 7. It allows the Java application to communicate with the HTML5 WebSocket clients.

Java EE 7 continues the theme that was started in the earlier editions of the platform: improvements for ease-of-development and allowing the developers to write POJOs.

Xentracker JavaServer Faces

Let's move into the development mode now. We will look at a JSF example that I created for my earlier book. The project is called **XenTracker**. The code is available at `https://github.com/peterpilgrim/javaee7-developer-handbook`. The following is the JSF view (`xentracker-basic/src/main/webapp/views/index.xhtml`):

```
<!DOCTYPE html>
<html xmlns="http://www.w3.org/1999/xhtml"
      xmlns:ui="http://xmlns.jcp.org/jsf/facelets"
      xmlns:h="http://xmlns.jcp.org/jsf/html"
      xmlns:f="http://java.sun.com/jsf/core">

  <ui:composition template="/views/template.xhtml">
    <f:metadata>
      <f:viewParam name="id"
        value="#{taskListViewController.id}" />
```

```
      <f:event type="preRenderView"
        listener="#{taskListViewController.findProjectById}"/>
  </f:metadata>

  <ui:define name="content">

    <div class="entry-form-area">

      <h1>Task List for Project</h1>

      <p>
        <h:outputText value="Task list for this project:"/>
      </p>

      <h:link styleClass="btn btn-primary" outcome=
        "createTask.xhtml?id=#{taskListViewController.id}">
      <f:param name="id"
        value="#{taskListViewController.id}" />
      Create New Task
      </h:link>

      <table class="table table-striped table-bordered" >
        <tr>
          <td>Title:</td>
          <td><strong>
            #{taskListViewController.project.name}
          </strong></td>
        </tr>
        <tr>
          <td>Headline:</td>
          <td> 
          #{taskListViewController.project.headline}</td>
        </tr>
        <tr>
          <td>Description:</td>
          <td> 
          #{taskListViewController.project.description}</td>
        </tr>
      </table>
      <!-- form table grid see below -->
    </div>
  </ui:define>
 </ui:composition>
</html>
```

At first glance, this looks like standard HTML5; the specific JSF tags and the Expression Language syntax are not so obvious. The name of the file in the project is called `projectTaskList.xhtml`, which serves a big clue to the type of view this file represents. This view is actually a JSF Facelet template. The file type refers to an older XHTML standard, as sanctioned by the **World Wide Web Consortium** (**W3C**) after the creation of the HTML 4.01 standard. XHTML is the same as HTML4, but restricted by an XML schema and, therefore, is genuinely an XML document.

In order to render any output from JSF, the specification stipulates the provision of a **Page Description Language** (**PDL**). It is possible to have more than one type of PDL. The standard PDL is a view called a Facelet view template. The Facelet framework was a separate open source API external to the JCP, but since JSF 2.0 it has been brought into the fold. Facelet templates are designed to be lightweight and work natively with the JSF framework. Facelets have implicit knowledge of the JSF lifecycle and have access to the UI components through expression language, and they provide decorators to standard HTML elements. The Facelets templating solution performs very well in servlet engines. It may eventually feature in its own specification for Java EE 8.

The templating in the preceding example is illustrated by the specific Facelet tags, namely `<ui:define>` and `<ui:composition>`. Briefly, the `<ui:composition>` tag refers to a template view that defines the layout of the page. One can think of this as the master view. The `<ui:define>` tag defines the actual content, which will be inserted into the template to form the final page output. We will comprehensively tackle JSF and Facelets in later chapters of this book.

By inspecting the opening XML definition at the top of the view definition, we can see a few namespace declarations. The `xmlns:ui` namespace, as you have already seen, refers to the Facelet extensions. The `xmlns:f` namespace refers to the core JSF tags and `xmlns:h` namespace refers to the JSF components that render the HTML elements. You are warned not to expect a complete one-to-one match as you will understand later on. For instance, the `<h:outputText>` tag simply prints out the content; you can almost think of it as the echo function in PHP.

The really observant among you will see that it is definitely possible to build modern websites with JSF. There is a `<div>` element in the markup, and yes, as you may have guessed correctly, Bootstrap CSS is definitely being used. It is important to stress that JSF is a server-side templating solution and a view technology.

Look at the following section again:

```
<h:link styleClass="btn btn-primary"
  outcome="createTask.xhtml?id=#{taskListViewController.id}">
```

This is approximately the equivalent to this straight HTML5:

```
<a style="btn btn-primary"
  href="JSF_munged_createTask.xhtml?id=jsf_fizz_12345">
```

In JSF, the syntactic delimiters denote `Expressions`: `#{...}`. The expression language is parsed in the JSF runtime during the rendering phase of the lifecycle. We will discuss the life cycle in the following chapters.

The previous view is incomplete, because we are missing the tabular view component. Although HTML tables are frowned upon due to the layout of content of the web pages, tables are still extremely important for their original purpose, that is, to display tabular data.

The following is the missing table view that should be inserted in the correct place:

```
<h:form>
  <h:dataTable id="projects"
    value="#{taskListViewController.project.tasks}"
      styleClass="table table-bordered" var="task">
    <h:column>
      <f:facet name="header">
        <h:outputText value="Task Name" />
        </f:facet>
        <h:outputText value="#{task.name}"/>
    </h:column>
    <h:column>
      <f:facet name="header">
        <h:outputText value="Target Date" />
      </f:facet>
        <h:outputText value="#{task.targetDate}">
          <f:convertDateTime pattern="dd-MMM-yyyy" />
        </h:outputText>
    </h:column>
    <h:column>
      <f:facet name="header">
        <h:outputText value="Completed" />
      </f:facet>
      <h:outputText value="#{task.completed}"/>
    </h:column>
    <h:column>
      <f:facet name="header">
        <h:outputText value="Action" />
      </f:facet>
      <h:link styleClass="btn"
        outcome="editTask.xhtml?taskId=#{task.id}">
        <f:param name="taskId" value="#{task.id}" />
        <i class="icon-edit"></i>
```

```
        </h:link>
        <h:link styleClass="btn"
          outcome="removeTask.xhtml?taskId=#{task.id}">
          <f:param name="taskId" value="#{task.id}" />
            <i class="icon-trash"></i>
        </h:link>
      </h:column>
    </h:dataTable>
    <hr/>
    <h:commandLink styleClass="btn btn-primary btn-info"
      immediate="true"
        action="#{taskListViewController.returnToProjects}">
      Return to Projects</h:commandLink>
  </h:form>
```

The preceding code exemplifies the JSF style of content. The `<h:form>` tag corresponds to a HTML Form element. The `<h:dataTable>` tag denotes the table component grid that renders the data from the managed JSF bean. The value attribute denotes the data that is retrieved from a server component named `taskListViewController`. This controller accesses the list collection of Task objects using the expression language, and translates it to the Java reflection invocation of `taskListViewController.getProjects().getTasks()`. It is worth noticing once more the Bootstrap CSS in the attribute `styleClass="table table-bordered"`.

The `<h:dataTable>` JSF component essentially iterates over a Java Collection, array, iterator, or enumerator, sets the current element defined by the attribute `var`, and processes the content in its body. It builds an HTML table. The `<h:column>` tag declares the content in each column of the row and `<f:facet>` tag declares the content specifically to go into the table header rows.

The `<h:outputText>` tag is also flexible enough to accept another usual tag `<f:convertDateTime>`, which formats the particular data value into a date time format.

Finally, we have the `h:commandLink` tag that renders an HTML anchor tag, which behaves like a form submit button. The `h:commandLink` tag is optionally associated with a backing bean, which in our case is the `taskListViewController`. Certain components of the JSF HTML tags like `h:dataTable` and `h:commandLink` are contained in an `h:form` tag in order to be processed correctly.

> Bootstrap CSS (`http://getbootstrap.com`) is a very popular CSS, component, and front-end framework for developing responsive websites. It is particularly suited for mobile by default projects, because it builds against a flexible and fluid grid system. The CSS and JavaScript are easily added to the web application; Bootstrap is genuinely a kick-starter for many projects.

Application servers

At the time of writing, there are several popular application servers that are certified as Java EE 7 compliant: GlassFish, WildFly, Payara, Cosminexus, and TMax Jeus 8. The reference implementation for the entire umbrella specification is GlassFish 4.1 (`https://glassfish.java.net/`). In 2013, I devoted the entire sister book and source code example, *Java EE 7 Developer Handbook*, to GlassFish, because it was the only server available. GlassFish is built on open source, there is a public issue tracker, many forums on various Java EE topics, and because Oracle supports the host and the repository of the source code, it works out of the box.

In order to be certified as a Java EE 7 application server, the vendor or open source provider must pass the Test Compatibility Kit, which guarantees a certification list of compliance (`http://www.oracle.com/technetwork/java/javaee/overview/compatibility-jsp-136984.html`). The code written only against Java EE 7 standard APIs must be able to run against a compliant server else the word *standard* wouldn't hold any meaning. The basic principle of Java: write once run-everywhere, ought be achievable. The fly in the ointment is when the code relies on vendor-specific features that are not part of the standard. It is also worth pointing out that TCK is not free. In fact, I know a very good source of information, who mentioned the cost to be at least $250 K. Therefore, this barrier to entry is beyond the remit of the majority of open source projects or **Small & Medium Enterprises** (**SME**), without significant investment from angels or kick-starter funds.

At the beginning of 2014, Oracle announced that it would be removing the commercial support for the GlassFish server. This news had the Java EE community up-in-arms about the future of the application server. Oracle clarified later that there was a roadmap for GlassFish 5, and it was still on the agenda to be the reference implementation for Java EE 8. The database vendor and Java steward instead recommended the avenue of upgrading to Oracle WebLogic for production. In 2014, Oracle released WebLogic 12.1.3 with selected Java EE 7 compliant components.

WildFly 9 (`http://wildfly.org/`) is the next generation of application servers from Red Hat. The server features a modular architecture based on a new class loader infrastructure in an attempt to avoid the issue of conflicting dependencies between the third party JARs and the infrastructure within the server itself. There are two key benefits to WildFly: the new high performance HTTP server, which is called Undertow (`http://undertow.io/`) and the reduction of administration ports. The ports are 8080 for web traffic, Servlets, REST, and WebSocket endpoint and 9990 for server administration. With WildFly it is possible to invoke the EJB remote methods through the de facto HTTP port 8080, which adds some interesting possibilities for enterprise applications.

The modular approach in WildFly 9 appears to be suitable for end sites that prefer to have a strict control over the deployment of their enterprise architecture. WildFly has a download option called the *core* distribution, which allows developers to configure the modules that they require in an application server runtime. The final benefit of WildFly is that it is the first Java EE 7 server that is compatible with Java SE 8 (Lambdas and default interfaces). Only GlassFish 4.1 releases are compatible with Java SE 8.

After the debacle of the professional support for GlassFish, another corporation entered the space. C2B2 Consulting offered an open source adaptation of GlassFish called Payara Server (`http://payara.co.uk`) with 24/7 production support.

I should quickly mention one other server that is gaining track with the server-side Java community and that is worth keeping an eye on in the near future. The Apache Software Foundation has an open source project called Tom EE (`http://tomee.apache.org/`). Tom EE (pronounced *Tommy*) is, essentially, Apache Tomcat 7 with additional extensions, which are already configured, to support JSF, JPA JAX-RS, CDI, and EJB. David Blevins, a popular speaker and an ASF committer, was the founder of the Tom EE project. At the time of writing, Tom EE is only certified against Java EE 6 Web Profile; however, there are plans to add support to Java EE 7. Business stakeholders can obtain commercial and production support for Tom EE through vendors like Tomi Tribe (`http://www.tomitribe.com/`).

Since GlassFish, WildFly, and Payara are the only application servers certified as Java EE 7-compliant at the time of writing, we will concentrate only on them for the rest of this book. The source code examples work with both these servers. Wherever necessary, we will point out the differences and explain the features appropriately. Let us now continue our journey into the digital web with Java EE 7.

Summary

In this chapter, we discussed the role of the digital worker, that is, you, the engineer and how you fit into the new marketing role as a creative person. We looked at the skills and the tool chain set that is certainly expected in the years 2015 and 2016. We covered how the Java platform and JVM fit into this picture.

Being a Digital Java EE 7 worker is more than just developing the server-side Java code; you are expected to understand JavaScript programming at an elementary level. Some of you may already have basic JavaScript knowledge and some others will understand a lot more about programming in the client space. JavaScript, for all its warts and mishaps, is a professional language that deserves respect, and we covered some of the frameworks that you are expected to know. Whilst this book does not teach you JavaScript and is aimed at Java EE development, I recommend that you brush up on your skills apropos module patterns and applying advanced libraries.

In this chapter, we looked at the Java EE 7 architecture and the specifications that are part of the platform. Finally, we pored over the code of a simple JavaServer Faces example. In particular, we inspected a Facelet view code. We noticed that much of the view resembles standard HTML.

In the upcoming chapters, we will delve deeply into the JSF and build a simple **Create Retrieve Update Delete (CRUD)** example. We will be generating the example in a couple of different ways. As the saying goes, we have to crawl before we can walk, and walk before we can run. Our crawling is over, now let's starting walking.

Exercises

In order to aid those in the field of education: students, teachers, and lecturers, questions have been provided at the end of each chapter in the book.

1. Grab a sheet of paper; outline the core Java EE 7 specifications, which include the Servlets CDI, EJB, JPA, JMS, JAX-RS, and JSF. On a scale of 1-10 (1 being novice and 10 expert) ask yourself how much do you honestly know?

2. When was the last time you looked at Java EE? If you still think of enterprise development as the term J2EE, then you definitely need to take a look at the book, *Java EE Developer Handbook*. Make a note of the specifications that you do not know quite so well and plan to learn them.

3. Test your understanding of the Java EE platform by matching the parts of the specification to a recent web application that you have been involved in. Describe how each specification can provide benefits, including productivity gains.

4. Now switch to the other side and dissent against Java EE. Some voices in the community are for and some are decidedly against standardization. The detractors say that the standardization process is too slow for a world of need and innovation. What do you think are the potential pitfalls of relying on the Java EE platform? Think of areas beyond software development, such as education, training, hiring, and the wider community. What would be the ideal state of Java where you can do what you like and without responsibility?

5. You probably already have a favorite website, which you visit regularly, perhaps everyday. Draw or outline the basic (high level) information architecture for it. Chances are that your favorite website has a lot of rich content and has been around for a long time. What changes have you noticed with the information architecture that you know today?

6. How good is your JavaScript knowledge? On a scale of 1 (beginner) and 10 (expert), how do you rate it as a skill? How does your JavaScript compare against your Java programming?

7.   Did you know that you can examine HTML, CSS, and JavaScript dynamically from a modern web browser with Developer Tools (Chrome Developer Tools `https://developer.chrome.com/devtools` or Christopher Pederick's Web Developer Tools `http://chrispederick.com/work/web-developer/` or similar)? Have you ever learnt to debug JavaScript through these tools? Why not learn to simply add a break point to the code? How about using the inspector to examine the computed CSS?

8.   Using the distributed version control system, Git, to clone the book source code from GitHub (`http://github.com/peterpilgrim/digitaljavaee7`), and examine the code around the simple JSF example given in this chapter. Download and setup the GlassFish 4.1 (`https://glassfish.java.net/`) or WildFly 9 (`http://wildfly.org/`) application servers and get the first examples running.

9.   How good are your image-editing skills in web design (using a commercial application Adobe Photoshop or Firework or Xara Edit)? Do you partake in this activity at work or at home, or do you delegate this effort to another person, like a creative designer? Would it benefit your wider career plans to have better knowledge in this area? Ask yourself, would it make you be a better digital worker?

10. The digital teams practicing Agile software development tend to work with the stakeholders. It they are lucky, they are in direct contact with the stakeholder. The stakeholder is the customer, a representative of the business end users, to which these teams are delivering software. Have you ever had conversations directly with the stakeholder(s)? What was the outcome of these discussions? How did they go? Did you ever wish to be more involved? Did you ever feel like running away? How could your efforts in these talks have been better, retrospectively? Put yourself in your stakeholder's shoes to understand how he perceives you.

2
JavaServer Faces Lifecycle

"No two people on earth are alike, and it's got to be that way in music or it isn't music"

Billie Holiday

Java has been a complete success in the server side for a long time: since the year 2000. Businesses have trusted the JVM, Java programming language, and abundance of frameworks as their platform of choice for enterprise software. So, are we correct in continuing to put our trust in the JVM as digital web engineers? I think the answer to that question, and because you are reading this book, is yes!

This chapter is an expansive overview of the **JavaServer Faces** (**JSF**) concepts. We will start with the history and purpose of JSF and how it relates to the fundamental design pattern: the **Model-View-Controller** (**MVC**). We will explore the life cycle concepts in JSF, which is one of the key concepts that separates it from the other Java web application frameworks. Moreover, we will examine some JSF code, including the nefarious concept of managed beans. We will also cover how a JSF application navigates between the POJOs and pages. To sweeten this, we will meander in the powerful expression language for page authors. By the time we finish the chapter, we will have built a solid foundation of knowledge.

Introduction to JSF

JSF is a specification to build a web user interface from a component model. It encompasses a MVC and templating framework. JSF is a standard library of the Java EE platform. The **Java Community Process** (**JCP**) controls the specifications, and the current version is JSF 2.2, which is defined by **Java Specification Request** (**JSR**) 334 (`https://www.jcp.org/en/jsr/detail?id=344`).

Originally, the promise behind JSF was to bring rapid user interface development to server-side Java. This statement was true when JSF was first conceived; but of course, it is still useful if you would rather not write a lot of JavaScript code and hand crafted boilerplate so as to handle the transformation of an HTTP request to the Java invocations and back-to-page responses. Web technology and, in particular, digital development has leaped off the web pages since JSF 1.0 was conceived in 2004. Back then, JavaScript was not taken as a programming language so seriously as it is now; there was no responsive web design and there was certainly less demand for mobile web programming. Nowadays, it is common to see terms such as mobile first or digital by default. This means that websites consider all sorts of screen sizes and devices and recognize that people can view the content on a smartphone or tablet. Some people (your target customers) do not have access to a desktop PC or laptop.

> See Cameron Moll's pioneering—but now slightly dated—e-book on mobile web design (`http://mobilewebbook.com/`). The UK government places great emphasis on the term, Digital by Default (`https://www.gov.uk/service-manual/digital-by-default`), which has been followed up by the expansive Default to Open term from the United States Digital Service (`https://playbook.cio.gov/`).

JSF was conceived as a user interface technology that could allow even a Java engineer to build frontend in the same way as a JavaFX (or Swing) application. The idea was to allow the developers (not designers) to assemble an HTML page using a custom editor. The JSF applications were designed to be themed. The intention of the framework was to allow a render kit to produce different forms of output. A render kit might generate a PDF output, another type would generate an HTML output, and yet another would generate specific mobile content in the form of **Wireless Application Protocol (WAP)** (WAP was a technology that was afforded much attention before Apple produced the first iPhone in 2007). Technology has moved on in leaps and bounds!

Although there is much criticism of JSF as web technology to produce serious applications, it has the support of the Java EE platform. Facelets is a useful template framework to build sharable components and partial content for web pages. JSF has a lifecycle model that integrates into a POJO, and this means that it works seamlessly with the Context and Dependency Injection (CDI) beans. Moreover, JSF has been kept up to date with the changes taking place in the digital landscape. JSF 2.2 supports HTML5 friendly markup. It supports AJAX events and allows the events to be queued. It allows a W3C sanction ID attribute for all the elements for the HTML5 content. JSF 2.2 introduces Faces Flow, which adds the ability to take the user through the sets of screens, workflows, and wizards. Above all, JSF 2.2 (JSR 334) represents a commitment to continually support a standard component-based framework for the Java EE platform.

> **Mojarra 2.2**
>
> In order for JSF to become a standard of the Java EE platform, it requires a JSR and reference implementation. For JSF, the reference implementation project is called Mojarra. The software is open source and supported by the Oracle Corporation (`https://javaserverfaces.java.net/`). The reference implementation is part of the GlassFish 4 application server.

JSF 1.0 and 2.0 history

The concept of JSF was first discussed around 2001. It was a part of the Sun Microsystems project called Project Rave and then announced as JSR 127. The technology, although an improvement over the action-request-based framework of the era such as Apache Struts, was met with lukewarm fanfare in 2003 and 2004. A maintenance version 1.1 was released in 2004, but only in 2006 did the JSF 1.2 specification become an official part of the umbrella specification: Java EE 5.

By this time, however, the developer mindshare had already evolved into the AJAX techniques, partial applications, and non-JVM software such as Ruby and Ruby on Rails. JSF 1.2 was encumbered by the default templating technology of the platform, JavaServer Pages. JSP proved unsuitable for JSF because the life cycle of the interception of the requests and the generation of the responses were essentially incompatible. The search for alternatives led to the creation of Facelets, which were designed to work explicitly with JSF.

In 2009, Facelets became the default template solution in JSF 2.0 (JSR 314), which was also a part of Java EE 6. JSF 2.0 added annotations for validation and conversion. JSF 2.0 defined a standard AJAX component life cycle and it also added improvements for graphical editors. JSF 2.0 introduced a resource handle for the web content, including images, JavaScript, and CSS files.

Key JSF 2.2 features

The big ticket features of the JSF 2.2 specification are as follows:

- It provides the support for the HTML5 friendly markup, which is a boon to web designers and interface developers.
- The Resource Library Contracts is a new system in JSF to build reusable themes through bundling the Facelet views, components, style sheets, and other resources including internationalization.

- It provides the new URI locators that are consistent with the Java EE 7 umbrella specification. The Oracle Corporation purchased Sun Microsystems in 2010, and so, the old URIs of the form `http://java.sun.com/jsf/core` were transformed to `http://xmlns.jcp.org/jsf/core` reflecting the namespace of the JCP web domain.

- Faces Flows allow an application to be modeled as a directed graph of pages and views. With Faces Flows, we can build the basis of a workflow application in terms of the user interface. As a digital engineer, we can assemble a subdivision of the applications in a greater whole. These types of workflows lend themselves to the conversational scope of the CDI beans. You will learn more about flows in detail in *Chapter 6, JSF Flows and Finesse.*

- Stateless Views allow the developers to build the components that have no server-side state. Usually, the JSF components will save the state of the user interface component on either the server or the client, but sometimes a view does not require this extra resource, and thus, having a stateless view affords the scalability of the web application on servers.

- It provides the ability to correctly handle the content of the browser from the client window: tab, browser window, pop-up dialog, or modal dialog.

JSF 2.2 is backward compatible with Faces 2.1 and 2.0. An application built against Faces 2.0 or 2.1 will not require changes in order to run with Faces 2.2; however, going the other way and using specific 2.2 features will not run in these older environments.

JSF is based on the following Java API specifications:

- JavaServer Pages 2.2 and JavaServer Pages Tag Library (JSTL) 1.2
- Java Servlet 3.0
- Java SE 7
- Java EE 7
- Java Beans 1.01

Why choose JSF over alternatives?

JSF is the only Java web application framework that is certified as a JCP standard so far. Of course, there are alternatives; in fact, there may be as many as 100 different Java web frameworks, and the majority of them will be open source. However, they will vary according to the vision, implementation, age of the code base, and who actually maintains it as a repository. It is no good for a business if the web framework that your application works against is built with yesterday's technology because the web is constantly evolving. Equally, the web framework has to evolve with the times or it will eventually become irrelevant. Businesses trust that JSF is a standard that has the guarantees that the technology will be supported for the long term.

> In fact, MVC (JSR 371) will be the other standard web
> application framework in Java EE 8. You will learn about
> MVC in *Chapter 9, Java EE MVC Framework*.

It is perfectly understandable that an application architect may want to choose a web framework other than JSF for their business requirements. Apache Struts 2, Spring MVC, and Apache Wicket are a few that I would mention in passing. Apache Struts 2 and Spring MVC are generally considered to be request-oriented frameworks. Apache Wicket is a component-oriented framework and a direct competitor to JSF. Apache Struts was one of the most famous web application frameworks in the early 2000s and certainly the first to break the mold.

The world of web frameworks does not stop with Java. Most developers will have heard of Ruby on Rails, which is an off-JVM technology. A few engineers will know about the Play framework for both the Java and Scala developers, and then there are solutions based around the Groovy language such as Grails.

Whatever framework you choose for a web application essentially dictates the Java-based frontend architecture for your developer. Whatever you do, my strong recommendation is not to invent your own web application framework. The strength of open source is the community of developers that is diverse with from thousands of different companies, endeavors, and cultures.

If you choose JSF, then it is more than likely that you, as a customer, want to maintain your investment in the Java platform. The core strength of your JSF enterprise application is the rich components, and you rely on the model to add the default benefits such as easier validation, type conversion, and mapping of HTTP request parameters so as to bean the properties. Many experienced Java EE engineers will have experience in the JSF framework, so you will be in great company.

The MVC design pattern

The MVC design describes a set of design patterns that aim to separate the concerns of a user interface from the application logic that semantically binds them. The Model describes the business logic. The View denotes the presentation—the abstract surface that the user senses and also interacts with. The Controller denotes the component that handles the interaction between the model and view. The original idea of MVC stemmed from Trygve Reenskaug, who introduced the concept in the Smalltalk programming language during the 1970s. The pattern was subsequently implemented and popularized in the Smalltalk-80 before it was adopted in the wider software engineering community. MVC is famous for its ideas about the division of labor and the separation of responsibilities between the components.

We call it MVC patterns because the plural term describes a set of related derivatives of the classic pattern as group patterns.

The MVC pattern has subsequently evolved, giving rise to variants such as the **Hierarchical model–view–controller (HMVC)**, **Model-view-presenter (MVP)**, **Model View ViewModel (MVVM)**, and others that adapted MVC to different contexts.

MVC in JSF

How does the MVC map to JSF? This has been answered in the following points:

- **Model**: In JSF and Java EE, the model is the component or a set of components that handles the business data and logic. The model is either a CDI bean, EJB, or some other component that is compatible with the life cycle of the web container and the JSF framework.

- **Controller**: A lot of the responsibility of the controller logic in the classic design pattern is taken care of by the framework. In JSF, one can consider the start of the controller as FacesServlet, which is responsible for dispatching the incoming HTTP request to the correct managed bean.

- **View**: In JSF, the view is the rendering group that contains the UI components and their respective beans. Usually, the view is described in a page description language, for which JSF 2.0 is Facelets. The render kit of JSF composes the UI components and beans in a full page.

The following diagram illustrates the MVC patterns in a perspective of the JSF framework:

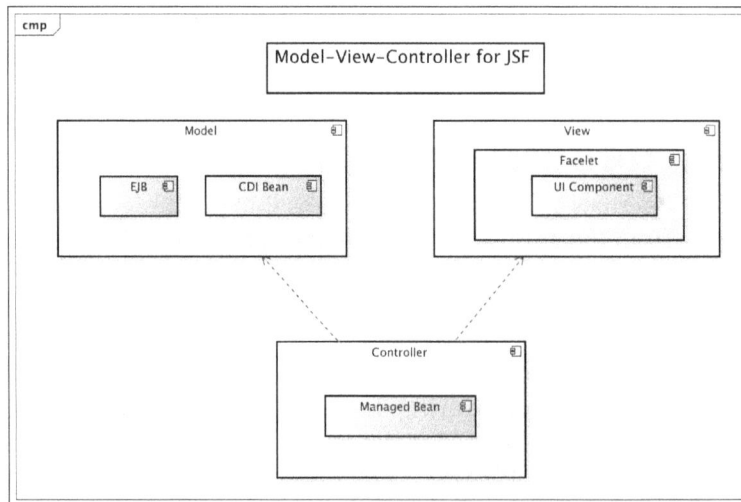

The Model View Controller pattern is terms of JSF framework

Facelets

The JSF specification defines a **View Declaration Language** (**VDL**) to render the output of the pages. In JSF 1.0, this was JavaServer Pages; but in JSF 2.0, the VDL was changed to Facelets by default. Facelets are the default view handler for JSF 2.0 and are defined as XHTML files.

Facelets can be used in a templating situation. A Facelets file can reference a master template as a composition, and the view can provide the content that will look like a cookie cutter being supplied to the template. A Facelet that utilizes a reference template is known as a template client. The placeholder content in the template client will override the default content in the master template. In this way, Facelets can be reused in order to share the content. The template clients may become master templates and thus, a hierarchy of views can be derived.

Facelets also provide reuse by the custom tags. It is possible for engineers to write their own custom tags through the XHTML files and metadata. The designer and developer will provide the content through a tag library descriptor file.

The final option to template that Facelets provide is the Composite Component Composition. This mechanism allows a composition to be reused in the other Facelet views so that they appear like first-class components. The template files, however, must be created in a special directory in order to allow the internal composition handler to succeed.

The request processing lifecycle

JSF has a request-response processing lifecycle that is built around the HTTP protocol. JSF is built on top of the Java Servlet specification that takes care of translating the request user agent, which in the majority of the cases, is a web browser to a known endpoint. For JSF, the first port of call is `javax.faces.webapp.FacesServlet`. This servlet will simply dispatch the incoming request to the controller, and this component can elect to generate a response or delegate the output to the internal JSF controller implementation.

There are three circumstances for JSF in the request processing lifecycle. The first is the invocation to the JSF controller with a Faces request, which ultimately generates a Faces response.

The second is a request to retrieve a resource such as a CSS or JavaScript file or image or some other media file. However, a Faces resource request, which does not require the execution of logic, causes the JSF framework to furnish the output as a Faces resource response.

The last one is a page request to retrieve the content that has nothing to do with JSF, and this is called a Non-Faces request and subsequently derives a Non-Faces response. An HTTP request to a JAX-RS service endpoint is an example of a Non-Faces request and response. Let's have a look at the following figure:

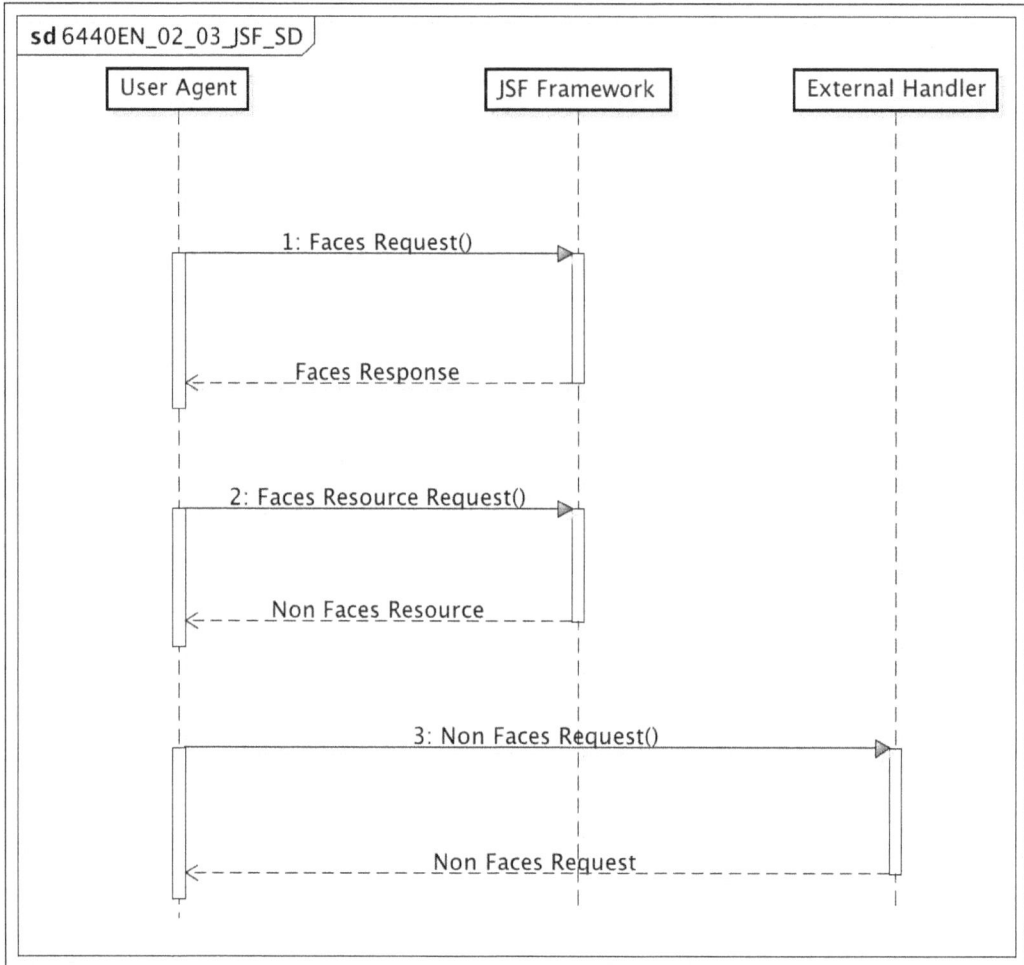

JSF request and response processing

The JSF framework first determines if the incoming request is for a resource. If it is, then the framework serves up the resource and sends the bytes, content type, and data to the user agent.

The interesting work happens when the incoming request is treated as a Face request; the JSF framework handles this processing in a linear workflow. This process is known as the execute and render lifecycle.

The execute and render lifecycle

The following diagram shows the JSF lifecycle to process a Faces request:

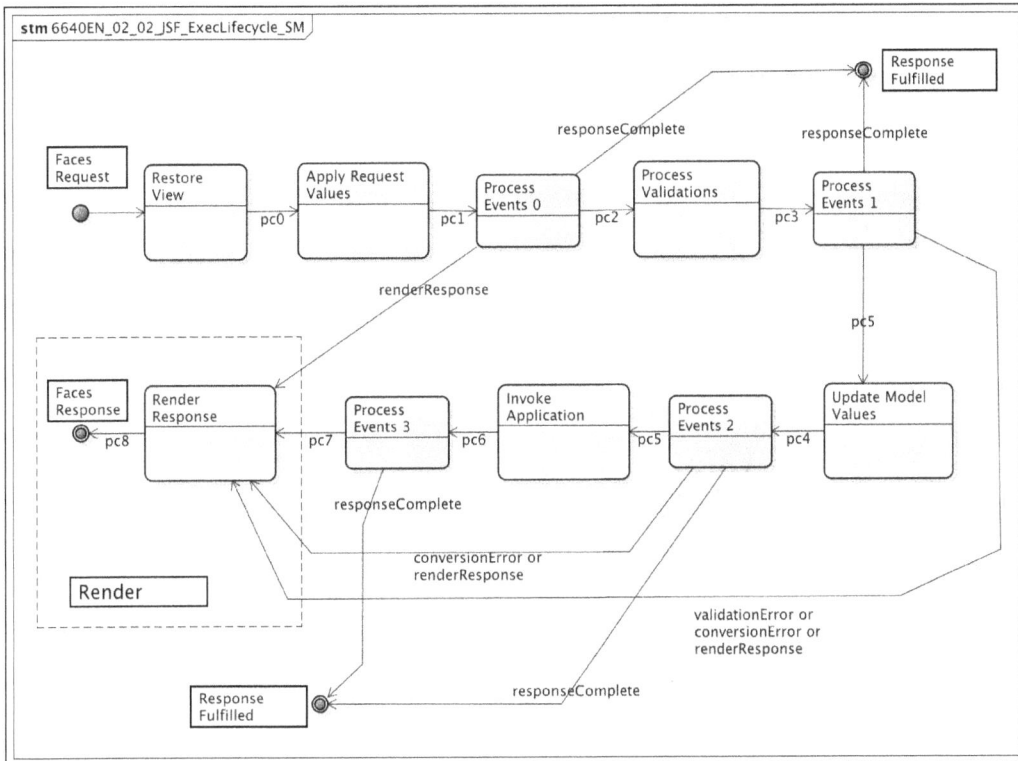

The execute and render lifecycle phases inside the JSF framework

The standard request processing lifecycle starts with a Faces request stimulus to the **Restore View** stage. JSF maintains a `javax.faces.context.FacesContext` instance for the lifecycle. This object instance contains all of the information that is associated with a single Faces request. FacesContext is passed along to the various stages.

Restore View

Restore View is a phase of the lifecycle where the JSF framework ensures that the tree of the components and their states match the form when the view was originally generated at the response. In other words, JSF has to rebuild the view accurately before it can start inserting the changes and apply the form property values from the Faces request. The reason for this phase to exist is that the state of the overall input can change dynamically between requests. What follows is the technical depth description.

Restore View determines if the request is a postback or an initial request according to the algorithm. Every view in JSF has its unique identifier, `viewId`, and this is usually stored in a map collection internally in the framework's implementation. The framework calls the `initView()` method on the `javax.faces.application.ViewHandler` instance, which is associated with the view. Restore View constructs or retrieves the view so as to display to the user agent.

If the view already exists, then the request is a postback. JSF will then restore the view with `viewId` using the previously saved state. The state can be stored on the server or client. This behavior is configured from the Web XML deployment behavior for the application.

For an entirely new view, JSF creates a new instance of the type `javax.faces.component.UIViewRoot`, which is initially empty and sets the associated properties on it, such as the locale and character set. JSF then populates the view with the UI components in a tree data structure.

Apply Request Values

After the component tree is restored, JSF maps the request information parameters to the component properties. The framework iterates over the component objects in the tree. Each component retrieves the data from the request object, which are usually the request parameters but can be cookies, session attributes, or even header parameters. Hence, the new values are stored with the UI component locally. The values are extracted from the request information, and at this phase, the values are still strings. This stage is called the Apply Request Values phase.

During this stage, JSF will attempt to apply conversion on the component properties where it is appropriate. If the conversion or validation fails, then the error message is queued on FacesContext.

The Apply Request Values phase adds events to an internal JSF event queue when a command button or link is clicked on. JSF has certain special conditions in which an event handler is allowed to break the linear flow of processing and skip to the final stage: Render Response.

Process Validations

The Process Validation phase is the stage where the submitted string values, which are stored with the component, are converted to local values. These local values can be Java objects of any type. It is in this phase that the validators that are associated with the component can verify the value of the local values. If the validation passes and all the required validators are invoked successfully, then the JSF life cycle continues to the next phase. If the validation fails or there have been conversion errors from the previous lifecycle phase—the Apply Request Values phase—then the JSF framework skips directly to the Render Response phase. The web user then has a chance to enter the correct data in, say, an HTML input form.

As a JSF developer, it is up to you to attach validators to the UI components with inputs, which are important to check.

Update Model Values

After the conversion and validation phases, JSF enters the Update Model Values stage. At this point, the local values are considered as safe so as to update the model. Remember that in JSF versus MVC parlance, the model is likely to be your managed backing bean, CDI bean, or an EJB or aggregate object. JSF updates the beans that are referenced by the component.

Invoke Application

In the life cycle, we arrive at the phase where the model has been updated, and conversion and validation has been applied. JSF calls this the Invoke Application phase, and here, finally, business logic is invoked. JSF calls the method that is named by the action method of the command button or link component. The Invoke Application phase is a result of the user submitting an HTML form or invoking a navigation anchor link, so the JSF framework executes the corresponding method of the backing bean.

The method may elect to return a simple outcome string. Since JSF 2.0, methods are allowed to return a simple string that refers to the view by its name. Alternatively, the method may build its own response programmatically using the FacesContext instance or may return the navigation view ID that is passed to a navigation handler, which in turn looks up the next page.

Render Response

The last phase in the lifecycle is the Render Response phase. This stage has the requirement to encode the Faces response and the JSF framework sends this output to the requesting user agent, which is usually a web browser. As soon as the data is sent down the network to the client, the life cycle is complete for the request and response. A new lifecycle begins on the next request.

Event handling

Between certain phases, you will have noticed the Process Event stages. JSF allows the listeners to be registered against the framework in order to observe events. These are called Phase Listeners. They are special because they can be active in behavior and cause the lifecycle to skip or they can be passive in behavior to just monitor some aspects of the user interface that is interesting to the application. These mini-extension points are quite useful and powerful for application builders and thus are a major differentiator between JSF and the other web frameworks.

A basic JSF example

We have covered just enough theory on the JSF framework. I think it is time for my readers to see some code. The first code is the XHTML file to display a basic web page on a site. The source code is available on the book's website in the author's public GitHub account at `http://github.com/peter_pilgrim/digital_javaee7`.

Here is the XHTML source code for the initial Facelets view, and the file is called `index.xhtml`:

```
<?xml version="1.0" encoding="UTF-8"?>
<!DOCTYPE html PUBLIC "-//W3C//DTD XHTML 1.0 Transitional//EN"
  "http://www.w3.org/TR/xhtml1/DTD/xhtml1-transitional.dtd">
<html xmlns="http://www.w3.org/1999/xhtml"
      xmlns:h="http://xmlns.jcp.org/jsf/html"
      xmlns:ui="http://xmlns.jcp.org/jsf/facelets"
      xmlns:f="http://xmlns.jcp.org/jsf/core">

  <h:head>
    <title>Digital Java EE 7 - Sample JSF</title>
  </h:head>
  <h:body>
    This is the simplest JSF example possible.

    <h:form>
```

```
    <h:commandButton action="#{basicFlow.serveResponse}"
      value="Invoke Action" />
  </h:form>

  <h:link outcome="composition1.xhtml">
    Composition 1
  </h:link>
 </h:body>
</html>
```

It is worth reminding you that this file is not an HTML5 document; although JSF 2.2 can cope with the document grammar, we must walk before we can run. XHTML is a format of HTML that uses an XML schema namespace to add additional tags. Hence, there are JSF-specific namespaces for HTML, UI, and F. See further onward for a description of these namespaces.

The <h:head>, <h:body>, and <h:form> custom tags resemble the standard HTML element tags that everyone knows about in web development. This is because they are designed to reflect this purpose deliberately. In fact, these are the JSF customs tags that add the functionalities and in the end, render the equivalent HTML element output.

You are probably wondering that what an earth is a <h:link> element. This is simply JSF's way of rendering an HTML anchor tag. The outcome tag attribute references another XHTML directly, and after JSF 2.0, developers are allowed to write this in code.

The <h:commandButton> tag is an example of a JSF form button that ultimately renders an HTML submit element tag. This tag accepts an action attribute that refers to a special string. The string is an example of the expression language; it references a method name of a bean.

Here is the code for the JSF managed bean, BasicFlow:

```
package uk.co.xenonique.digital.javaee.jsfcomps;

import javax.enterprise.context.RequestScoped;
import javax.inject.Named;

@Named
@RequestScoped
public class BasicFlow {
    public String serveResponse() {
        return "endState.xhtml";
    }
}
```

`BasicFlow` is a CDI bean with the request scope life cycle as declared by the `@javax.enterprise.context.RequestScoped` annotation. The bean is created by the CDI framework at the beginning of the servlet request lifecycle and is finished and left for the garbage collection once the servlet response is complete.

In JSF 2.2, we will use the `@javax.inject.Named` annotation to specify the bean that is available to the JSF framework. We can explicitly write the annotation as `@Named("basicFlow")`, but the default is the camel case identifier of the simple class name. We recommend that a digital developer should not use the older `@javax.faces.bean.ManagedBean` annotation as it is now targeted for deprecation in a future JSF specification.

> Make sure that your POJOs are actually CDI beans. Confusion can abound with JSF if you are using the wrong import for JSF. At deployment time, you will be unable to inject or find the backing bean in an expression like `#{basicFlow.serveResponse}`. Check that you are importing `javax.enterprise.context.RequestScoped` and not importing the deprecated `javax.faces.bean.RequestScoped` annotation.

The `#{basicFlow.serveResponse}` string is an example of the **Expression Language (EL)**, which is a mechanism for the page content to communicate with the backing beans while maintaining a separation of concerns. The first `BasicFlow` element refers to the backing bean instance and the second `serverResponse` element refers to the `serveResponse()` method. So, this is an EL expression that references the backing bean method. We will learn a lot more about expression languages later in this chapter.

You can see that the response is a simple string, which is the next VDL file: `endState.xhtml`. Strictly speaking, the suffix can be left off and the JSF framework will determine the correct view.

The `endState.xhtml` Facelet view file looks as follows:

```
<html xmlns="http://www.w3.org/1999/xhtml"
      xmlns:h="http://xmlns.jcp.org/jsf/html">
  <h:head>
    <title>Digital Java EE 7 - End State</title>
  </h:head>
  <h:body>
    <p>
      This is the <strong>end state</strong>.
    </p>
    <h:link outcome="index.xhtml">
      Go back to the start
```

```
      </h:link>
    </h:body>
  </html>
```

This is a JSF view that allows the user to go back to the start view with an
<h:link> element.

A web deployment descriptor

In order to get the best out of the JSF framework, we recommend configuring a
web application deployment descriptor. This file is a special XML document that
declaratively describes the entry servlet endpoints, servlet mapping, and other
environment resources. The code for the XML file is as follows:

```xml
<?xml version="1.0" encoding="UTF-8"?>
<web-app xmlns="http://xmlns.jcp.org/xml/ns/javaee"
    xmlns:xsi="http://www.w3.org/2001/XMLSchema-instance"
    xsi:schemaLocation="http://xmlns.jcp.org/xml/ns/javaee
    http://xmlns.jcp.org/xml/ns/javaee/web-app_3_1.xsd"
    version="3.1" metadata-complete="false">

  <display-name>
    jsf-compositions-1.0-SNAPSHOT
  </display-name>

  <servlet>
    <servlet-name>Faces Servlet</servlet-name>
    <servlet-class>
      javax.faces.webapp.FacesServlet
    </servlet-class>
    <load-on-startup>1</load-on-startup>
  </servlet>

  <servlet-mapping>
    <servlet-name>Faces Servlet</servlet-name>
    <url-pattern>*.xhtml</url-pattern>
  </servlet-mapping>

  <context-param>
    <param-name>javax.faces.PROJECT_STAGE</param-name>
    <param-value>Development</param-value>
  </context-param>

  <welcome-file-list>
```

```
      <welcome-file>index.xhtml</welcome-file>
   </welcome-file-list>
</web-app>
```

The preceding file has the `WEB-INF/web.xml` path. In order to activate the JSF framework, the deployment descriptor declares the servlet with a fully qualified class name; `javax.faces.webapp.FacesServlet`. Note that the servlet is mapped to serve the `*.xhtml` files.

We will define the active phase of the current project with the context parameter `javax.faces.PROJECT_STAGE` and an appropriate value. In the preceding example, the stage is set to `Development` but after the application goes live, then we might want to switch the value to `Production`. Switching to `Production` improves the performance and disables some of the debugging output.

You will find the deployment descriptor in the book's source code as part of the project `ch02/jsf-compositions`. Once you add the project to an IDE—say, IntelliJ, Eclipse, or NetBeans—you can view the output from the application server at the URL `http://localhost:8080/jsf-compositions-1.0-SNAPSHOT/`.

JSF XML namespaces

Here is a table describing the common JSF and related namespaces:

Namespace	Description
h	`http://xmlns.jcp.org/jsf/html`
	This defines the standard tag JSF library for the HTML renderers and components such as `h:link`, `h:commandButton`, and so on.
f	`http://xmlns.jcp.org/jsf/core`
	This defines the standard tag JSF library for the core functionality that is independent of any render kit. This library includes the tags to handle the validation and conversion.
ui	`http://xmlns.jcp.org/jsf/facelet`
	This defines the standard tag JSF library to template the support including the composition of the views.
cc	`http://xmlns.jcp.org/jsf/composite`
	This defines the standard `tag` library to build the composite components.
jsf	`http://xmlns.jcp.org/jsf`
	This defines the tags to support HTML5 friendly output.

p	`http://xmlns.jcp.org/jsf/passthrough`
	This defines the tags to support the HTML5 friendly output with the pass-through `tag` attributes.
c	`http://xmlns.jcp.org/jsp/jstl/core`
	This defines the JSTL 1.2 tag library for the JSP core behaviors. These tags include `<c:forEach>`, `<c:if>`, `<c:choose>`, and `<c:catch>`.
fn	`http://xmlns.jcp.org/jsp/jstl/ficmtion`
	This defines the JSTL 1.2 tag library for the JSP functions. These tags include `<fn:upperCase>`, `<fn:length>`, and `<fn:contains>`.

An abbreviated name such as `fn` must be added to the root XML document element, which in the majority of cases is an HTML element.

A Composition example

Let's delve into some code to demonstrate the JSF composition before we close this chapter. We will start with a simple JSF template that lies out a web page in two areas: a top area and the main area.

This `template-top.xhtml` file is the JSF view that performs the following:

```
<?xml version="1.0" encoding="UTF-8"?>
<!DOCTYPE html PUBLIC "-//W3C//DTD XHTML 1.0 Transitional//EN"
        "http://www.w3.org/TR/xhtml1/DTD/xhtml1-transitional.dtd">
<html xmlns="http://www.w3.org/1999/xhtml"
      xmlns:h="http://xmlns.jcp.org/jsf/html"
      xmlns:ui="http://xmlns.jcp.org/jsf/facelets">

  <h:head>
    <title>Digital Java EE 7 - Sample JSF</title>
    <meta name="viewport"
      content="width=device-width, initial-scale=1.0"/>
    <meta name="description" content="XeNoNiQUE"/>
    <meta name="author" content="Peter Pilgrim"/>

      <h:outputStylesheet library="styles"
        name="main.css" rel="stylesheet"/>
      <h:outputStylesheet name="/styles/top.css"
        rel="stylesheet"/>
  </h:head>

  <h:body>
    <div id="content">
```

```
        <div id="top" class="topContent">
          <ui:insert name="top">
            Reserved for Top Content
          </ui:insert>
        </div>

        <div id="main" class="mainContent">
          <ui:insert name="content">
            Reserved for Main Content
          </ui:insert>
        </div>
      </div>
    </h:body>
</html>
```

The preceding code is the template master. So far so good. This resembles a standard web page with HTML elements and we can see that the page uses the nested DIV elements to structure the content. I will draw your attention to the `<h:outputStylesheet>` tag, which denotes that we should include a couple of cascading style sheets as resources.

The `ui:insert` tag is the composition JSF tag that denotes an area of the template that will be replaced by a placeholder in a client template. An insertion placeholder must have a name and we have two in this example, namely top and content. Note that the `ui:insert` tags are inserted in the body content of the HTML `div` elements.

Here is the code for the client template as `composition1.xhtml`:

```
<?xml version="1.0" encoding="UTF-8"?>
<!DOCTYPE html PUBLIC "-//W3C//DTD XHTML 1.0 Transitional//EN"
        "http://www.w3.org/TR/xhtml1/DTD/xhtml1-transitional.dtd">
<html xmlns="http://www.w3.org/1999/xhtml"
      xmlns:h="http://xmlns.jcp.org/jsf/html"
      xmlns:ui="http://xmlns.jcp.org/jsf/facelets">
  <ui:composition template="/template-top.xhtml">
    <ui:define name="top">
      <h1>layout composition 1</h1>
    </ui:define>

    <ui:define name="content">
      The is the main content
      <h:form>
        <h:commandButton
          action="#{basicFlow.serveResponse}"
            value="Invoke Action" />
```

```
      </h:form>
    </ui:define>
  </ui:composition>
</html>
```

Downloading the example code

You can download the example code files for all
Packt books you have purchased from your account
at http://www.packtpub.com. If you purchased
this book elsewhere, you can visit http://www.
packtpub.com/support and register to have the
files e-mailed directly to you.

The key annotation in this file is the `<ui:composition>` JSF custom tag that
references the master template that is being used. The template attribute refers the
path to the file.

The two `<ui:define>` tags define the name placeholders with the content that
substitutes for the default content in the master template. In this example, the
placeholders are top and content.

Here are the screenshots of this process. The first screenshot is the initial Facelets
view, `index.xhtml`:

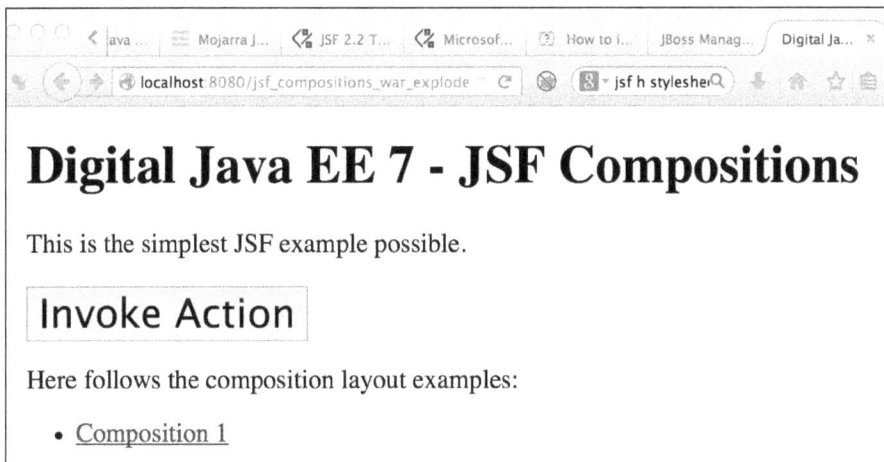

The second is the second Facelets view, `endState.xhtml`:

JSF serving resources

JSF expects our web resources to be placed in the `resources` folder by default. A quick look at the following file directory will help you understand:

`jsf-composition`

`jsf-composition/src/main/webapp`

`jsf-composition/src/main/webapp/resources`

`jsf-composition/src/main/webapp/resources/images`

`jsf-composition/src/main/webapp/resources/javascripts`

`jsf-composition/src/main/webapp/resources/styles`

`jsf-composition/src/main/webapp/WEB-INF`

`jsf-composition/src/main/webapp/WEB-INF/classes`

`jsf-composition/src/main/webapp/WEB-INF/lib`

In this simplified view of the Gradle project, we can see the folders, images, JavaScript, and CSS files that are placed under the `resource` folder. Let's remind ourselves of the JSF view code again, as follows:

```
<h:outputStylesheet library="styles"
                    name="main.css" rel="stylesheet"/>
<h:outputStylesheet name="/styles/top.css"
                    rel="stylesheet"/>
```

These tags are essentially referring to two files: `resources/style/top.css` and `resources/style/main.css`.

In order for these tags to work, the resource must be placed under the resources folder or it can be placed in the `META-INF/resources` folder of a web application JAR file that is deployed with the web application. The specification lists the following two options:

```
<ROOT>/resources/<RES-ID>
```

Otherwise, you can use this:

```
<ROOT>/WEB-INF/lib/<DEPENDANT-JAR>/META-INF/resources/<RES-ID>
```

Here, `<ROOT>` is the project web root, `<DEPENDANT-JAR>` is a third-party dependent JAR, and `<RES-ID>` is the resource identifier.

`<RES-ID>` can be further broken up into formal parts, as follows:

```
<RES-ID> ::=
    [ <LOCALE-PREFIX> / ] +
    [ <LIBRARY-NAME> / ] [ <LIBRARY-VERSION> / ] +
    <RESOURCE-NAME> [ / <RESOURCE-VERSION> ]
```

The term parts inside [] are optional except for the resource name. It is therefore possible to have a resource identifier that is completely internationalized, versioned, and modularized in a library. Perhaps your project might utilize the following resource:

```
/en_us/sportsBulletin/v1_2_3/top_masters_golfer/2015_may.png
```

What happens if you want to buck the trend and change the default location for the resources in JSF 2.2? It is possible to configure an alternative folder in the `web.xml` deployment descriptor file. You can set a context parameter variable: `javax.faces. WEBAPP_RESOURCES_DIRECTORY`.

Here is an extract of the descriptor that defines the resources folder as asset:

```
<context-param>
```

```
        <param-name>
        javax.faces.WEBAPP_RESOURCES_DIRECTORY</param-name>
        <param-value>assets</param-value>
    </context-param>
```

We will cover the full extent of the JSF custom tags and how to submit the HTML forms in *Chapter 3, Building JSF Forms* and *Chapter 4, JSF Validation and AJAX*.

Expression language

The expression language version 3.0 is now a separate specification in Java EE 7. It allows the page author to reference the bean properties, invoke methods, and perform arithmetic operations in the page description language. Originally, EL was a part of the JavaServer Pages specification, and it also became useful for the JSF technology. There are two types of EL: immediate evaluation and deferred evaluation. JSP relied on the immediate form, whereas JSF — because of its lifecycle management of request and response — required a deferred form. EL 3.0 represents the final unification of these strategies.

EL is useful for the page authors so that the digital developer can reference the properties in the managed beans, CDI components, and reference methods in a controller. EL is also used to invoke methods in a controller. EL is used to retrieve values from the beans but it can also set values.

Immediate and deferred expressions

The syntax of an expression has two forms: `${expression}` and `#{expression}`. The beginning dollar character denotes an expression that is evaluated immediately. The beginning hash character denotes an expression that is deferred later.

An immediate expression is always evaluated immediately, and as a consequence, they can only be used to read the values and not to set them. The evaluation takes place when the page is rendered, which is normally the case for JavaServer Pages.

As we are building applications with JSF, we will mostly use deferred expressions in the book. A deferred expression means that the technology behind the scenes is responsible for taking the literal text and interpreting it into a result or invoking a function that returns a result.

Let's quickly jump ahead a little and introduce a JSF custom tag called `<h:inputText>`. This tag renders an HTML input element with a type as text. The tag accepts an `id` attribute to specify an HTML identifier; however, I want to draw your attention to the value attribute, which specifies an EL value expression.

We can write a value expression that is immediately evaluated as in JSP. Here is the code snippet:

```
<h:inputText id="firstName" value="${employee.firstName}"/>
```

This would work as a read-only value. However, it is not possible to apply the value to the employee bean using JSF because the expression is not evaluated in any life cycle state.

If we change the expression from an immediate to a deferred form, then we will see the following behavior:

```
<h:inputText id="firstName" value="#{employee.firstName}"/>
```

With this change, the EL is evaluated immediately during the Render Response phase of the lifecycle. The JSF implementation performs the evaluation and retrieves the value of the `firstName` property from the bean called employee.

When the form is posted back to the server as a Faces request, which by the way is also known as a `postback` event, the JSF implementation has a chance to retrieve the value at a deferred time. It is at these later life cycle states—Apply Request Values, Process Validation, and Update Model—that the value expression is evaluated and the value from the Faces request is injected into the target bean property.

Value expressions

A value expression is one that returns a single result. The value is retrieved from the object graph in the implementation that manages the collections of the Java instances. For Java EE, this is either JSF or JSP provider, and for application servers, it is a Context and Dependency Injection provider. CDI maintains a set of collections internally of the `@javax.inject.Named` beans. (Please wait for the explanation of the named beans or head straight for *Chapter 3, Building JSF Forms*.) In particular, JSF traditionally keeps a record of the managed beans annotated with `@javax.faces.bean.ManagedBean`.

JSP will search for the named object in the page scope, request scope, session scope, and then the application scope of the servlet container. Behind the scenes, there is a subclass of the abstract class `javax.el.ELResolver`, which is responsible for evaluation. This class has useful methods, such as `getValue()`, `setValue()`, `isReadOnly()`, and `invoke()` that developers can use to add evaluation to their own applications programmatically.

In any case, the first port of call of value expressions is the object instance with an identified name. This is known as the initial term. Afterwards, the evaluation logic can traverse through the object graph through a named property using the dot-notation (`.`). The evaluation continues through the subsequent terms in the expression. Let's stick with JSF for the moment and consider that the `#{employee.firstName}` expression will evaluate a deferred search for the object named employee in the scope. The EL resolver will then look up the property in the bean named `firstName`, which in turn will be a call to the `getFirstName()` method. The job will be completed and the EL resolver returns the result value of the property.

EL also works with Java Collections. In particular, the `java.util.Map` collections are treated specially. A standard EL assumes that the collection has a key of a String type we can think of this as `Map<String,Object>`. The entries in Map may be accessed using the dot notation or square bracket notation `[]`.

The following table of value expressions will make this scheme clear for more complex expressions:

Expression	Meaning
`Employee`	This finds the initial term associated with the name `employee`
`employee.firstName`	This resolves the named instance and invokes `getFirstName()`
`employee.department.name`	This resolves the object, invokes `getFirstName()`, retrieves the next object, and invokes `getName()` on this object
`employee["firstName"]`	This is equivalent to the dot notation `employee.firstName`
`employee['firstName']`	This is equivalent to the dot notation `employee.firstName`
`capitalCities['Brazil']`	This finds the name instance and, assuming that `capitalCities` is a type of `java.util.Map`, retrieves the value with the key `Brazil`
`capitalCities["Brazil"]`	This is a map expression equivalent to the previous

The square bracket notation `[]` is very useful with the string that contains dashes and/ or a period character. This notation helps when you want to extract a message from a resource bundle for internationalization purposes. You can write a value expression as: `appMessages["registeredTraveller.applicant.firstName.required"]`.

The square bracket notation allows us to write peculiar expressions. We can write the following value expression:

```
${employee['class'].simpleName}
```

This translates to the following equivalent Java code:

```
employee.getClass().getSimpleName()
```

Map expressions

The EL handles the Map objects seamlessly with the square bracket notation `[]`. If the expression evaluates to a reference that accesses or reads the value associated with Map key on the right-hand-side (an `rvalue`), then the EL resolver translates to a `Map.get("key")` call. The following are the expressions to read a value:

```
${capitalCitiesMap['France']}
  // translates to capitalCitiesMap.get("France")
#{capitialCitesMap['France']}  // ditto, but deferred
```

If the expression is bound to the left-hand side (an `lvalue`), then the EL resolver translates to `Map.put("key", newValue)`.

List expressions

The EL can retrieve objects from an index array with the square bracket notation. It works exactly like a Map expression except that the key must evaluate to a literal integer. In EL, the array index number starts at zero, as expected.

So, these following value expressions are valid if departmentList is a type of java.util.List and departmentArray is a primitive array:

```
${departmentList[0].name}
${departmentArray[0].name}
```

These are the equivalent pseudo Java statements:

```
List<Department> department = resolve(...)
departmentList.get(0).getName()

Department departmentArray[] = resolve(...)
departmentArray[0].getName()
```

Resolving the initial term

The EL relies on the ability to look up the initial term from the servlet container, JSF list of the managed beans, and CDI scopes with the named beans. Essentially, you can give a JSF bean any name that you want, except you should avoid predefined objects. The initial term is the first part of an expression.

In the servlet container, you can refer to several predefined objects. As an example, `requestScope` is a map collection of all the request scope attributes on a page. The request is also a predefined object in the EL that represents the `javax.servlet.http.HttpServletRequest` instance that is passed to the JSF view. We can use this to retrieve the web application context path in an `lvalue` expression, as follows:

```
<link href="#{request.contextPath}/resources/styles/main.css"
    rel="stylesheet"/>
```

The preceding code is extremely helpful to ensure that the resources can be found in a JSF application. It is used to create reliable relative URLs. We will explain more in *Chapter 4*, *JSF Validation and AJAX*.

Resolution of the initial term begins by checking whether the initial term in the expression is a predefined object or not. If it is a predefined object, then the resolver continues this object. If it is not, then the JSF implementation searches for the object name in one of the servlet container scopes in this order: `requestScope`, `sessionScope`, or `applicationScope`.

If the object is not found by name, the JSF 2.2 framework will delegate to `ELResolver`, which will search for the equivalent CDI scopes for the instance and will then look at the registered or annotated managed beans.

The following table lists the predefined object instances in the expression language:

Predefined Name	Description
`applicationScope`	This is a Map collection of the application scope attributes (`javax.servlet.ServletContext.getAttributes()`)
`application`	This refers to the `ServletContext` instance
`cookie`	This is a Map collection of the cookie names and values
`facesContext`	This is the `javax.faces.context.FacesContext` instance of this page and life cycle
`header`	This is a Map collection of the HTTP header parameters that only yield the first elements of the multiple values
`headerValues`	This is a Map collection of the HTTP header parameters yielding a `String[]` array of values

Predefined Name	Description
`initParam`	This is a Map collection of the web application initialization parameters
`param`	This is a Map collection of the HTTP request parameters with only the first element in any array of values
`paramValue`	This is a Map collection of the HTTP request parameters yielding a `String[]` array of values
`requestScope`	This is a Map collecction of the request scope attributes (`HttpServletRequest.getAttributes()`)
`request`	This refers to the `HttpServletRequest` instance
`sessionScope`	This is a Map collection of the session scope attributes (`HttpSession.getAttributes()`)
`session`	This refers to the `HttpSession` instance
`View`	This is the `javax.faces.component.UIViewRoot` instance of the page

Let's move on to method expressions.

Method expressions

EL also permits the association to a method on an object instance. This type of reference is called a method binding expression. The JSF framework permits method expressions to reference the action methods, validators, converters, and phase listeners. A method expression invokes a method on a named object instance and then returns the results, if any.

A good example of a method expression is an action handler on a managed bean, which you already witnessed in the basic JSF example in this chapter.

```
<h:commandButton action="#{basicFlow.serveResponse}"
    value="Invoke Action" />
```

The `#{basicFlow.serverResponse}` expression is a method binding that refers to the controller, the CDI bean named `BasicFlow`, and the `serveResponse()` method.

Parameterized method expressions

EL also supports method invocation with parameters. The parameters can be literal constants. They can also be names of the terms in the scope of the page. This provides a very powerful way to build applications with the list collections and other complicated data structures.

Here is an example of the expression that uses the method parameters code:

```
<h:inputText
  action="#{complexFlow.process('SALE',productLine)}"
    value="Purchase Products/>
```

The `process()` method is invoked on the object instance that is resolved with the `complexFlow` initial term. The first parameter is a literal string. The second parameter is the value of the `subterm`, `productLine`, which we will assume is available to the EL resolver.

It is also possible to get the size of the collection by definition because this is a no-arguments call. This expression looks like `#{genericSearchResult.size()}`, assuming that the initial term references a type of `java.util.Collection` or `java.util.Map`.

Arithmetic expressions

We can use arithmetic operators to perform calculations in the expressions. The expressions may also feature the relational and logical operators.

In EL, the following are the reserved operators:

- Arithmetic operators: + - * / div % mod
- Relational operators: == or eq, != or ne, < or lt, > or gt, <= or le, >= or ge
- Logical operators: && and, || or, ! not
- Empty operator: empty

Here is an example of some of these arithmetic expressions in use:

```
<p> The expression \#{1+5*2-3/4} evaluates to:
  #{1+5*2-3/4} </p>
<p> The expression \#{(2014 div 4) mod 3} evaluates to:
  #{(2014 div 4) mod 3} </p>
<p> The expression \#{2018 lt 2022} evaluates to:
  #{2018 lt 2022} </p>
<p> The expression \#{0.75 == 3/4} evaluates to:
  #{0.75 == 3/4} </p>
```

Note the use of the escape character – the backslash (\), which prevents the JSF view from interpreting the expression. We can also render the expressions directly on the page without the need for a `<h:outputText/>` custom tag. This is a nice treat for the page authors.

> **Preserve the MVC Model**
>
> It is better to place business logic in a controller bean rather than populating the page with complicated conditions.

Page navigation

After JSF 2, it is very easy to provide navigation in a controller. In the `BasicFlow` controller from the earlier JSF example, we relied on implicit page navigation. The developer can specify the next page to render simply by returning a simple string.

Here is the controller class again:

```
@Named @RequestScoped
public class BasicFlow {
    public String serveResponse() {
        return "endState.xhtml";
    }
}
```

In JSF 1, the page navigation was determined explicitly in a Faces Configuration XML file: `/WEB-INF/faces-config.xml`, which made the development harder because of the enforced cognitive indirection. The purpose of `faces-config.xml` is to define the configuration for a JSF web application. The developer can define the navigation rules, inject bean properties, define the properties file, and declare the resource bundles and locales. They can register the converters, validators, and renderer components.

Explicit page navigation is useful for the defined information architecture paths. Writing the page navigation is easier to share in a team. It can be incredibly quick to make prototypes for business stakeholders. However, explicit navigation is probably redundant if your controllers and rendered pages map directly in a one-to-one relationship.

The navigation rules

JSF also supports explicit navigation rules in the Faces Configuration XML file. I should warn you that this is the old style in JSF 1.*x* to describe the navigation between the pages explicitly. In JSF 2.*x*, navigation rules are no longer required, and if you want to describe the page navigation better, remind yourself to learn about Faces Flows (See *Chapter 6, JSF Flows and Finesse*). However, there is a reasonable chance that, in your professional work, you will encounter older JSF applications, and therefore, you will need to learn how the JSF navigation rules are designed.

With this in mind, here is how navigation works explicitly. Suppose that we have a simple page where we can choose between a collection of fruits and vegetables in a set of pages. We can also elect to cancel the choice.

Here is a representation of these rules in the standard Faces Configuration file, `faces-config.xml`. This file is normally found in `src/main/webapp/WEB-INF` in Maven and Gradle projects:

```xml
<?xml version="1.0" encoding="UTF-8"?>
<faces-config xmlns="http://xmlns.jcp.org/xml/ns/javaee"
  xmlns:xsi="http://www.w3.org/2001/XMLSchema-instance"
  xsi:schemaLocation="http://xmlns.jcp.org/xml/ns/javaee
   http://xmlns.jcp.org/xml/ns/javaee/web-facesconfig_2_2.xsd"
  version="2.2">
  <navigaton-rule>
    <from-view-id>/order-start.xhtml</from-view-id>
    <navigation-case>
      <from-outcome>cancel</from-outcome>
      <to-view-id>/cancel.xhtml</to-view-id>
    </navigation-case>
  <navigation-case>
      <from-outcome>fruit</from-outcome>
      <to-view-id>/fruit.xhtml</to-view-id>
    </navigation-case>
  <navigation-case>
      <from-outcome>vegetable</from-outcome>
      <to-view-id>/vegetable.xhtml</to-view-id>
    </navigation-case>
  </navigation-case>
</faces-config>
```

Explicit navigation is determined by a set of rules that the JSF framework applies. The developers will write a series of compound elements in the `<navigation-rule>` tag. The context of the rule is determined by the `<from-view-id>` element, which references a specific view page, `/order-start.xhtml`, or it can be a wildcard rule (asterisk *) that applies to more than one navigation case. Each navigation rule has a collection of the `<navigation-case>` elements. Each case requires a `<from-outcome>` and `<to-view-id>` element. The outcome identifies the literal string, which is returned by the controller method and the view ID is the destination view. So, in the cancellation case, the outcome string identified by cancel will navigate to the `/cancel.xhtml` view.

The advantage of the indirection mapping of the outcome to the view page is obvious. The outcome code in the controller remains the same but the destination view can change.

We can write a JSF controller that handles these navigation rules. This is an extract of the `ProductTypeController` class:

```
@Named @ViewScoped
public class ProductTypeController {
  public String productType;
  /* ... getter and setter omitted */

  public String cancel() { return "cancel";}
  public String navigate() {
    if ("fruit".equalsIgnoreCase(productType)) {
      return "fruit";
    }
    else {
      return "vegetable";
    }
  }
}
```

The `cancel()` method simply returns the cancel outcome, which JSF maps to the `/cancel.xhtml` page because the navigation case matches the outcome. The `navigate()` method sets outcome depending on the `productType` property. There can only be two outcomes in the `fruit` and `vegetable` methods, and the navigation case ensures that the `fruit.xhtml` and `vegetable.xhtml` pages are rendered respectively.

Wildcards

Navigation rules may also have wildcard views. A wildcard navigation rule occurs where the asterisk (*) character prepends to the URI path in the `<from-view-id>` element.

Suppose we have a website with protected pages that should not be displayable unless the user is logged in as a registered user. We can write a navigation rule that is shared for all the pages under the protected area. Let's say we want to secure any web pages under the URI `/secured`:

```
<faces-config ...>
  <navigaton-rule>
    <from-view-id>/secured/*</from-view-id>
    <navigation-case>
      <from-outcome>login</from-outcome>
      <to-view-id>/login.xhtml</to-view-id>
    </navigation-case>
    <navigation-case>
      <from-outcome>register</from-outcome>
      <to-view-id>/register.xhtml</to-view-id>
```

```
    </navigation-case>
  </navigation-case>
  ... more rules ...
</faces-config>
```

The wildcard `from-view-id` `/secured/*` identifies all the pages that start with the `/secured/` prefix. You are allowed to have only one wildcard in a URI path.

Using wildcards in an outcome brings forth the question of precedence. When does a wildcard `view id` take precedence over a direct outcome? Here is a navigation case extract of the Faces Configuration XML where we set the source page view:

```
<from-view-id>stocks.xhtml</from-view-id>
// Has higher precedure than
<from-view-id>*</from-view-id>
```

A direct `view id` always has a higher precedence over an equivalent wildcard view. JSF chooses the navigation case of a direct view, `stocks.xhtml`, over the wildcard view, as follows:

```
<from-view-id>/secured/portfolio/*</from-view-id>
// Has higher precedure than
<from-view-id>/secured/*</from-view-id>
```

If there are multiple wildcard views that are in competition for a match, then the longest match is chosen. JSF chooses the navigation case in the longest matching view, which is in the illustration `/secured/portfolio/*`.

Conditional navigation

A JSF explicit page navigation also supports the idea of conditional navigation in the Faces configuration file. This allows the developer to declaratively set up the navigation rules based on the dynamic state of the application. Conditional navigation is achieved by using the `<if>` element tag, as shown in the next example:

```
<faces-config>
  <navigaton-rule>
    <from-view-id>/shopping-cart.xhtml</from-view-id>
    <navigation-case>
      <from-outcome>nextPage</from-outcome>
      <if>#{user.registered}</if>
      <to-view-id>/existing-customer.xhtml</to-view-id>
    </navigation-case>
    <navigation-case>
      <from-outcome>nextPage</from-outcome>
      <if>#{!user.registered}</if>
```

```
        <to-view-id>/new-customer.xhtml</to-view-id>
    </navigation-case>
  </navigation-case>
</faces-config>
```

The body content of `<if>` is a deferred value expression, which is evaluated in the JSF lifecycle and should return a Boolean value. In the code, the `#{user.registered}` expression is evaluated to the bean with the current logged-in user profile bean and property called registered. The `#{!user.registered}` expression evaluates the negation—note the use of the exclamation character for the operator.

Static navigation

To complete the digital developer story about page navigation, it is time to look at static navigation with JSF. Static navigation allows us to traverse from one JSF page to another without invoking a managed bean controller. It is useful for the page views where there is no requirement for a server-side Java code or where there are no HTML input elements. Static navigation is achieved from a combination of markups on the Facelets view and explicit navigation rules.

In the earlier `Basic JSF` example, we had a page view with `<h:link>`. Let's change this to `<h:commandButton>`:

```
<h:form>
  ...
  <h:commandButton action="your-next-view">
      Composition 1
  </h:commandButton>
</h:form>
```

The action attribute specifies the name of outcome to navigate. We will replace the old element with the `<h:commandButton>` JSF tag. The action attribute specifies the value expression. JSF looks for the initial term in several contexts but it will also search the Faces configuration to match the navigation rule. For this traversal to work, we also require a navigation rule in the Faces configuration:

```
<navigation-case>
  <from-outcome>your-next-view</from-outcome>
  <to-view-id>/shopping-cart.xhtml</to-view-id>
</navigation-case>
```

The navigation rule matches the `your-next-view` outcome from the Facelets view, and so JSF can navigate to the destination page.

I think we will stop here regarding the page navigation topic. We will continue our developer digital journey with page navigation in *Chapter 4, JSF Validation and AJAX*.

Summary

This chapter has been a robust adventure in the world of JSF. You should be able to understand the theory of how the framework has been put together. We covered the key features of JSF such as an HTML5 friendly markup and a templating engine. JSF is a part of the Java EE platform and is available on many application servers and servlet containers. We learned how the JSF framework relates to the Model-View-Controller design pattern.

You should be able to understand the request and response processing lifecycle and the phase change state model in JSF under the execute and render lifecycle.

Towards the middle chapter, we inspected the JSF basic pages, custom tag libraries, Facelets views, and a simple backing bean. We also observed a composition layout with both the master and client templates.

We also went in detail in the powerful EL framework, which is a part of Java EE 7 and JSF 2.2. EL is a very important facility for the server-side Java applications, especially if they are built against Faces. To finish the journey, we looked at both implicit and explicit page navigation.

We now have enough knowledge to constitute a JSF foundation. In the next chapter, we will look at beefing up our JSF knowledge with the HTML forms and set the ground running with validation. In the subsequent chapters, we will definitely lose the XHTML documents and add HTML5 so that we can develop more modern websites.

Exercises

Here are the questions for this chapter:

1. Where else in computer science might one find the Model-View-Controller design pattern?

2. Why do you think that keen computer scientists and architects wanted to separate business logic from the presentation view code?

3. Consider a situation where you have been contracted by the municipal government for a local territory.

4. You have been asked to write an electoral roll web application for the voters to replace the traditional paper trail. Instead of sending official letters to the citizens and waiting to receive the filled-in forms, the citizens will be able to register for the electoral roll online. What constitutes the Model-View-Controller in this application?

5. What parts of the JSF life cycle map to the Model-View-Controller pattern?

6. Describe when and where the framework will encounter the Restore View phase.

7. Describe the process of an HTML form submission. What happens in JSF transferring the contents of an HTML form to the Java POJOS?

8. When a customer enters an invalid value in a form, describe the phases of the JSF life cycle that will process the Faces request. What do you think is added to the Faces response? Why?

9. Why have the JSF specification writers explicitly designed a special Render Response phase?

10. JSF has explicitly separated the valuation from the invocation of business logic in a backing bean (or action controller). Other web frameworks have a validation code in the backing beans. Outline the pros and cons of both the approaches.

11. Download the code for chapter 2 and study how the web application is laid out. If you are feeling brave, modify one of the project examples. Add another string property to the backing bean, and then add a JSF form text field (hint: `<f:inputText>`). What happens? If your changes go wrong, you can always revert the changes.

3
Building JSF Forms

"It's the whole thing. The way something actually works on so many different levels. Ultimately, of course, design defines so much of our experiences."

Sir Jony Ive, Senior Vice President of Design, Apple USA

JavaServer Faces is an example of a component-oriented web application framework, as opposed to Java EE 8 MVC (See *Chapter 9, Java EE MVC Framework*), WebWork, or Apache Struts, which are known as request-oriented web application frameworks.

A request-oriented framework is one where the information flow is from the web request to the response. Such frameworks provide you with an ability and structure above the `javax.servlet.http.HttpServletRequest` and `javax.servlet.http.HttpServletResponse` objects, but there are no special user interface components. With additional help, the application user must program the mapping of the parameters and attributes to the data entity models. The developer, therefore, has to write parsing logic.

It is important to understand that component-oriented frameworks, such as JSF, have their detractors. The quick inspection of the code resembles the components found in a standalone client such as Java Swing or even JavaFX, but the very same `HttpServletRequest` and `HttpServletResponse` lurk behind the scenes. Hence, a competent JSF developer has to be aware of the Servlet API and underlying servlet scopes. This was a valid criticism in 2004, and in the digital marketing age, a digital developer has to know not only Servlet, but also we can presume that they would be open to learning other technologies such as JavaScript. Based on the knowledge obtained from *Chapter 2, JavaServer Faces Lifecycle*, we will learn about building the JSF forms.

Create, Retrieve, Update, and Delete

In this chapter, we will solve an everyday problem with JSF. The Java EE framework and enterprise application are about solving data entry issues. Unlike social networking software that is built with a different architecture and non-functional requirements such as scalability, performance, statelessness, and eventual consistency, Java EE applications are designed for stateful work flows, as shown in the following screenshot:

Screenshot of the page view to create contact details

The preceding screenshot is the JSF application, `jsf-crud`, which shows the create contact details form.

As a reminder, you can find the entire code for this application with the book's source code.

Typically, an enterprise application captures the information from a web user, stores it in a data store, and allows this information to be retrieved and edited. There is usually an option to delete the user's information. In software engineering, we call this idiom Create, Retrieve, Update, and Delete (CRUD).

> What constitutes the actual deletion of the user and customer data is a matter that ultimately affects the business owners who are under the pressure to conform to the local and international laws that define privacy and data protection.

A basic create entity JSF form

Let's create a basic form that captures the user's name, e-mail address, and date of birth. We will write this code using HTML5 and take advantage of Bootstrap for the modern day CSS and JavaScript. Refer to `http://getbootstrap.com/getting-started/`.

The following is the JSF Facelet view, `createContact.xhtml`:

```
<!DOCTYPE html>
<html xmlns="http://www.w3.org/1999/xhtml"
      xmlns:ui="http://xmlns.jcp.org/jsf/facelets"
      xmlns:h="http://xmlns.jcp.org/jsf/html"
      xmlns:p="http://xmlns.jcp.org/jsf/passthrough"
      xmlns:f="http://xmlns.jcp.org/jsf/core">
    <h:head>
        <meta charset="utf-8"/>
        <title>Demonstration Application </title>
        <link href="#{request.contextPath}/resources/styles/bootstrap.
css" rel="stylesheet"/>
        <link href="#{request.contextPath}/resources/styles/main.css"
rel="stylesheet"/>
    </h:head>

    <h:body>
        <div class="main-container">
            <div class="header-content">
                <div class="navbar navbar-inverse"
                role="navigation">
                  ...
                </div>
```

```
        </div><!-- headerContent -->

        <div class="mainContent">
            <h1> Enter New Contact Details </h1>

            <h:form id="createContactDetail"
                styleClass="form-horizontal"
                p:role="form">
                ...
            </h:form>

        </div><!-- main-content -->

        <div class="footer-content">

        </div> <!-- footer-content -->
      </div> <!-- main-container -->
    </h:body>
    <script src="#{request.contextPath}/resources/javascripts/jquery-
1.11.0.js"></script>
    <script src="#{request.contextPath}/resources/javascripts/
bootstrap.js"></script>
    <script src="#{request.contextPath}/resources/app/main.js">
    </script>
</html>
```

You should already recognize the `<h:head>` and `<h:body>` JSF custom tags. As the type is a Facelet view, (`*.xhtml`), the document must actually be well-formed like an XML document. You should have noticed that certain HTML5 element tags such as `<meta>` are closed and completed; the XHTML document must be well-formed in JSF.

> **Always close the XHTML elements**
>
> The typical e-commerce application has web pages with standard HTML with the `<meta>`, `<link>`, and `<br>` tags. In the XHTML and Facelet views, these tags, which web designers normally leave open and hanging, must be closed. **Extensible Mark-up Language (XML)** is less forgiving and XHTML, which is derived from XML, must be well-formed.

The new `<h:form>` tag is a JSF custom tag that corresponds to the HTML form element. A JSF form element shares many of the attributes of the HTML partner. You can see that the `id` attribute is just the same. However, instead of the `class` attribute, we have the `styleClass` attribute in JSF, because in Java, the `java.lang.Object.getClass()` method is reserved and therefore, cannot be overridden.

What is the JSF request context path expression?

The curious markup around the links to the style sheets, JavaScript, and other resources is the expression language: `#{request.contextPath}`. The expression reference ensures that the web application path is added to the URL of the JSF resources. Bootstrap CSS itself relies on the font glyph icons in a particular folder. The JSF images, JavaScript module files, and CSS files should be placed in the resources folder of the web root.

The `p:role` attribute is an example of the JSF `passthrough` attribute, which informs the JSF render kit to send through the key and value to the rendered output. The `passthrough` attributes are key additions in JSF 2.2, which is a part of Java EE 7. They allow JSF to play well with the recent HTML5 frameworks such as Bootstrap and Foundation (`http://foundation.zurb.com/`).

Here is an extract of the rendered HTML source output:

```
<h1> Enter New Contact Details </h1>
<form id="createContactDetail" name="createContactDetail"
  method="post"
    action="/jsf-crud-1.0-SNAPSHOT/createContactDetail.xhtml"
      class="form-horizontal"
        enctype="application/x-www-form-urlencoded"
          role="form">
<input type="hidden" name="createContactDetail"
value="createContactDetail" />
```

JSF was implemented before Bootstrap was created in Twitter. How could the JSF designer retrofit the framework in order to be compatible with the recent HTML5, CSS3, and JavaScript innovations? This is where the `passthrough` attribute helps. By declaring the XML namespace in XHTML with the URI `http://xmlns.jcp.org/jsf/passthrough`. We can enable the feature for the page view. As you can see, the attribute name and value, `role="form"`, is simply passed through to the output. The `passthrough` attributes allow JSF to easily handle the HTML5 features such as placeholders in the text input fields, which we will exploit from now onwards.

If you are brand new to web development, you might be scared of markup that appears to be overcomplicated. There are lots and lots of DIV HTML elements, which are often created by page designers and Interface Developers. This is the historical effect and just the way that HTML and the web has evolved over time. The practices of 2002 have no bearing on 2016. I recommend that you read the *Appendix C, Agile Performance – Working inside Digital Teams*.

Let's take a deeper look at `<h:form>` and fill in the missing details. Here is the extracted code:

```
<h:form id="createContactDetail"
   styleClass="form-horizontal"
   p:role="form">
   <div class="form-group">
     <h:outputLabel for="title" class="col-sm-3 control-label">
        Title</h:outputLabel>
     <div class="col-sm-9">
       <h:selectOneMenu class="form-control"
         id="title"
         value="#{contactDetailController.contactDetail.title}">
         <f:selectItem itemLabel="--" itemValue="" />
         <f:selectItem itemValue="Mr" />
         <f:selectItem itemValue="Mrs" />
         <f:selectItem itemValue="Miss" />
         <f:selectItem itemValue="Ms" />
         <f:selectItem itemValue="Dr" />
       </h:selectOneMenu>
     </div>
   </div>
   <div class="form-group">
     <h:outputLabel for="firstName" class="col-sm-3 control-label">
       First name</h:outputLabel>
     <div class="col-sm-9">
       <h:inputText class="form-control"
        value="#{contactDetailController.contactDetail.firstName}"
        id="firstName" placeholder="First name"/>
     </div>
   </div>
   ... Rinse and Repeat for middleName and lastName ...
   <div class="form-group">
     <h:outputLabel for="email" class="col-sm-3 control-label">
     Email address </h:outputLabel>
     <div class="col-sm-9">
       <h:inputText type="email"
        class="form-control" id="email"
        value="#{contactDetailController.contactDetail.email}"
        placeholder="Enter email"/>
     </div>
   </div>
   <div class="form-group">
     <h:outputLabel class="col-sm-3 control-label">
```

```
      Newsletter
    </h:outputLabel>
    <div class="col-sm-9 checkbox">
      <h:selectBooleanCheckbox id="allowEmails"
    value="#{contactDetailController.contactDetail.allowEmails}">
          Send me email promotions
      </h:selectBooleanCheckbox>
    </div>
  </div>
  <h:commandButton styleClass="btn btn-primary"
    action="#{contactDetailController.createContact()}"
    value="Submit" />
</h:form>
```

This form is built using the Bootstrap CSS style, but we will ignore the extraneous details and concentrate purely on the JSF custom tags.

The <h:selectOneMenu> tag is a JSF custom tag that corresponds to the HTML form select element. The <f:selectItem> tag corresponds to the HTML form select option element. The <h:inputText> tag corresponds to the HTML form input element. The <h:selectBooleanCheckbox> tag is a special custom tag to represent the HTML select with only one checkbox element. Finally, <h:commandButton> represents the HTML form submit element.

The JSF HTML output label

The <h:outputLabel> tag renders the HTML form label element in the following way:

```
<h:outputLabel for="firstName" class="col-sm-3 control-label">
    First name</h:outputLabel>
```

The developers should prefer this tag in conjunction with the other associated JSF form input tags because the special for attribute targets the correct sugared identifier for the element.

Here is the rendered output:

```
<label for="createContactDetail:firstName"
    class="col-sm-3 control-label"> First name</label>
```

We could have written the tag using the value attribute, as follows:

```
<h:outputLabel for="firstName" class="col-sm-3 control-label"
    value="firstName" />
```

It is also possible to take advantage of internationalization at this point; so just for illustration, we could rewrite the page content as follows:

```
<h:outputLabel for="firstName" class="col-sm-3 control-label"
    value="${myapplication.contactForm.firstName}" />
```

For more information about internationalization and resource bundles in JSF, please see the *Appendix A*, *JSF with HTML5, Resources, and Faces Flows*. Let's move on to the input fields.

The JSF HTML input text

The `<h:inputText>` tag allows data to be entered in the form like text, as shown in the following code:

```
<h:inputText class="form-control"
    value="#{contactDetailController.contactDetail.firstName}"
        id="firstName" placeholder="First name"/>
```

The value attribute represents a JSF expression language, and the clue is that the evaluation string starts with a hash character. The Expression Language value references a scoped backing bean `ContactDetailController.java` with the name of `contactDetailController`. In JSF 2.2, there are now convenience attributes to support the HTML5 support so that the standard `id`, `class`, and `placeholder` attributes work as expected.

The rendered output is as follows:

```
<input id="createContactDetail:firstName" type="text"
    name="createContactDetail:firstName" class="form-control" />
```

Note that the sugared `createContactDetails:firstName` identifier matches the output of the `<h:outputLabel>` tag.

The JSF HTML select one menu

The `<h:selectOneMenu>` tag generates a single select drop-down list. In fact, it is a part of a family of selection type custom tags. See *JSF HTML select Boolean checkbox* in the next section.

In the code, we have the following code:

```
<h:selectOneMenu class="form-control"
        id="title"
        value="#{contactDetailController.contactDetail.title}">
    <f:selectItem itemLabel="--" itemValue="" />
    <f:selectItem itemValue="Mr" />
```

```
        <f:selectItem itemValue="Mrs" />
        <f:selectItem itemValue="Miss" />
        <f:selectItem itemValue="Ms" />
        <f:selectItem itemValue="Dr" />
    </h:selectOneMenu>
```

The `<h:selectOneMenu>` tag corresponds to an HTML Form select tag The `value` attribute is again a JSF expression language string.

In JSF, we can use another new custom tag, `<f:selectItem>`, which adds a child javax.faces.component.UISelectItem to the nearest parent UI component. The `<f:selectItem>` tag accepts an `itemLabel` and `itemValue` attribute. If you set the `itemValue` and do not specify the `itemLabel`, then the value becomes the label. So, for the first item, the option is set to -- but the value submitted to the form is a blank string because we want to hint to the user that there is a value that ought be chosen.

The rendered HTML output is instructive, as follows:

```
<select id="createContactDetail:title" size="1"
  name="createContactDetail:title" class="form-control">
  <option value="" selected="selected">--</option>
  <option value="Mr">Mr</option>
  <option value="Mrs">Mrs</option>
  <option value="Miss">Miss</option>
  <option value="Ms">Ms</option>
  <option value="Dr">Dr</option>
</select>
```

The JSF HTML select Boolean checkbox

The `<h:selectBooleanCheckbox>` custom tag is a special case of selection where there is only one item that the user can choose. Typically, in a web application, you will find such an element in the final terms and conditions form or usually in the marketing e-mail section in an e-commerce application.

In the targeted managed bean, the only value must be a Boolean type, as shown in the following code:

```
<h:selectBooleanCheckbox for="allowEmails"
  value="#{contactDetailController.contactDetail.allowEmails}">
    Send me email promotions
</h:selectBooleanCheckbox>
```

The rendered output for this custom tag looks as follows:

```
<input id="createContactDetail:allowEmails" type="checkbox"
  name="createContactDetail:allowEmails" />
```

The JSF HTML command button

The `<h:commandButton>` custom tags correspond to the HTML form submit element. They accept an action attribute in JSF that refers to a method in a backing bean. The syntax is again in the JSF expression language:

```
<h:commandButton styleClass="btn btn-primary"
  action="#{contactDetailController.createContact()}"
    value="Submit" />
```

When the user presses this **Submit** button, the JSF framework will find the named managed bean corresponding to `contactDetailController` and then invoke the no-arguments method: `createContact()`.

> In the expression language, it is important to note that the parentheses are not required because the interpreter or Facelet automatically introspects whether the meaning is an action (`MethodExpression`) or a value definition (`ValueExpression`). Be aware that most of the examples in the real world do not add the parentheses as a short hand.

The `value` attribute denotes the text for the form **Submit** button. We can write the tag in an alternative way and achieve the same result, as follows:

```
<h:commandButton styleClass="btn btn-primary"
    action="#{contactDetailController.createContact()}" >
    Submit
</h:commandButton>
```

The value is taken from the body content of the custom tag. The rendered output of the tag looks as follows:

```
<input type="submit" name="createContactDetail:j_idt45"
  value="Submit" class="btn btn-primary" />
<input type="hidden" name="javax.faces.ViewState"
  id="j_id1:javax.faces.ViewState:0"
    value="-3512045671223885154:3950316419280637340"
      autocomplete="off" />
```

The preceding code illustrates the output from the JSF renderer in the Mojarra implementation (`https://javaserverfaces.java.net/`), which is the reference implementation. You can clearly see that the renderer writes an HTML submit and hidden element in the output. The hidden element captures information about the view state that is posted back to the JSF framework (postback), which allows it to restore the view.

Finally, here is a screenshot of the contact details form:

The contact details input JSF form with additional DOB fields

There are many more JSF custom tags to consider, and you will find a full table list of all the tags later in the chapter. Now, let's examine the backing bean that is also known as the controller.

The backing bean controller

For our simple POJO form, we need a backing bean or, in modern day JSF developer parlance, a managed bean controller.

The following is the entire code for ContactDetailController:

```
package uk.co.xenonique.digital;
import javax.ejb.EJB;
import javax.inject.Named;
import javax.faces.view.ViewScoped;
import java.util.List;
```

```
@Named("contactDetailController")
@ViewScoped
public class ContactDetailController {
  @EJB ContactDetailService contactDetailService;

  private ContactDetail contactDetail =
    new ContactDetail();

  public ContactDetail getContactDetail() {
      return contactDetail;
  }

  public void setContactDetail(
    ContactDetail contactDetail) {
      this.contactDetail = contactDetail;
  }

  public String createContact() {
      contactDetailService.add(contactDetail);
      contactDetail = new ContactDetail();
      return "index.xhtml";
  }

  public List<ContactDetail> retrieveAllContacts() {
      return contactDetailService.findAll();
  }
}
```

For this managed bean, let's introduce you to a couple of new annotations. The first annotation is called `@javax.inject.Named` and it declares this POJO to be a CDI-managed bean, which also simultaneously declares a JSF controller. Here, we will explicitly declare the value of the name of the managed bean as `contactDetailController`. This is actually the default name of the managed bean, so we could have left it out.

We can also write an alternative name, as follows:

```
@Named("wizard")
@ViewScoped
public class ContactDetailController { /* .. . */ }
```

Then, JSF would give us a bean with the name `wizard`. The name of the managed bean helps in the expression language syntax.

When we are talking about JSF, we can interchange the term backing bean with managed bean freely. Many professional Java web developers understand that both the terms mean the same thing!

The `@javax.faces.view.ViewScoped` annotation denotes that the controller has scoped the lifecycle of the view. The scoped view is designed for a situation where the application data is preserved just for one page until the user navigates to another page. As soon as the user navigates to another page, JSF destroys the bean. JSF removes the reference to the view-scoped bean from its internal data structure and the object is left for the garbage collector.

The `@ViewScoped` annotation is new in Java EE 7 and JSF 2.2 and fixes a bug between the Faces and CDI specifications. This is because CDI and JSF were developed independently. By looking at the Javadoc, you will find an older annotation: `@javax.faces.bean.ViewScoped`, which comes from JSF 2.0 and was not part of the CDI specification.

For now, if you choose to write the `@ViewScoped` annotated controllers, you probably should use `@ManagedBean`. We will explain `@ViewScoped` beans later in this chapter.

`ContactDetailController` also has a dependency on an **Enterprise Java Bean (EJB)** service endpoint: `ContactDetailService` and most importantly, has a bean property: `ContactDetail`. Note the `getter` and `setter` methods and we will also ensure that the property is instantiated during the construction time.

We will now turn our attention to the methods, as follows:

```
public String createContact() {
  contactDetailService.add(contactDetail);
  contactDetail = new ContactDetail();
  return "index.xhtml";
}

public List<ContactDetail> retrieveAllContacts() {
  return contactDetailService.findAll();
}
```

The `createContact()` method uses EJB to create a new contact detail. It returns a string, which is the next Facelet view: `index.xhtml`. This method is referenced by `<h:commandButton>`.

The `retrieveAllContacts()` method invokes the data service to fetch the list collection of the entities. This method will be referenced by another page.

Data service

The controller relies on an entity bean: `ContactDetail`. Here is the code for this bean, which has been simplified:

```java
package uk.co.xenonique.digital;
import javax.persistence.*;
import java.util.Date;

@Entity
@Table(name="CONTACT")
@NamedQueries({
  @NamedQuery(name="ContactDetail.findAll",
    query = "select c from ContactDetail c " +
            "order by c.lastName, c.middleName, c.firstName")
})
public class ContactDetail {
  @Id
  @GeneratedValue(strategy = GenerationType.AUTO)
  @Column(name="CONTACT_ID", nullable = false,
          insertable = true, updatable = true,
          table = "CONTACT")
  private long id;

  private String title="";
  private String firstName;
  private String middleName;
  private String lastName;
  private String email;

  @Temporal(TemporalType.DATE)
  private Date dob;

  private Boolean allowEmails;

  public long getId() { return id; }
  public void setId(long id) { this.id = id; }

  public String getTitle() { return title; }
  public void setTitle(String title) { this.title = title; }

  // Other getters and setters omitted

  // equals, hashCode, toString omitted
}
```

It uses the **Java Persistence API (JPA)** annotation to map the Java properties to a relational database.

There are a set of annotations that declare against the entity itself. The `@Entity` annotation marks this POJO as a persistence capable object. The `@Table` annotation overrides the default database table name for the entity—instead of `CONTACT_DETAIL`, it becomes `CONTACT`. The `@NameQueries` and `@NameQuery` annotations define the name queries in the **Java Persistence Query Language (JPQL)**.

The remaining annotations declare the metadata that is associated with the database table columns. The `@Id` annotation specifies the property that will be the primary key, which is the `id` field. The `@GenerationValue` annotation declares that the primary key is automatically generated. The JPA provider generates a unique value if there is a `0` or null value. The other annotation on this property—`@Column`—renames the default database table column name from `ID` to `CONTACT_ID` and sets certain constraints.

Finally, JPA must specify the date time type for a field with the `@Temporal` annotation. The annotation value can be `Temporal.DATE`, `Temporal.TIME`, or `Temporal.TIMESTAMP`.

You will learn about the JPA in my book, Java EE 7 Developer Handbook, where there are several concise and devoted chapters on the subject. However, this book concerns the web application development.

It should be apparent now that the entity bean can be directly used in a JSF form. Do you remember the JSF expression language for the form properties? Look at the following first name field:

```
<h:inputText class="form-control"
  value="#{contactDetailController.contactDetail.firstName}"
    id="firstName" placeholder="First name"/>
```

As the JSF framework knows about `contactDetailController` by name, which has a class type of `ContactDetailController`, it can move through the object graph and determine the property. The controller has a property called `contactDetail` of the `ContactDetail` type, which has a `firstName` property of the String type.

The key requirement for a controller is that the entity should be instantiated by the time the form is submitted and when the data is retrieved from the form for the `remembered` values. Let's have a look at the following code:

```
private ContactDetail contactDetail = new ContactDetail();
```

There are a number of possibilities that the developer can make use of for a large object hierarchy. Lazy loading and lazy creation of the data structure can help in these situations.

Let's look now at the enterprise service bean, `ContactDataService`:

```
package uk.co.xenonique.digital;
import javax.ejb.Stateful;
import javax.persistence.*;
import java.util.List;

@Stateful
public class ContactDetailService {
  @PersistenceContext(unitName = "applicationDB",
      type = PersistenceContextType.EXTENDED)
  private EntityManager entityManager;

  public void add(ContactDetail contactDetail) {
    entityManager.persist(contactDetail);
  }

  public void update(ContactDetail contactDetail) {
    ContactDetail contactDetailUpdated
        = entityManager.merge(contactDetail);
    entityManager.persist(contactDetailUpdated);
  }

  public void delete(ContactDetail contactDetail) {
    entityManager.remove(contactDetail);
  }

  public List<ContactDetail> findAll() {
    Query query = entityManager.createNamedQuery(
        "ContactDetail.findAll");
    return query.getResultList();
  }
}
```

This class is an example of a stateful session EJB, which is essentially a poolable remote service endpoint in an application server with a conversational state. A stateful session bean is associated with a calling client.

`ContactDetailService` has a dependency on a JPA provider, as we can see with the injection of the entity manager through the `@PersistenceContext` annotation. Note that we are using the extended variety of the persistence context because the conversation can live for more than one request-response cycle.

In a non-extended persistence conversation, EntityManager will live only as long as there is a JTA transaction. Once the transaction is finished in the Java EE model, all of the persistence objects are detached from `EntityManager` and they become unmanaged.

An extended persistence conversation is one where EntityManager can outlive the scope of a **Java Transaction API (JTA)** transaction. In fact, it can survive over several transactions. The persistence objects do not become detached from EntityManager in this case; the data is only saved to the database when it is flushed explicitly or through the special demarcation of states that the application server provides around the stateful session beans. For this reason, the extended persistence contexts can be used only in the stateful session beans.

For more information about the permission and stateful session beans, see my sister book, *Java EE 7 Developer Handbook*.

For now, we should only concern ourselves with the methods in `ContactDataService`. The `add()` method inserts a new record in the database. The `update()` method amends an existing record and `delete()` removes the record. The `findAll()` method retrieves all of the `ContactDetail` records from the underlying database. It uses the named JPQL query: `Contact.findAll`.

You might be wondering where in the user interface is the JSF field that sets up the `Date of Birth (DOB)` property, as seen in the `ContactDetail` entity bean. We will add these fields later on.

JSF custom tags

As you have seen, JSF comes with a wealth of custom tag libraries. In order to get the best out of the framework, a digital developer should learn about them and their abilities. The tags can be divided into namespaces as we have previously seen.

The HTML render kit custom tags

The first set of tags in JSF 2.2 relate to the rendering of the HTML elements. They are in the name space: `http://xmlns.jcp.org/jsf/html`. The default implementation of the render kit in the JSF framework contains component tags for `javax.faces.component.UIComponent`.

Here is a table of the HTML render kit tags:

JSF custom tag	Description
`<h:column>`	This renders an instance of `javax.faces.component.UIColumn` that represents a single column of data in a parent UIData component. This custom tag is used in `<h:dataTable>`.
`<h:commandButton>`	This renders an HTML input element with the submit or rest type.
`<h:commandLink>`	This renders an HTML anchor element that performs like a submit button, and therefore, the tag must be added in an `<h:form>` tag.
`<h:dataTable>`	This renders an HTML table with rows and columns including the table headers and table column cells.
`<h:form>`	This renders an HTML form element.
`<h:graphicImage>`	This renders an HTML image element.
`<h:inputFile>`	This renders an HTML form input element with a file type and allows an application to upload a file from the client's operating system.
`<h:inputHidden>`	This renders an HTML form input element with a hidden type.
`<h:inputSecret>`	This renders an HTML form input element with a password type.
`<h:inputText>`	This renders an HTML form input element with a text type.
`<h:inputTextarea>`	This renders an HTML form text area element.
`<h:link>`	This renders an HTML anchor element that performs an HTTP GET request to the application.
`<h:outputFormat>`	This tag renders the parameterized text with formatted parameters.
`<h:outputLabel>`	This renders an HTML label element.
`<h:outputLink>`	This renders an HTML anchor element that is typically used for non-JSF application links.
`<h:outputText>`	This tag renders the output to the view.
`<h:message>`	This renders a single message to a page for a specific component. The tag allows internationalization through a resource bundle.
`<h:messages>`	This renders a series of messages to a page from the Faces Context.

JSF custom tag	Description
`<h:panelGrid>`	This custom tag renders components into a grid. The default JSF implementation uses the HTML table element.
`<h:panelGroup>`	This custom tag organizes the nested JSF tags into defined groups where the layout produces and generates a single entity.
`<h:selectBooleanCheckbox>`	This renders an HTML input element with a checkbox type and is designed for Boolean properties.
`<h:selectManyCheckbox>`	This renders a list of the HTML input elements with the type as checkbox.
`<h:selectManyListbox>`	This renders a list of the HTML select option elements.
`<h:selectManyMenu>`	This renders a list of the HTML select option elements.
`<h:selectOneListbox>`	This renders a list of the HTML select option elements.
`<h:selectOneMenu>`	This renders a list of the HTML select option elements.
`<h:selectOneRadio>`	This renders a list of the HTML input elements with the type as radio.

The JSF HTML tags are divided into different kinds, such as commands, inputs, outputs, and types in order to handle the selection of items. There are also additional tags to handle special cases such as `<h:graphicImage>` to render the `<img>` tags and `<h:dataTable>` to render the `<table>` information.

The core JSF custom tags

The core JSF custom tags add the features that are independent to the HTML render kit tags. The namespace for these tags is `http://xmlns.jcp.org/jsf/core`. The JSF framework is extendable. If you want an alternative render kit, then all you have to do is add it. The core JSF custom tags will still work.

Here is a table of the JSF Core tags:

JSF custom tag	Description
`<f:actionListener>`	This registers an `ActionListener` instance.
`<f:attribute>`	This adds an attribute to `UIComponent` with the closest parent `UIComponent` action.
`<f:convertDateTime>`	This registers `DateTimeConverter` to `UIComponent`.
`<f:convertNumber>`	This registers `NumberConverter` to `UIComponent`.

JSF custom tag	Description
`<f:converter>`	This renders an HTML anchor element that performs like a submit button, and therefore, the tag must be added in `<h:form>`.
`<f:facet>`	This adds a facet to a component.
`<f:loadBundle>`	This loads a resource bundle that is localized for Locale of the current view and stores the properties as `java.util.Map`.
`<f:metadata>`	This declares the metadata facet for this view.
`<f:param>`	This adds a parameter to `UIComponent`.
`<f:phaseListener>`	This registers a `PhaseListener` instance to the page.
`<f:selectItem>`	This specifies an item for a select one or select many component.
`<f:selectItems>`	This specifies items for a select one or select many component.
`<f:setProperty-ActionListener>`	This registers `ActionListener` to the component for a particular property.
`<f:subview>`	This creates another JSF naming context (See `<f:view>`).
`<f:validateDoubleRange>`	This registers `DoubleRangeValidator` to the component.
`<f:validateLength>`	This registers `LengthValidator` to the component.
`<f:validateLongRange>`	This registers `LongRangeValidator` to the component.
`<f:validateRegex>`	This registers a regular expression validator to the component. If the entire pattern matches, then it is valid.
`<f:validateRequired>`	This ensures that a value in a component is present when a form is submitted.
`<f:validator>`	This registers a named Validator instance to the component.
`<f:valueChangeListener>`	This registers `ValueChangeListener` to the component.
`<f:verbatim>`	This adds a markup to a JSF page and allows the body content to pass directly to the rendered output.
`<f:view>`	This sets parameters on the JSF current naming context for the page. Use this tag to override the locale, encoding, or content type.
`<f:viewParam>`	This adds a view parameter to the metadata of a facet so that the page has access to query the parameters in a GET request. This tag can be used only in `<f:metadata>`.

The purpose of many core JSF tags is to enhance and configure an `UIComponent` instance. You have already seen this example used with the `<f:selectItem>` tag in `<h:selectOneMenu>` in the previous code example, `createContact.xhtml`. (See the section *Basic JSF form*).

For most circumstances, the developer can add attributes, listeners, converters, facets, parameters, and selections to the components using the core JSF tag.

The template composition custom tags

The library of the template JSF custom tags provides you with the ability to compose pages with content from the other pages. Templating allows the content to reused and shared across an entire JSF application. Best of all, the templates can be adapted by specifying the parameters so that there is adaptability and flexibility in the mix. The namespace for these tags is `http://xmlns.jcp.org/jsf/facelets`, which underlines the technology of the Facelet view behind the scenes.

Here is a list of the template tags in JSF 2.2:

JSF custom tag	Description
`<ui:component>`	This defines a template component and specifies the filename for the component.
`<ui:composition>`	This defines a page composition, which encapsulates the JSF content that optionally uses a template.
`<ui:debug>`	This creates and adds a special component to the current page that allows the debugging output to be shown.
`<ui:define>`	This defines the JSF content that is inserted into a page by a composition template.
`<ui:decorate>`	This defines the content that decorates specific regions of a JSF page.
`<ui:fragment>`	This defines a template fragment in a way that is similar to the `<ui:composition>` tag, except that this tag preserves the content outside the body instead of discarding it.
`<ui:include>`	This includes inserting another JSF page into the current page.
`<ui:insert>`	This inserts a named content definition into the current page. This tag is used in conjunction with `<ui:define>`.
`<ui:param>`	This passes parameters to an included file that is specified with `<ui:include>` or a template reference such as `<ui:composition>` or `<ui:include>`.
`<ui:repeat>`	This iterates over a list collection from the bean property or method. This tag is an alternative way to loop through a collection similar to `<h:dataTable>` or `<c:forEach>`.
`<ui:remove>`	This removes specific marked content from a page.

We have seen the operation of `<ui:composition>`, `<ui:define>`, and `<ui:insert>` in *Chapter 2, JavaServer Faces Lifecycle*. We will definitely be using the template JSF tags for the remainder of the book concerning JSF.

Common attributes

The JSF standard tags share many common attributes. The following table is a reference and some of these attributes are available for most of the HTML render kit tags:

Attribute Name	Description
id	This specifies the HTML element identifier. JSF developers should use this attribute every time.
binding	This binds a tag to a component instance in a managed bean. The JSF framework binds a component's reference in the component tree to a scoped variable.
Immedate	This specifies to a Boolean value, if set `true`, it causes the JSF framework to skip the processing of validations, conversions, and events after the Apply Request Value stage in the JSF lifecycle.
rendered	This specifies to a Boolean value, which usually defaults to true, whether the component should be rendered.
required	This specifies to a Boolean value whether this input element is required for input validation.
styleClass	This specifies the HTML class attribute for a rendered tag.
stylestyle	This specifies the HTML style attribute for the rendered tag.
valuevalue	This specifies a String value or expression language reference.

Now that we have seen the JSF tags, we will move back to our CRUD example.

Displaying a list collection of objects

For CRUD examples, we are often faced with the practical problem of displaying the data in the application in a meaningful context that the user can understand. One of the easiest ways is to just print out a list of items for the fairly simple data. Another way is to display a tabular view of the data. There are other solutions worthy of consideration if your data is a tree structure or a graph.

For our case, we will choose the second path and display the list of contact details in a table. In JSF, we can use the `<h:dataTable>` HTML component. This custom tag iterates over each object in the list and displays the specified values. The `<h:dataTable>` component is a very powerful and flexible tag because the Java web engineer can configure it in order to render the custom styles in a variety of layouts.

Let's take a look at another JSF Facelet view, `index.html`, in the `jsf-crud` project. As a reminder, we are using Bootstrap CSS to style. Now, here is the extracted code, as follows:

```
<div class="main-content">
  ...
  <h2> List of Contact Details </h2>

  <h:dataTable id="contactTable"
    value="#{contactDetailController.retrieveAllContacts()}"
    styleClass="table-striped table-bordered user-table"
    var="contact">
    <h:column>
      <f:facet name="header">
        <h:outputText value="Title" />
      </f:facet>
        <h:outputText value="#{contact.title}"/>
    </h:column>
    <h:column>
        <f:facet name="header">
            <h:outputText value="First name" />
        </f:facet>
        <h:outputText value="#{contact.firstName}"/>
    </h:column>

    ... (repeat for Middle name and Last Name) ...

    <h:column>
      <f:facet name="header">
        <h:outputText value="Email" />
      </f:facet>
        <h:outputText value="#{contact.email}"/>
    </h:column>
    <h:column>
      <f:facet name="header">
        <h:outputText value="D.O.B" />
      </f:facet>
        <h:outputText value="#{contact.dob}"/>
```

```
      </h:column>
      <h:column>
        <f:facet name="header">
          <h:outputText value="Allow emails?" />
        </f:facet>
          <h:outputText value="#{contact.allowEmails}"/>
      </h:column>
    </h:dataTable>

    <hr class="subfeaturette-divider" />
  </div><!-- main-content -->
```

The first thing that you will notice is that the `<h:dataTable>` tag accepts a value attribute, which is the JSF expression language reference to the controller's `retrieveAllContacts()` method. `ContactDetailController` delegates this request to `ContactDetailService`, the stateful session EJB that we saw earlier.

The `var` attribute specifies the name of the JSF scope variable, which is the element that is created each time a component iterates through the list collection. The type of the element in the view is the entity bean: `ContactDetail`.

The `styleClass` attributes add specific CSS styles from the Bootstrap framework, and of course, every component can have an `id` attribute.

The `<h:dataTable>` component requires the nested delineated `<h:column>` tags that describe the column data for the table.

If you want header rows for the table, then you must place and add a core JSF tag called `<f:facet>` in the `<h:column>` tag. This tag name must be given a special name attribute with the `header` value. If you were to ask me: why must I write tags using different XML namespaces? Then my answer would be that this was the way the JSF designers foresaw that the core tags could be reusable to the other rendering kits. Hence, the tag name is `<f:facet>` and not something like `<h:headerColumn>`.

In order to show the user the information for each row, we use the `<h:outputText>` element. This tag accepts another expression language statement, namely, the reference to the property in the entity bean such as `#{contact.firstName}`.

Here is a screenshot of the `index.html` list view:

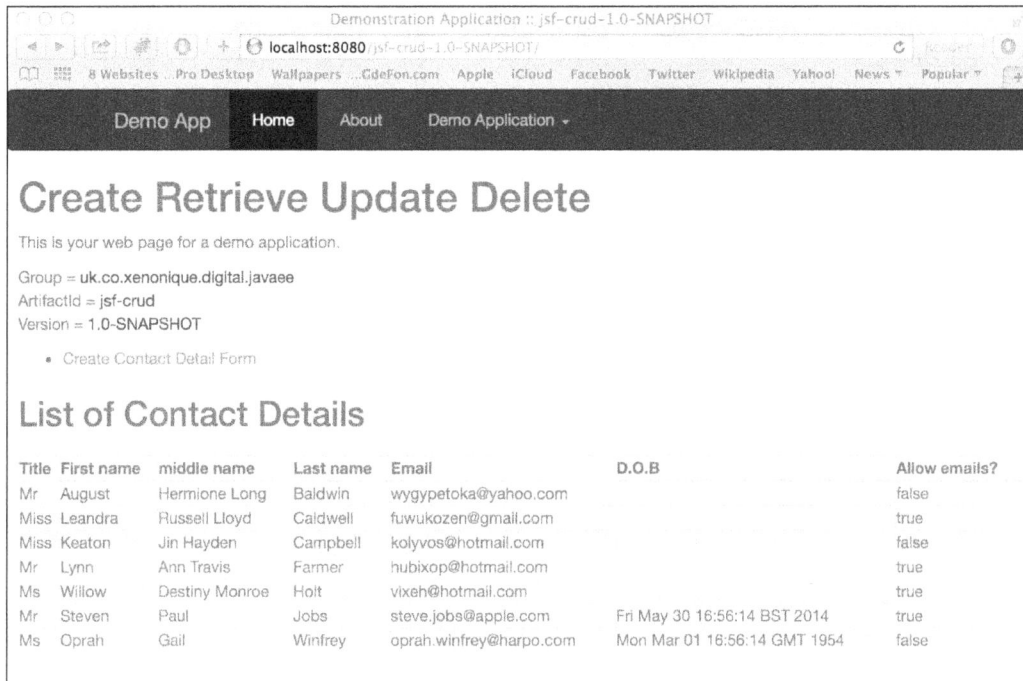

A screenshot of the list view for the CRUD application

Enhanced date time entry

If you notice, we neglected to add the JSF controls so that a user can add his or her date of birth to the contact details form. Let us presume that we have a directive from the UX person in our agile team and that the input has to be in two drop-down lists. The business wants two drop-down elements for the days of the month and months of the year respectfully. They also want a text entry for the year.

We have already covered some of the HTML selection custom tags so far in our JSF journey, such as `<h:selectOneMenu>` and `<h:selectBooleanCheckbox>`. Now, we will learn how to generate data for these tags programmatically from our managed bean. If we can help it — and we surely can — we truly don't want to repeat writing `<f:selectItem>` 31 times in a JSF view.

We will need to add extra logic to `ContactDetailController`. These are the enhancements for the JSF managed bean, which provide the methods accessible to the page view through the expression language, which is mentioned as follows:

```
@ManagedBean(name = "contactDetailController")
@ViewScoped
public class ContactDetailController {
  // ... same as before

  public String createContact() {
      Calendar cal = Calendar.getInstance();
      cal.set(Calendar.DAY_OF_MONTH, dobDay);
      cal.set(Calendar.MONTH, dobMonth-1 );
      int year = Integer.parseInt(dobYear);
      cal.set(Calendar.YEAR, year);
      contactDetail.setDob(cal.getTime());
      contactDetailService.add(contactDetail);
      contactDetail = new ContactDetail();
      return "index.xhtml";
  }

  // ...

  private int dobDay;
  private int dobMonth;
  private String dobYear;

  public int getDobDay() { return dobDay; }
  public void setDobDay(int dobDay) {
      this.dobDay = dobDay; }
  // ... getter and setter for dobMonth and dobYear

  private static List<Integer> daysOfTheMonth
    = new ArrayList<>();
  private static Map<String,Integer> monthsOfTheYear
    = new LinkedHashMap<>();

  static {
```

```
    for (int d=1; d<=31; ++d) {
        daysOfTheMonth.add(d);
    }

    DateFormatSymbols symbols =
            new DateFormatSymbols(Locale.getDefault());
    for (int m=1; m<=12; ++m) {
        monthsOfTheYear.put(symbols.getMonths()[m-1], m );
    }
}

public List<Integer> getDaysOfTheMonth() {
    return daysOfTheMonth;
}
public Map<String,Integer> getMonthsOfTheYear() {
    return monthsOfTheYear;
}
}
```

We will add three new bean properties: dobDay, dobMonth, and dobYear to the controller. Note that dobYear is a string, whereas the other two are integers because the year field is a text field. When an integer is used, the default value shown in the front end is 0, which detracts and confuses the user. We want the user to see an empty text field. There are getters and setters for these new properties.

We enhance the createContact() method to take into account the date of birth from the three separate fields and convert them to a DOB value using a java.util. Calendar instance. Before the entity bean is saved to the database, we will set a property on the entity with the computed value of a java.util.Date type.

There are two bean property methods, getDaysOfTheMonth() and getMonthsOfTheYear(), which will return the static collections that are built in the static initializer of the class. The daysOfTheMonth field is a list collection of integers from 1 to 31, and the monthsOfTheYear field is a map collection of the entries and strings associated with integers, which represent the months of the year.

We use JDK's DateFormatSymbols class to retrieve the long names of the months that are set to the application's default locale.

With these backend changes, we can adapt the JSF view in order to add the ability to set the applicant's date of birth.

Here are the updated changes in the JSF view, `createContactDetails.xhtml`:

```
<label class="control-label"> Your Date of Birth</label>
<div class="row  my-group-border">
  <div class="col-sm-3">
    <label class="control-label" for="dobDay">Day</label>
    <div class="controls">
      <h:selectOneMenu id="dobDay"
          value="#{contactDetailController.dobDay}"
          label="Registration Day">
        <f:selectItem itemLabel="----"  itemValue=""/>
        <f:selectItems
          value="#{contactDetailController.daysOfTheMonth}"
          var="day"
           itemLabel="#{day}" itemValue="#{day}" />
        <f:validateRequired/>
      </h:selectOneMenu>
      <h:message for="dobDay" styleClass="form-error"/>
    </div>
  </div>
  <div class="col-sm-3">
    <label class="control-label" for="dobMonth">Month</label>
    <div class="controls">
      <h:selectOneMenu id="dobMonth"
          value="#{contactDetailController.dobMonth}"
          label="Registration Month">
        <f:selectItem itemLabel="----"  itemValue=""/>
        <f:selectItems
          value="#{contactDetailController.monthsOfTheYear}" />
        <f:validateRequired/>
      </h:selectOneMenu>
      <h:message for="dobMonth" styleClass="form-error"/>
    </div>
  </div>
  <div class="col-sm-3">
    <label class="control-label" for="dobYear">Year</label>
    <div class="controls">
      <h:inputText id="dobYear"
          value="#{contactDetailController.dobYear}"
          label="Registration Year">
        <f:validateRequired/>
      </h:inputText>
      <h:message for="dobYear" styleClass="form-error"/>
    </div>
```

```
    </div>
  </div>
  <h:commandButton styleClass="btn btn-primary"
    action="#{contactDetailController.createContact()}"
      value="Submit" />
```

Well, hopefully I did not scare you off and have you running up the hill! We are using Bootstrap CSS v3.11 here, so this is the reason you see a lot of the `<div>` elements in HTML with the specifically named CSS selectors such as `control-label`, `col-sm-6` and `row`. Bootstrap is popular framework for HTML5, CSS and JavaScript that helps designers and developers build responsive web sites.

As a component framework, JSF provides the basis to encapsulate the `<div>` layer, CSS, and JavaScript. There are a few approaches that can help. First, the teams can develop their custom components; second, they can leverage a third-party component system that has the features and customization that is required, and finally, the team can act as a library writer and therefore, create their own bespoke HTML render kit. The custom components are a lot easier to program, which we will talk about in *Chapter 5, Conversations and Journeys*.

> If your team is interested in the component libraries, then you may want to look at vendor solutions such as Rich Faces (`http://richfaces.jboss.org/`) and particularly, Prime Faces (`http://primefaces.org/`).

Let's concentrate on the `<h:selectOneMenu>` tags. This HTML custom tag from the JSF namespaces specifies a drop-down selection list where the user can choose only one item. The `value` attribute references a property in the controller bean. So, the expression language for the first field is `#{contactDetailController.dobDay}`.

In the parent tag, you see the `<f:selectItem>` and `<f:selectItems>` custom tags. The `<f:selectItem>` tag defines one menu item. It accepts an `itemLabel` and `itemValue` attribute. We can use it to define a default empty option.

The `<f:selectItems>` tag defines many menu items and accepts another value attribute, which is the expression language `#{contactDetailController.daysOfTheMonth}`. This expression refers to the controller getter method, `getDaysOfTheMonth()`, which returns `List<Integer>`. We will use `var`, `itemLabel`, and `itemValue` to configure how this collection renders each menu option, as follows.

```
  <f:selectItems
    value="#{contactDetailController.daysOfTheMonth}"
      var="day" itemLabel="#{day}" itemValue="#{day}" />
```

Just as with the `<h:dataTable>` tag, we can define a JSF scope variable using the `var` attribute and iterate effectively through the collection.

The markup for the months of the year dropdown is slightly different in
`<f:selectMenu>`. As `getMonthsOfTheYear()` already returns a `Map<String,Integer>`
collection, there is no need to provide the configuration of the labels and values. The
custom tag already knows that it has to render the map collections.

The last field for the DOB year is `<h:inputText>`, and by now, you already know
how these tags work. There are a couple of surprises that you may have noticed.

The `<f:validateRequired>` tag is a validation custom tag, which specifies that the
bean properties must be defined by the time the form is submitted. The `<h:message>`
tag specifies an area in the HTML where we want a specific validation error to
appear, as follows:

```
<h:message for="dobYear" styleClass="form-error"/>
```

The `<h:message>` tag accepts a compulsory for attribute that refers to the JSF HTML
form property. We can set the CSS style with the `styleClass` attribute, which is a
form error from Bootstrap. In the next chapter, we will look at the validation properly.

Here is a screenshot of the new form:

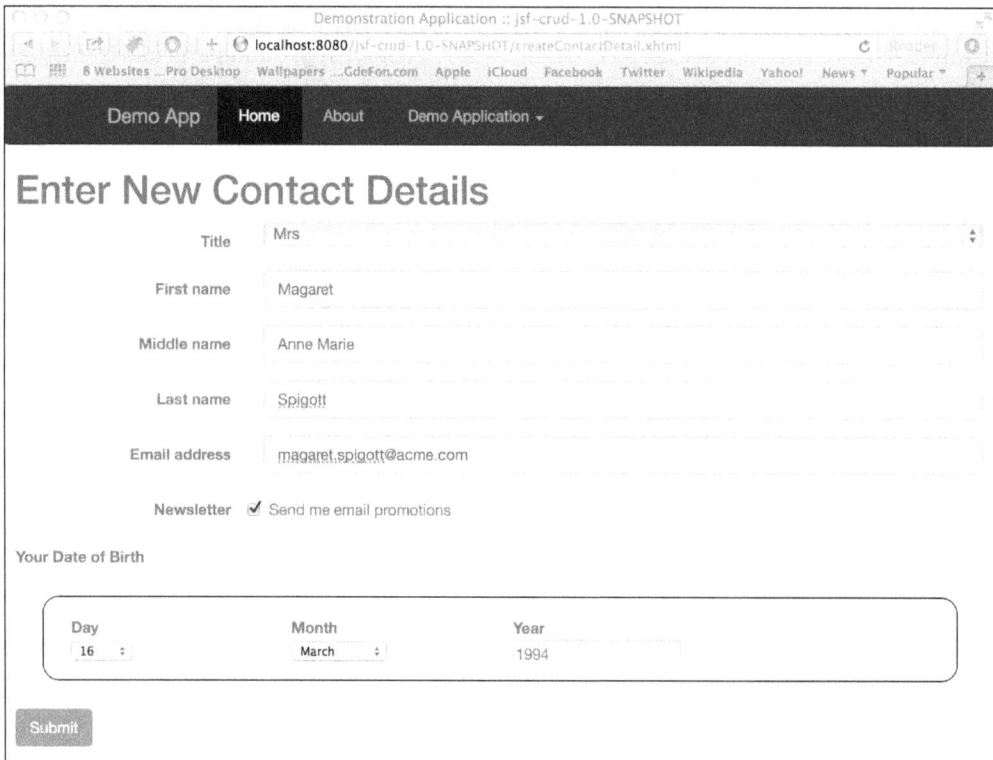

A screenshot of the create page view for the contact data application

Editing data

Now, let's add one more JSF `index.xhtml` to allow the users to edit and delete the contact details. Before we can edit a contact detail, we must add some JSF links to the list view so that the user can navigate to the edit and remove pages.

Let's modify the `<h:dataTable>` section in the `index.xhtml` view and add an additional column. The code looks as follows:

```
<h:dataTable id="contactTable"
  ... other columns as before ...
  <h:column>
    <f:facet name="header">
      <h:outputText value="Action" />
    </f:facet>
    <h:link styleClass="btn"
      outcome="editContactDetail.xhtml?id=#{contact.id}">
      <f:param name="id" value="#{contact.id}" />
      <span class="glyphicon glyphicon-edit"></span>
    </h:link>
    <h:link styleClass="btn"
      outcome="removeContactDetail.xhtml?id=#{contact.id}">
      <f:param name="id" value="#{contact.id}" />
      <span class="glyphicon glyphicon-trash"></span>
    </h:link>
  </h:column>

</h:dataTable>
```

We have two `<h:link>` tags that generate two HTML anchor element links to two new pages: `editContactDetail.xhtml` and `removeContactDetail.xhtml`.

The `<h:link>` custom tag has an outcome attribute to generate the URL using the JSF navigation rules. The `value` attribute specifies the text on the link or you may specify the body text. The tag is clever enough that if the link does not exist, then it will generate a `<span>` element instead. This is a useful feature for prototyping.

Here is some of the rendered output for `<h:link>`:

```
<td>
  <a href="/jsf-crud-1.0-SNAPSHOT/editContactDetail.xhtml?id=5"
    class="btn">
    <span class="glyphicon glyphicon-edit"></span></a>
  <a href="/jsf-crud-1.0-SNAPSHOT/deleteContactDetail.xhtml?id=5"
    class="btn">
    <span class="glyphicon glyphicon-trash"></span></a>
</td>
```

The glyphicon, glyphicon-edit, and glyph-trash class are markups from Bootstrap to show the icon buttons.

With the links in place, we must now allow the editing of the contract details on the server side. We will adapt ContactDetailController with new properties and methods. The first property that we will introduce is id so that we can track the primary key of the contact ID in the database. We will also require a getter and setter for the JSF framework.

On second thoughts, it would be nice to allow the user to cancel the task. So, we will introduce a cancel() method in the controller. We will also add a couple of methods: findByContactId() and editContact().

This is the following code of ContactDetailController as it now stands:

```
import javax.faces.application.FacesMessage;
import javax.faces.context.FacesContext;

public class ContactDetailController {
  // ... as before ...
  private int id;

  public int getId() { return id; }
  public void setId(int id) { this.id = id; }

  public String cancel() {
      return "index.xhtml";
  }

  public void findContactById() {
    if (id <= 0) {
      String message =
        "Bad request. Please use a link from within the system.";
      FacesContext.getCurrentInstance().addMessage(null,
        new FacesMessage(
          FacesMessage.SEVERITY_ERROR, message, null));
      return;
    }

    ContactDetail item = contactDetailService.findById(id).get(0);
    if (item == null) {
      String message =
        "Bad request. Unknown contact detail id.";
      FacesContext.getCurrentInstance().addMessage(null,
        new FacesMessage(
```

```
                FacesMessage.SEVERITY_ERROR, message, null));
        }
        contactDetail = item;
        Calendar cal = Calendar.getInstance();
        cal.setTime(contactDetail.getDob());
        dobDay = cal.get(Calendar.DAY_OF_MONTH);
        dobMonth = cal.get(Calendar.MONTH)+1;
        dobYear = Integer.toString(cal.get(Calendar.YEAR));
    }

    public String editContact() {
        Calendar cal = Calendar.getInstance();
        cal.set(Calendar.DAY_OF_MONTH, dobDay);
        cal.set(Calendar.MONTH, dobMonth-1);
        int year = Integer.parseInt(dobYear);
        cal.set(Calendar.YEAR, year);
        contactDetail.setDob(cal.getTime());
        contactDetail.setId(id)
        contactDetailService.update(contactDetail);
        contactDetail = new ContactDetail();
        return "index.xhtml";
    }

    // ...
}
```

The `cancel()` method simply returns the next view: `index.xhtml`. It does nothing, which is not an error in the code, but is in fact the purpose: to go back to the start.

The `findContactById()` method uses the `id` property to look up the contact details using the `ContactDataService` EJB. This method makes use of the `Calendar` instance in order to pull apart the `dob` property from the `ContactDetail` entity in the constituent `dobDay`, `dobMonth`, and `dobYear` properties.

The `javax.faces.context.FacesContext` type is an aggregate object that stores the current request and response information. `FacesContext` can be retrieved using the factory method only. In the example, we will add an error message to the Faces response, which can be displayed in the view. The `javax.faces.application.FacesMessage` type is a representation of the error validation or it can be defined as a message resource from a external resource bundle. See *Appendix A, JSF with HTML5, Resources, and Faces Flows*.

The `editContact()` method is almost the same as `createContect()` because it reconstructs the `dob` property in the entity. The difference is that the `id` property in the entity is set from the controller property: `id`. Setting the correct primary key is extremely important because the user does not want to see duplicate entries. The `editContect()` method now invokes the database using `update()` instead of `create()`.

We will now adapt the `ContactDetail` entity with a new named query. The following is the modification:

```
@Entity
@Table(name="CONTACT")
@NamedQueries({
  @NamedQuery(name="ContactDetail.findAll",
    query = "select c from ContactDetail c " +
      "order by c.lastName, c.middleName, c.firstName"),
        @NamedQuery(name="ContactDetail.findById",
          query = "select c from ContactDetail c where c.id =
            :id"),
})
public class ContactDetail { /* ... as before ... */ }
```

The named `ContactDetail.findById` query uses a JPQL statement with a key parameter, which is denoted in the string as `:id`. We will now add an extra method to the EJB.

Here is the additional `ContactDetailService` method with the following code:

```
@Stateful
public class ContactDetailService {
  // ... as before ...

  public List<ContactDetail> findById(Integer id) {
    Query query = entityManager.createNamedQuery(
      "ContactDetail.findById").setParameter("id", id);
    return query.getResultList();
  }
}
```

The `findById()` method makes use of the named query and invokes the JPA query in order to retrieve a list collection of the `ContactDetail` elements. There should only be one element in the collection by definition as we are querying by a primary key.

With these change in the backend, all we need are a few changes in the page view, which is almost the same as `createContactDetail.xhtml`.

Here is an extract of the Facelet view, `editContactDetail.xhtml`:

```
<h:body>
  <f:metadata>
    <f:viewParam name="id"
      value="#{contactDetailController.id}" />
    <f:event type="preRenderView"
      listener="#{contactDetailController.findContactById()}"/>
```

```
      </f:metadata>

      ...

      <div class="main-content">
        <h1> Edit Contact Details </h1>
        <h:form id="editContactDetail"
          styleClass="form-horizontal"
          p:role="form">
            <h:inputHidden value="${contactDetailController.id}" />

            <div class="form-group">
              ...
            </div>

            <h:commandButton styleClass="btn btn-primary"
              action="#{contactDetailController.editContact()}"
              value="Submit" />
             
             
            <h:commandButton styleClass="btn btn-default"
              action="#{contactDetailController.cancel()}"
              immediate="true" value="Cancel"/>
        </h:form>

        <hr class="subfeaturette-divider" />

      </div><!--  "main-content" -->
      ...
    </h:body>
```

There are JSF custom tags used here. The `<f:metadata>` tag is a container tag that declares a metadata facet for the current page.

The `<f:viewParam>` tag attaches a GET request parameter for the page as metadata for the current view. We will use it to attach the query parameter to the controller property. The name attribute specifies the query parameter name. The value attribute specifies the JSF expression language reference. Giving a URL request such as `/jsf-crud-1.0-SNAPSHOT/editContactDetail.xhtml?id=4` will cause the framework to populate the `id` property in `ContactDetailController` with the value of `4`. This call happens in the Restore View phase of the JSF lifecycle.

> As the `<f:metadata>` tag declares the metadata for a single page view, it must be placed near the root element view of the page. The `<f:metadata>` tag must be placed in `<ui:define>` if it is used in a JSF template composition. In the example, the tag is just after `<h:body>`.

The `<f:event>` custom tag associates a JSF Faces event with a component. The official documentation describing this tag says that it installs a `ComponentSystemEventListener` instance on a target component in a page. Here, we can simply say that the tag associates a prerendering event with the `findByContactId()` method in the controller. In other words, `<f:event>` prepopulates the form with the data from the underlying database.

In the `<h:form>` content, we will use the `<h:hidden>` custom tag so as to store the current ID of the contact details. The value attribute is an expression reference. In this way, the identifier is propagated back to the controller when the user submits the form.

Finally, there are two `<h:submit>` buttons and they reference the `editContact()` and `cancel()` methods in the controller respectively. The intermediate attribute in the second `<h:submit>` button specifies that the JSF life cycle should skip the Process Validation state. JSF then does not apply the validation when the form is submitted. Instead, the life cycle moves from Apply Request Values directly to the Render Response state.

> **Adding HTML entity characters to XHTML**
>
> Facelets only support five predefined XML entity characters: `&lt`, `&gt`, `&amp`, `&quot`, and `&apos`. The only way to add an HTML element is through the hexadecimal or octal notation. The ` ` entity represents the Unicode character ` ` for break space.

Here is a screenshot of the `editContactDetail.xhtml` view:

A screenshot of the edit page view for the contact details application

Removing data

Our user is able to create the contact details and she can now update the entries. To complete our customer's journey, we should allow her to remove the entries as a good Net citizen. Why there are so many companies out there that want to block the access to delete the user's data by putting in hazards or extra hassles to make such a simple task so difficult is beyond me! However, we can do this for our contact detail application and it is now straightforward as we have the building blocks in place.

We will add a `removeDetail()` method to `ContactDetailController`. Here is the extra method:

```
public class ContactDetailController {
  // ... as before ...
  public String removeContact() {
    contactDetail = contactDetailService.findById(id).get(0);
    contactDetailService.delete(contactDetail);
    contactDetail = new ContactDetail();
    return "index.xhtml";
  }
}
```

This method searches for `contactDetail` by a fresh `id`. The `id` field is the controller's property, which is set in a hidden form field. By invoking the data services `findById()` method at the form submission, we will ensure that we retrieve the latest information from the persistence context. Maybe the user went off to lunch and came back and then submitted the form. With the entity found, we can then call the data service to remove it.

Here is an extract of the `removeContactDetail.xhtml` view:

```
<div class="main-content">
  <h1> Delete Contact Details </h1>
  <table class="table table-striped table-bordered">
    <tr>
      <th> Item</th> <th> Value</th>
    </tr>
    <tr>
      <td> Title </td>
      <td>
      #{contactDetailController.contactDetail.title} </td>
    </tr>
    <tr>
      <td> First Name </td>
      <td>
      #{contactDetailController.contactDetail.firstName} </td>
    </tr>
    <tr>
      <td> Middle Name </td>
      <td>
      #{contactDetailController.contactDetail.middleName} </td>
    </tr>
    <tr>
      <td> Last Name </td>
```

```
    <td>
      #{contactDetailController.contactDetail.lastName} </td>
  </tr>
  <tr>
    <td> Allows Email? </td>
    <td>
      #{contactDetailController.contactDetail.allowEmails} </td>
  </tr>
  <tr>
    <td> Email </td>
    <td> #{contactDetailController.contactDetail.email} </td>
  </tr>
  <tr>
    <td> Date of Birth </td>
    <td>
      <h:outputText
        value="#{contactDetailController.contactDetail.dob}" >
        <f:convertDateTime type="date" pattern="dd-MMM-yyyy"/>
      </h:outputText>
    </td>
  </tr>
</table>

<h:form id="editContactDetail"
  styleClass="form-horizontal"
  p:role="form">
  <h:inputHidden value="${contactDetailController.id}" />

    <h:commandButton styleClass="btn btn-primary"
      action="#{contactDetailController.removeContact()}"
      value="Submit" />
     
     
    <h:commandButton styleClass="btn btn-default"
      action="#{contactDetailController.cancel()}"
      immediate="true" value="Cancel"/>
  </h:form>
</div>
```

If you look at this carefully, then you will see the `<table>` element that displays
the properties of the `ContactDetail` entity; but wait a minute, where have the
`<h:outputText>` elements gone? Well, in JSF 2, you no longer have to write
`<h:outputText>`, just output the authoring content for the JSF managed bean and
you can immediately write the expression directly in place.

Hence, one simply writes as follows:

```
<td> #{contactDetailController.contactDetail.title} </td>
```

Instead of:

```
<td>
  <h:outputText
    value="#{contactDetailController.contactDetail.title}"/>
</td>
```

Which of the preceding authoring contents would you prefer to program with?

However, the DOB is a field where we will use the `<h:outputText>` element. The `<f:convertDateTime>` tag formats a `java.util.Date` type to a readable format. The pattern attribute specifies the date format pattern. This tags relies on the `java.text.SimpleDateFormat` class.

The `<h:form>` tag is still required in order to allow the user to submit the form. It encloses the two `<h:commandButton>` tags. When the form is submitted, JSF invokes the `removeContact()` method in the controller.

Finally, the page also requires the `<f:metadata>` stanza that was mentioned earlier in the *Editing data* section of this chapter in order to fetch the contact details before the page is rendered.

We have come to the end of our customer's journey with this basic digital-by-default JSF example. We can create, retrieve, update, and delete a contact detail from a database using a web form. It is really so straightforward. We have also taken advantage of the HTML5 framework like Bootstrap, and therefore, we can quickly adapt our application to a responsive web design.

Here is the screenshot for the `deleteContent.xhtml` view:

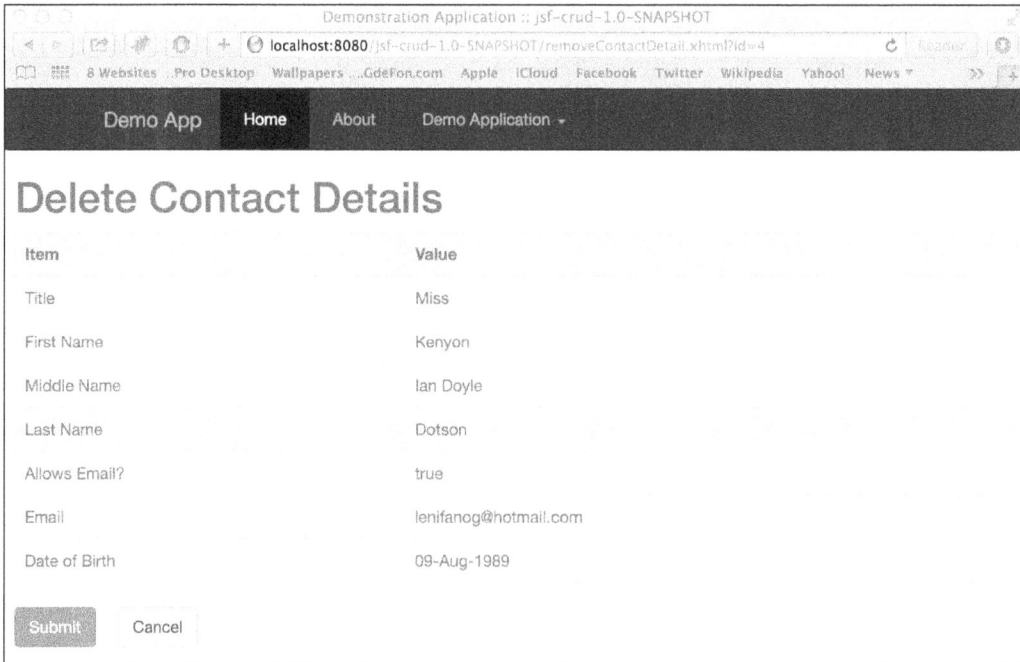

The delete page view for the contact details application

Before we close this chapter, we will have a short interlude on the JSF and CDI scopes.

JSF and CDI scopes

There has been some confusion before Java EE 7 about which annotations are correct to declare the managed beans. The issues are that the JavaServer Faces specification predates the later standard from the CDI and the fact that the scoping overlaps. The history of scopes comes from the original design and definition of the servlet container and providing convenience to the application developer. A scope is simply a map collection of name/value pairs. It helps to think of them as `java.util.Map` type hash map collections. The scopes differ in their life span.

For CDI, the package name is `javax.enterprise.context`, and for JSF managed beans, the package is `javax.faces.bean`.

Bean scopes

An `@RequestScoped` annotation denotes a controller with a lifecycle that has the duration for the Faces request and response. The request-scope is short-lived. It begins when the web client submits an HTTP request and is then processed by the servlet container. The scope ends when the response is sent back to the client.

The `@SessionScoped` annotation denotes a lifecycle of many requests and responses. The session scope is designed to get around the stateless protocol of HTTP. The servlet containers enhance the HTTP protocol with the ability to store and retrieve the objects that live longer than one request and response cycle. For this reason, the session scope long-lived. A session scope can expire after a time-out or may become invalid if the service is restarted.

The `@ApplicationScoped` annotation denotes a life cycle that exists for as long as the web application is running and available. The application scope, more importantly, is shared across all the requests, sessions, and conversation and custom scopes. This scope begins as soon as the web application starts up. It ends when the web application is shut down.

The request, session, and application scopes are classic versions of the scope model. JSF and CDI also have additional scopes.

The `@javax.enterprise.context.ConversationScoped` annotation denotes a lifecycle that has a duration greater than one or more request and response cycles and yet is shorter than the session scope. CDI defines a scope called a conversation scope. It is a scope between the request and session scopes but also has a contextual association to the beans that it encapsulates. We will discuss the conversation scope in a later chapter.

JSF 2.0 has defined a scope called `@javax.faces.bean.ViewScoped` that is similar to the conversation scope because it also has a longer life span than the request scope. The view scope begins when the client submits an HTTP request. It stays around until the user navigates to another page. This makes the `@ViewScoped` bean a broader and more reasonable choice for the managed bean controller than the `@RequestScoped` variety. A `@ViewScoped` annotation is appropriate to manage a one-user story, as we have seen with the CRUD example.

> The `@ViewScoped` annotation is not available for the CDI beans. If you are using a version of JSF before 2.2 and Java EE 7, then this annotation will not work with the `@javax.inject.Named` annotated beans. You have to use `@javax.faces.bean.ManagedBean` instead.

In JSF 2.2, there is the `@javax.faces.flow.FlowScoped` annotation, which is a CDI sanctioned extension. The flow scope is also similar to the conversation scope with a life span that is greater than the request-scope but shorter than the session scope; however, it is designed for workflow management operations. The flow scope allows the developer to create a set of pages with a well-defined entry and an exit point. One can think of this scope as being appropriate to the Wizard data-entry applications.

Finally, let's learn about the two remaining scopes. There is the POJO annotation, `@javax.faces.beanCustomScoped`, which allows the managed bean to evaluate the values at the runtime. For a custom scope, the JSF implementation will defer to the implementation, and so, any EL expression may be customized depending on the code-based values. The `@javax.faces.bean.NoneScoped` annotation is a special scope that implies that a managed bean has no scope at all. JSF will instantiate these types of none scope managed beans every time they are referenced. You might wonder why JSF should sanction such types of beans? A none scope bean might be useful in a security context or in situations where you do not want a bean to maintain a state.

> **Where are the other HTML tags?**
>
> There are many examples of an older version of JSF on the Internet. You might wonder why we have not seen tags such as `h:panel` and `h:panelGrid`. These tags are used to lay out the content, especially in JSF 1.*x*. The default HTML implementation of these tags generates the content with the HTML table elements. The modern digital engineer knows that building sites with the ubiquitous table elements are not recommended. For this reason, I chose not to build my examples with these tags.

Summary

In this chapter about JSF forms, we explored the HTML and core JSF custom tags to build the answer to one of the most sought-after questions on the Internet: how on earth do I—as a digital developer—write a CRUD application? It is surprising that this simple idea is considered difficult to program.

We built a digital JSF form that initially created a contact detail. We saw the Facelet view, the managed bean controller, the stateful session EJB, and the entity. We are modern because we took advantage of the recent HTML5 advances such as the Bootstrap CSS framework. We displayed a list collection of objects with a `<h:dataTable>` tag, which is a powerful and flexible component. We then added the ability to edit and remove the contact details from the application.

In the next chapter, we will look at form validation extensively and throw in a mix of an AJAX communication in JSF. We have already—sort of—looked in the territory of validation with `<f:validateRequired>`, `<h:messages>`, and `<h:message>`.

Exercises

These are the questions for Chapter 3:

1. What are the differences between the HTML5 render kit and core custom tags in JSF?

2. What are the common attributes that are shared among the JSF custom tags?

3. The web applications for a business tend to be of two types: data submission and case working. Data submissions simply capture the data and have some limited validation. The other mode provides you with full control to enter new records, amend them, and often delete data. What do you think are the reasons for these two types?

4. The idiom **Create Read Update Delete** (**CRUD**) is de rigueur for a business facing an e-commerce application. Where have you encountered these applications? Are these applications exclusive to the web? Given a second chance, what can be done to improve the state of art of these applications? How can better digital transformations help these businesses and more importantly, their customers?

5. Write a simple JSF application that basically uses an HTML form element, `<h:form>`, with a command button, `<h:commandButton>`. Your task is to write a registration application for a local Hobby Book Club of avid readers of fiction. Your participants have to register online before they can attend. Start with the backing bean (managed controller). Think of the properties that you need to record. (Your `Registration.java` POJO will need contact details such as names, age, and e-mail.) At this stage, you do not have to persist any information to a database but it would be helpful if you create a book data record (`Book.java`), which contains the properties `title` (String), `author` (String), `genre` (String), `publisher` (String), and `publication year` (Integer). Write a design specification using the MVC design pattern.

6. In the first iteration with an imaginary stakeholder, you are required to only write a simple JSF form. Create a backing bean that captures the book title and author. You will need to `<h:outputLabel>` and `<h:inputText>`. In the book's source site, you will find an empty project directory with empty JSF placeholder pages and Bootstrap CSS and JavaScript libraries such as jQuery already set up. You can copy and rename this folder to get started quicker.

7. In order to use Bootstrap CSS in JSF, we can apply almost all of the JSF HTML components to the `styleClass` attribute. What are the other common attributes?

8. Take the Hobby Book Club application and add some other components such as a drop-down list: `<h:selectManyMenu>`. You will need to add properties to the backing bean. (This could be the genre of the book such as crime, science fiction, thriller, or romantic). You will need a POJO to serve as a data record for the registrants (perhaps a class name of `Registrant.java` will serve us well).

9. What happens if you find a rare book that defies a genre? How would you model this property bean and which JSF HTML custom tags would you use?

10. Adapt your hobby application in order to use the other elements of the JSF HTML custom tags such as `<h:selectBooleanCheckbox>`. You might add a Boolean value to a property to capture the state when somebody in the group has reviewed the book.

11. What is the difference between `<h:selectOneMenu>` and `<h:selectManyCheckbox>`? Explain what the customer will see when confronted with `<h:selectOneListbox>` and `<h:selectManyListbox>`?

12. In a modern digital web design, why should we avoid composing a web user interface with the `<h:panelGroup>` elements?

13. To finish the hobby book application, we might allow a registered user to add a comment to their application form. They want to say what their particular specialty is, and it could be anything from futuristic cyberpunk Doctor Who to historical marine warfare around ancient Greece and Rome. What is the difference between `<h:inputText>` and `<h:inputTextArea>`? Can you optimize this control with the modern CSS frameworks?

14. What happens when two customers want to edit the same contact detail record in the web database? How do think the application should behave? What features would you add? How do you think the customer will feel about your ideas?

4
JSF Validation and AJAX

"It always seems impossible until it is done."

Nelson Mandela

So far, we have created a digital customer journey that accomplishes the common create, retrieve, update, and delete, that is, the famous CRUD requirement. The results are attractive to the stakeholder and to the product owner, but the user members of our team are not satisfied with the form, because it lacks the ability to verify the data entries made by members of the general public.

When we think about it, validation is important for the user as he or she is the one entering the data in a web application. It saves time and frustration for the user, because they know that the entry is wrong as they enter the data. It avoids the costs incurred for fixing of the wrongly submitted data by the database administrator. Validation improves the efficiency of a web application that works 24/7 over the Internet. As more of our daily lives get dependent on the digital adaptation of traditional services, e-commerce is now a necessity; it is essential that we give the general public the right information at the right time, that is, at the point-of-sale or point-of-capture.

Validation methods

In this chapter, taking the basic JSF form as a base, we will learn how to apply validation on the server side and on the client-server side. There are certain advantages to both the strategies; we will learn about the pros and cons of both the approaches.

Server-side validation

Form validation can be achieved on the server-side in a Java EE application running on the application server or the servlet container. The information is sent from the web browser to the web application as a normal HTTP form submission. In this mode, the form is submitted as a traditional HTML form element. The web framework, in this case Java EE, validates the input and sends back a response to the client. If the form fails the validation, the page that contains the web form is redisplayed and error messages are shown.

The server-side quick validation is secure in the sense that it will protect the database even if JavaScript is disabled or unavailable in a web browser. On the other hand, this type of validation requires a round trip from the client to the server side. The users will not get feedback about the form data until they submit the form.

There always seems to be an exception to a rule. If the server-side form validation is submitted using AJAX, then we can get around the slow response. AJAX validation is a nice compromise, because the form can be validated as and when the user enters the data on the form. On the other hand, AJAX requires JavaScript to be enabled in the web browser.

Client-side validation

The user-experience person in our team really prefers the client-side validation, but this type of validation requires the presence of JavaScript in the browser (or an equivalent type of dynamic scripting technology). Client-side validation affords a more responsive and richer user interaction with the form.

Client-side validation ensures that the form is always correct before the user is allowed to submit the form. With JavaScript being a progressive language, there are many ways to inform the user how to better interact with the form submission process. Technologies such as jQuery allow the programmers to add hinting and validation error messages in flight as the user types the data.

There are situations where JavaScript is disabled or unavailable in the web browser. I can readily think of government security or specialist centers where the sandbox is strictly controlled. When JavaScript is turned off by the user or by the administrator of the device, client-side validation will certainly fail, and the user is able to bypass the validation.

> **Combine client-side and server-side validation**
>
> In professional applications for businesses, I strongly recommend that you combine both the approaches to validation in order to get the best of both worlds. Client-side validation provides a faster and richer experience and server-side validation protects your data and database from bad data and hacking.

Before we go through the technical topic of validation, we must understand how messages are represented in JSF.

Faces messages

The JSF provides two custom tags to display error messages. The `<h:message>` tag displays messages that are bound to specific components. The `<h:messages>` tag displays messages that are not bound to specific components.

We saw our first use of `<h:message>` in *Chapter 3, Building JSF Forms*. The tag is typically associated with a form control. We can add messages to our JSF pages with the following:

```
<h:messages globalOnly="false" styleClass="alert alert-danger" />
```

The tag is added to the top of the content. The attribute `globalStyle` is a Boolean value, and it specifies whether the tag should display messages that are not associated with a component. Here, we are using the Bootstrap CSS selectors again.

The following is a table of the attributes that are shared between the JSF tags, `<h:messages>` and `<h:message>`:

Attribute	Description
Id	Specifies the unique identifier
errorClass	Specifies the CSS class selectors for error messages
errorStyle	Specifies the style for error messages
infoClass	Specifies the CSS class selector for information messages
infoStyle	Specifies the CSS styles for information messages
for	Specifies the component that a message is associated with
rendered	Sets a Boolean value to specify whether the tag is rendered to the page or not
style	Defines the CSS selectors for all the message types
styleClass	Defines the CSS style for all the message types

Behind the scenes, these tags render the content from the `javax.faces.HtmlMessages` and `javax.faces.HtmlMessages` components respectively, which in turn, rely on the list collection of the `javax.faces.application.FacesMessage` elements. As a JSF digital developer, we do not have to worry too much about the `HtmlMessage` and `HtmlMessages` components from day-to-day, as they lie under the car bonnet. If we were in the business of writing a new JSF renderer or an extension, then we would have to look at the Javadoc and JSF specifications.

In *Chapter 3*, *Building JSF Forms*, you were introduced to the application, `FacesMessage`, for creating the JSF CRUD style forms. In the Controller, we can create a validation error message that is not associated to any `UIComponent` in the form. Therefore this validation error is accessible only through global error messages. Here is code that generates such a validation error:

```
public void findContactById() {
  if (id <= 0) {
    String message =
      "Bad request. Please use a link from within the system.";
    FacesContext.getCurrentInstance().addMessage(null,
      new FacesMessage(
        FacesMessage.SEVERITY_ERROR, message, null));
    return;
  }
  /* ... */
}
```

The `FacesMessage` object represents a validation message with a severity level. We add it to the `FacesContext` object. The `FacesMessage` constructor is of the form:

```
public FacesMessage(Severity severity, String summary,
                    String detail)
```

The severity can be of four static constants defined in the `FaceMessages` class, which are `SEVERITY_INFO`, `SERVERITY_WARNING`, `SEVERITY_ERROR`, and `SEVERITY_FATAL`. These values are actually instantiations of a private inner class `Severity` that, unfortunately, is not accessible outside the enclosing class, so we can invent our own severities.

A Faces message also requires a summary of the message and, optionally, details about the invalidation message.

`javax.faces.context.FacesContext` is an aggregate holder for the current incoming request and the potential response. The object instance is instantiated on the initial JSF incoming request (Faces Request), and it will stay alive until the subsequent JSF `release()` method is triggered, which is usually deep inside the framework. `FacesContext` is the place from where a `FacesMessage` is added and from where the list collection of messages can be retrieved.

`FacesContext` has several interesting methods including `isValidationFailed()`, which is useful to detect any validation failure earlier in the JSF lifecycle. We shall see an example of this call later with Bean Validation. There are other methods as well like using `getViewRoot()` to get the view root, `getCurrentPhaseId()` to get the current phase in the JSF lifecycle, and `getRenderKit()` to retrieve the render kit form. With the `isPostback()` method, we can find out if the request was an HTML form and if the JSF framework is about to send the data back to the same form. There is much more to the context objects.

The method to add a faces message to the context looks as follows:

```
public abstract void addMessage(
    String clientId, FacesMessage message);
```

If the `clientId` attribute is null, the message is a globally available message and is not associated with any view component.

Now that we've understood how to generate JSF- specific messages, let's delve into the validation of a JSF application.

Validation

There are a two main ways of achieving validation on the server side. One route to follow is through the use of Bean Validation version 1.1 from the Java EE 7 specification, and the other traditional route takes you through JSF validation.

Constraining form content with Bean Validation

Bean Validation is a specification that allows the developers to annotate the POJOs and entity beans and then call a custom validator instance to verify the properties. The validation framework works with Java annotation and thus, the digital engineer can firmly say how a property or even a method is validated.

I devoted an entire chapter to Bean Validation in the *Java EE 7 Developer Handbook*; nevertheless, I will run through the basics with you here, in this Digital Web Application book. There are several annotations in the Bean Validation 1.1 standard that you can use straightaway. However, if your platform allows or if you decide to add Hibernate Validator, then many more useful validation annotations are available. The developer can also create custom validations.

Let's use the `ContactDetail` entity again, but this time we have added Bean Validation annotations to the properties, as follows:

```
package uk.co.xenonique.digital;
import javax.persistence.*;
import javax.validation.constraints.*;
import java.util.Date;

@Entity @Table(name="CONTACT")
/* ... */
public class ContactDetail {
  @Id /* ... */ private long id;

  @NotNull(message = "{contactDetail.title.notNull}")
  private String title;

  @Size(min = 1, max = 64,
        message = "{contactDetail.firstName.size}")
  private String firstName;

  private String middleName;

  @Size(min = 1, max = 64,
        message = "{contactDetail.lastName.size}")
  private String lastName;

  @Pattern(regexp =
      "^[_A-Za-z0-9-\\+]+(\\.[_A-Za-z0-9-]+)*@"
      + "[A-Za-z0-9-]+(\\.[A-Za-z0-9]+)*(\\.[A-Za-z]{2,})$",
      message = "{contactDetail.email.pattern}")
  private String email;

  @NotNull( message = "{contactDetail.dob.notNull}")
  @Temporal(TemporalType.DATE)
  @Past( message="{contactDetail.dob.past}" )
  private Date dob;

  /* ... as before ... */
}
```

We added the annotations `@Pattern`, `@Past`, `@NotNull`, and `@Size` to the properties of the `ContactDetail` entity. The annotations can be found in the Java package `javax.validation.constraints`, reserved for Bean Validation.

The following is a table of the important Bean Validation annotations:

Constraint Name	Description	Allowed Types
`@Null`	Specifies that the element must be a null reference pointer.	Any
`@NotNull`	Specifies that the element must not be a null reference pointer.	Any
`@Min`	Specifies that the element must be a number value that is greater than or equal to the minimum value supplied. Because of floating arithmetic rounding errors, float and double are not supported.	`BigDecimal, BigInteger, byte, short, int, and long`
`@Max`	Specifies that the element must be a number value that is less than or equal to the minimum value supplied. Because of floating arithmetic rounding errors, float and double are not supported.	`BigDecimal, BigInteger, byte, short, int, and long`
`@DecimalMin`	Similar to `@Min` but adds the ability to set the value as a String parameter. The number value must be greater than or equal to the supplied value. FP restriction also applies here.	`BigDecimal, BigInteger,` `CharSequence, byte, short, int, and long`
`@DecimalMax`	Similar to `@Max` but adds the ability to set the value as a String parameter. The number value must be less than or equal to the supplied value. FP restriction also applies here.	`BigDecimal, BigInteger,` `CharSequence, byte, short, int, and long`
`@Size`	The element's size must be inside the supplied inclusive boundary limits.	`CharSequence, Collection, Map and primitive array`
`@Past`	The element must be a date in the past according to the current time of the Java Virtual Machine.	`java.util.Date and java.util. Calendar`
`@Future`	The element must be a date in the future according to the current time of the Java Virtual Machine.	`java.util.Date and java.util. Calendar`
`@Pattern`	The element must match against a supplied regular expression pattern that conforms to the Java convention.	`CharSequence`

Bean Validation annotations typically accept a message attribute, which is the validation message for the user, or it can be a value in brackets, which is a trigger for the validation framework to search for a message from `java.util.ResourceBundle`. Certain annotations like `@Min`, `@Max`, `@DecimalMin`, and `@DecimalMax` have additional attributes like `min` and `max` to specify the obvious boundaries.

We can define an `@NotNull` constraint on the property with the validation message, as follows:

```
@NotNull( message = "The office reference must not be null")
private String officeReference;
```

It is a good approach, possibly for prototyping a website; but as we know from our knowledge of software archaeology. This could be a maintenance nightmare, because we are writing a digital copy directly into Java code. It is far better to write a text copy inside a property file that can be picked up by the standard `ResourceBundle`, which Bean Validation uses. Jenny, our resident digital strategist and copywriting expert, will thank us for sending her a property file instead of Java source code.

So let's rewrite this constraint on the property as follows:

```
@NotNull( message = "{mydataform.officeReference.notNull}")
private String officeReference;
```

Bean Validation can be integrated with JSF by placing the messages at a specific location. The programmer need only create a `ValidationMessages.properties` file in the folder `WEB-INF/classes`.

The following is an extract of the message properties file for the `ContactDetail` entity:

```
contactDetail.title.notNull = Title cannot be blank or empty
contactDetail.firstName.size = First name must be between {min} and
{max} characters
contactDetail.middleName.size = Middle name must be between {min} and
{max} characters
contactDetail.lastName.size = Last name must be between {min} and
{max} characters
contactDetail.email.pattern = You must supply a valid email address
contactDetail.dob.past=Your Date of Birth must be in the past
```

With Bean Validation, we can add placeholders that are denoted with curly brackets to enrich the messages that the user will see. The placeholders are specific like {min} and {max}. The other advantage of property files is that the ResourceBundle in the JDK already handles the tricky topic of internationalization for different locales.

There are big disadvantages to just relying on Bean Validation using JSF. It is great for protecting a database from poorly entered data, and with the Java EE 7 application server that the digital developer gets almost for free, validation is added or amended to the database before each record. However, the Bean Validation has no connection to the JSF frontend. The framework does not have any association with the page author's content. Nor would we want this dependency between the presentation and the model layer in modern day software engineering. One of the best practices in object-oriented programming is the SOLID principle. We certainly want the layers to be singularly responsible for a purpose; open to extension, but closed to modification and, most importantly, to prevent the leaky abstractions that cause a technical debt in the software as it ages.

Another disadvantage about just relying on Bean Validation is that the verification of the data depends solely on the skills of the Java digital engineer. It means that the page author or designer cannot innovate, edit, or remove validation on the road to a better user-centric experience.

Bean Validation is great for adding validation in the application logic. You can ensure that the contact detail's title is never blank, if this is a business requirement. Complex and group validations for properties can be achieved. Refer to my book, *Java EE 7 Developer Handbook*, for further details.

The following screenshot shows `bean-validation/createContactDetail.xhtml` in action from the book source code. The screenshot shows what happens when the user just submits the form without filling it in:

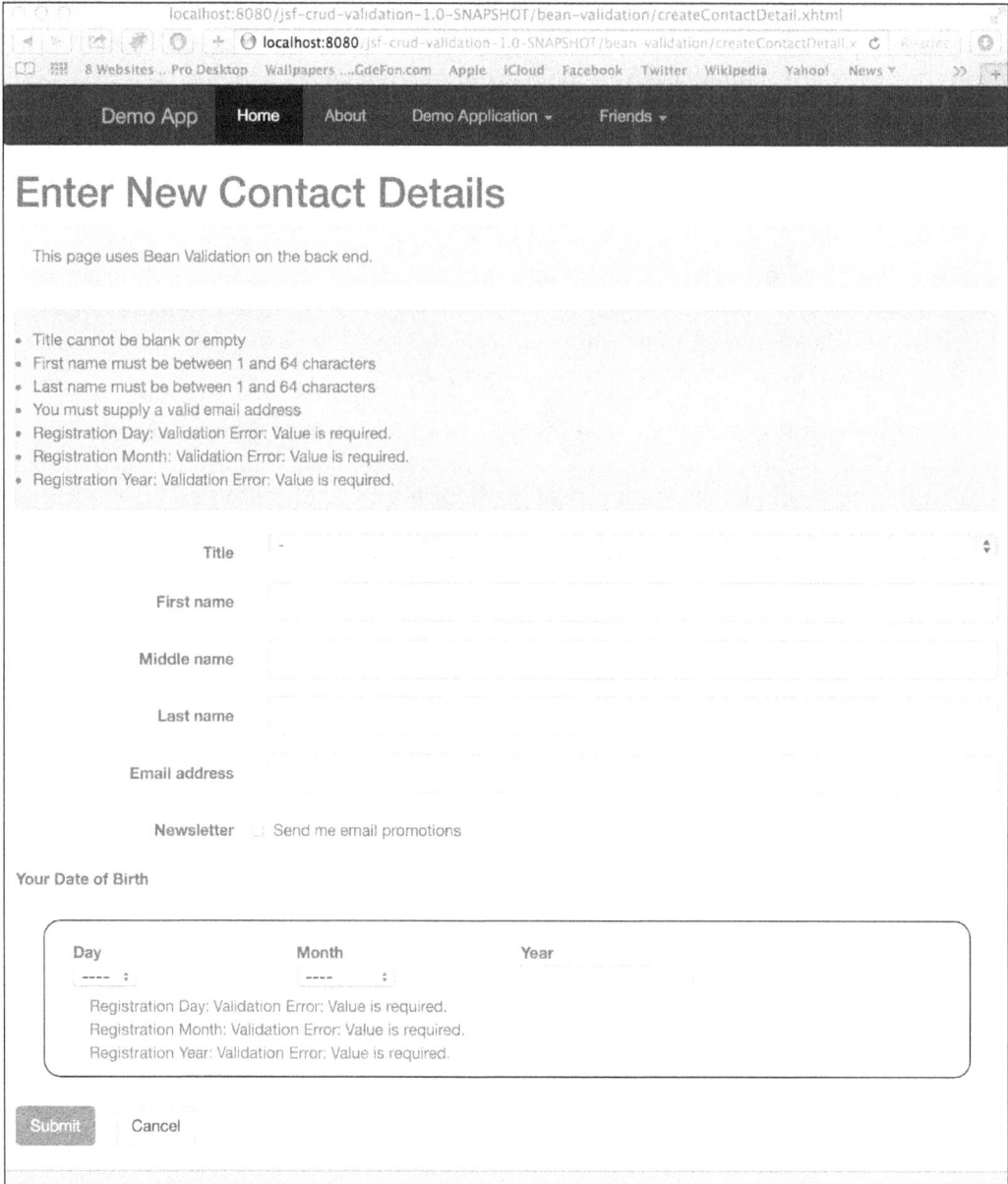

Screenshot of Bean Validation on the contact details application

The <h:messages> tag with the setting globalStyle=true shows the output of the validation messages that the framework discovers in the ContactDetail entity.

Validating user input with JSF

JSF has always had a validation framework since its inception in 2004. It was a feature that separated JSF from the de facto Apache Struts web framework, at the time, as the latter had no built-in support for validation.

It is helpful to remember that conversion and validation occur at different phases of the JavaServer Faces lifecycle (review the diagram from *Chapter 2, JavaServer Faces Lifecycle, The execute and render lifecycle* section). As a reminder, JSF will set the values in a component during the Apply-Request values phase and then use various conversions, if required, to transform the input String values to the target object. Validation occurs during the Process-Validations phase and this lifecycle follows by design. In order to transform the input data from the HTML request, JSF attempts and checks whether the parameters can be set in the backing bean. The Update-Model-Values phase follows the earlier phases. If a validation or a conversion error occurs in the lifecycle, then it is effectively shortened. JSF moves directly to the Render-Response phase and it converts the properties in the backing bean to Strings so that the web client can display them.

JSF provides a small set of prebuilt validator tags, which you can apply to mark up as a page author, A table of the Core JSF Custom Tags has been given in *Chapter 3, Building JSF Forms*. Some of them are as follows: <f:validateDoubleRange>, <f:validateLength>, <f:validateLongRange>, <f:validateRegex>, and <f:validateRequired>.

We can apply these tags to the contact detail CRUD example. So let's start with the createContact.xhtml page. The following is a short extract from the page:

```
<h:form id="createContactDetail"
  styleClass="form-horizontal" p:role="form">
  <div class="form-group">
    <h:outputLabel for="title" class="col-sm-3 control-label">
      Title</h:outputLabel>
    <div class="col-sm-9">
      <h:selectOneMenu class="form-control"
        label="Title" id="title"
        value="#{contactDetailControllerBV.contactDetail.title}">
      <f:selectItem itemLabel="-" itemValue="" />
      <f:selectItem itemValue="Mr" />
```

```
                <f:selectItem itemValue="Mrs" />
                <f:selectItem itemValue="Miss" />
                <f:selectItem itemValue="Ms" />
                <f:selectItem itemValue="Dr" />
                <f:validateRequired/>
            </h:selectOneMenu>
            <h:message for="title" styleClass="alert validation-error"/>
        </div>
    </div>
    <div class="form-group">
        <h:outputLabel for="firstName" class="col-sm-3 control-label">
            First name</h:outputLabel>
        <div class="col-sm-9">
            <h:inputText class="form-control" label="First name"
             value="#{contactDetailControllerBV.contactDetail.firstName}"
             id="firstName" placeholder="First name">
                <f:validateRequired/>
                <f:validateLength maximum="64" />
            </h:inputText>
            <h:message for="firstName" styleClass="alert validation-error"/>
        </div>
    </div>
    <!-- . . . -->
    <div class="form-group">
        <h:outputLabel for="email" class="col-sm-3 control-
            label">Email address
        </h:outputLabel>
        <div class="col-sm-9">
            <h:inputText type="email"
             label="Email" class="form-control" id="email"
             value="#{contactDetailControllerBV.contactDetail.email}"
             placeholder="Enter email">
                <f:validateRequired/>
                <f:validateLength maximum="64" />
            </h:inputText>
            <h:message for="email" styleClass="alert validation-error"/>
        </div>
    </div>
    <!-- . . . -->

    <label class="control-label"> Your Date of Birth</label>
```

```
<!-- . . . -->
<div class="row  my-group-border">
  <div class="col-sm-12">
    <h:message for="dobDay" styleClass="alert validation-error"/>
  </div>
  <div class="col-sm-12">
    <h:message for="dobMonth" styleClass="alert validation-error"/>
  </div>
  <div class="col-sm-12">
    <h:message for="dobYear" styleClass="alert validation-error"/>
  </div>
</div>
</h:form>
```

We placed the `<f:validateRequired>`, `<f:validateLength>`, and `<f:validateLongRange>` tags inside the body content of the JSF HTML rendering tags like `<h:inputText>` and `<h:selectOneMenu>`. The `validateLength` tag verifies the length of String property. The tag accepts a maximum parameter, but it can also take a minimum attribute.

We also added a `<h:message>` tag close to its respective HTML input field. The `styleClass` attribute specifies a custom CSS selector that forces the validation message on a separate new line. The CSS for this looks like as follows:

```
.validation-error {
    display: block;
    margin: 5px 15px 5px 15px;
    padding: 8px 15px 8px 15px;
    color: #a94442;
    background-color: #f2dede;
    border-color: #ebccd1;
}
```

In order to avoid JSF sugared names like `<jsf_form>:<form_property_name>` to the validation error message, which would give a result like `contactDetail:title -Validation Error: Value is required`, we specify the label attribute for each HTML render tag. The title input field has an attribute setting `label="Title"`.

The `<f:validateLongRange>` tag checks if the actual content of the String is a numerical value between the minimum and maximum attributes. We use this tag in the `date-of-birth` fields.

The following extract is the authoring for the day field in the DOB group:

```
<h:selectOneMenu id="dobDay"
  value="#{contactDetailControllerBV.dobDay}"
    label="Registration Day">
    <f:selectItem itemLabel="----"  itemValue=""/>
    <f:selectItems
      value="#{contactDetailControllerBV.daysOfTheMonth}"
      var="day"
     itemLabel="#{day}" itemValue="#{day}" />
    <f:validateRequired/>
    <f:validateLongRange minimum="1" maximum="31" />
</h:selectOneMenu>
```

The preceding code demonstrates how the `<f:validateLongRange>` tag enforces the day-of-the month field in the form. We rinse and repeat for the other DOB fields.

The `<f:validateRegex>` tag matches the input property string against a regular expression. We use this tag for the `email` property. The following is the code for this validation check:

```
<div class="col-sm-9">
  <h:inputText type="email"
    label="Email" class="form-control" id="email"
    value="#{contactDetailControllerBV.contactDetail.email}"
    placeholder="Enter email">
     <f:validateRequired/>
     <f:validateLength maximum="64" />
     <f:validateRegex pattern="^[_A-Za-z0-9-\+]+(\.[_A-Za-z0-9-]+)*@
[A-Za-z0-9-]+(\.[A-Za-z0-9]+)*(\.[A-Za-z]{2,})$" />
    </h:inputText>
    <h:message for="email" styleClass="alert validation-error"/>
  </div>
```

It is interesting to note that the overbearing pattern attribute value, the regular expression, is almost exactly the same as in the Bean Validation `@Pattern`. We had to convert the double backslash characters to single backslash, because we do not need to escape the literal in a normal regular expression, not set in Java code.

The following is a screenshot of the page `jsf-validation/createContactDetail.`
`xhtml`:

A screenshot demonstrating JSF built-in validation rules

Customizing JSF validation

If you have played around with the source code and ran the example, I bet you would have noticed some glaring issues with the JSF validation. For instance, when the email field has a value that is not a valid e-mail address, you will see a validation message like this:

```
Regex pattern of '^[_A-Za-z0-9-\\+]+(\\.[_A-Za-z0-9-]+)*@
[A-Za-z0-9-]+(\\.[A-Za-z0-9]+)*(\\.[A-Za-z]{2,})$' not matched
```

Clearly, this very detailed application message fails the user-centric design and clean language for the public. What can we do with JSF to avoid these messages?

There are three attributes that can be applied to the HTML rendering tags for input fields like <h:inputText> and <h:selectOneMenu>. The following table shows the attributes that can help customize the JSF validation messages:

Attribute	Description
requiredMessage	Defines a value-based expression that will be used as a message text if the field is required.
validatorMessage	Defines a value-based expression that will be used as a validation text if the field and property fails validation.
conversionMessage	Defines a value-based expression that will be used as a message if the field can be converted to the target type.

With this information, we can easily solve our issue with the messages by applying the requiredMessage attribute to our field:

```
<h:inputText type="email"
    label="Email" class="form-control" id="email"
    value="#{contactDetailControllerBV.contactDetail.email}"
    validatorMessage="Value must be in the format of an email address"
    converterMessage="Value should be in the format in an email
address"
    placeholder="Enter email">
  <f:validateRequired/>
  <f:validateLength maximum="64" />
  <f:validateRegex pattern=". . ." />
</h:inputText>
```

The `requiredMessage`, `validatorMessage`, and `conversionMessage` override any message that is set by the JSF validator on the server side. Note that these attributes can accept value expressions. This is great for page authors to dictate the method. On the other side of the fence though, our e-mail address field has two validation constraints, a regular expression check and a length-of-field constraint. The message is not appropriate for `validateLength`. So we have a problem there if we use more than one type of validator following this approach.

There is another approach that we could take. How about overriding the validation messages globally in the JSF framework? We can configure our own version of the JSF validator messages. In order to achieve this goal, first, we configure the framework with the information regarding the location for loading these messages. We set up a message bundle in the `WEB-INF/faces-config.xml` file, as follows:

```
<?xml version="1.0" encoding="UTF-8"?>
<faces-config xmlns="http://xmlns.jcp.org/xml/ns/javaee"
    xmlns:xsi="http://www.w3.org/2001/XMLSchema-instance"
    xsi:schemaLocation="http://xmlns.jcp.org/xml/ns/javaee
    http://xmlns.jcp.org/xml/ns/javaee/web-facesconfig_2_2.xsd"
    version="2.2">
  <application>
      <message-bundle>
          uk.co.xenonique.digital.JSFVMessages
      </message-bundle>
  </application>
</faces-config>
```

This configuration file defines the Faces resources for the application, and here we can configure a message bundle that references a property file. The path to the property file is actually `uk/co/xenonique/digital/JSFVMessages.properties`, which you find in the project resources `ch04/jsf-crud-validation/src/main/resources`.

Secondly, we supply our own message-bundle file. The contents of this property file `JSFVMessages.properties` are simply the following property definitions:

```
javax.faces.validator.RegexValidator.NOT_MATCHED = Input value does not
conform to according expected format.

javax.faces.validator.RegexValidator.PATTERN_NOT_SET = A pattern must be
set for validate.

javax.faces.validator.RegexValidator.MATCH_EXCEPTION = The pattern is not
a valid regular expression.

javax.faces.validator.LengthValidator.MAXIMUM = {1}: This field can
accept up to ''{0}'' characters long.
```

```
javax.faces.validator.LengthValidator.MINIMUM = {1}: This field must have
at least ''{0}'' characters long.
```

```
javax.faces.validator.LongRangeValidator.MAXIMUM = {1}: This value must
be less than or equal to ''{0}''
```

```
javax.faces.validator.LongRangeValidator.MINIMUM = {1}: This value must
be greater than or equal to ''{0}''
```

```
javax.faces.validator.LongRangeValidator.NOT_IN_RANGE = {2}: This value
must be between of {0} and {1} inclusive.
```

```
javax.faces.validator.LongRangeValidator.TYPE = {0}: Unable to convert
this value to a decimal number.
```

```
javax.faces.component.UIInput.REQUIRED = {0}: This value is required
```

As you can see, we have overridden the property `RegexValidator.NOT_MATCHED` to provide a new message. The original definitions are found in the JAR file in the application server or bundle as a third party JAR in your servlet container. The definitions can be found in the package of the JAR (`jsf-api-2.2.jar`) `javax/faces/Messages.properties`.

The original definitions for the regular expression validator look like this:

```
javax.faces.validator.RegexValidator.NOT_MATCHED = {1}: Validation Error:
Value not according to pattern ''{0}''
```

```
javax.faces.validator.RegexValidator.PATTERN_NOT_SET = A pattern must be
set for validate.
```

```
javax.faces.validator.RegexValidator.MATCH_EXCEPTION = The pattern is not
a valid regular expression.
```

```
javax.faces.validator.LengthValidator.MAXIMUM = {1}: Validation Error:
Length is greater than allowable maximum of ''{0}''
```

```
javax.faces.validator.LengthValidator.MINIMUM = {1}: Validation Error:
Length is less than allowable minimum of ''{0}''
```

```
javax.faces.validator.LongRangeValidator.MAXIMUM = {1}: Validation Error:
Value is greater than allowable maximum of ''{0}''
```

```
javax.faces.validator.LongRangeValidator.MINIMUM = {1}: Validation Error:
Value is less than allowable minimum of ''{0}''
```

```
javax.faces.validator.LongRangeValidator.NOT_IN_RANGE = {2}: Validation
Error: Specified attribute is not between the expected values of {0} and
{1}.
```

```
javax.faces.validator.LongRangeValidator.TYPE = {0}: Validation Error:
Value is not of the correct type.
```

You can examine this file in the source code at `http://svn.apache.org/repos/asf/myfaces/core/branches/2.0.x/api/src/main/resources/javax/faces/Messages.properties`. As you can see, they are quite technical and user-unfriendly. Many property definitions in the message bundle do accept placeholders for the parameters. The `NOT_MATCHED` accepts two parameters: the first parameter {0} is the pattern and the second parameter {1} is the label of the input field.

> In Java EE 7, the placeholders for parameterization in JSF validation are different from those in the Bean Validation framework. JSF uses integer indices, whereas Bean Validation can use named placeholders.

At the time of writing, there is a bug in the reference implementation of the JSF validator, which prevents the developers from using some of the placeholders in a message property. We would have enjoyed a property definition like this:

```
javax.faces.validator.RegexValidator.NOT_MATCHED = Input value {1}
does not conform to according expected format.
```

Sadly, the current bug in Mojarra prevents us from writing this out as production code.

There is an alternative strategy to customizing the JSF validation. We can define our own validators in order to extend the functionality of the framework.

Custom validation methods

JSF allows the digital engineer to configure a method in a managed bean controller that will be called to validate a field. Adding the attribute validator to the HTML render tags accomplishes this strategy, and it is a value expression.

The following is a way to add a custom validation method to the `emailAddress` property of the contact detail form:

```
<h:inputText type="email"
 label="Email" class="form-control" id="email"
 value="#{contactDetailControllerBV.contactDetail.email}"
 validator="#{contactDetailControllerJV.validateEmailAddress}"
 placeholder="Enter email">
    <f:validateRequired/>
</h:inputText>
```

The attribute validator references the method `validateEmailAddress()` in the modified `ContactDetailControllerJV` bean. This method looks like the following:

```
public void validateEmailAddress(
    FacesContext context, UIComponent component, Object value) {
    String text = value.toString();
    if ( text.length() > 64 ) {
      throw new ValidatorException(
        new FacesMessage(
          FacesMessage.SEVERITY_ERROR,
          "The value must be less than 64 chars long.", null));
    }
    final String REGEX =
        "^[_A-Za-z0-9-\\+]+(\\.[_A-Za-z0-9-]+)*@"
        + "[A-Za-z0-9-]+(\\.[A-Za-z0-9]+)*(\\.[A-Za-z]{2,})$";
    Pattern pattern = Pattern.compile(REGEX);
    Matcher matcher = pattern.matcher(text);
    if ( !matcher.matches() ) {
      throw new ValidatorException(
        new FacesMessage(
          FacesMessage.SEVERITY_ERROR,
          "The value must be a valid email address.", null));
    }
}
```

In the preceding method `validateEmailAddress()`, the incoming parameters are the `FacesContext`, the component being validated is of type UIComponent, and the pending value to be checked is of type Object. This method is validating two constraints: it checks that the length of the field is not too long and that the field is an e-mail address. We use the JDK standard library `javax.regex` package to fulfill this. To assert the validation errors, if any, we create the `FacesMessage` objects and add them to the current `FacesContext` instance.

Defining custom validators

Writing validators in controllers or a CDI named bean is a helpful strategy. However, the disadvantage is that you always need an indirect POJO in your application. There is another strategy where JSF allows us to define custom validators, which are integrated within the framework. A developer may choose to write a POJO that is declared with the annotation javax.faces.validator.FacesValidator. The POJO must implement the interface javax.faces.validator.Validator.

Let's move our e-mail address checking code into a custom validator. The code for FacesEmailAddressValidator is as follows:

```java
package uk.co.xenonique.digital;
import javax.faces.application.FacesMessage;
import javax.faces.component.UIComponent;
import javax.faces.context.FacesContext;
import javax.faces.validator.*;
import java.util.regex.*;

@FacesValidator("emailValidator")
public class FacesEmailAddressValidator implements Validator {
  public static final String EMAIL_REGEX =
    "^[_A-Za-z0-9-\\+]+(\\.[_A-Za-z0-9-]+)*@"
  + "[A-Za-z0-9-]+(\\.[A-Za-z0-9]+)*(\\.[A-Za-z]{2,})$";

  @Override
  public void validate(FacesContext context,
    UIComponent component, Object value)
    throws ValidatorException
  {
    String text = value.toString();
    Pattern pattern = Pattern.compile(EMAIL_REGEX);
    Matcher matcher = pattern.matcher(text);
    if ( !matcher.matches() ) {
      throw new ValidatorException(
        new FacesMessage(
          FacesMessage.SEVERITY_ERROR,
          "The value must be a valid email address.", null));
    }
  }
}
```

This class is annotated with @FacesValidator, and the single argument identifies the name of the validator in the page view. The method validate() implements the design by constraint in the validator interface. JSF passes in the FacesContext, the associated component with the input value, and the value itself.

We retrieve the input value as a text string. The regular expression code that validates the e-mail address is almost the same as before except for the message key. The error key is {application.emailAddress.pattern}.

With our POJO custom validator in place, we can rewrite the HTML on the page view to use it. The following is the extract view from login.xhtml:

```
<div class="form-group">
  <h:outputLabel for="email" class="col-sm-3 control-label">
    Email</h:outputLabel>
  <div class="col-sm-6">
    <h:inputText class="form-control" label="Email"
        value="#{loginControllerJV.email}"
        id="email" placeholder="Password"
        validator="emailValidator">
       <f:validateRequired/>
    </h:inputText>
    <h:message for="email" styleClass="alert validation-error"/>
  </div>
</div>
```

The only difference is the validator attribute in the <h:inputText> element. This attribute specifies the custom validator by name as emailValidator. As we can see, we can combine the custom validator with the default standard validators. There is still a <f:validateRequired> element.

The following screenshot shows the rendered output of `LoginControllerJV`:

A front-end page view demonstration two-factor security login and validation

Validating groups of properties

Now that we have knowledge of the JSF custom validators, we can write a custom validator to verify the group Date-of-Birth input fields. We can achieve this goal, because the FacesContext has been passed. It is possible to look up the UI components individually, separate from the context.

We shall use the JSF technique called binding inside a page view. Binding effectively publishes the instance of javax.faces.component.UIInput in JSF value and makes it available elsewhere in a page. The attribute binding on the HTML rendering JSF tags binds a component's reference in the component tree to a scoped variable. The following is the relevant JSF code. In particular, pay close attention to the JSF hidden input element at the start of the code extract from jsf-validation/createContact.xhtml.

```
<label class="control-label"> Your Date of Birth</label>
<h:inputHidden id="aggregateDobHidden"
               label="hiddenField1" value="true">
  <f:validator validatorId="dateOfBirthValidator" />
  <f:attribute name="dob_dotm" value="#{dob_dotm}" />
  <f:attribute name="dob_moty" value="#{dob_moty}" />
  <f:attribute name="dob_year" value="#{dob_year}" />
</h:inputHidden>

<div class="row  my-group-border">
  <div class="col-sm-3">
    <label class="control-label"
      for="dobDay">Day</label>
    <div class="controls">
      <h:selectOneMenu id="dobDay"
        value="#{contactDetailControllerJV.dobDay}"
        binding="#{dob_dotm}"
        label="Registration Day">
        <f:selectItem itemLabel="----"  itemValue=""/>
        <f:selectItems
          value="#{contactDetailControllerJV.daysOfTheMonth}"
var="day"
          itemLabel="#{day}" itemValue="#{day}" />
        <f:validateRequired/>
        <f:validateLongRange
          minimum="1" maximum="31" />
      </h:selectOneMenu>
    </div>
  </div>
  <div class="col-sm-3">
```

```
      ...
          <h:selectOneMenu id="dobMonth"
            value="#{contactDetailControllerJV.dobMonth}"
             binding="#{dob_moty}"
             label="Registration Month">
             ...
          </h:selectOneMenu>
      </div>
      <div class="col-sm-3">
        ...
          <h:inputText id="dobYear"
            value="#{contactDetailControllerJV.dobYear}"
               binding="#{dob_year}"
               label="Registration Year">
               ...
          </h:inputText>
      </div>
    </div>
    ...
    <div class="col-sm-12">
      <h:message for="aggregateDobHidden"
        styleClass="alert validation-error"/>
    </div>
  </div>
```

We utilize the hidden field, which is identified as `aggregateDobHidden` with a dummy form parameter name `hiddenField1`. It always sends a true value. The `<f:attribute>` element appends additional binding information to this UI component. We need three attributes with the names `dob_dotm` (day of the month), `dob_moty` (month of the year), and `dob_year`. These attributes are value expressions for the similarly-named page scope variables `#{dob_dotm}`, `#{dob_moty}`, and `#{dob_year}` respectively.

We add a binding attribute to each of the JSF selection components. Look at the following first field, again:

```
<h:selectOneMenu id="dobDay"
    value="#{contactDetailControllerJV.dobDay}"
  binding="#{dob_dotm}"
```

The attribute binding associates the component to the view and makes it available in the page scope variable defined by the literal String definition #{dob_dotm}. This is an instance of the javax.faces.component.UIInput class, which has a getSubmittedValue() method to get the submitted value. We repeat adding the binding for the other two properties. During a form submission, hiddenField1 has the record of bound values for each of the individual properties. This property is different from the individual day, month, and year properties.

This trick with the binding allows us to group properties together for form validation. The following source code shows the validation on the server side:

```
package uk.co.xenonique.digital;
import javax.faces.component.*;
import javax.faces.context.FacesContext;
import javax.faces.validator.*;
import java.util.*;


@FacesValidator("dateOfBirthValidator")
public class FacesDateOfBirthValidator implements Validator {
  @Override
  public void validate(FacesContext context,
  UIComponent component, Object value)
  throws ValidatorException {
    UIInput dayComp   = (UIInput)
      component.getAttributes().get("dob_dotm");
    UIInput monthComp = (UIInput)
      component.getAttributes().get("dob_moty");
    UIInput yearComp  = (UIInput)
      component.getAttributes().get("dob_year");

    List<FacesMessage> errors = new ArrayList<>();
    int day = parsePositiveInteger(
      dayComp.getSubmittedValue());
    if ( day < 1 || day > 31 ) {
      errors.add(new FacesMessage(
        FacesMessage.SEVERITY_ERROR,
        "DOB day must be in the range of 1 to 31 ", null));
    }
    int month = parsePositiveInteger(
      monthComp.getSubmittedValue());
```

```
    if ( month < 1 || month > 12 ) {
      errors.add(new FacesMessage(
        FacesMessage.SEVERITY_ERROR,
        "DOB month must be in the range of 1 to 12 ", null));
    }

    Calendar cal = Calendar.getInstance();

    cal.setTime(new Date());
    cal.add(Calendar.YEAR, -18);
    Date eighteenBirthday = cal.getTime();

    cal.setTime(new Date());
    cal.add(Calendar.YEAR, -100);
    Date hundredthBirthday = cal.getTime();

    int year = parsePositiveInteger(
      yearComp.getSubmittedValue());
    cal.set(year,month,day);
    Date targetDate = cal.getTime();
    if (targetDate.after(eighteenBirthday) ) {
      errors.add(new FacesMessage(
        FacesMessage.SEVERITY_ERROR,
        "DOB year: you must be 18 years old.", null));
    }
    if ( targetDate.before(hundredthBirthday)) {
      errors.add(new FacesMessage(
        FacesMessage.SEVERITY_ERROR,
        "DOB: you must be younger than 100 years old.", null ));
    }
    if ( !errors.isEmpty()) {
      throw new ValidatorException(errors);
    }
  }

  public int parsePositiveInteger( Object value ) { /*...*/ }
}
```

The POJO `FacesDateOfBirthValidator` verifies the three DOB properties. It does this using a technique in JSF called binding in the page view, which we will see in a minute. Binding allows JSF input properties to be propagated to another named scope variable that can be used elsewhere on the page. As for the validator, we use an HTML hidden element as a vehicle to retrieve these bounded values as attributes. This is the purpose of the code that casts the component to `javax.faces.component.UIInput` and then extracts a value.

```
UIInput dayComp   = (UIInput)
      component.getAttributes().get("dob_dotm");
int day = parsePositiveInteger(
      dayComp.getSubmittedValue());
```

We have a helper method, `parsePositiveInteger()` for converting the text value to an integer. Before that, we create a list collection to store any error messages. We then validate the boundary for the day-of-the month from 1 to 31. The logic is almost identical for the month property.

For the year property, we take a different step. Using the JDK Calendar and Date classes, we build two Date instances: one represents the current date exactly 100 years ago and the other represents the current date 18 years ago. We can then compare if the user's entry date falls inside these two birthday limits.

If there are any errors at the end of the method `validate()`, then it raises a `ValidatorException` exception with the error collections. Note that we elect to use the alternative constructor.

To complete the validator, the helper method `parsePositiveInteger()` can be written as follows:

```
public int parsePositiveInteger( Object value ) {
  if ( value == null ) return -1;
  try {
      return Integer.parseInt( value.toString().trim());
  }
  catch (NumberFormatException nfe) {
      return -1;
  }
}
```

The following is a screenshot of the contact detail that demonstrates the group
validator in use:

A screenshot of the date of birth validators

Converters

The standard JSF validators allow the digital developer to achieve a lot of functionality. There are circumstances when the requirements exceed the default behavior. Converters are JSF classes that convert between strings and objects. Similar to the way in which annotations define the custom validator, JSF permits the registration of custom convertors. A converter is associated with a JSF component.

The annotation `@java.faces.convert.FacesConverter` denotes that a POJO is a custom JSF converter. This type must implement the `javax.faces.convert.Converter` interface, which has the following methods:

```
public Object getAsObject( FacesContext context,
  UIComponent component, String newValue);

public String getAsString( FacesContext context,
  UIComponent component, Object value);
```

The method `getAsObject()` converts a string representation from the client to the target object. The other method `getAsString()` converts the object to the string representation, which is rendered in the client browser.

We shall exemplify the custom JSF converter with one that converts a string to the suits of playing cards. We can write this using a simple Java enumeration class:

```
public enum FrenchSuit {
    HEARTS, DIAMONDS, CLUBS, SPADES
}
```

The following is the full listing for the custom converter `FrenchSuitConverter` class:

```
package uk.co.xenonique.digital;
import javax.faces.application.FacesMessage;
import javax.faces.component.*;
import javax.faces.context.FacesContext;
import javax.faces.convert.*;
import static uk.co.xenonique.digital.FrenchSuit.*;

@FacesConverter("frenchSuitConverter")
public class FrenchSuitConverter implements Converter {
  @Override
  public Object getAsObject(FacesContext context,
    UIComponent component, String value) {
    String text = value.trim();
    if ( text.length() == 0 ) {
      text = ((UIInput)component).getSubmittedValue().toString();
```

```
          }
          text = text.toUpperCase();
          switch (text) {
            case "HEARTS": return HEARTS;
            case "DIAMONDS": return DIAMONDS;
            case "CLUBS": return CLUBS;
            case "SPADES": return SPADES;
            default:
              throw new ConverterException(
                new FacesMessage(
                  FacesMessage.SEVERITY_ERROR,
                  "Unable to convert object to string", null));
          }
        }


        @Override
        public String getAsString(FacesContext context,
          UIComponent component, Object value) {
          if ( value instanceof String ) {
            return value.toString();
          }
          else if ( !(value instanceof FrenchSuit)) {
            throw new ConverterException(
              new FacesMessage(
                FacesMessage.SEVERITY_ERROR,
                "Unable to convert object to string", null));
          }
          switch ((FrenchSuit)value) {
            case HEARTS: return "Hearts";
            case DIAMONDS: return "Diamonds";
            case CLUBS: return "Clubs";
            case SPADES: return "Spades";
          }
          throw new IllegalStateException(
              "PC should never reach here!");
        }
      }
```

The POJO is the annotated @FacesConverter, and the value becomes the identifier in the page view.

JSF invokes the `getAsObject()` method with the text representation, which is trimmed and transformed to the uppercase in order to make the comparisons easier. At the beginning of the method, there is a possibility that the new value could be a blank string. If this is true, then we retrieve the text representation from the already submitted value. For this particular converter, the use case of an empty value is a possibility, so we add the guard. If there is an issue with the process, the method raises an exception, `javax.faces.convert.ConverterException`.

JSF calls the `getAsString()` method in order to convert the object representation to a String. Depending on the object type, the method defends against the different types of input. The input value may be just a string, or it may be an instance of the `FrenchSuit` enumeration. If the input value is not one of these, the method raises `ConverterException`.

In the real world, we know that there will always be four suits in a set of playing cards, and therefore, we can be fairly confident about the maintainability of our enumeration. As a digital developer, you may not have such luxuries, and hence, applying the principle of defensive programming in a converter and a validator can go a long way to tracking down bugs.

The following is an extract from the page `/jsf-validation/french-suit.xhtml` that exercises the custom converter:

```
<h:form id="cardForm"
        styleClass="form-horizontal"
        p:role="form">
  ...
  <div class="form-group">
    <h:outputLabel for="suit" class="col-sm-3 control-label">
        Card Suit</h:outputLabel>
    <div class="col-sm-9">
      <h:selectOneMenu class="form-control"
          label="Suit" id="suit"
          value="#{frenchSuitController.suit}" >
        <f:converter converterId="frenchSuitConverter" />
        <f:selectItem itemLabel="-" itemValue="" />
        <f:selectItem itemValue="#{frenchSuitController.
suitEnumValue('HEARTS')}" />
        <f:selectItem itemValue="#{frenchSuitController.
suitEnumValue('CLUBS')}" />
        <f:selectItem itemValue="#{frenchSuitController.
suitEnumValue('DIAMONDS')}" />
        <f:selectItem itemValue="#{frenchSuitController.
suitEnumValue('SPADES')}" />
        <f:validateRequired/>
```

```
        </h:selectOneMenu>
        <h:message for="suit" styleClass="alert validation-error"/>
      </div>
    </div>

    <h:commandButton styleClass="btn btn-primary"
       action="#{frenchSuitController.doAction()}"
       value="Submit" />
    ...
  </h:form>
```

In the preceding view, we are using a dropdown menu `<h:selectOneMenu>` that allows the user to select a card suit. The code should be very familiar to you by now. The difference lies in the value expressions for each card suit, which are all method invocations with a String-literal parameter. The Expression Language allows you to call methods with parameters. Therefore, the expression: `#{frenchSuitController.suitEnumValue('HEARTS')}` translates to a method call on the controller.

Inside the body content of `<h:selectOneMenu>`, we explicitly reference the custom converter by an identifier, and associate it with the UI component through the following:

```
    <f:converter converterId="frenchSuitConverter" />
```

JSF then invokes the custom converter in order to translate the individual FrenchSuit enumeration to a String from the page view. It sounds like a roundabout way to show a list of values, but this example demonstrates that the method getAsString() in FrenchSuitConverter is being called. Additionally, it illustrates how to reference Java enumeration in a page view and in a controller in a robust manner.

Let's examine the controller now:

```
    package uk.co.xenonique.digital;
    import javax.faces.context.Flash;
    import javax.faces.context.FacesContext;
    import javax.faces.view.ViewScoped;
    import javax.inject.Named;

    @Named("frenchSuitController")
    @ViewScoped
    public class FrenchSuitController {
        private String firstName;
        private String lastName;
        private FrenchSuit suit;

        public String doAction() {
```

```
            Flash flash = FacesContext.getCurrentInstance().
                   getExternalContext().getFlash();
            flash.put("firstName",firstName);
            flash.put("lastName",lastName);
            flash.put("suit", suit);
            return "/jsf-validation/french-suit-complete?redirect=true";
        }

    public String cancel() {
        return "/index.xhtml?redirect=true";
    }

    public FrenchSuit  suitEnumValue( String name ) {
        return FrenchSuit.valueOf(name);
    }

    // Getters and setters omitted
}
```

We are jumping ahead slightly with this code for `FrenchSuitController`. First, let me draw your attention to the method `suitEnumValue()`, which converts a String literal to the enumeration type `FrenchSuit`. This is a nice handy trick for obtaining enumerations in the page view, because Expression Language does not allow direct access to the Java enumerations. It will especially work with enumerations that change over time through different project releases.

The `doAction()` and `cancel()` methods return the URI with a special query parameter `redirect=true`. This is an instruction for JSF to return a bookmarkable URL; we shall cover this topic much later in this chapter.

Within `doAction()` we are making use of the Flash scope in JSF for the first time. The Flash scope is a temporary context that allows the controllers to pass on data to the next navigation view. Remember that the View scope is only valid for the current controller that navigates to the same page view. The `@ViewScoped` managed beans go out of scope when the `FacesContext` moves to the next page view. The methods set a key value association in the `javax.faces.context.Flash` instance.

The final piece of the puzzle demonstrates how we use the Flash scope in a page view. This code can be found in the file `/jsf-validation/french-suit-complete.xhtml`. The following code is an extract from the same:

```
<ui:define name="mainContent">
  <h1> House of Card with JSF Validation</h1>
  ...
  <div class="jumbotron">
```

```
    <h1> Complete </h1>
    <p>
      Terrific! You completed the French suit action.
      Your first name is <b>#{flash['firstName']}</b> and
      your last name is <b>#{flash['lastName']}</b> and
      you chose <b>#{flash['suit']}</b> as the playcard suit.
    </p>
  </div>
  ...
</ui:define>
```

In this page view, we use the map expression to retrieve values from the Flash scope. The expression `#{flash['suit']}` is the suit that the user selected. The reader is also directed to look at the documentation for the default JSF converter `javax.faces.convert.EnumConverter`. In the same package, there are other standard converters such as `BigDecimalConverter`, `BigIntegerConverter`, `DateTimeConverter`, `ByteConverter`, `LongConverter`, and `DoubleConverter`.

I will leave you with the screenshot for the form view `french-suit.xhtml`:

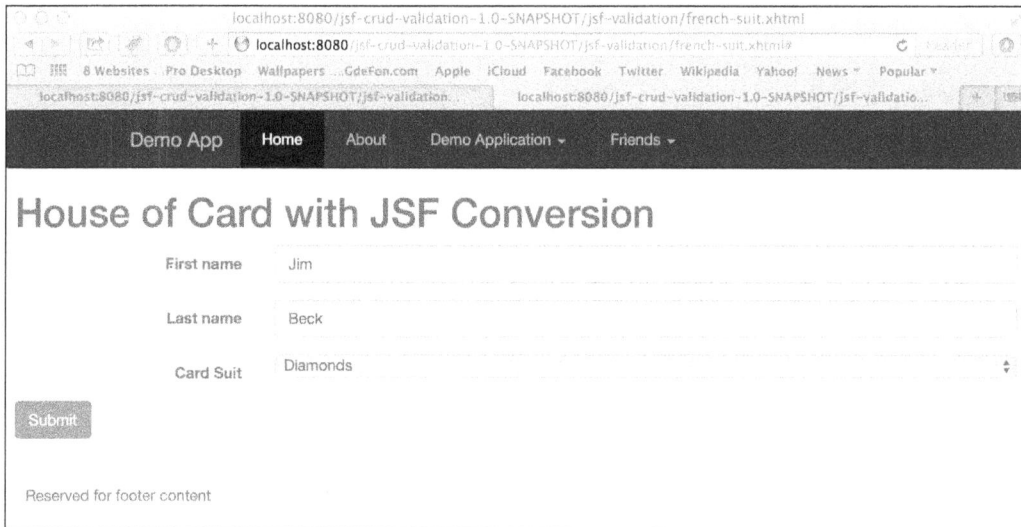

A screenshot of the suites of cards with the JSF convertor

The following is a screenshot showing the end state of `french-suit-complete.xhtml`. The mark up shows nice visuals in the CSS jumbotron style from Bootstrap.

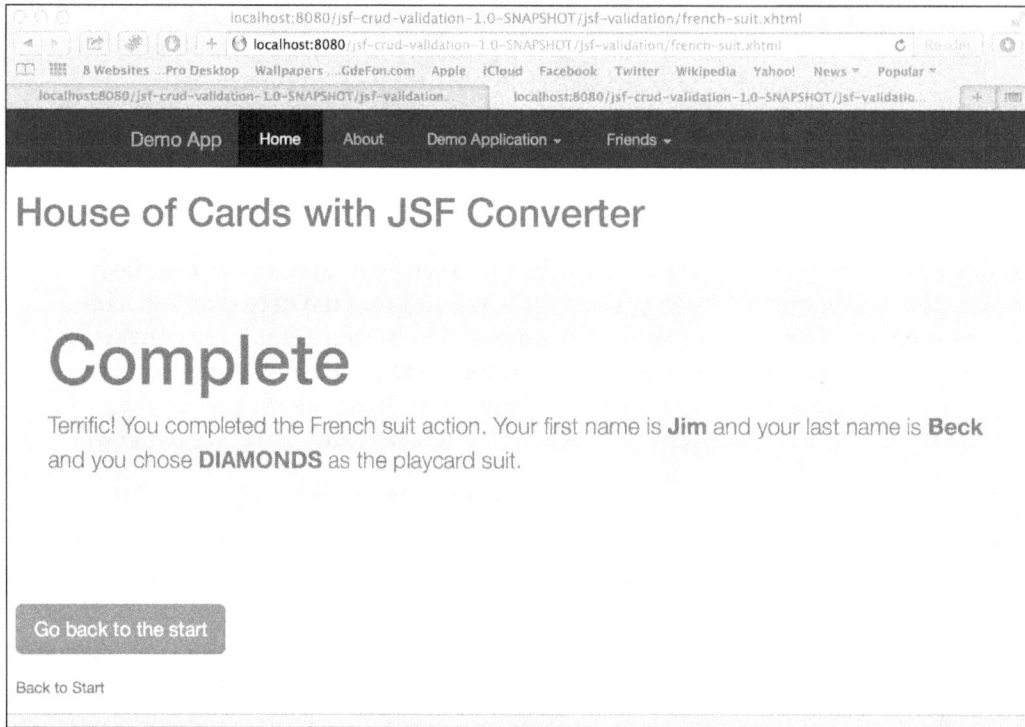

The second screen from the house of cards example after form submission and validation

We have covered a lot of validation that happens on the server side. Let's now move on to AJAX validation.

Validating immediately with AJAX

Asynchronous JavaScript and XML (**AJAX**) is a group of technologies that together solve the restriction to the retrieving of partial updates to a web page and that provide a rich interactive user experience. The key to AJAX is the term *asynchronous*, which builds on a **World Wide Web Consortium** (**W3C**) standard namely, the `XmlHttpRequest` object. It was introduced in the Internet Explorer in 2006 and all modern web browsers by now support this object. The asynchronous mode allows the browser to make a data transfer request to the server on a separate connection; the enterprise backend response responds with a data result, usually JSON or XML. These AJAX data transfers tend to be smaller in comparison to reloading the entire page each time.

JSF has built-in support for AJAX requests and responses; the developer does not have to know the finer details of XmlHttpRequest and JavaScript programming to get the benefit of an immediate response. The digital developer can start with the default JavaScript library for performing AJAX interaction.

It is very easy to get started with AJAX in JSF with the <f:ajax> tag. This Core JSF tag registers the AJAX behavior with a UI component, and it is used to perform validation on a field. Developers are only required to place the tag inside the body content of an HTML JSF tag that represents a component, which requires validation.

The following code shows how to use this tag with the contact details application:

```
<f:ajax event="blur" render="firstNameError"/>
```

The tag attribute event establishes when the framework would invoke the AJAX validation. The blur value denotes that it occurs when the user moves from this component field to the next input field. So when the user presses the *Tab* key on a desktop computer or navigates the UI on a phone or a tablet, validation occurs immediately, because JavaScript fires an AJAX request to the server. The second attribute, render, informs the framework about the specific UI component to render the error message to, if any. JSF receives an AJAX response, and if there is an error, it knows the HTML component ID to update with the validation message.

Let's look at the project ch04/jsf-crud-ajax-validation, which is the full extract of the page view jsf-validation/createContactDetail.xhtml:

```
<h:form id="createContactDetail"
    styleClass="form-horizontal"
    p:role="form">
    <div class="form-group">
      <h:outputLabel for="title" class="col-sm-3 control-label">
          Title</h:outputLabel>
      <div class="col-sm-9">
        <h:selectOneMenu class="form-control"
            label="Title" id="title"
          value="#{contactDetailControllerJV.contactDetail.title}">
          <f:selectItem itemLabel="-" itemValue="" />
          <f:selectItem itemValue="Mr" />
          <f:selectItem itemValue="Mrs" />
          <f:selectItem itemValue="Miss" />
          <f:selectItem itemValue="Ms" />
          <f:selectItem itemValue="Dr" />
          <f:validateRequired/>
          <f:ajax event="blur" render="titleError"/>
        </h:selectOneMenu>
```

```
            <h:message id="titleError"
                    for="title" styleClass="alert validation-error"/>
        </div>
    </div>
    <div class="form-group">
        <h:outputLabel for="firstName" class="col-sm-3 control-label">
            First name</h:outputLabel>
        <div class="col-sm-9">
            <h:inputText class="form-control" label="First name"
          value="#{contactDetailControllerJV.contactDetail.firstName}"
            id="firstName" placeholder="First name">
                <f:validateRequired/>
                <f:validateLength maximum="64" />
                <f:ajax event="blur" render="firstNameError"/>
            </h:inputText>
            <h:message id="firstNameError"
                for="firstName" styleClass="alert validation-error"/>
        </div>
    </div>
    <div class="form-group">
        <h:outputLabel for="middleName" class="col-sm-3 control-label">
            Middle name</h:outputLabel>
            ...
    </div>
    <div class="form-group">
        <h:outputLabel for="lastName" class="col-sm-3 control-label">
            Last name</h:outputLabel>
        <div class="col-sm-9">
            <h:inputText class="form-control"
          value="#{contactDetailControllerJV.contactDetail.lastName}"
            label="Last name"
            id="lastName" placeholder="Last name">
                <f:validateRequired/>
                <f:validateLength maximum="64" />
                <f:ajax event="blur" render="lastNameError"/>
            </h:inputText>
            <h:message id="lastNameError"
                for="lastName" styleClass="alert validation-error"/>
        </div>
    </div>
    ...
</h:form>
```

This page view exemplifies that adding the AJAX validation to a page is extremely easy in JSF. The `<f:ajax>` Core JSF tag is embedded in the corresponding HTML JSF tag, as you can see for the first and last name fields. The other difference between the non-AJAX and AJAX page for contact details is the addition of the identifiers such as `firstNameError` and `lastNameError` to the `<h:message>` tag. We need to add the HTML identifier elements for allowing JavaScript to look up the HTML element by ID from the browser's **Document Object Model (DOM)**.

The page has an AJAX validation added to all the properties except for the middle name and the newsletter HTML checkbox field. AJAX validation also works with custom validators and converters.

The following screenshot illustrates the single property AJAX validation:

A screenshot demonstrating single validations for each input fields

Validating groups of input fields

So far we have seen the JSF AJAX validation on single instances of input fields. The `<f:ajax>` tag also works with validation on a group of components. We can enclose the tag around one or more JSF input fields and then the `<f:ajax>` tag becomes the parent of the UI component. This causes JSF to apply the AJAX validation to multiple components.

Let's add the group validation to the Date-of-Birth fields in the contact details form with the following page view:

```
<h:inputHidden id="aggregateDobHidden"
            label="hiddenField1" value="true">
  <f:validator validatorId="dateOfBirthValidator" />
  <f:attribute name="dob_dotm" value="#{dob_dotm}" />
  <f:attribute name="dob_moty" value="#{dob_moty}" />
  <f:attribute name="dob_year" value="#{dob_year}" />
</h:inputHidden>

<f:ajax event="blur" render="dobDayError dobMonthError dobYearError">
  <div class="row  my-group-border">
    <div class="col-sm-3">
      <label class="control-label" for="dobDay">Day</label>
      <div class="controls">
        <h:selectOneMenu id="dobDay" value="#{contactDetailController
JV.dobDay}"
                       binding="#{dob_dotm}"
                       label="Registration Day">
          . . .
        </h:selectOneMenu>
      </div>
    </div>
    <div class="col-sm-3">
      <label class="control-label" for="dobMonth">Month</label>
      <div class="controls">
        <h:selectOneMenu id="dobMonth" value="#{contactDetailControlle
rJV.dobMonth}"
                       binding="#{dob_moty}"
                       label="Registration Month">
          . . .
        </h:selectOneMenu>
      </div>
    </div>
```

```
    <div class="col-sm-3">
      <label class="control-label" for="dobYear">Year</label>
      <div class="controls">
          ...
      </div>
    </div>
    <div class="col-sm-12">
      <h:message id="dobDayError"
        for="dobDay" styleClass="alert validation-error"/>
    </div>
    <div class="col-sm-12">
      <h:message id="dobMonthError"
        for="dobMonth" styleClass="alert validation-error"/>
    </div>
    <div class="col-sm-12">
      <h:message id="dobYearError"
        for="dobYear" styleClass="alert validation-error"/>
    </div>
    <div class="col-sm-12">
      <h:messages for="aggregateDobHidden"
         styleClass="alert validation-error"/>
    </div>
  </div>
</f:ajax>
```

As you can see, we surround the DOB input fields with an encompassing `<f:ajax>` tag. The event attribute is still set to `blur`. The render attribute is set to a list of the HTML element IDs for specific validation messages, namely `dobDayError`, `dobMonthError`, and `dobYearError`.

The `aggregationDobHidden` HTML hidden element is kept the same as in the non-AJAX example in order to illustrate that the validation does not interfere with the custom validation.

To recap, use the `<f:ajaxTag>`, and embed it inside any JSF component. To validate over a group of multiple components, surround the components with `<f:ajaxTag>`.

The following screenshot depicts the multiple component AJAX validation around the DOB fields. The month-of-the-year component had the browser's focus last and hence, the corresponding validation message depicts the `onblur` DOM JavaScript event. Similarly, tabbing across this set of fields produces the error messages one by one.

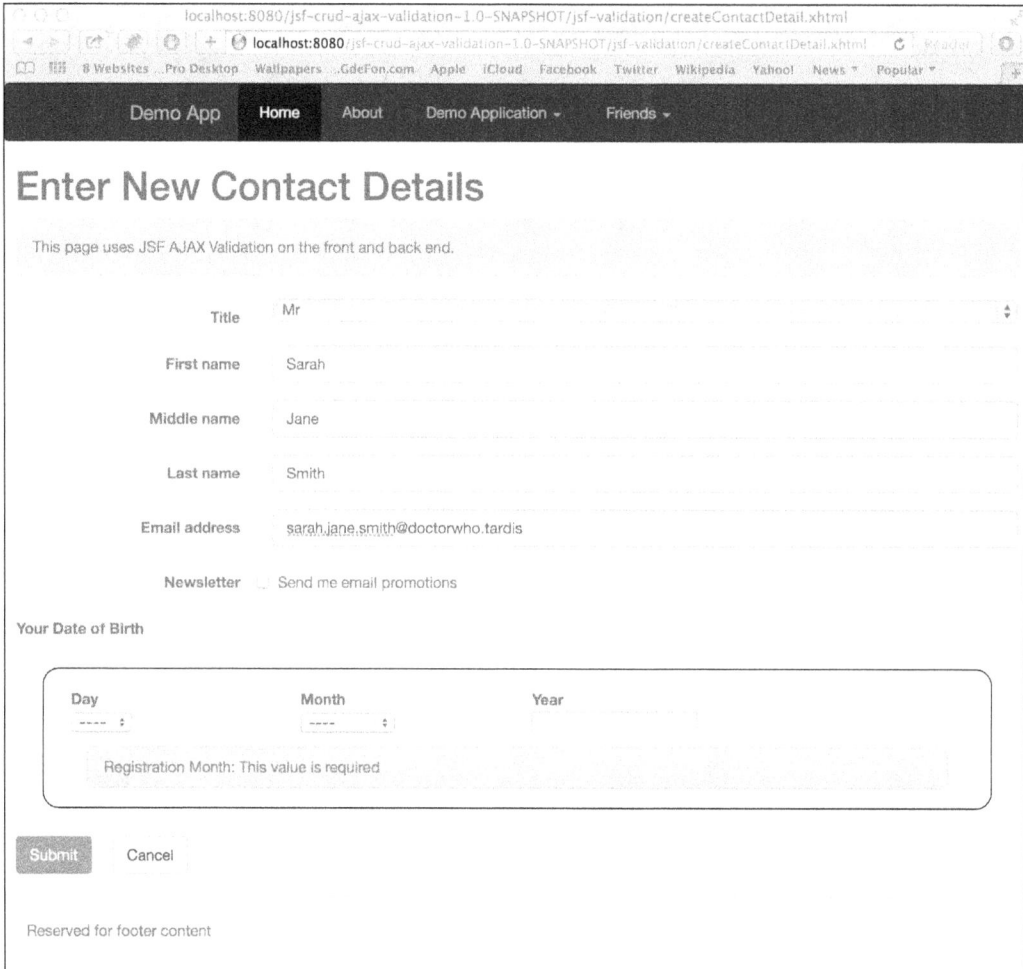

A screenshot of the group validation for date of birth input fields

AJAX custom tag in depth

It is useful to understand the attributes that can be applied to this Core JSF custom tag. The following table describes the attributes for `<f:ajax>`.

Attribute	Description
delay	Specifies the delay in milliseconds between sending multiple AJAX requests to the server. Requests are queued up by the JSF implementation. Setting the value to none disables the feature.
disabled	Specifies a Boolean value to indicate the tag status. If set to true, then the AJAX behavior is not rendered. The default value is false.
event	Defines a String enumeration that represents the event type of the AJAX action. By default, JSF determines the event name for the component.
execute	Enumerates a space-delimited collection of names that represent the components that are executed on the server. The value can be a string or a value expression. The default value is @this, which indicates the parent component of the AJAX behavior.
immediate	States a Boolean value that indicates whether the input value is processed early in the JSF lifecycle.
listener	Indicates the name of the listener method that will be called during a broadcast event, namely AjaxBehaviorEvent.
onerror	Specifies the name of a JavaScript function that will accept errors.
onevent	Specifies the name of a JavaScript function that will handle the UI events.
render	Enumerates a collection of UI components that will be rendered on the client when the AJAX behavior completes. This value can be a space-delimited collection of component identifiers, or it can be a value expression. The default value is @none, which means that no components are rendered.

From this preceding table, you will notice that the execute and render attributes may indicate additional meaningful values. The execute attribute stipulates the components to be executed on the server. The render attribute determines the affected UI components for when the AJAX behavior completes. The following table lists the attribute values:

Value	Description
@all	Specifies that all the components are executed or rendered in the view.
@form	Specifies that only the components that are the children of the form are executed or rendered.
@none	Specifies that no components are executed or rendered.

Value	Description
`@this`	Specifies that only the current component that triggered the AJAX request is executed or rendered.
`List of component identifiers`	Enumerates the identifiers of the UI components that are explicitly executed or rendered as an AJAX request.
`Expression language`	Specifies a value expression that ultimately returns a collection of Strings, which indicates the UI components that are executed or rendered as an AJAX request-response.

A partial JSF lifecycle

The JSF lifecycle is, in effect, for all Faces requests and responses including those that emanate from the AJAX-enabled components. Behind the scenes, JSF instantiates a special object, `javax.faces.context.PartialViewContext` for the AJAX requests and responses, and that is entered into the processing lifecycle. This context object contains the information that allows JSF to update the component model on the server-side. Based on the partial context, JSF decides whether to accomplish partial processing of the selected UI component and/or partial rendering of the UI components. Partial processing corresponds to the Apply-Requests-Values, Process-Validations, and Update-Model-Values phases of the lifecycle. Partial rendering refers to the Render-Response phase.

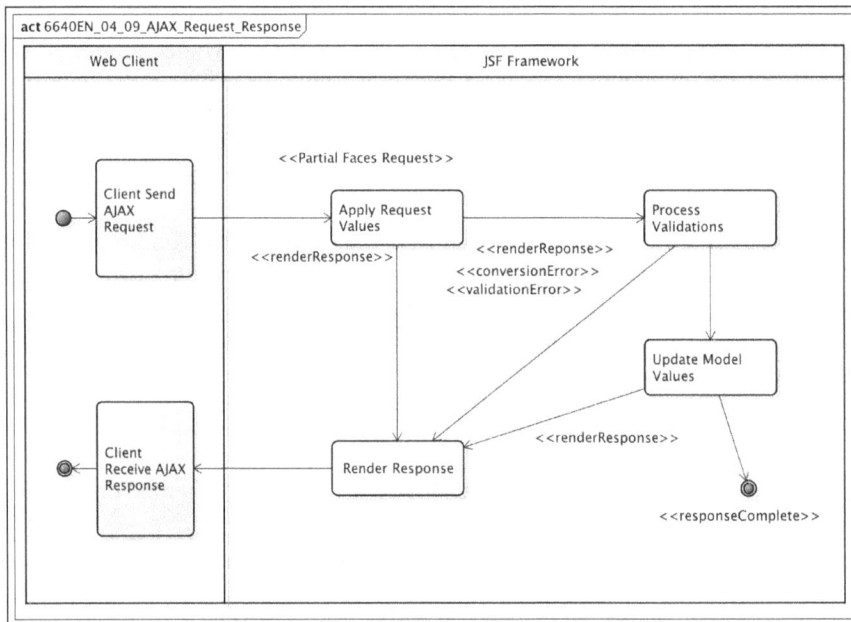

Partial request – response lifecycle for AJAX submissions

The preceding diagram encapsulates our understanding of the partial context for the AJAX request and response in the JSF lifecycle.

Handling views

In this chapter, we've chiefly examined the validation of the users' input with JSF. There were some miscellaneous concepts regarding navigation that we glossed over. Let's now talk about handling views and navigation.

Invoking controller methods

There are several ways to invoke the controller from a page view with parameters. For many situations in the digital e-commerce applications, developers need to retrieve a particular data record, trigger a server-side action, or save a certain state from the client-side at the backend.

Parameterized method invocations

JSF allows the developer to pass parameters to methods in the page view using the Expression Language . The first feature given in *Chapter 3*, *Building JSF Forms* is called Method Expression Invocation, which was introduced in JSF 2.0.

The following is an extract from the page view /jsf-miscellany/examplar-methods.xhtml:

```
<h:form id="methodExampler"
        styleClass="form-horizontal"
        p:role="form">
  ...
  <div class="form-group">
    <div class="col-sm-9">
    <p>
        Invoke JSF controller with 3 literal arguments
    </p>
    <p class="monospace">
        \#{examplarController.methodThreeArgs(
          'Obiwan','Ben','Kenobi')}
    </p>
    <h:commandButton styleClass="btn btn-primary"
        action="#{examplarController.methodThreeArgs(
          'Obiwan','Ben','Kenobi')}"
```

```
        value="Invoke" />
    </div>
  </div>
  ...


  </h:form>
```

The preceding code depicts the `<h:commandButton>` tag with an action value expression, which is `#{examplarController.methodThreeArgs('Obiwan','Ben', 'Kenobi')}`. This is a method invocation with three arguments of literal string.

The arguments can also be references to other JSF scope instances. The following is another invocation with only two arguments that show this off:

```
<h:commandButton
    styleClass="btn btn-primary"
    action="#{examplarController.methodTwoArgs(
        examplarController.city, examplarController.country)}"
      value="Invoke" />
```

The arguments are dynamically set from the controller bean properties. Let's look at the controller `ExamplarController` now:

```
@Named("examplarController") @ViewScoped
public class ExamplarController {
  private String city = "London";
  private String country="United Kingdom";

  public String methodOneArg( String alpha ) {
    Flash flash = FacesContext.getCurrentInstance().
      getExternalContext().getFlash();
    flash.put("result",
      String.format("executed methodOneArg(\"%s\")",
        alpha ));
    return "examplar-methods-complete?redirect=true";
  }

  public String methodTwoArgs(
    String alpha, String beta ) {
    Flash flash = FacesContext.getCurrentInstance().
      getExternalContext().getFlash();
    flash.put("result",
      String.format("executed methodTwoArgs(\"%s\", \"%s\")",
        alpha, beta ));
```

```
      return "examplar-methods-complete?redirect=true";
   }

   public String methodThreeArgs(
      String alpha, String beta, String gamma ) {
      Flash flash = FacesContext.getCurrentInstance().
         getExternalContext().getFlash();
      flash.put("result",
         String.format("executed methodThreeArgs(\"%s\", \"%s\",
\"%s\")",
         alpha, beta, gamma ));
      return "examplar-methods-complete?redirect=true";
   }

   ...
   // Getters and setters omitted
}
```

There are three methods that are called `methodOneArg()`, `methodTwoArgs()`, and `methodThreeArgs()`. The names are self-explanatory for the number of arguments that can be passed; each one saves an output result in the JSF Flash scope, before moving to the next page view, `/jsf-miscellany/examplar-methods-complete.xhtml`.

The following is the extract of the end state Facelet view, `exemplar-methods-complete.xhtml`:

```
<ui:composition template="/basic_layout.xhtml">
   <ui:define name="title">
      <title> JSF Method Invocation Example </title>
   </ui:define>

   <ui:define name="mainContent">
      <h1> Method Invocations Complete</h1>
      <h:messages globalOnly="true"
                  styleClass="alert alert-danger" />
      <div class="jumbotron">
         <h1> Complete </h1>
         <p>
            Terrific! You completed the action.
            The result message was <b>#{flash['result']}</b>.
         </p>
      </div>
      ...
   </ui:define> <!--name="mainContent" -->
</ui:composition>
```

Passing parameters to the controller

Before the JSF 2.0 specification was created, it was possible to send parameters to a backing bean controller using the `<f:param>` tag inside of the body of a `<h:commandLink>`, `<h:commandButton>`, or `<h:link>` tag. Although this technique is superseded by the method invocation expressions in JSF 2.0, it is still a useful technique to send out-of-bounds communication to the controller.

The following code shows the recipe, and we embed two `<f:param>` elements in a `<h:commandButton>` custom tag:

```
<div class="form-group">
  <div class="col-sm-9">
    <p>
        Invoke JSF controller method with parameters
    </p>
    <p class="monospace">
      \#{examplarController.methodPassingAttribute()
      <br/>
          name="callToActionText" value="FindNearestDealer"
      <br/>
      name="customerType" value="Motorbikes"
    </p>
    <h:commandButton styleClass="btn btn-primary"
      action="#{examplarController.methodPassingParameters()}"
      value="Invoke" >
      <f:param name="callToActionText"
              value="FindNearestDealer"/>
      <f:param name="customerType"
              value="Motorbikes"/>
    </h:commandButton>
  </div>
</div>
```

The authoring on this page view invokes the controller's no argument method, `methodPassingParameters()`. JSF passes two parameters to the target method through the Faces request with the key names `callToActionText` and `customerType`.

Let's look at the controller method that handles this invocation:

```
public String methodPassingParameters() {
  Map<String,String> params = FacesContext.getCurrentInstance()
      .getExternalContext().getRequestParameterMap();
  String ctaText = params.get("callToActionText");
  String custType = params.get("customerType");
  Flash flash = FacesContext.getCurrentInstance().
```

```
          getExternalContext().getFlash();
      flash.put("result",
        String.format("executed methodPassingParameters() " +
          "ctaText=\"%s\", custType=%s", ctaText, custType ));
      return "examplar-methods-complete?redirect=true";
  }
```

Inside the method `methodPassingParameters()`, we retrieve the parameters from the `FacesContext` instance by using the nested call `getRequestParameterMap()`. It is then straightforward to access the parameters from the map collection of type `Map<String, String>`. It is interesting to note that the parameters can only be Strings, and that this technique can be combined with method parameters invocations in JSF 2.0 and later.

The following screenshot displays the page to demonstrate the method invocation techniques described in this section:

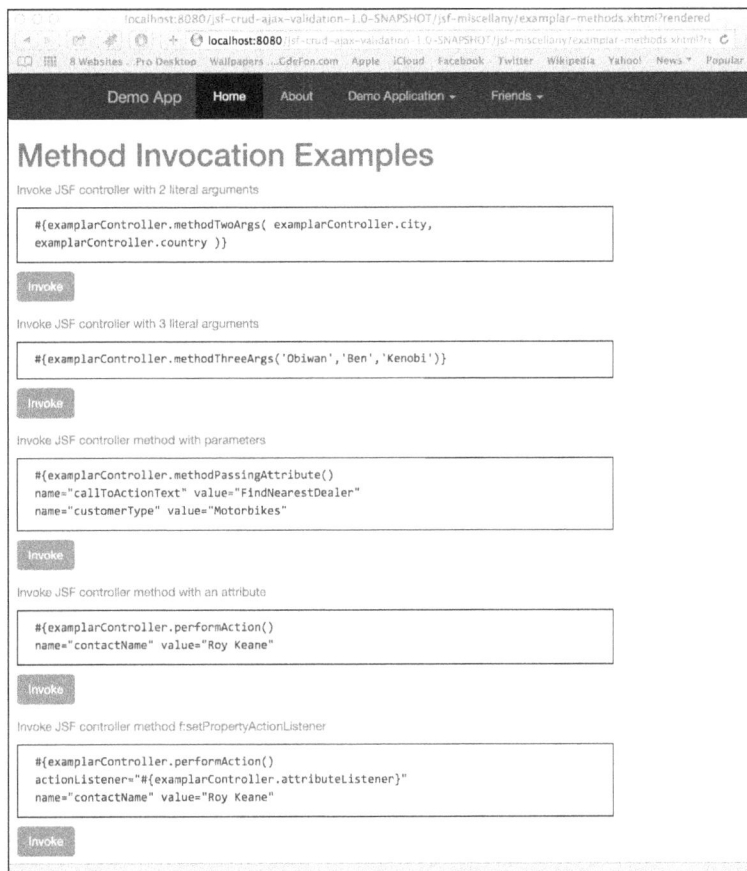

A screenshot of the method invocation JSF example

Invoking an action event listener

The final technique for handling views invokes an action listener in the controller. Any instance method that accepts a single argument of `javax.faces.event.ActionEvent` can be an action event listener. An action listener is associated with a UI component in the page markup. JSF invokes action listeners before invoking the actions, so this technique is helpful for hooking in the business logic and setting up data for the action call.

The following is an extract from the method invocation page that enacts this technique. We will dispense with the Bootstrap CSS markup in this code:

```
<h:commandButton styleClass="btn btn-primary"
  action="#{examplarController.performAction}"
  actionListener="#{examplarController.attributeListener}"
  value="Invoke">
 <f:attribute name="contactName" value="Roy Keane" />
</h:commandButton>
```

The `<h:commandButton>` tag has an additional `actionListener` attribute set to the expression that references the action listener method, `attributeListener()`. The tag also embeds an `<f:attribute>` to define a passed attribute. The action attribute references the method `performAction()`.

Let's examine our `ExamplarController` backing bean to see the code:

```
private String contactName;

public void attributeListener(ActionEvent event){
  contactName = (String) event.getComponent()
    .getAttributes().get("contactName");
}

public String performAction() {
  Flash flash = FacesContext.getCurrentInstance()
    .getExternalContext().getFlash();
  flash.put("result",
    String.format("executed performAction()
      contactName=\"%s\" ", contactName ));
  return "examplar-methods-complete?redirect=true";
}
```

On submission of the command button, JSF invokes the method `attributeListener()` first with an `ActionEvent` instance. We can find the component responsible for the invocation and retrieve the attributes stored on it. In this case, we retrieve the value for the attribute keyed in as `contactName`. This value is stored in the controller's instance variable. (We must be careful with this technique if the scope of our backing bean is set to a scope other than `@RequestScope` or `@ViewScope`, because the instance variable will be shared between multiple requests over time!)

After the action listener returns, eventually, JSF invokes the action method `performAction()`. The instance variable `contactName` is available and has the current value from the page. The method proceeds to the next page view.

Redirection pages

If you have been following the examples in this chapter, you must have noticed that the page views have been suffixed with a query parameter `redirect=true` (or `faces-redirect=true`, according to the official JSF specification). This is an instruction to JSF for sending an HTTP Response back to the web client to be redirected to a URL. Why is this suffix required? It allows the user to bookmark page views, because the JSF framework effectively hides the current page view from the user by just rendering the output. The main issue is internal page forwarding that makes it difficult for the customers using a digital application to remember or bookmark their location. If the customer has a deeply nested site of information architecture, the ability to provide page redirection is key. The secondary issue is that if your web application exercises a flow of process in a linear fashion, then the web browser's URL is updated, but always shows the previous page in the process.

Redirection works in controller methods `examplar-methods-complete?redirect=true` that cause JSF to send an HTTP Response Redirect to the browser. The web browser interprets the redirect to another HTTP GET request for a URL such as `http://localhost:8080/jsf-crud-ajax-validation-1.0-SNAPSHOT/jsf-miscellany/examplar-methods.xhtml`. The consequence of the redirection is that there are at least two request-response events occurring for each page navigation or action. If you remember, the scope of `@ViewScoped` or `@RequestScoped` bean is available only for a short duration. By the time JSF processes the HTTP GET from the redirection instruction, the original bean has already disappeared. This is the reason why the examples use the Flow scope; that scope guarantees that the data from the controller business logic survives till the next page view is displayed.

The other way to specify page redirection is through `faces-config.xml` for particular navigation cases. We can define a case as follows:

```
<navigation-rule>
  <from-view-id>epayment.xhtml</from-view-id>
  <navigation-case>
    <from-outcome>payment-delivery</from-outcome>
    <to-view-id>payment-deliver.xhtml</to-view-id>
    <redirect />
  </navigation-case>
  <navigation-case>
    <from-outcome>payment-creditcard</from-outcome>
    <to-view-id>payment-credit.xhtml</to-view-id>
    <redirect />
  </navigation-case>
</navigation-rule>
```

This style of configuration can be useful in setting up third-party JSF packages. Of course, it also provides flexibility for library writers, and it does not pollute the Java-managed bean redirect strings. I suppose it is a horses-for-courses situation and, therefore, depends on the purpose of the project.

Finally, the developer can set redirection directly to page views through submission links and buttons. The following code shows this technique:

```
<h:commandButton style="btn bth-primary"
  action="epayments.xhtml?faces-redirect=true"
  value="Proceed to Paymemt" />
```

Debugging the JSF content

Maybe I should have introduced this feature of JSF earlier, because learning to develop with JSF can be puzzling to beginners. It is possible to get debuggable output in a JSF application if you include the `<ui:debug/>` custom tag element inside one of the template views. Actually, the Facelet view renderer output of the framework is responsible for this feature.

By embedding a single `<ui:debug>` inside a `<ui:insert>` tag causes JSF to add a special UI component to the UI hierarchy tree. This debug component captures the Facelet view information and current state of the UI hierarchy, including any scoped variables in the application. Information is captured at the time of rendering . If the user presses the keys *Ctrl + Shift + D*, JSF opens a separate browser window showing the debuggable information, which is really useful in tough situations. The main template of the application is the best place to add the `<ui:debug>` tag.

The `<ui:debug>` tag accepts the following attributes:

Name	Type	Description
hotkey	String	Defines the single character of the hotkey that causes the debuggable window to open. The default is d.
rendered	ValueExpression	Specifies if the debug component is rendered or not. It must be a value expression or a String literal that evaluates to true or false.

The following screenshot shows the exemplar method invocations:

Clicking on the plus (**+**) symbols expands the content so that the developers see more information dynamically.

Summary

This chapter focused on the different forms of JSF validation, because it is extremely important for the user to know if the data has been entered correctly. We examined the two forms of validation methods: client side and server side. We looked at the `FacesMessage` instances and learnt how to create them. Afterwards, we proceeded to cover validation from the server side, particularly, the Bean Validation framework in Java EE 7. We then took an extended developer journey into JSF validation. We learnt how to create custom validators and converters. We also learnt how to perform immediate mode validation with AJAX and understood the partial context life cycle. Finally, we spent a good deal of time on handling views and passing information from the page view to the controller. Along the way, we addressed the JSF flow scope and page redirection.

In the next chapter, we will turn our attention to conversational scopes and start putting the useful process flow applications together. At this point, we add finesse and sophistication to our burgeoning digital JSF applications. I will you see there.

Exercises

1. What is the fundamental difference between the `<h:outputLink>` and `<h:commandButton>` elements? How do you style the control elements appropriately with a CSS framework such as Bootstrap?

2. In the previous chapter, there were exercises around developing a web application for registering new people to a local hobbyist book-reading club. Did you happen to write content in separate pages with no reuse?

3. Apply the UI template compositing to your hobby book club project. Call this version two and save the first version for your reference. Make use of the Template Composition tags `<ui:define>`, `<ui:composition>`, and `<ui:insert>` only at this stage.

4. Add a `<ui:debug>` custom tag to master the template page. What does this special tag do for the developer?

5. An annoyed business stakeholder arrives at your office and tells you about an issue that they are having with spoof data. It seems that some naughty people on the Internet are faking data entry and this is causing more burden for the caseworkers. As a consultant with JSF, explain how you can protect the data in the backend database using validation. Would only a server-side validation work? Would only client-side validation work?

6. With reference to the previous Hobby Book Club application, let's now add validation to the JSF form elements that you created.

7. Add Bean Validation to the registrant class (`Registrant.java` — you may have named this class differently in your own project). Will your users be satisfied with the validation output?

8. What happens when you add only the server-side validation to an application?

9. What are the differences between Bean Validation and JSF validation?

10. What are the similarities between Bean Validation and JSF validation?

11. How appropriate are the error messages for Bean Validation and JSF validation according to the users ?

12. Start with the creation page. Validate against the registrant's name. You can validate with `<f:validateRequired>` and `<f:validateLength>` directly on the page view. Add appropriate `<h:messages>` to the page view.

13. Some registrants use social networks like Facebook, Twitter, and Instagram. Add some properties to the Registrant POJO. Add a URL validator to verify that the social network properties are correct. Use the regular expression validator to verify the Twitter account syntax or, perhaps, write your own custom validator.

14. Download the book's source code example and run the sample code for Chapter 4. Study how validation occurs from the server side.

15. Given that you have developed your project with server-side validation, you must take the Hobby Book Club web application up a notch. Add client-side validation with AJAX for control elements. You will need to add appropriate `<f:ajax>` elements to your JSF form control elements. Don't forget that each control requires an area to render a specific error message; so, you will not add a corresponding `<h:message>` element on the page in close proximity.

16. Download the Chrome Developer Web Tools or similar web page inspection development tools, and inspect the HTML content of the JSF application. What do you observe and notice about the naming of the various HTML elements, especially the forms?

17. Take a breather and add modern CSS styles to the Hobby Book Club application. Ask a colleague or friend to evaluate the user experience of your application and gather feedback. Act on the feedback; change the content around.

18. Add a cancel operation to your CRUD application; what do you need to ensure that JSF does not validate the input?

Conversations and Journeys

"Success is liking yourself, liking what you do, and liking how you do it."

Maya Angelou

In this chapter, we devote our attention to the JSF conversation scope. This scope defines the lifecycle of a managed backing bean that spans between the request and the session scope. This allows the data in the form to survive in a lifespan that sits between the request-scope and the session-scope. The conversation scope is also said to be contextual. This term is appropriated from the **Context and Dependency Injection (CDI)** specification, and it means that the life span of the beans marked with a conversation scope are treated as being part of a context. You can think of this as a dotted marker that the CDI container draws around the object instances to define them as a private group, which denotes a lifecycle. The CDI container does this job of gathering the object instances together as it associates one object bean with a dependency on another.

In CDI, Context represents the CDI container's ability to bind a group of object instances that are stateful components into well-defined and extendible lifecycles.

In CDI, Dependency Injection represents the CDI container's capability to inject components into an application with type safety in mind. The CDI container chooses, at runtime, the implementation of the Java interface that is to be injected.

JavaServer Faces integrates into the standard CDI scope, including the conversational scope. Examples of conversation include several types of contemporary digital customer journeys. You probably have seen this yourself whilst applying for a new job online, going through the shipping and delivery flow of an e-commerce website, or setting up a government resource or function like a tax assessment or return. In this chapter, we are going look at one example customer journey, where the developer or user is applying for an instant secured loan. You may have already seen these or actually have been fortunate, or unfortunate, to peruse a payday loan facility.

The conversation scope maintains a state with a client. The controller or POJO, which is demarcated with the conversation scope, and its component instances become part of its state.

The following diagram outlines the conversation scope around the managed bean controller that we will be studying in this chapter:

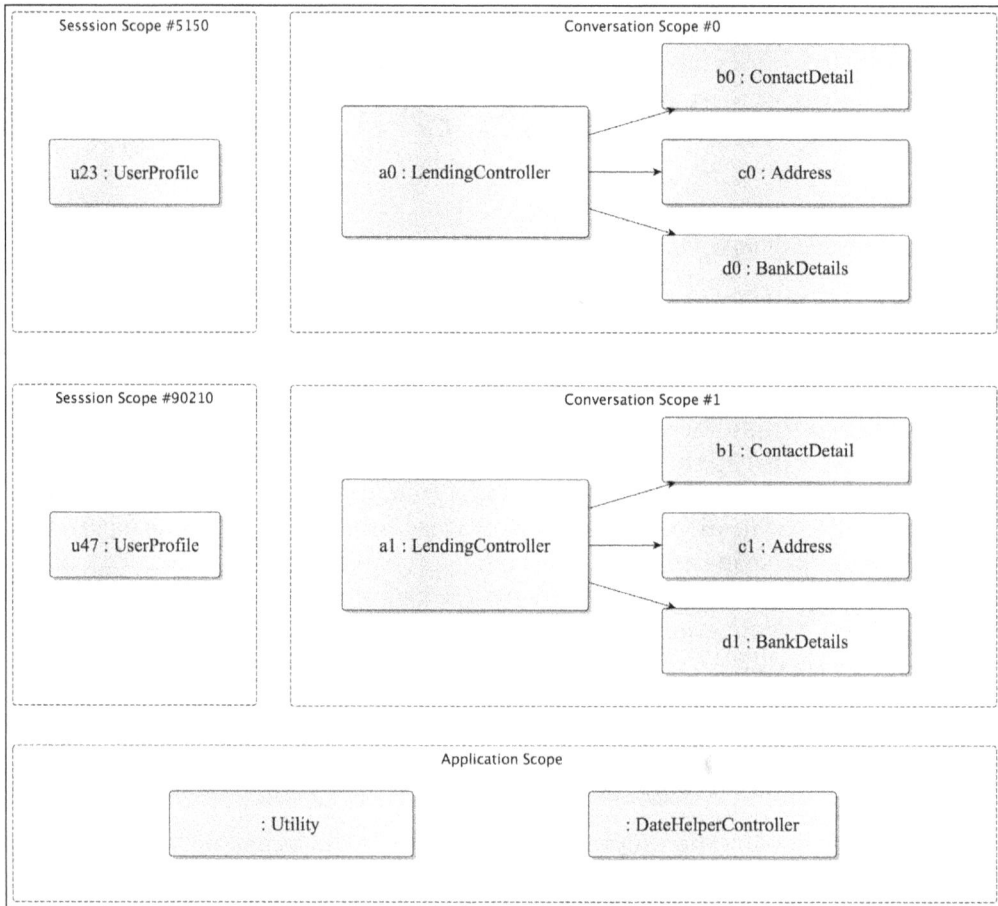

An illustration of the several bean instances with different CDI scopes

The preceding diagram shows two different customers, which are logged into the enterprise application. Starting from left to right, we have the **UserProfile** instances that capture the login information of the customer, which are stored in the CDI session scope. These beans are shared with only the particular customer associated with the `javax.servlet.http.HttpSession` object.

Moving over to the right, we have an object graph of bean instances, the **LendingController**, **ContactDetail**, and **BankDetails**, which are stored in the conversation scope.

At the bottom of the diagram, inside the application scope, we have the bean instances, **Utility** and **DataHelperController**. All web application users share the beans. The conversation beans are able to access the shared information in the current session scope and also in the application scope.

> For more information on CDI, please read the sister book, *Java EE 7 Developer Handbook, Packt Publishing.*

Digital e-commerce applications

Java EE applications are well-suited to digital sites that maintain state. If the site maintains any sort state with the user in their customer journey, then the users are usually involved with conversations. UX testing has shown that, for many enterprise sites where lots of interactions occur, there are several conversations. To paraphrase, a fellow Java Champion, Antonio Gonclaves, who was a member of the Java EE 7 expert group, if your intention is to build digital web applications, then it must be able to handle complex flow management.

An instant loan is not quite in the same league of the products that fast start-ups and entrepreneurs effectively provided as an end-state solution to the global economic credit crunch. With the rise in competition from these new agile upstarts, many domestic household banks in several of the developed nations have had to quickly assemble an instant loan facility product. In this chapter, we will develop an instant secure loan facility. Our product is not a full solution, but it shows the way to deliver the initial prototype for a digital customer. We do not integrate with the financial services, whereas a commercial solution would need management information reporting as well as integration with the commercial banking infrastructure.

Let's move on to the conversational scope more extensively.

Conversational scope

Conversational scope is defined by a lifecycle that spans many HTTP requests to the server. The developer determines when the scope begins and ends, and most importantly, it is associated with a user. The key annotation is defined by a CDI specification called `@javax.enterprise.context.ConversationScoped`. When you apply this annotation to a controller or POJO, remember to ensure that you implement the marker interface, `java.io.Serializable`.

CDI also defines an interface, javax.enterprise.context.Conversation that represents the conversation interface. A conversation can be two distinct states of existence: transient and long-running. The transient state means that the conversation is a temporary state. When you annotate a bean with @ConversationScoped, it will be in the transient state by default.

The developer controls when the conversation switches from the transient to the long-running state. The conversation, then, becomes active and it maintains the holds state of the HTTP user connection, which is usually associated with a particular web browser tab. Essentially, a conversation is a unit of work. A conversation is started and, eventually, ends.

The following is the definition of javax.enterprise.context.Conversation interface:

```
public interface Conversation {
  void begin();
  void begin(String id);
  void end();
  String getId();
  long getTimeout();
  void setTimeout(long milliseconds);
  boolean isTransient();
}
```

The methods, begin() initiate a conversation. A conversational scope POJO is marked for long running storage by the CDI container. A conversation has an identifier; the other method begin(String id) allows the developer to provide an explicit one.

The method end() terminates a conversation, the CDI container effectively discards the contextual information associated with the POJO, and the state returns to transient. In order to find out if a conversation is transient, the call isTransient() is used.

The following diagram illustrates the lifecycle of a CDI conversation scope bean:

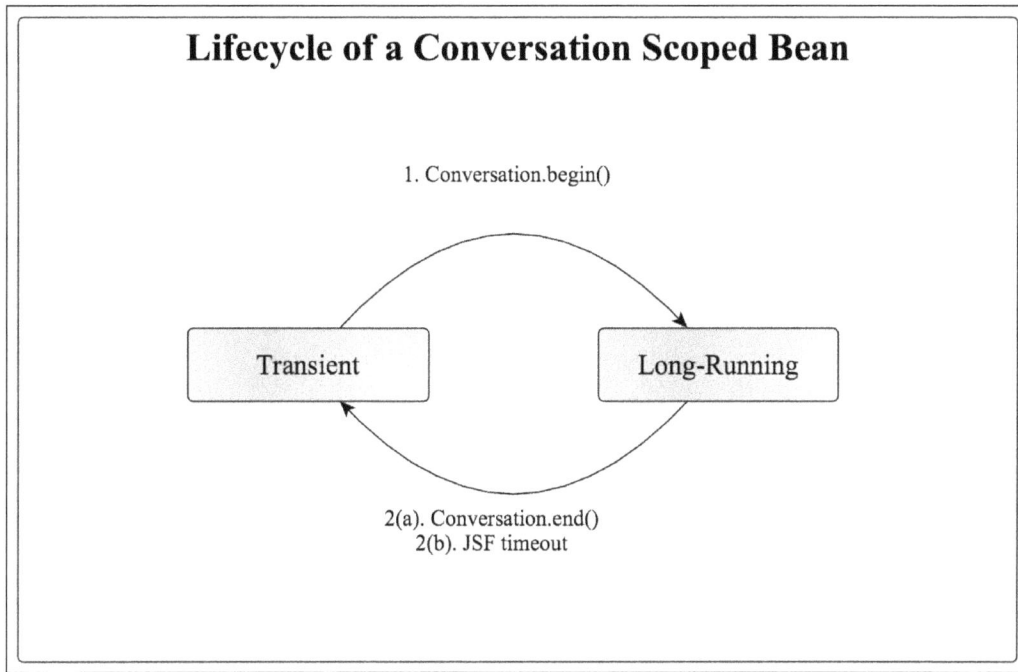

Conversation timeout and serialization

As we discussed earlier, the lifespan of a conversation scope is beyond the request scope, but cannot survive beyond the session scope. The CDI container can timeout a conversation scope and terminate the contextual information in order to preserve or recover a resource. This is partially the reason that an annotated bean with @ConversationScoped must be Serializable. A smart CDI container and servlet container may transfer a conversation to disk or even to another running JVM instance, but it could never attempt this without serialization.

The application developer can retrieve the timeout and set it with the methods, getTimeout() and setTimeout().

So now we know what are @ConversationScoped and Conversation. Let's put them to good use in our instant secure lending application.

The conversation scope controller

The heart of our digital customer journey is a managed bean called
LendingController. We will break it down gently into easier sections
as we go through this chapter.

The initial implementation looks like this:

```
package uk.co.xenonique.digital.instant.control;
import uk.co.xenonique.digital.instant.boundary.ApplicantService;
import uk.co.xenonique.digital.instant.entity.Address;
import uk.co.xenonique.digital.instant.entity.Applicant;
import uk.co.xenonique.digital.instant.entity.ContactDetail;
import uk.co.xenonique.digital.instant.util.Utility;
// imports elided

@Named("lendingController")
@ConversationScoped
public class LendingController implements Serializable {
  @EJB ApplicantService applicantService;
  @Inject Conversation conversation;
  @Inject Utility utility;

  public final static int DEFAULT_LOAN_TERM = 24;
  public final static BigDecimal DEFAULT_LOAN_AMOUNT = new
BigDecimal("7000");
  public final static BigDecimal DEFAULT_LOAN_RATE = new
BigDecimal("5.50");

  private int dobDay;
  private int dobMonth;
  private String dobYear;
  private BigDecimal minimumLoanAmount = new BigDecimal("3000");
  private BigDecimal maximumLoanAmount = new BigDecimal("25000");
  private BigDecimal minimumLoanRate  = new BigDecimal("3.0");
  private BigDecimal maximumLoanRate  = new BigDecimal("12.0");

  private String currencySymbol = "£";

  private BigDecimal paymentMonthlyAmount = BigDecimal.ZERO;
  private BigDecimal totalPayable = BigDecimal.ZERO;
  private Applicant applicant;

  public LendingController() {
    applicant = new Applicant();
```

```
        applicant.setLoanAmount( DEFAULT_LOAN_AMOUNT);
        applicant.setLoanRate( DEFAULT_LOAN_RATE );
        applicant.setLoanTermMonths( DEFAULT_LOAN_TERM );
        applicant.setAddress(new Address());
        applicant.setContactDetail(new ContactDetail());
    }

    public void checkAndStart() {
        if ( conversation.isTransient()) {
            conversation.begin();
        }
        recalculatePMT();
    }

    public void checkAndEnd() {
        if (!conversation.isTransient()) {
            conversation.end();
        }
    }
    /* ... */
}
```

This might appear a complicated controller on the first observation, however, there are two important items here. First, we annotate the LendingController with @ConversationScoped and second, we ask the CDI to inject a Conversation instance into this bean. We also implement the Serializable marker interface to allow the servlet container to have the freedom to persist and reload beans on the fly, if it so chooses and if the implementation supports this feature.

Pay particular attention to the helper methods, checkAndStart() and checkAndEnd(). The checkAndStart() method starts a new long-running conversation if the current state is transient. The checkAndEnd() method terminates a long-running conversation provided that the current Conversational instance is in the running state.

You can see that some elements of the previous contact detail application have made it into our instant lending application. This is by deliberate design.

The LendingController bean contains an instance member of Applicant, which is the domain master detail record. It is a JPA entity bean that stores the applicant's data. You have already seen the date-of-birth fields. The controller also has members related to the monthly payment amount and the total payable amount of the loan. It also contains the lower and upper limits for the loan amount and the rate, which are exposed as getters and setters.

Finally, the CDI injects a utility instance into `LendingController`. This is an application scoped POJO, which neatly lets us avoid writing a static singleton.
We shall see the details of the utility class later, but first we must side step into a design pattern.

The Entity-Control-Boundary design pattern

This instant lending application takes advantage of a particular design pattern called Entity-Control-Boundary. This is a pattern that separates the concerns and responsibilities for a group of objects in an application. The clue is in the imported package names for `LendingController`.

To explain very briefly, the notion of entities represents the data model in a software application. The control elements are the components in the software application that manage the flow of information. The boundary elements belong to the application system, but lie on the periphery of the system.

You are quite correct in your assumption that this pattern resembles the Model-View-Controller, except that the ECB is applicable to the entire software system and the control element is more responsible than the controller and user interfaces.

In this application, I placed `LendingController` in the control package, because the source code shows that it contains the majority of the business logic. Perhaps, for a proper production application, we could delegate our logic into another CDI bean or EJB. As a consultant once said to his client, *it depends on the situation*.

Inside the entity package, there is no controversy; I added the `Applicant`, `ContactDetail`, and `Address` classes. These are persistence capable objects. You have already seen the `ContactDetail` entity bean in *Chapter 4, JSF Validation and AJAX*.

I put the `ApplicantService` EJB in the boundary package, because it lies on the periphery and it is responsible for data access.

The customer journey

Let's delve back into `LendingController` and reveal our customer journey. We assume that we have sat with creative designers and the UX team and come up with a design. The application is based on a series of linear web pages organized into a wizard. For the sake of this basic example, we only allow the consumer to progress to the next page when they successfully enter valid information for the current page.

The following are the topographical titles for each page:

Step	Page	Description
1	Getting started	Provide the customers with information about the eligibility criteria
2	Your details	The customers enter their personal contact detail and date of birth
3	Your rate	The customers selects their loan amount and term
4	Your address	The customers enters their full home address and telephone numbers
5	Confirm	The consumers agree to the legal terms of service and view the summary
6	Completion	The consumers see an acknowledgement of their application form submission

This is now quite simple to implement in the controller with the following extract:

```
@Named("lendingController")
@ConversationScoped
public class LendingController implements Serializable {
  /* ... */

  public String cancel() {
      checkAndEnd();
      return "index?faces-redirect=true";
  }

  public String jumpGettingStarted() {
      return "getting-started?faces-redirect=true";
  }

  public String doGettingStarted() {
      checkAndStart();
      return "your-details?faces-redirect=true";
  }

  public String doYourDetails() {
      checkAndStart();
      Calendar cal = Calendar.getInstance();
      cal.set(Calendar.DAY_OF_MONTH, dobDay);
      cal.set(Calendar.MONTH, dobMonth-1);
      int year = Integer.parseInt(dobYear);
      cal.set(Calendar.YEAR, year);
```

```
            applicant.getContactDetail().setDob(cal.getTime());
            return "your-rate?faces-redirect=true";
    }

    public String doYourRate() {
        checkAndStart();
        return "your-address?faces-redirect=true";
    }

    public String doYourAddress() {
        checkAndStart();
        return "confirm?faces-redirect=true";
    }

    public String doConfirm() {
        /* ... */
        return "completion?faces-redirect=true";
    }

    public String doCompletion() {
        /* ... */
        return "index?faces-redirect=true";
    }

    /* ... */
}
```

The LendingController bean has several action methods that correspond to the user requirements, namely doGettingStarted(), doYourDetails(), doYourRate(), doYourAddress(), doConfirm(), and doCompletion(). These action methods progress the customer to the next page view by simply returning the name. For most of these methods, apart from doCompletion(), we ensure that the conversation is in a long-running state by calling checkAndStart(). In the doCompletion() and cancel() methods, we invoke checkAndEnd() to ensure that the conversation reverts to the transient state. The method doCompletion() utilizes ApplicationService to save the data, the Applicant entity instance, to the underlying database.

> In the example code, we are cheating slightly by applying checkAndStart() at the beginning of each action method. For production code, we should usually ensure that it is an error or a redirection if the user jumps into a bookmarkable URL that is supposed to have a conversation.

Let's examine the entities and fill in more of the blanks.

Entity classes

The entity `Applicant` is a master detail record. This is known as the core domain object. It stores the data for the customer's application for the instant secured loan. We capture the customer's loan information such as the contact details (`ContactDetail`), the address (`Address`), the telephone numbers (home, work, and mobile), and, most importantly, the financial details.

The `Applicant` entity would be as follows:

```
package uk.co.xenonique.digital.instant.entity;
import javax.persistence.*;
import java.math.BigDecimal;
import java.util.Date;

@Entity
@Table(name="APPLICANT")
@NamedQueries({
  @NamedQuery(name="Applicant.findAll",
          query = "select a from Applicant a " +
                  "order by a.submitDate"),
  @NamedQuery(name="Applicant.findById",
          query = "select a from Applicant a where a.id = :id"),
})
public class Applicant {
  @Id
  @GeneratedValue(strategy = GenerationType.AUTO)
  private long id;

  @OneToOne(cascade = CascadeType.ALL)
  private ContactDetail  contactDetail;
  @OneToOne(cascade = CascadeType.ALL)
  private Address  address;

  private String workPhone;
  private String homePhone;
  private String mobileNumber;

  private BigDecimal loanAmount;
  private BigDecimal loanRate;
  private int loanTermMonths;
  private boolean termsAgreed;

  @Temporal(TemporalType.TIMESTAMP)
```

```
        private Date submitDate;

        public Applicant() { }

        // Getters and setters omitted ...
        // hashCode(), equals(), toString() elided
    }
```

The `Applicant` entity stores the loan amount, rate, term, and also a submission date. It also contains the home, work, and mobile telephone numbers. An applicant has a one-to-one unidirectional relationship with both, the `ContactDetail` and `Address` entities.

For the financial properties such as `loanRate` and `loanAmount`, please note that we prefer to use `BigDecimal` rather than the primitive floating-point type for monetary accuracy during calculations.

The way to explain a domain object to the stakeholder would be: a customer has a loan rate, a loan term, and must agree electronically to the legal conditions. With this information, the system can compute the loan and how much the customer pays back each month, and displays it at the time of applying for the loan.

You have already seen the `ContactDetail` entity. It is exactly the same as before and only the package name has been refactored to entity. The following is the extract code of the `Address` entity bean:

```
package uk.co.xenonique.digital.instant.entity;
import javax.persistence.*;

@Entity
@Table(name="ADDRESS")
@NamedQueries({
  @NamedQuery(name="Address.findAll",
    query = "select a from Address a "),
  @NamedQuery(name="Address.findById",
    query = "select a from Address a where a.id = :id"),
})
public class Address {
    @Id
    @GeneratedValue(strategy = GenerationType.AUTO)
    @Column(name="ADDRESS", nullable = false,
            insertable = true, updatable = true,
            table = "ADDRESS")
    private long id;
```

```
      String houseOrFlatNumber;
      String street1;
      String street2;
      String townOrCity;
      String region;
      String areaCode;
      String country;

      // toString(), hashCode(), equalsTo() elided
      /* ... */
   }
```

The entity `Address` represents the applicant's correspondence and legal personal address. There is nothing special to see here. It is a bog standard entity bean that you will see in e-commerce applications.

May I remind you that the source code for the examples are online and are a part of this book for your reference.

Data service

How do we save the customer's input into persistence storage? Our application utilizes a stateful session EJB, and it provides methods to save and retrieve the `Applicant` entity records.

The class `ApplicantService` is as follows:

```
package uk.co.xenonique.digital.instant.boundary;
import uk.co.xenonique.digital.instant.entity.Applicant;
import javax.ejb.Stateful;
import javax.persistence.*;
import java.util.List;

@Stateful
public class ApplicantService {
  @PersistenceContext(unitName = "instantLendingDB",
    type = PersistenceContextType.EXTENDED)
  private EntityManager entityManager;

  public void add(Applicant applicant) {
    entityManager.persist(applicant);
  }

  /* ... */
```

```
    public List<Applicant> findAll() {
      Query query = entityManager.createNamedQuery(
          "Applicant.findAll");
      return query.getResultList();
    }

    public List<Applicant> findById(Integer id) {
      Query query = entityManager.createNamedQuery(
          "Applicant.findById").setParameter("id", id);
      return query.getResultList();
    }
  }
```

The `add()` method inserts a new applicant into the database. The `findAll()` and `findById()` are not used in the instant loan example. These query methods are there for illustrative purposes only. Presumably, one requires access to the applicant data in another part of the full application.

We have covered the entity, control, and boundary of our application. It is time to examine the page views.

Page views

The flow of control for the view is defined by the customer journey. Each page view represents a particular requirement that the business stakeholder wants to see. The index page view is a requirement, because the lender wants the customer to see a landing page. It is also a legal duty of compliance required by national government authorities. You will also notice that the customer journey maps to a linear flow, but not for all journeys.

> The Payday loan scheme must follow compliance requirements. Refer to the websites of the UK Financial Conduct Authority (https://goo.gl/NfbFbK) and the US Consumer Financial Protection Bureau (http://goo.gl/3V9fxk).

The following table outlines the relationship between the controller actions and the view pages:

View source	View target	Action method
index	getting-started	jumpGettingStarted()
getting-started	your-detail	doGettingStarted()
your-details	your-rate	doYourDetails()
your-rate	your-address	doYourRate()

View source	View target	Action method
`your-address`	`confirm`	`doYourAddress()`
`confirm`	`completion`	`doConfirm()`
`completion`	`index`	`doCompletion()`

All the view pages are suffixed with the extension `xthml` in the preceding table. It is quite clear there is a linear flow of work happening in the conversation. The conversation scope ideally begins when the customer enters the getting-started view through the `jumpGettingStarted()` action method.

An initial page view

Let's look at the initial `index.xhtml` page view. This is the landing page of the loan application. The following is a screenshot of our loan application and the landing page:

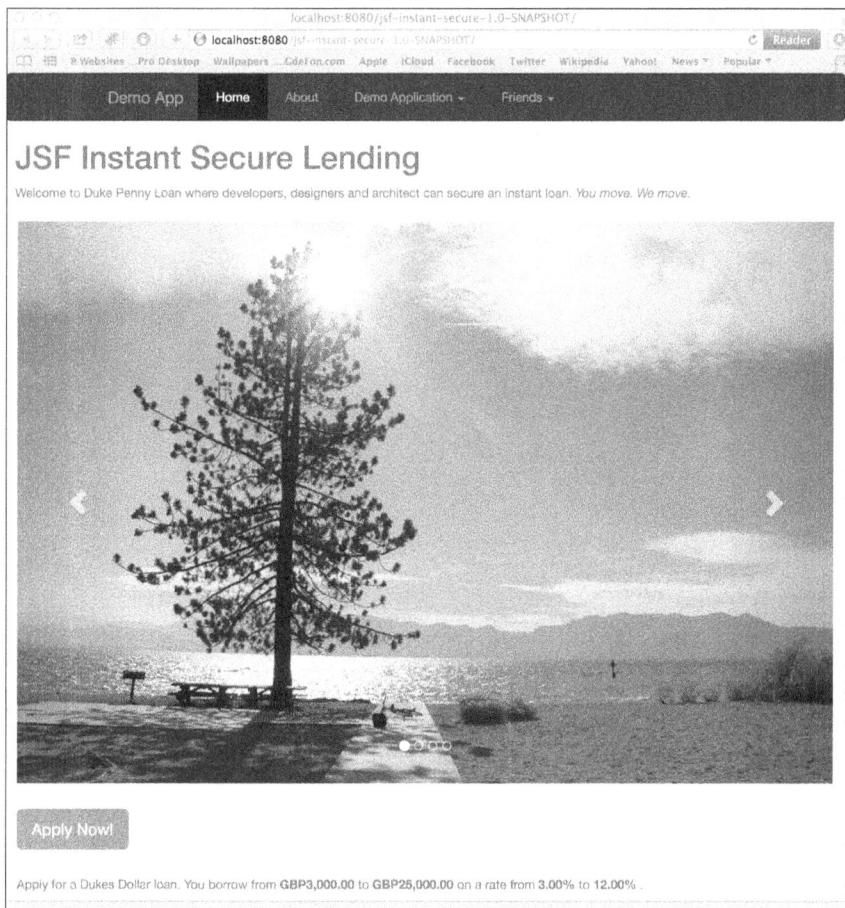

The view for this page index.xhtml is very straightforward. It features a basic link button component and features a Bootstrap carousel:

```
<!DOCTYPE html>
<html ...>
    <ui:composition template="/basic_layout.xhtml">
        ...
      <ui:define name="mainContent">
        <h1> JSF Instant Secure Lending</h1>
        <p>
            Welcome to Duke Penny Loan where developers,
            designers and architect can secure
            an instant loan. <em>You move. We move.</em>
        </p>

        <div class="content-wrapper   center-block">
          <div id="carousel-example-generic" class="carousel slide"
                data-ride="carousel"  data-interval="10000">
            <!-- Indicators -->
            <ol class="carousel-indicators">
                <li data-target="#carousel-example-generic" data-
slide-to="0" class="active"></li>
                <li data-target="#carousel-example-generic" data-
slide-to="1"></li>
                <li data-target="#carousel-example-generic" data-
slide-to="2"></li>
                <li data-target="#carousel-example-generic" data-
slide-to="3"></li>
            </ol>
            ...
          </div>
        </div><!-- content-wrapper  -->

        <div class="content-wrapper">
          <h:link styleClass="btn btn-primary btn-lg"
                outcome="#{lendingController.jumpGettingStarted()}">
            Apply Now!
          </h:link>
        </div>

    ...
      </ui:define> <!--name="mainContent" -->
    </ui:composition>
</html>
```

The `<h:link>` element is the most important feature of this view. The outcome of this custom tag references the `jumpGettingStarted()` method in the controller, which begins a long-running conversation.

Even at this stage, before a conversation begins, we can deliver information to the customer. So, in a further section of the page view, we tell the customer about the minimum and maximum loan amounts and the rates using expression language.

The following is the code, which is also a part of the page view `index.xhtml`:

```
<div class="content-wrapper">
  <p>
    Apply for a Dukes Dollar loan. You borrow from
    <b>
      <h:outputText
        value="#{lendingController.minimumLoanAmount}" >
        <f:convertNumber currencyCode="GBP" type="currency" />
      </h:outputText>
    </b>
      to
    <b>
      <h:outputText
        value="#{lendingController.maximumLoanAmount}" >
        <f:convertNumber currencyCode="GBP" type="currency" />
      </h:outputText>
    </b>
      on a rate from
    <b>
      <h:outputText
        value="#{lendingController.minimumLoanRate}" >
        <f:convertNumber pattern="0.00" />
      </h:outputText>&#37;
    </b>
      to
    <b>
      <h:outputText
        value="#{lendingController.maximumLoanRate}" >
        <f:convertNumber pattern="0.00" />
      </h:outputText>&#37;
    </b>.
  </p>
</div>
```

This page makes use of the JSF core tag `<f:convertNumber>` to format the floating numbers into monetary formats. The HTML entity character `&#37;` represents the percent character (`%`). Remember, the view technology is strictly Facelets and not HTML5.

Getting started page view

The getting started view is even simpler. We present the customer with information regarding their eligibility to apply for a loan. The customer must be 18 years or over; we repeat how much they borrow and for how long.

The view is called `getting-started.xhtml` and looks like the following screenshot:

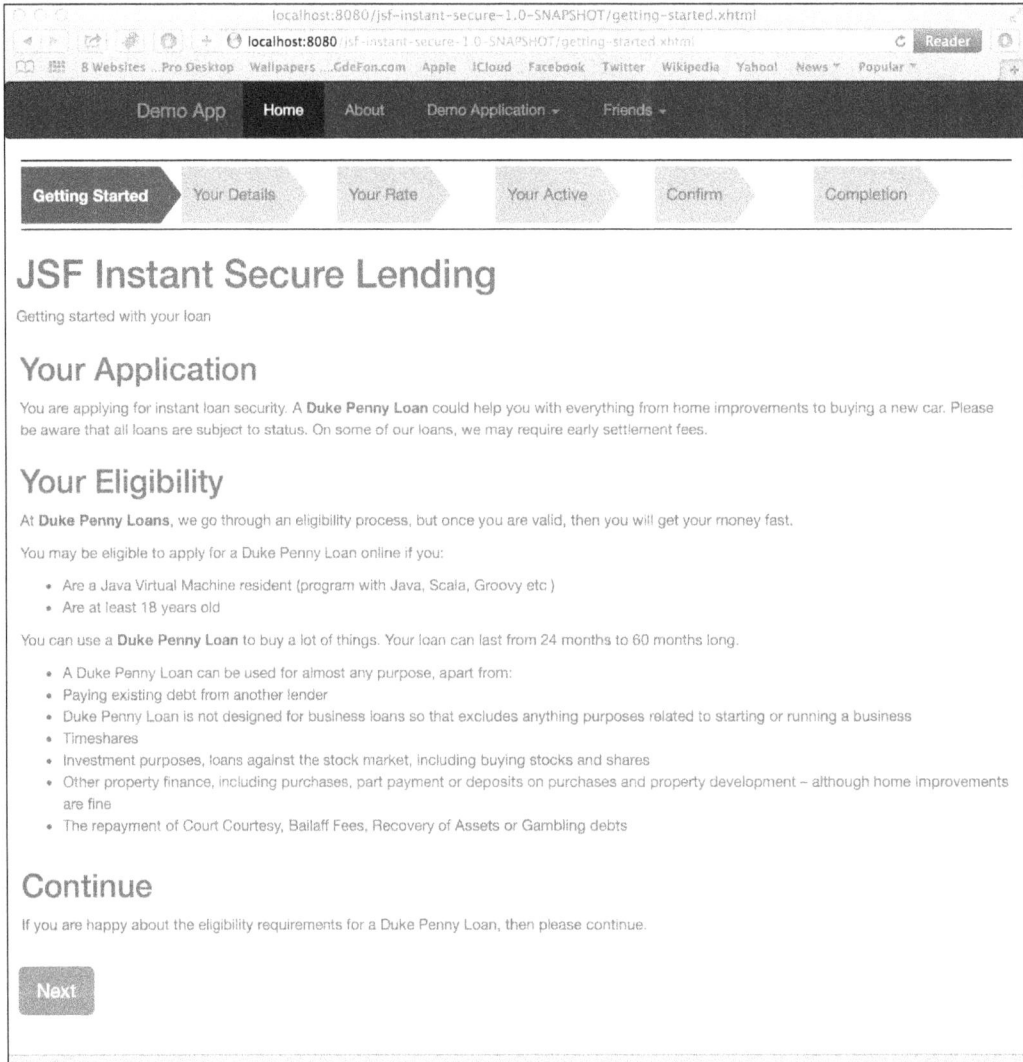

There is a single JSF form with a button to move the customer to the next page view, `your-details.xhtml`. There is no need to see the full source code for this view, because it is mainly mark-up HTML. However, we have another command link:

```
<h:link styleClass="btn btn-primary btn-lg"
  outcome="#{lendingController.doGettingStarted()}">
  Next</h:link>
```

Contact details page view

The next view is the familiar contact details screen. We've subsumed it from the previous chapters into the instant secure loan example. We've also repurposed the JSF expression language to reference the controller and the nested properties.

The page-authoring code for the first name field is as follows:

```
<h:inputText class="form-control" label="First name"
   value="#{lendingController.applicant.contactDetail.firstName}"
   id="firstName" placeholder="First name">
    <f:validateRequired/>
    <f:validateLength maximum="64" />
    <f:ajax event="blur" render="firstNameError"/>
</h:inputText>
```

The EL `#{lendingController.applicant.contactDetail.firstName}` refers to the relevant nested entity bean property. We also retain the AJAX JSF validation features from *Chapter 4, JSF Validation and AJAX* to provide a rich customer journey.

For this view, we use a JSF command button to submit the form:

```
<h:commandButton styleClass="btn btn-primary"
                 action="#{lendingController.doYourDetails()}"
                 value="Submit" />
 
 
<h:commandButton styleClass="btn btn-default"
                 action="#{lendingController.cancel()}"
                 immediate="true" value="Cancel"/>
```

We also have the obligatory cancel operation just in case the customer no longer wants to apply for the loan that day.

The following is a screenshot of the `your-details.xhtml` view, which allows the customer to enter their contact details:

Now it is time for something new. How about adding in some HTML5 goodness to the good old JavaServer Faces?

Your rate page view

The loan amount and rate page view relies on the HTML5 range control element, which, on most standard compliant browsers, is rendered as a horizontal slider. JSF has no built-in support for a range control; so for this view, we make use of the JSF HTML5 friendly support capability. The JSF specification allows us to write a markup that looks like a standard HTML component, but if we supply a special attribute, JSF treats it as a UI component. The pass-through ability works only with the markup that resembles the existing JSF core controls.

A picture is worth a thousand words, so let's take a look at the following screenshot of `your-rate.xhtml`:

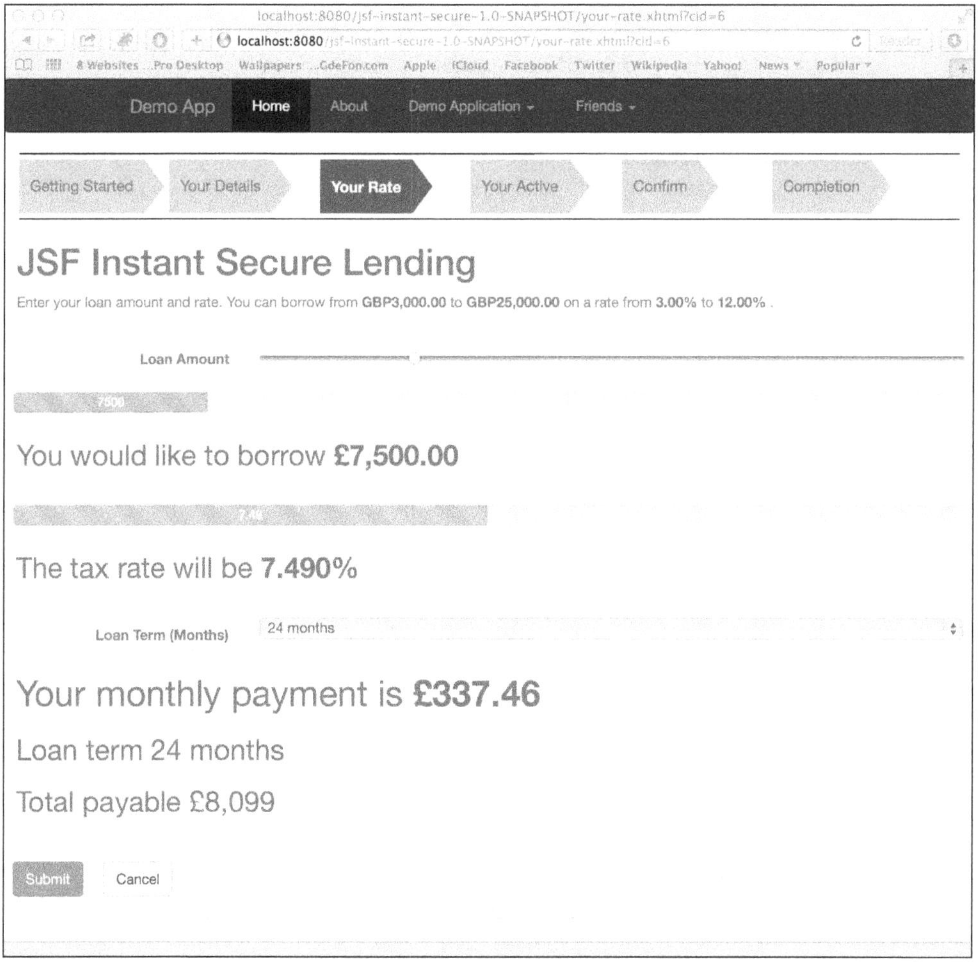

The view uses AJAX partial updates and the HTML5 friendly markup facility. Let me show you the code for the form:

```
<h:form id="yourRateForm"
   styleClass="form-horizontal"
     p:role="form">
   <div class="form-group">
     <h:outputLabel for="loanAmount"
       class="col-sm-3 control-label">
         Loan Amount</h:outputLabel>
     <div class="col-sm-9">
       <input class="form-control" jsf:label="Loan Amount"
         jsf:value="#{lendingController.applicant.loanAmount}"
           type="range"
         min="#{lendingController.minimumLoanAmount}"
         max="#{lendingController.maximumLoanAmount}"
         step="250"
         id="loanAmount" >
       <f:validateRequired/>
         <f:ajax event="blur" render="loanAmountError"/>
         <f:ajax event="valueChange"
                 listener="#{lendingController.recalculatePMT()}"
                 render="paymentMonthlyOutput loanRateOutput
totalPayableOutput" />
       </input>
       <h:message id="loanAmountError"
                 for="loanAmount" styleClass="alert validation-
error"/>
     </div>
   </div>
```

As with all JSF forms, we first declare a form called `yourRateForm` and style it using Bootstrap CSS. Concentrating on the control element, you will notice that it is written as `<input>` as not `<h:inputText>`. This is because the JSF `<h:inputText>` does not support the new HTML5 Range element. Ordinarily, the lack of access to a richer UI component would have been an issue for the instant secure lending.

The HTML5 Range Input element accepts a minimum, a maximum, and the current value. It also accepts a step size.

HTML5 friendly support

JSF 2.2 allows HTML5 friendly components with a new tag library URI for an XML namespace of `xmlns:jsf="http://xmlns.jcp.org/jsf"`. With the attributes `jsf:id`, `jsf:label`, and `jsf:attribute`, HTML5 tags have a visibility within the JSF framework.

The full XML namespace for `your-rate.xhtml` looks as follows:

```
<!DOCTYPE html>
<html xmlns="http://www.w3.org/1999/xhtml"
      xmlns:ui="http://xmlns.jcp.org/jsf/facelets"
      xmlns:p="http://xmlns.jcp.org/jsf/passthrough"
      xmlns:h="http://xmlns.jcp.org/jsf/html"
      xmlns:f="http://xmlns.jcp.org/jsf/core"
      xmlns:c="http://xmlns.jcp.org/jsp/jstl/core"
      xmlns:jsf="http://xmlns.jcp.org/jsf"
      xmlns:xen="http://xmlns.jcp.org/jsf/composite/components">
```

We will discuss composite components later in the chapter. The HTML5 friendly tag library exposes a standard HTML input component to the JSF lifecycle. It is also easier for the creatives, not experienced in JSF or Java, to understand a page view. We do not have to worry any longer about the special name mangling that JSF applies to the view IDs; this means that component IDs are useful for both, HTML and JavaScript.

Using AJAX for a partial update

In *Chapter 4*, *JSF Validation and AJAX*, we learnt how to validate the form properties using Ajax. JSF allows the developers to perform a partial page update using the `<f:ajax>` custom tag.

To enable a rich user example, whenever the customer changes the loan amount slider, we invoke the server side to recalculate the monthly payment amount. We achieve this by attaching an event listener to the change in value. The code for this would be as follows:

```
<f:ajax event="valueChange"
    listener="#{lendingController.recalculatePMT()}"
    render="paymentMonthlyOutput  loanRateOutput
           totalPayableOutput" />
```

A new addition to the code is the render attribute, which specifies the unique ID of the JSF UI components that will be re-rendered on an AJAX response. In other words, we declaratively specify the components to be re-rendered on the completion of an AJAX behavior to JSF, and thus, obtain a partial update.

Binding components

Let's see the other components that the HTML5 Range element, the loan amount in this case, binds with.

Take a look at the following code:

```
<c:set var="loanAmountWidth" value="#{100.0 * (lendingController.
applicant.loanAmount - lendingController.minimumLoanAmount)
/ (lendingController.maximumLoanAmount - lendingController.
minimumLoanAmount)}" />

  <div class="progress">
      <div id="loanAmountProgress" class="progress-bar  progress-bar-
success  progress-bar-striped"
            role="progressbar" aria-valuenow="#{lendingController.
applicant.loanAmount}"
            aria-valuemin="#{lendingController.minimumLoanAmount}"
            aria-valuemax="#{lendingController.maximumLoanAmount}"
            style="width: ${loanAmountWidth}%;">
          #{lendingController.applicant.loanAmount}
      </div>
  </div>

  <div class="content-wrapper">
    <p id="loanAmountText" class="monetary-text">
        You would like to borrow
        <b> #{lendingController.currencySymbol}
        <h:outputText value="#{lendingController.applicant.
loanAmount}" >
            <f:convertNumber pattern="#0,000" />
        </h:outputText> </b>
    </p>
  </div>
```

The progress markup is directly copied from the Bootstrap CSS component examples. We plugged in the value expressions to pull information from the LendingController and the Applicant instances.

Right at the top of the preceding code extract, we set the initial value of the progress bar with the JSTL core tag `<c:set>`.

```
<c:set var="loanAmountWidth" value="#{100.0 *  (lendingController.
applicant.loanAmount - lendingController.minimumLoanAmount)
/ (lendingController.maximumLoanAmount - lendingController.
minimumLoanAmount)}" />
```

This demonstrates that the unified expression language in EL 3.0 has the ability to retrieve the late bounded values in JSF to compute a result. The result is set in a page scope variable called loanAmountWide. This variable is accessed later with $(loanAmountWidth) and it sets the initial position value of the Bootstrap CSS progress bar component..

The HTML5 standard has no built-in support for displaying the value of an HTML5 Range element that works across all the top web browsers. At the time of writing, this feature was missing, and the W3C or WHATWG may tighten up this weakness in the HTML5 specification in the near future. Until then, we will use jQuery and JavaScript to fill the void.

If you noticed, the text is identified with `loanAmountText` and the progress component is denoted by `loanAmountProgress` in the preceding code. It is trivial to write the jQuery for binding the HTML5 Range elements to these fields.

We need a JavaScript module to achieve the binding. The complete code to `/resources/app/main.js` is given as follows:

```javascript
var instantLending = instantLending || {};

instantLending.Main = function()
{
  var init = function()
  {
    $(document).ready( function() {
      associateRangeToText(
        '#loanAmount', '#loanAmountProgress', '#loanAmountText',
        3000.0, 25000.0,
        function(value) {
            var valueNumber = parseFloat(value);
            return "You would like to borrow <b>£" +
                valueNumber.formatMoney(2, '.', ',') + "</b>";
        });
    });
  };

  var associateRangeToText = function( rangeElementId,
    rangeProgressId, rangeTextId, minimumValue,
    maximumValue, convertor) {
    var valueElem = $(rangeElementId);
    var progressElem = $(rangeProgressId);
    var textElem = $(rangeTextId);
    valueElem.change( function() {
      var value = valueElem.val();
      progressElem.html(value);
      progressElem.attr("aria-valuenow", value);

      var percentage = 100.0 * ( value - minimumValue) /
        ( maximumValue - minimumValue );
      progressElem.css("width", percentage+"%");
```

```
    var monetaryText = convertor( value )
    textElem.html( monetaryText );
  });
}

var oPublic =
{
  init: init,
  associateRangeToText: associateRangeToText
};

return oPublic;
}(jQuery);

instantLending.Main.init();
```

The module `instantLending.Main` defines a binding of an HTML Range element to two other components: a progress bar and a label text area. For a quick revision of the JavaScript module, refer to *Chapter 1, Digital Java EE 7*.

The module has an `init()` function that sets up the binding using the jQuery document loading mechanism. It calls a function called `associateRangeToText()`, which computes the percentage travelled for the progress bar and writes that value into the text element area. The function accepts the document ID for the relevant components: the range, progress, and text label components. It attaches an anonymous function to the range element; when the user changes the component, it updates the associated component.

The module `main.js` also defines a helpful prototype method added to the JavaScript number type. The following code shows how it works:

```
// See http://stackoverflow.com/questions/149055/how-can-i-format-
numbers-as-money-in-javascript
Number.prototype.formatMoney = function(c, d, t){
  var n = this,
      c = isNaN(c = Math.abs(c)) ? 2 : c,
      d = d == undefined ? "." : d,
      t = t == undefined ? "," : t,
      s = n < 0 ? "-" : "",
      i = parseInt(n = Math.abs(+n || 0).toFixed(c)) + "",
      j = (j = i.length) > 3 ? j % 3 : 0;
  return s + (j ? i.substr(0, j) + t : "") +
      i.substr(j).replace(/(\d{3})(?=\d)/g, "$1" + t) +
      (c ? d + Math.abs(n - i).toFixed(c).slice(2) : "");
};
```

The method `formatMoney()` formats a floating-point value type to the monetary output as a String. This code has been contributed by Patrick Desjardins to Stack Overflow. The following code illustrates how to invoke this function:

```
var p = 128500.99
console.log(p.formatMoney(2, '.', ',') ) // 128,500.99
```

The first parameter is the fixed fraction size, the second parameter determines the decimal symbol, and the third specifies the thousand-unit character.

With this module, we bound the HTML5 Range element to other elements in the page, thus demonstrating the HTML5 friendly support within JSF.

Updating areas with AJAX partial updates

How does JSF update an area of the page with an AJAX response? The developer specifies the UI components that are updated with the render attribute of the `<f:ajax>` tag. In modern web design, which component can be treated as an HTML Layer element `<div>` inside the standard JSF rendering kit? The answer for this is to use the `<h:panelGroup>` JSF custom tag. We can supply this UI component with a unique identifier, and when the AJAX behavior completes, JSF renders this component.

The following is the code extract for the instant loan rate where the div element is identified by `loanRateOutput`:

```
<c:set var="loanRateWidth" value="#{100.0 * (lendingController.
applicant.loanRate - lendingController.minimumLoanRate) /
(lendingController.maximumLoanRate - lendingController.
minimumLoanRate)}" />

<h:panelGroup layout="block" id="loanRateOutput">
  <div class="progress">
    <div id="loanRateProgress" class="progress-bar  progress-bar-
      info progress-bar-striped"
      role="progressbar" aria-
        valuenow="#{lendingController.recalculateLoanRate()}"
        aria-valuemin="#{lendingController.minimumLoanRate}"
        aria-valuemax="#{lendingController.maximumLoanRate}"
        style="width: ${loanRateWidth}%;">
      #{lendingController.applicant.loanRate}
    </div>
  </div>
  <div class="content-wrapper">
    <p id="loanRateText" class="monetary-text">
      The tax rate will be
```

```
      <b> <h:outputText
        value="#{lendingController.applicant.loanRate}" >
        <f:convertNumber pattern="0.000" />
      </h:outputText>&#37;</b>
    </p>
  </div>
</h:panelGroup>
```

The `<h:panelGroup>` renders a div layer by default and thus contains the progress bar component and the text output content. The div is rendered after an invocation to the method `recalculatePMT()` in `LendingController`. Refer to the preceding sections for a reminder of this code.

The functions `recalclulatePMT()` and `recalculateLoanRate()` look as follows:

```
public BigDecimal recalculatePMT() {
  recalculateLoanRate();
  paymentMonthlyAmount =
    new BigDecimal(utility.calculateMonthlyPayment(
      applicant.getLoanAmount().doubleValue(),
      applicant.getLoanRate().doubleValue(),
      applicant.getLoanTermMonths()));

  totalPayable = paymentMonthlyAmount.multiply(
    new BigDecimal( applicant.getLoanTermMonths()));
  return paymentMonthlyAmount;
}

public BigDecimal recalculateLoanRate() {
  applicant.setLoanRate(
    utility.getTaxRate(applicant.getLoanAmount()));
  return applicant.getLoanRate();
}
```

The function `recalculatePMT()` uses the classic mathematical formula to evaluate the monthly payment amount for the loan based on the principal amount, length of the term and, of course, the rate.

The function `recalculateLoanRate()` uses a utility, an application-scoped CDI bean, to work out the rate according to a table of rate limits that vary according to the loan account.

So let's recap. The JavaScript module `instantLending::Main` updates on the client side. When the customer changes the loan amount then this module changes the progress bar component and the text content. Simultaneously, JSF invokes an AJAX request to the server side and invokes the action event listener, `recalculatePMT()`. The framework eventually receives the AJAX response and then re-renders the loan rate, term control, and the summary area.

To complete the XHTML, let's inspect the remaining content on this page view, your-`rate.xhtml`. The following is the content for the loan term, which is a drop-down component:

```
<div class="form-group">
  <h:outputLabel for="loanTerm" class="col-sm-3 control-label">
    Loan Term (Months)</h:outputLabel>
  <div class="col-sm-9">
    <h:selectOneMenu class="form-control"
      label="Title" id="loanTerm"
        value="#{lendingController.applicant.loanTermMonths}">
      <f:selectItem itemLabel="12 months" itemValue="12" />
      <f:selectItem itemLabel="24 months" itemValue="24" />
      <f:selectItem itemLabel="36 months" itemValue="36" />
      <f:selectItem itemLabel="48 months" itemValue="48" />
      <f:selectItem itemLabel="60 months" itemValue="60" />
      <f:validateRequired/>
      <f:ajax event="blur" render="loanTermError"/>
      <f:ajax event="valueChange"
        listener="#{lendingController.recalculatePMT()}"
        render="paymentMonthlyOutput loanRateOutput
          monthTermsOutput  totalPayableOutput" />
    </h:selectOneMenu>
    <h:message id="loanTermError"
      for="loanTerm" styleClass="alert validation-error"/>
  </div>
</div>
```

The component also features a `<f:ajax>` custom tag that invokes the recalculation event listener. Therefore, if the customer selects a different term for the loan, `loanRateOutput` and `paymentMonthlyOutput` also change along with the summary due to a partial AJAX update.

Finally, let's see the content for the summary area:

```
<div class="content-wrapper" >
  <div class="row">
    <div class="col-md-12">
```

```
        <p class="monetary-text-large">
          Your monthly payment is <b>
          #{lendingController.currencySymbol}<h:outputText
            id="paymentMonthlyOutput"
            value="#{lendingController.recalculatePMT()}">
            <f:convertNumber pattern="#0.00" />
          </h:outputText></b>
        </p>
      </div>
    </div>
    <div class="row">
      <div class="col-md-6">
        <p class="monetary-text">
          Loan term
          <h:outputText id="monthTermsOutput"
          value="#{lendingController.applicant.loanTermMonths}"/>
           months
        </p>
      </div>
      <div class="col-md-6">
        <p class="monetary-text">
          Total payable
          #{lendingController.currencySymbol}<h:outputText
            id="totalPayableOutput"
            value="#{lendingController.totalPayable}">
              <f:convertNumber pattern="#0,000" />
          </h:outputText>
        </p>
      </div>
    </div>
  </div>
```

In the preceding code extract, we use `<h:outputText>` instead of `<h:panelGroup>` to update only certain parts of the content using partial AJAX updates. A JSF output text element is a JSF UI component, so it works by asking for the AJAX behavior to be re-rendered.

The address page view

The address page view captures the customer's primary home address. This page also features an AJAX validation on the client side.

This code is so similar to the contact details form that we will leave out the code extract and the trees here. I will only show the first houseOrFlatNumber fields in the following code:

```
<h:form id="yourAddressForm"
        styleClass="form-horizontal"
        p:role="form">
  <div class="form-group">
    <h:outputLabel for="houseOrFlatNumber"
      class="col-sm-3 control-label">
        House number</h:outputLabel>
    <div class="col-sm-9">
      <h:inputText class="form-control"
        label="House or Flat Number"
          value="#{lendingController.applicant.address.
houseOrFlatNumber}"
         id="houseOrFlatNumber" placeholder="First name">
        <f:validateLength maximum="16" />
        <f:ajax event="blur" render="houseOrFlatNumberError"/>
      </h:inputText>
      <h:message id="houseOrFlatNumberError"
        for="houseOrFlatNumber"
        styleClass="alert validation-error"/>
    </div>
  </div>
  ...
</h:form>
```

The following is a screenshot of the `your-address.xhtml` pageview.

The confirmation page view

The confirmation page view is where the customer sees all the details about their instant loan. In this view, they have a chance to read the terms and conditions of the contract. The customer must either select the checkbox to accept the agreement, or they can hit the cancel button to terminate the conversation. The cancel button invokes the `cancel()` method in `LendingController`, which, in turn, invokes `checkAndEnd()`.

The only relevant code here is for the terms of agreement checkbox. The code extract is as follows:

```
<h:form id="yourConfirmForm"
    styleClass="form-horizontal" p:role="form"> ...
```

```
<div class="form-group">
  <h:outputLabel for="tocAgreed" class="col-sm-6 control-label">
    Do you agree with the <em>Terms of Conditions</em>?
  </h:outputLabel>
  <div class="col-sm-6">
    <h:selectBooleanCheckbox class="form-control"
        label="TOC Agreement" id="tocAgreed"
        value="#{lendingController.applicant.termsAgreed}"
      validator="#{lendingController.validateTermsOrConditions}" >
        <f:ajax event="blur" render="tocAgreedError"/>
    </h:selectBooleanCheckbox>
    <h:message id="tocAgreedError"
        for="tocAgreed" styleClass="alert validation-error"/>
  </div>
</div>
...
</h:form>
```

We use `<h:selectBooleanCheckBox>` with immediate AJAX validation on the blur event. This ensures that the Boolean property is set to true on the server side. However, we must still verify on form submission, as we see in the action controller method:

```
public String doConfirm() {
  if ( applicant.isTermsAgreed()) {
    throw new IllegalStateException(
      "terms of agreements not set to true");
  }
  recalculatePMT();
  applicant.setSubmitDate(new Date());
  applicantService.add(applicant);
  return "completion?faces-redirect=true";
}
```

Inside the `doConfirm()` method, we recalculate the monthly payment term just to be sure. We check that the the applicant's data values have not changed, set the date of submission, and then we invoke the `ApplicationService` to insert a new record into the database. After this method, the customer is said to have applied successfully.

We include a manual check on `isTermsAgreed()`, because it is a legal requirement in the contract for the customer to accept the terms and conditions. It is probably controversial to raise an application error `IllegalStateException` here. More likely, the developer would print a message to an error log, and also raise an exception. The servlet specification allows different exceptions to be trapped and sent to a certain error page. Therefore, if we created a custom runtime exception such as `LegalTermsAgreementException`, we could responsibly handle such conditions.

In a production system, the end of this sequence would probably trigger an additional business process. For instance, the work message might be sent to another case working area using a messaging bus, JMS. In a modern digital application, the customer should expect an e-mail to be sent with the confirmation and the loan contract details. Of course, this is an additional exercise for the reader to deliver this requirement.

The following is a screenshot for the confirmation view, `confirm.xhtml`:

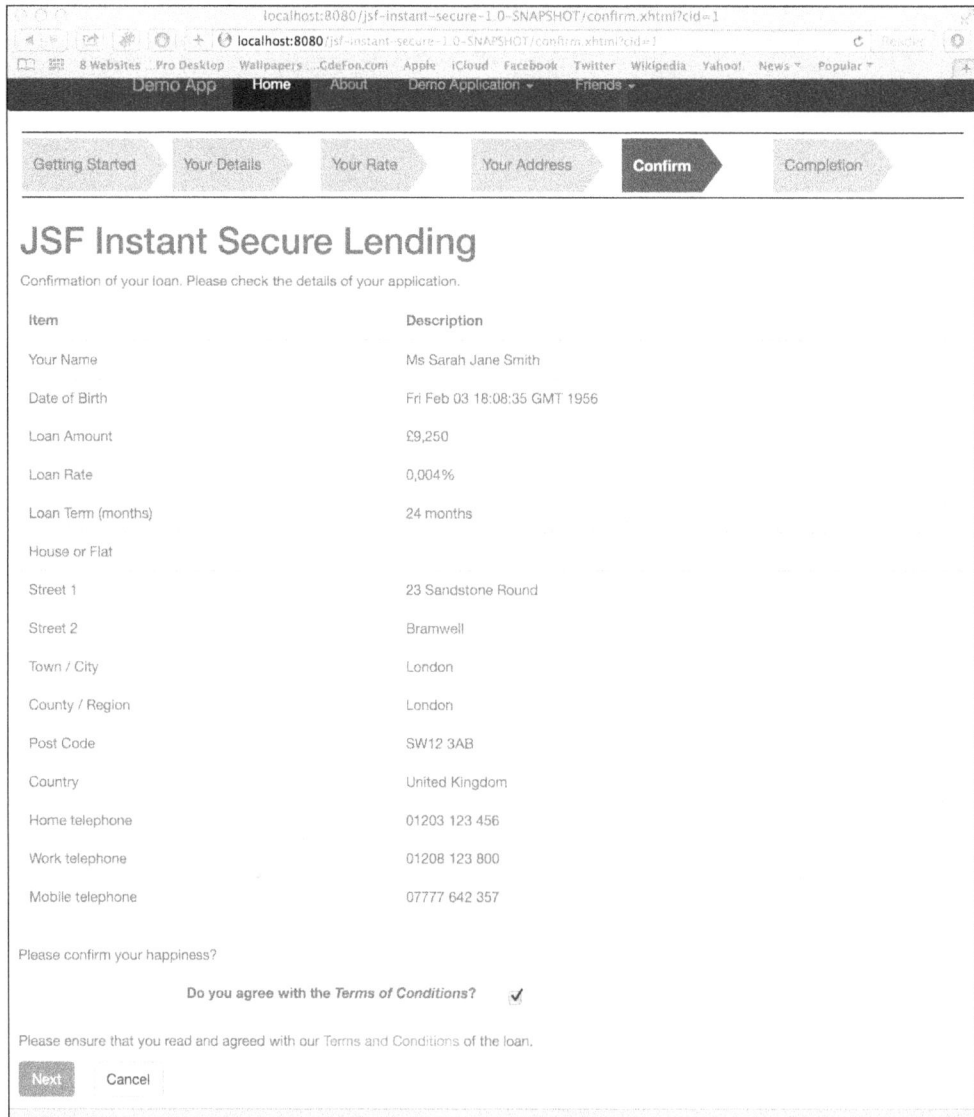

Let's move to the final page view of completion.

The completion page view

The complete stage is straightforward. The customer has submitted his application, so we only need to inform him or her about this and then the conversation ends. The following is the full code for the doCompletion() method in LendingController:

```
public String doCompletion() {
  checkAndEnd();
  return "index?faces-redirect=true";
}
```

This method simply ends the conversation scope, because the user's digital customer journey is finished by then.

Now we have a complete flow, a digital customer journey. What is missing? We should add the steps to accept a valid bank account, a bank sorting code, IBAN number, and an integration into the national bank infrastructure! Of course, we would also need a certain level of financial capital, enough money to satisfy the regulators; in the United Kingdom, this would be the Financial Conduct Authority (http://www.fca.org.uk/).

A screenshot of this page view, completion.xhtml, is as follows:

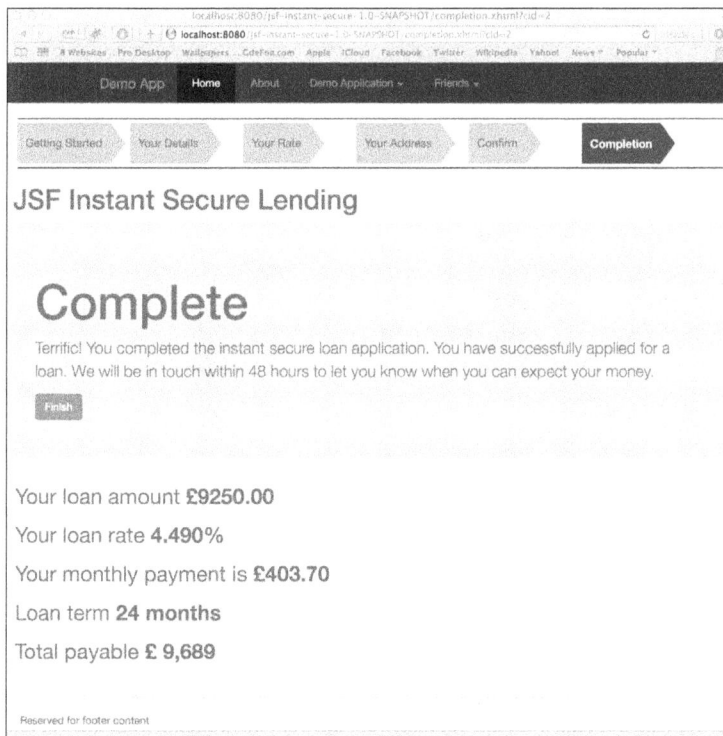

Utility classes

Often in applications, we refactor common methods and properties into a separate utility class, which has features so common that they do not make sense in any particular package domain. We often place these concepts inside static methods in a singleton. With Java EE, we can do much better than that. Since CDI supports application scope, we can simply move our commons methods into a POJO and make CDI inject the bean into dependent objects. It is the smart way to handle the data, the time and monthly payment term calculation in the `LendingController` example.

The application scope bean `DateTimeController` acts as a helper for the page author views:

```java
package uk.co.xenonique.digital.instant.control;
import javax.annotation.PostConstruct;
import javax.enterprise.context.ApplicationScoped;
import javax.inject.Named;
import java.io.Serializable;
import java.text.DateFormatSymbols;
import java.util.*;

@Named("dateHelperController")
@ApplicationScoped
public class DateHelperController implements Serializable {
  private List<Integer> daysOfTheMonth = new ArrayList<>();
  private Map<String,Integer> monthsOfTheYear
    = new LinkedHashMap<>();

  @PostConstruct
  public void init() {
    for (int d=1; d<=31; ++d) { daysOfTheMonth.add(d); }
    DateFormatSymbols symbols =
      new DateFormatSymbols(Locale.getDefault());
    for (int m=1; m<=12; ++m) {
        monthsOfTheYear.put(symbols.getMonths()[m-1], m );
    }
  }

  public List<Integer> getDaysOfTheMonth() {
    return daysOfTheMonth;
  }
  public Map<String,Integer> getMonthsOfTheYear() {
    return monthsOfTheYear;
  }
}
```

The DateHelperController method is used in your-details.view, and it generates the data for the drop-down day and month of the date-of-birth fields. This code was originally a part of the ContactDetailsController method in *Chapter 4, JSF Validation and AJAX*. It has been refactored for reuse.

There is an other POJO with an application scope and it is called Utility.

```java
package uk.co.xenonique.digital.instant.util;
import javax.enterprise.context.ApplicationScoped;
import java.io.Serializable;
import java.math.BigDecimal;
import java.util.*;

@ApplicationScoped
public class Utility implements Serializable {
  protected List<LoanRateBounds> bounds = Arrays.asList(
      new LoanRateBounds("0.0",       "4500.0",    "22.50"),
      new LoanRateBounds("4500.0",    "6000.0",    "9.79"),
      new LoanRateBounds("6000.0",    "9000.0",    "7.49"),
      new LoanRateBounds("9000.0",    "11500.0",   "4.49"),
      new LoanRateBounds("11500.0",   "15000.0",   "4.29"),
      new LoanRateBounds("15000.0",   "20000.0",   "5.79"),
      new LoanRateBounds("20000.0",   "25000.0",   "6.29"),
      new LoanRateBounds("30000.0",   "50000.0",   "6.99")
      );

  public BigDecimal getTaxRate( BigDecimal amount ) {
    for ( LoanRateBounds bound : bounds ) {
      if ( bound.getLower().compareTo(amount) <= 0 &&
           bound.getUpper().compareTo(amount) > 0 ) {
        return  bound.getRate();
      }
    }
    throw new IllegalArgumentException("no tax rate found in bounds");
  }

  public double calculateMonthlyPayment( double pv, double apr, int np
) {
    double ir = apr / 100 / 12;
    return (pv * ir) / (1 - Math.pow(1+ir, -np));
  }
}
```

In the preceding code, the method `calculateMonthlyPayment()` calculates the monthly payment amount. The arguments are `pv` (that specifies the principal value), `apr` (that specifies the annual percentage rate), and the `np`, which stands for the notice period measured in months.

The method `getTaxRate()` looks up the appropriate tax rate given the principal value, that is, the loan amount that the customer wants. The class `LoanRateBounds` is a simple POJO, as shown in the following code:

```java
package uk.co.xenonique.digital.instant.util;
import java.math.BigDecimal;

public class LoanRateBounds {
  private final BigDecimal lower;
  private final BigDecimal upper;
  private final BigDecimal rate;

  public LoanRateBounds(String lower, String upper, String rate) {
    this(new BigDecimal(lower), new BigDecimal(upper),
        new BigDecimal(rate));
  }

  public LoanRateBounds(final BigDecimal lower,
    final BigDecimal upper, final BigDecimal rate) {
      this.lower = lower;
      this.upper = upper;
      this.rate = rate;
  }

  // toString(), hashCode(), equals() and getters omitted
}
```

This `LoanRateBounds` POJO is an immutable object and is thread-safe.

Composite custom components

JSF also features custom components that you, the developer, can write. In fact, the instant secure lending example uses one: the top header of each page view in the conversation. It is a hint that informs the customer where he or she is in the flow. I've called it the `WorkerBannerComponent`.

In JSF, a custom component describes a reusable piece of page content that may insert into a Facelet view many times over. A custom component may or may not have a backing bean, and it may or may not group together a set of properties into a form. As mentioned in *Chapter 2, JavaServer Faces Lifecycle*, we can use custom components to build repeated page content that takes advantage of the latest HTML frameworks such as Bootstrap and that abstracts away the deeper details. Businesses can use custom components to establish a common structure for the page content and markup.

Components with XHTML

The WorkerBannerComponent is a backing bean for the logic of the display header, which identifies the section of the flow that the customer is active in. The code for the custom component is as follows:

```
package uk.co.xenonique.digital.instant.control;
import javax.faces.component.*;
import javax.faces.context.FacesContext;
import java.io.IOException;

@FacesComponent("workerBannerComponent")
public class WorkerBannerComponent extends UINamingContainer {
  private String gettingStartedActive;
  private String yourDetailsActive;
  private String yourRateActive;
  private String yourAddressActive;
  private String confirmActive;
  private String completedActive;

  @Override
  public void encodeAll(FacesContext context) throws IOException {
    if (context == null) {
        throw new NullPointerException("no faces context supplied");
    }
    String sectionName =
      (String)getAttributes().get("sectionName");
    gettingStartedActive = yourDetailsActive =
      yourRateActive = yourAddressActive =
        confirmActive = completedActive = "";

    if ( "gettingStarted".equalsIgnoreCase(sectionName)) {
        gettingStartedActive = "active";
    }
    else if ( "yourDetails".equalsIgnoreCase(sectionName)) {
        yourDetailsActive = "active";
    }
    else if ( "yourRate".equalsIgnoreCase(sectionName)) {
```

```
        yourRateActive = "active";
    }
    else if ( "yourAddress".equalsIgnoreCase(sectionName)) {
        yourAddressActive = "active";
    }
    else if ( "confirm".equalsIgnoreCase(sectionName)) {
        confirmActive = "active";
    }
    else if ( "completed".equalsIgnoreCase(sectionName)) {
        completedActive = "active";
    }
    super.encodeAll(context);
}

// Getters and setters omitted
}
```

We apply the annotation `@javax.faces.component.FacesComponent` to the POJO `WorkerBannerComponent`. This annotation declares to the JSF that we have a custom component with the name `workerBannerComponent`. The `@FacesComponent` is expanded in JSF 2.2, so that we can write all the code for generating the output HTML in Java. Fortunately, we do not require the ability to create a custom component that also registers its own custom tag, because it is quite handy to control the markup in a lightweight editor like Sublime or VIM.

Our `WorkerBannerComponent` extends `javax.faces.component.UINamingContainer`, which is a custom component supplied by JSF with the ability to add a unique identifier. In the JSF parlance, a naming container is a bucket for a component that has a unique name and which can also store the child components with the same characteristics.

The overridden method `encodeAll()` is usually the place to render the output of a custom tag that provides its own markup. Here, we second the intent with the logic that decides which worker tab is active and which is not. Similar to the custom event handling in the previous chapter (*Chapter 4, JSF Validation and AJAX, Invoking an action event listener* section), we can interrogate the attributes in order to retrieve the parameters that are passed to our component from the page content.

Let's examine the page content for this component. The name of the file is `worker-banner.xhtml`, and the extracted page content looks like the following:

```
<!DOCTYPE html>
<html xmlns="http://www.w3.org/1999/xhtml"
      xmlns:h="http://xmlns.jcp.org/jsf/html"
      xmlns:c="http://xmlns.jcp.org/jsp/jstl/core"
      xmlns:cc="http://xmlns.jcp.org/jsf/composite" >
```

```
<cc:interface componentType="workerBannerComponent">
  <cc:attribute name="sectionName" required="true"/>
</cc:interface>

<cc:implementation>
  <div class="workflow-wrapper">
    <div class="workflow-column">
      <div class="workflow-title  #{cc.gettingStartedActive}
        pull-left" >
          Getting Started
      </div>
      <div class="workflow-arrow-right
        #{cc.gettingStartedActive}  pull-left"></div>
    </div>

    <div class="workflow-column">
      <div class="workflow-title  #{cc.yourDetailsActive}
        pull-left" >
          Your Details
      </div>
      <div class="workflow-arrow-right  #{cc.yourDetailsActive}
        pull-left"></div>
    </div>

    <div class="workflow-column">
      <div class="workflow-title  #{cc.yourRateActive}
        pull-left" >
          Your Rate
      </div>
      <div class="workflow-arrow-right  #{cc.yourRateActive}
        pull-left"></div>
    </div>

    <div class="workflow-column">
      <div class="workflow-title  #{cc.yourAddressActive}
        pull-left" >
          Your Address
      </div>
      <div class="workflow-arrow-right  #{cc.yourAddressActive}
        pull-left"></div>
    </div>

    ...

    </div>
  </div>
</cc:implementation>
</html>
```

In JSF, the custom composite component content must be placed into the special directory, /resources. The full path for this content is /resources/components/workflow-banner.xhtml. The composite components are registered under an XML namespace, namely http://xmlns.jcp.org/jsf/composite. A custom component requires an interface and an implementation. Facelets define two tags <cc:interfaces> and <cc:implementation>.

The library tag <cc:interface> declares a composite component, and the attribute componentType references the name with the Java component. Here, it refers to the WorkerBannerComponent. The outer tag also encompasses a set of <cc:attribute> tags that declare the attributes that a component accepts. In our component, we only accept a sectionName attribute, which allows the page author to state where the customer is in their journey.

The tag <cc:implementation> declares the actual implementation, which is the rendered output. The tag also places a specially named variable called cc, which stands for composite component, into the JSF page scope. We can use it to access the properties in the custom composite component, and this special variable is only accessible inside the body content of the <cc:implementation> tag. Therefore, the value expression #{cc.gettingStartedActive} accesses the property called gettingStartedActive in WorkerBannerComponent. The logic ensures that only the named section will be highlighted as active through CSS. The logic is placed in a bean, because we need it to execute in the Render-Response phase of the JSF lifecycle rather than in the build time. JSF also adds another special variable into the page scope called component. This variable refers to the actual component being processed during the rendering phase.

> **Why does JSTL not work?**
>
> You might have thought that we could have dispensed with the server-side component and solved our banner problem with the good old **JavaServer Pages Tag Library** (**JSTL**). Unfortunately, this will fail to work, because JSF operates with lifecycles and therefore, the later binding of the frameworks makes working with the core JSTL tags such as <c:if>, <c:choose>, and <c:set> unworkable. Besides, good software engineers know that best practice means separating the presentation mark-up from business logic.

Although not shown in this section, it is possible to access the supplied attributes on the custom component inside the <cc:implementation> body content. The value expression cc.attrs provides such access. So if we wanted to write a component to access the input attributes, then we could have retrieved the section name in the markup using #{cc.attrs.sectionName}.

That is all there is to writing a composite component. In order to use it, we need to add an XML namespace, which is associated with the tag to the page that uses it. Let's see how to use it from the page content for `your-rate.xhtml` from our instant secure loan application, as shown in the following code:

```
<html xmlns="http://www.w3.org/1999/xhtml"
    xmlns:ui="http://xmlns.jcp.org/jsf/facelets"
    xmlns:p="http://xmlns.jcp.org/jsf/passthrough"
    xmlns:h="http://xmlns.jcp.org/jsf/html"
    xmlns:f="http://xmlns.jcp.org/jsf/core"
    xmlns:c="http://xmlns.jcp.org/jsp/jstl/core"
    xmlns:jsf="http://xmlns.jcp.org/jsf"
    xmlns:xen="http://xmlns.jcp.org/jsf/composite/components">

    <ui:composition template="/basic_layout.xhtml">
      <ui:define name="mainContent">
        <xen:workflow-banner sectionName="yourRate"/>
        ...

</html>
```

The namespace is `http://xmlns.jcp.org/jsf/composite/components`, and it is identified by the name **xen**. The special directory `/resources/components` is significant, because JSF searches for the custom components at this location by default.

Now we can directly use the component by the element name `<xen:workflow-banner>`. Under the counter, JSF knows that it has to look up a custom component definition called `workflow-banner.xhtml`; it then associates the component type, `WorkerBannerComponent`.

To recap, a composite component allows the JSF developers to create reusable dynamic content. A custom component uses an XHTML Facelet view and, usually, a backing bean or another action controller. A composite component may include other template views. There are no restrictions on the sort of markup as long as it is well formed and valid XHTML Facelets. The page author can use this composite component in many pages. Best of all, these composite components have the full support of the JSF action listeners, validators, and convertors.

Composite components and custom components

As mentioned in the preceding section, the JSF custom components make a distinction between the composite parent and the component in the render phase. Inside <cc:implementation>, one can access the composite parent with the variable cc and the actual processed component with the variable component.

An example of the distinction will make it abundantly clear. Let's create a custom composite component with just an XHTML markup. The path of the file, under the web root, is /resources/components/component-report.xhtml.

```
<!DOCTYPE html>
<html xmlns="http://www.w3.org/1999/xhtml"
  xmlns:h="http://xmlns.jcp.org/jsf/html"
  xmlns:cc="http://xmlns.jcp.org/jsf/composite" >

  <cc:interface/>

  <cc:implementation>
    <div class="alert alert-info">
      <h:outputText value="Own ID: #{component.id}, parent composite
ID: #{cc.id}" />
      <br/>
      <h:outputText value="Own ID: #{component.id}, parent composite
ID: #{cc.id}" />
      <br/>
      <h:outputText value="Own ID: #{component.id}, parent composite
ID: #{cc.id}" />
    </div>
  </cc:implementation>
</html>
```

By default, JSF references the XHTML with the basename, component-report. This component just dumps the component and the composite ids to the page . The component is one of the three <h:outputText> tags. The parent of these is the composite component itself. In fact, the component can be derived programmatically by invoking the static helper method, getCompositeComponentParent(), on the abstract class, javax.faces.component.UIComponent.

Let's inspect the page view that uses the composite component, /composite-demo.xhtml:

```
<!DOCTYPE html>
<html xmlns="http://www.w3.org/1999/xhtml"
  xmlns:ui="http://xmlns.jcp.org/jsf/facelets"
```

```
xmlns:h="http://xmlns.jcp.org/jsf/html"
xmlns:pro="http:/www.xenonique.co.uk/jsf/instant/lending"
xmlns:xen="http://xmlns.jcp.org/jsf/composite/components">

<ui:composition template="/basic_layout.xhtml">
  <ui:define name="mainContent">
    <h1> Custom Composite Demonstations</h1>

    <xen:workflow-banner sectionName="gettingStarted"/>
    <pro:infoSec message="The definition of digital transformation"
/>

    <xen:component-report/>

    <a class="btn btn-primary btn-lg"
      href="#{request.contextPath}/index.xhtml"> Home </a>

  </ui:define> <!--name="mainContent" -->
  </ui:composition>
</html>
```

The XHTML element `<xen:component-report>` represents the custom component. It is defined with the namespace `http://xmlns.jcp.org/jsf/composite/ components`, the same one as before.

The following is a screenshot of the page view illustrating the identifiers for the composite and component tags:

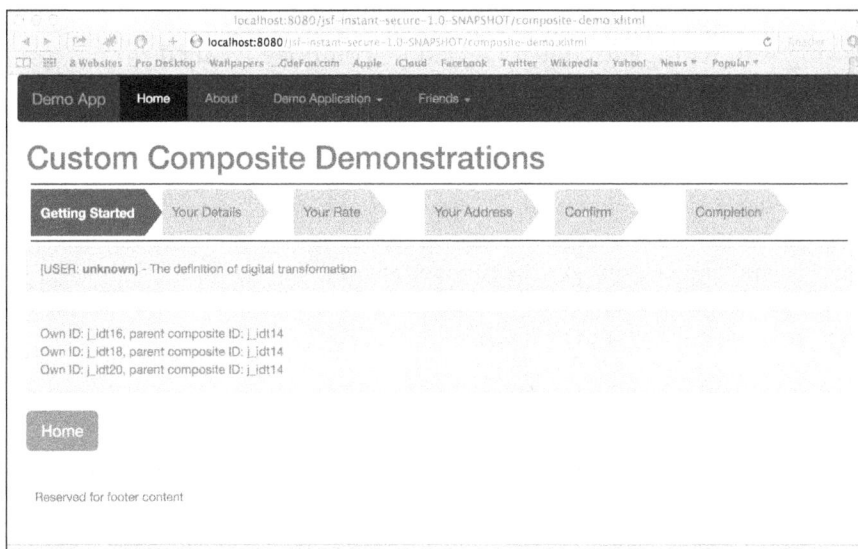

You can see the component ID changes per processing.

Composite component with self-generating tag

In JSF 2.2, @FacesComponent has the ability to generate the custom tag without specifying any XML declaration. This feature is in contrast to the previous versions of the specification, where it was a lot harder to write maintainable and reusable custom components. JSF 2.2 adds three additional attributes, including the attribute createTag.

The following table outlines the attributes for the @FacesComponent annotation:

Attribute	Type	Description
value	String	The value of this expression is the name of the custom component. By default, it is the camel case of the POJO class with the first character in lowercase, like any Java identifier.
createTag	Boolean	If true, then JSF creates a custom tag for this component.
tagName	String	Specifies the tag name for the custom component.
namespace	String	Specifies the namespace for the custom component. If none is given, the default is http://xmlns.jcp.org/jsf/component.

By way of example, we will write a basic security information custom tag, which is a custom component.

The following is the complete code for a custom component called **InfoSecurityComponent**:

```
package uk.co.xenonique.digital.instant.control;
import javax.faces.component.FacesComponent;
import javax.faces.component.UINamingContainer;
import javax.faces.context.FacesContext;
import javax.faces.context.ResponseWriter;
import java.io.IOException;
import java.security.Principal;

@FacesComponent(
  value="informationSecurity",
  namespace = "http:/www.xenonique.co.uk/jsf/instant/lending",
  tagName = "infoSec", createTag = true)
public class InfoSecurityComponent extends UINamingContainer {
  private String message;
```

```
@Override
public String getFamily() {
  return "instant.lending.custom.component";
}

@Override
public Object saveState(FacesContext context) {
  Object values[] = new Object[2];
  values[0] = super.saveState(context);
  values[1] = message;
  return ((Object) (values));
}

@Override
public void restoreState(FacesContext context, Object state) {
  Object values[] = (Object[]) state;
  super.restoreState(context, values[0]);
  message = (String) values[1];
}

public void encodeBegin(FacesContext context)
      throws IOException {
  ResponseWriter writer = context.getResponseWriter();
  writer.startElement("div", this);
  writer.writeAttribute("role", "alert", null );
  Principal principal = FacesContext.getCurrentInstance()
      .getExternalContext().getUserPrincipal();
  String name;
  if ( principal !=null ) {
    writer.writeAttribute("class","alert  alert-success",null);
    name = principal.getName();
  }
  else {
    writer.writeAttribute("class","alert  alert-danger",null);
    name = "unknown";
  }
  writer.write(
    String.format("[USER: <strong>%s</strong>] - %s",
    name, message));
}

public void encodeEnd(FacesContext context)
        throws IOException {
```

```
    ResponseWriter writer =
      context.getResponseWriter();
    writer.endElement("div");
    writer.flush();
  }
  // Getter and setter omitted
}
```

Once again, our `InfoSecurityComponent` component extends the class `UINamingContainer`, because this handles many useful JSF interfaces such as `NamingContainer`, `UniqueIdVendor`, `StateHolder`, and `FacesListener`. We annotate with `@FacesComponent`, and this time, we supply the namespace, `createTag`, and value tag.

The `getFamily()` method specifies the collection that this component belongs to. It is helpful if you are creating a reusable library of components for distribution, and effectively aids the third-party programming tools.

The `saveState()` and `restoreState()` methods demonstrate how we persist the state of a component over multiple HTTP requests. The reason for the existence of `StateHelpert` is the impedance between the JSF lifecycle and the stateless nature of HTTP. As you already know by now, JSF builds a dynamic graph of the component tree for a page. The state of this tree changes during the transition between the JSF phases. Saving the states allows JSF to preserve the information from the web form, when the user submitted the page. If there is a failure during conversion or validation, JSF can restore the state of the view.

In the `saveState()` method, we create an `Object[]` array of the necessary size and fill it with values. The first element of the array must be the saved context.

On the other hand, JSF invokes the `loadState()` method with the object state, which is also an `Object[]` array. We ignore the first element, because this is an irrelevant and, probably, a stale context from the previous request. We reassign the properties from the remaining elements of the array.

The methods `encodeBegin()` and `encodeEnd()` are where the real fun happens. These methods are designed for rendering the markup of the custom component, the tag's output. Because the custom component may embed other components, it is a good idea to split the rendered output. Here, we are using `javax.faces.context.ResponseWriter` to build up the HTML output. The abstract class has methods called `startElement()` and `endElement()` to render the content at the beginning and at the end of the markup element respectively. The method `writeAttribute()` handles the markup attributes of the element.

So `InfoSecurityComponent` renders a div layer element with the Bootstrap CSS alert classes. It attempts to retrieve the name of the current Java EE security principal, if one has been defined, and displays that information to the customer.

When given the XHTML page view:

```
<html xmlns="http://www.w3.org/1999/xhtml"
    ...
    xmlns:pro="http:/www.xenonique.co.uk/jsf/instant/lending"
    xmlns:xen="http://xmlns.jcp.org/jsf/composite/components">

...

    <pro:infoSec message="Hello world component" />
```

The output HTML should look like this:

```
<div class="alert alert-success" role="alert">
  [USER: <strong>unknown</strong>] - Hello world component
</div>
```

Note that the namespace in the XHTML matches the custom tag's annotation.

Take a look at the following screenshot of the view of `your-rate.xhtml` running on an iOS Simulator. It demonstrates the responsive web design features of the application:

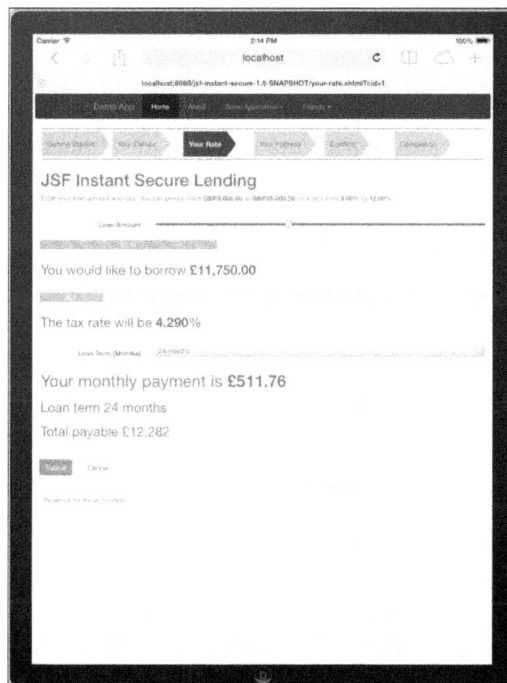

Summary

We made tremendous strides in this chapter towards a working application by examining a popular and contemporary business model. We looked at how conversational scope could help drive an instant secure lending application. Conversation scope allows us to easily write the customer journey and the wizard form that takes the user gradually through a process. Conversation scope ensures that data is stored over a lifecycle between the request and the session scopes.

We talked very briefly about a useful design pattern called Entity-Control-Boundary. It was revealed how this pattern is similar to the MVC pattern.

Along the way, we saw a JavaScript module that linked an HTML5 range component together with a Bootstrap CSS Progress element. We studied how JSF provides AJAX with partial updates of a view. We also learnt that we could replace static singleton classes with the CDI application-scoped POJOs.

Finally, we took a deep dive into custom composite components. We now know how to write a section banner component and even provide information about the Java EE security principal to a page view. JSF 2.2 is definitely a fun standard to play with. I think by now you agree that it fits the modern web architecture very well.

In the next chapter, we will look at Faces Flow.

Exercises

1. Describe, in simple steps, the digital customer journey for change of address for your local bank. You might start with the identification step first. Don't be tempted to drill down deep into banking security; instead remain at the altitude of 30,000 features, and list or tabulate steps on what you might expect to see.

2. At this stage of the study, you need to know how to persist data to a backing store. If you haven't done so already, revise your favorite persistence layer, be it JPA, Hibernate, Mongo DB, or something else. Do you know how to retrieve, save, amend, and remove entities from your persistence store?

3. Copy and rename the blank application, and write a simple conversational scope bean that captures web comments like a guest book.

4. Ensure that your backing bean uses `@ConversationScoped`. What happens to the guest book before a conversation starts? Is the information retained? (A guest book in the early digital stage was a very simple web application that allowed an Internet user to write a comment on a web page. The list of comments would grow and grow until the machine restarted or crashed. Nowadays nobody would write such a professional application and deploy it on a website.)

5. Open another browser and point it to the same guest book application. Do you see the same guest entries as before or afterwards?

6. Let's return to the Hobby Book Club application that you have been building through the previous chapters. We will add to it now by allowing books to be reviewed as a conversation. We'll keep it simple with user stories:

    ° As a reviewer, I want to be able to add my book reviews to the club's website

    ° As a reviewer, I want to see other people's reviews of the books including my own

    ° As a reviewer, I want to edit any reviews

    ° As a reviewer, I want to delete any reviews

7. Write a `@ConversationScoped` backing bean that handles the customer journey of adding a book review, amending, and removing it. To break this task down to easier milestones, you might prefer to first store the data records using the basic Java collection, without persistence into memory. After building the functionality, you can use a real database.

8. The Conversation scope is ideal for data-capture applications, especially where the user is entering information across several complex sections. Consider a business website that captures résumés (curriculum vitaes): CV Entry Application. Write the output of the customer journey, given the following sections:

    ° Personal information (full name, qualification)

    ° Address (home address, e-mail, and phone numbers)

    ° Skills matrix (professional industry skills)

    ° Work experience (places of employment)

    ° Achievements (awards)

    ° Education (education)

9. Map out the customer journey for the CV Entry Application. Build a website project using `@ConversationScoped` that captures this information. Apply the KISS (Keep It Simple Stupid) principle. You only need to demonstrate the conversation state across multiple pages and not build a complete professional application.

10. In the CV Entry Application, have you taken care of tracking the user journey in the page views? How does the user know where he or she is in the process? Write a custom component that enables this UX feature.

11. What is the difference between a custom component and a composite component? Do any of these component types require backing beans?

12. In the CV Entry Application, there are probably other areas where content reuse can be applied. Write a composite component that captures the skill set entry. You probably require a collection: `Collection<SkillSet>`, where the SkillSet entity has the properties: `title (String)`, `description (String)`, and `years or months of experience (Integer)`. How did you organize the data structure so that the order of the skills presented remain exactly the same as the user entered them? Is this an embellishment for an advanced skill-set a CRUD by itself?

6
JSF Flows and Finesse

"I've had a chance to fly a lot of different airplanes, but it was nothing like the shuttle ride."

Commander Chris Hadfield

This chapter is about Faces Flow, a new feature in JSF 2.2. The idea of flows stems from the concepts of workflows and business process management. A workflow is often an orchestrated and a repeatable sequence of business activities performed in order to do a unit of achievable work efficiently. The unit of work can involve transformation of state, processing of data, and/or provision of a service or information.

The checkout process in many web e-commerce applications is a good example of a workflow as it appears to the user. When you buy a product from Amazon, the site takes you to a separate area of the website for entering details. Behind the scenes, Amazon will gracefully move you from the micro service, which is responsible for handling products in the electronic and photography section, to the micro service that is the first step in the checkout workflow. You log in to your account or create a new one, and then you decide on the shipping address. Next, you pay with your credit or debit card, and Amazon will challenge you with an invoice address. Finally, you can choose how you want your products to be delivered. You can choose to group items together and also select express or regular delivery. Amazon is a complicated workflow to replicate; however, JSF allows the digital developer to build up from the fundamental simple flows.

Workflows also appear in rich user client applications for people who use desktop computers, especially in the government and financial services industry. You may have witnessed workflow-like applications that are case working systems, trading systems, and warehouse systems. The idea is essentially the same, which is to guide the employee through separate steps in a business process from start to finish.

In JSF 2.2, Faces Flow provides the basic programming API to create a behavior and user experience that resembles the workflow in general applications. Open source frameworks such as Apache MyFaces CODI (Orchestration module), Spring Web Flow, and the proprietary Oracle **Application Development Framework (ADF)** inspired the design of Faces Flow.

What is Faces Flow?

Faces Flow is the encapsulation of backing beans having a special scope with the related pages into a module. A Faces Flow is a module with a single, well-defined entry point and one or more exit points. The application developer determines how a Faces Flow is comprised and how it would function. In other words, Faces Flow is a low-level API, whereas other frameworks, with BPM in particular, feature higher-level configurations and macro-level processes.

- A JSF Faces Flow is modular in execution; a flow can invoke another flow in a nested fashion.

- Faces Flow can pass parameters to another nested flow and the nested flow can also return data through a special map property called the Flow Scope.

- Application developers can package a flow with the corresponding pages into a module, which may be distributed to a third-party developer.

- There is a brand new scope called `FlowScoped`, which denotes whether a POJO is a flow-scoped bean. The annotation for this is `@javax.faces.flow.FlowScoped`. A flow-scoped bean is compatible with CDI; so you can use the familiar Java EE annotations and order inject references to other beans and EJB elements.

- You can write action-controller methods and handle the logic inside the flow-scoped beans as you would with `@RequestScoped`, `@ConversationScoped`, `@SessionScoped`, and `@ApplicationScoped` beans.

Flow definitions and lifecycle

Faces Flows use the `@FlowScoped` beans where the user can enter a single page, which is known as the start page. After entering the flow, the user can navigate the pages, which are associated with the flow. The user can exit the flow at predefined points. A flow can invoke a nested flow.

The lifecycle of the @FlowScoped beans is greater than the @ViewScoped beans, but shorter than that of @SessionScoped. Therefore, we can compare flow scoped beans to their conversational brethren. A @ConversationalScoped bean maintains a state for all the views and web page tabs in a browser. Like their conversation mates, the @FlowScoped beans survive multiple requests; in fact, they are even better, because they have different instances for multiple windows in a session. The flow-scoped bean is not shared between browser tabs.

As the user enters and leaves the flows in the application, Faces Flows has a dedicated CDI scope, which the JSF framework implementation uses to activate and passivate the data of the bean.

As soon as the user leaves a flow, that instance is susceptible to garbage collection by the JVM. Therefore, in comparison to @SessionScoped and @ConversationalScoped beans, flows tend to have lower memory demands.

The following diagram illustrates the scope of a Faces Flow.

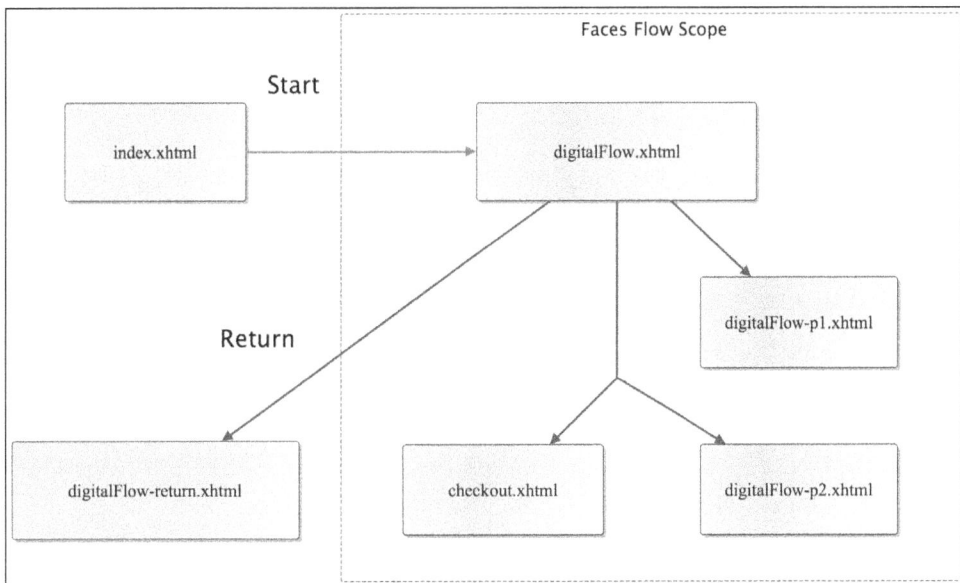

Simple Implicit Faces Flows

It is relatively straightforward to create an Implicit Faces Flow with just a folder name, an empty XML configuration, and some Facelet pages. A flow is a folder name in your web application, preferably at the root directory. We start with the basic flow in the directory of the same name called digitalFlow. Your flow must match the name of the folder.

In order to define an implicit flow, we create an empty XML file with the common basename and a suffix: `digitalFlow/digitalFlow-flow.xhtml`.

We now create a start page in the folder with the common basename. This file is a Facelet view page called `digitalFlow/digitalFlow.xhtml`.

We can create other pages in the flow inside the folder, and they can have any name we like. We might have `digitalFlow/digitalFlow1.xhtml`, `digitalFlow/checkout.xhtml`, or `digitalFlow/song.xhtml`. Only the defined flow `digitalFlow` can ever access these pages. If an outside call does attempt to access any of these pages, the JSF implementation will report an error.

In order to exit the implicit flow, we must provide a special page, `/digitalFlow-return.xhtml`, in the root folder of the web application, which means that the file is located outside of the folder.

Implicit navigation

Let's put this knowledge to good use with our first Faces Flow navigation example. In the source code, the project is called `jsf-implicit-simple-flow`. It is helpful to examine the file layout for this project, which is as follows:

`src/main/java`

`src/main/webapp`

`src/main/webapp/WEB-INF/classes/META-INF`

`src/main/webapp/index.xhtml`

`src/main/webapp/assets/`

`src/main/webapp/resources/`

`src/main/webapp/basic-layout.xhtml`

`src/main/webapp/view-expired.xhtml`

`src/main/webapp/digitalFlow/`

`src/main/webapp/digitalFlow/digitalFlow.xml`

`src/main/webapp/digitalFlow/digitalFlow.xhtml`

`src/main/webapp/digitalFlow/digitalFlow-p2.xthml`

`src/main/webapp/digitalFlow/digitalFlow-p2.xthml`

`src/main/webapp/digitalFlow/digitalFlow-p4.xthml`

`src/main/webapp/digitalFlow-return.xhtml`

As you study the preceding layout, you notice that the project has a standard home page called `index.xhtml`, as we would expect. It has a `digitalFlow` folder, which is the special area of the website dedicated for this Faces Flow. Inside this directory, there are a bunch of Facelet files and a configuration. The start page is called `digitalFlow.xhtml`, and there is an empty XML file reserved for a flow definition, `digitalFlow.xml`.

By now you are already aware of the purpose of the assets and resources folders, but the we will come back to the `view-expired.xhtml` file shortly. How do we ensure that our folder structure is treated as a Faces Flow?

A Flow scoped bean

With the annotation `@javax.faces.flow.FlowScoped`, we define a POJO as a flow scoped bean. The following is the code for our first Faces Flow, which is a backing bean:

```
package uk.co.xenonique.digital.flows.control;
import javax.faces.flow.FlowScoped;
import javax.inject.Named;
import java.io.Serializable;

@Named
@FlowScoped("digitalFlow")
public class DigitalFlow implements Serializable {
    public String debugClassName() {
        return this.getClass().getSimpleName();
    }

    public String gotoPage1() {
        return "digitalFlow.xhtml";
    }

    public String gotoPage2() {
        return "digitalFlow-p2.xhtml";
    }

    public String gotoPage3() {
        return "digitalFlow-p3.xhtml";
    }

    public String gotoPage4() {
        return "digitalFlow-p4.xhtml";
    }
```

```
        public String gotoEndFlow() {
            return "/digitalFlow-return.xhtml";
        }
    }
```

The simple controller class, DigitalFlow, has action methods such as gotoPage1() and gotoPage2() to move the user to the appropriate page in the flow. The method gotoEndFlow() navigates to the return Facelet view that JSF detects in order to exit the flow.

The annotation of @FlowScoped requires a single String value parameter, which in this case matches the name of the folder digitalFlow. We shall now move to the views.

Facelet views

We use flow-scoped beans in the Facelet views just as we use any other CDI scoped bean. The following is an extract of the home page, index.xhtml:

```
<!DOCTYPE html>
<html xmlns="http://www.w3.org/1999/xhtml"
      xmlns:ui="http://xmlns.jcp.org/jsf/facelets"
      xmlns:p="http://xmlns.jcp.org/jsf/passthrough"
      xmlns:h="http://xmlns.jcp.org/jsf/html"
      xmlns:f="http://xmlns.jcp.org/jsf/core" >

  <ui:composition template="/basic_layout.xhtml">
    <ui:define name="mainContent">
      <h1> JSF Implicit Simple Flow</h1>

      <p>
        Welcome to a simple Faces Flow...
      </p>

      <div class="content-wrapper">
        <h:form>
          <h:commandButton styleClass="btn btn-primary btn-lg"
            action="digitalFlow" value="Enter Digital Flow" />
        </h:form>
      </div>

      <!-- ... -->

    </ui:define> <!--name="mainContent" -->
  </ui:composition>
</html>
```

In the preceding view, the `<h:commandButton>` defines an action with the name of the flow, `digitalFlow`. Invoking this action causes JSF to enter the Faces Flow, which matches the corresponding annotated name of the backing bean.

JSF recognizes that a flow has implicit navigation, because the XML Flow Definition file `digitalFlow.xml` is empty. This file must exist; otherwise, the implementation reports an error. You do not need the start or end tags inside the file either.

When a user invokes the button, JSF instantiates a flow scoped bean before it is forwarded to the start page. The following is an extract from the start page of the flow `digitalFlow.xhtml`:

```
<html xmlns="http://www.w3.org/1999/xhtml" ...>
<ui:composition template="/basic_layout.xhtml>
  <ui:define name="mainContent">
    <!-- ... -->
    <div class="content-wrapper">
      <h1>Page <code>digitalFlow.xhtml</code></h1>
      <p>View is part of a flow scope? <code>
      #{null != facesContext.application.flowHandler.currentFlow}
      </code>.</p>

      <table class="table table-bordered table-striped">
        <tr>
          <th>Expression</th>
          <th>Value</th>
        </tr>
        <tr>
          <td>digitalFlow.debugClassName()</td>
          <td>#{digitalFlow.debugClassName()}</td>
        </tr>
      </table>

      <h:form prependId="false">
        <h:commandButton id="nextBtn1"
          styleClass="btn btn-primary btn-lg"
          value="Next Direct" action="digitalFlow-2" />
         
        <h:commandButton id="nextBtn2"
          styleClass="btn btn-primary btn-lg"
          value="Next Via Bean" action="#{digitalFlow.gotoPage2()}" />
         
        <h:commandButton id="exitFlowBtn1"
          styleClass="btn btn-primary btn-lg"
          value="Exit Direct" action="/digitalFlow-return" />
```

```
         
        <h:commandButton id="exitFlowBtn2"
          styleClass="btn btn-primary btn-lg"
          value="Exit Via Bean" action="#{digitalFlow.gotoEndFlow()}"
  />
         
      </h:form>
    </div>

  </ui:define> <!--name="mainContent" -->
</ui:composition>
</html>
```

The view demonstrates the invocation of the flow scoped bean with the familiar Expression Language as well as direct page-to-page navigation. To allow the user to move to the second page in the flow, we have two command buttons. The command button with the attribute action and value `digitalFlow-2` is page navigation direct without validation of any form input whatsoever. The command button with the attribute action and the expression language value, `#{digitalFlow.gotoPage2()}` is an invocation to the flow scoped bean's method, which means that the entire JSF lifecycle is executed.

> See *Chapter 2, JavaServer Faces Lifecycle*, if you have forgotten the different phases in the lifecycle.

In this view, we also generate the output, `#{digitalFlow.debugClassName()}`, in order to illustrate that we can invoke arbitrary methods in a flow-scoped bean.

Let me also draw your attention to the expression language that establishes if a view is a part of the flow or not through the following practical content:

```
#{null != facesContext.application.flowHandler.currentFlow}
```

This is functionally equivalent to the following Java statement:

```
null == FacesContext.getCurrentInstance().getApplication()
    .getFlowHandler().getCurrentFlow()
```

The other pages, `digitalFlow-p2.xhtml` and `digitalFlow-p3.xhtml`, are very similar, because they just add the command buttons to navigate back to the previous views. You can see the full code as part of the book's source distribution.

> In digital work, we often provide well-known identifiers (IDs) to certain HTML elements, especially form controls. This helps when we are writing testing scripts for web automation testing, especially with the Selenium Web Driver framework (`http://www.seleniumhq.org/`).

We shall jump to the final view, `digitalFlow-p4.xhtml` and just extract the form element for study:

```
<h:form prependId="false">
  <h:commandButton id="prevBtn1"
  styleClass="btn btn-primary btn-lg"
  value="Prev Direct" action="digitalFlow-p3" />
   
  <h:commandButton id="prevBtn2"
  styleClass="btn btn-primary btn-lg"
  value="Prev Via Bean" action="#{digitalFlow.gotoPage3()}" />
   
  <h:commandButton id="exitFlowBtn1"
  styleClass="btn btn-primary btn-lg"
  value="Exit Direct" action="/digitalFlow-return" />
   
  <h:commandButton id="exitFlowBtn2"
  styleClass="btn btn-primary btn-lg"
  value="Exit Via Bean" action="#{digitalFlow.gotoEndFlow()}" />
   
</h:form>
```

As we can see, the preceding content illustrates how to navigate directly and through the `DigitalFlow` backing bean. In order to exit the flow in an implicit navigation, the user must trigger an event that takes the JSF framework to the `/digitalFlow-return.xhtml` view, which causes the flow to finish. Directly navigating to the return mode avoids validation, and any data inside the form input elements is lost. If we want to validate the form input elements as a form request, we must invoke a method in the action controller, the backing bean.

And that is implicit navigation in JSF Faces Flow.

It really is that easy, so let's see some screenshots of this simple flow starting with the home page `/index.html`:

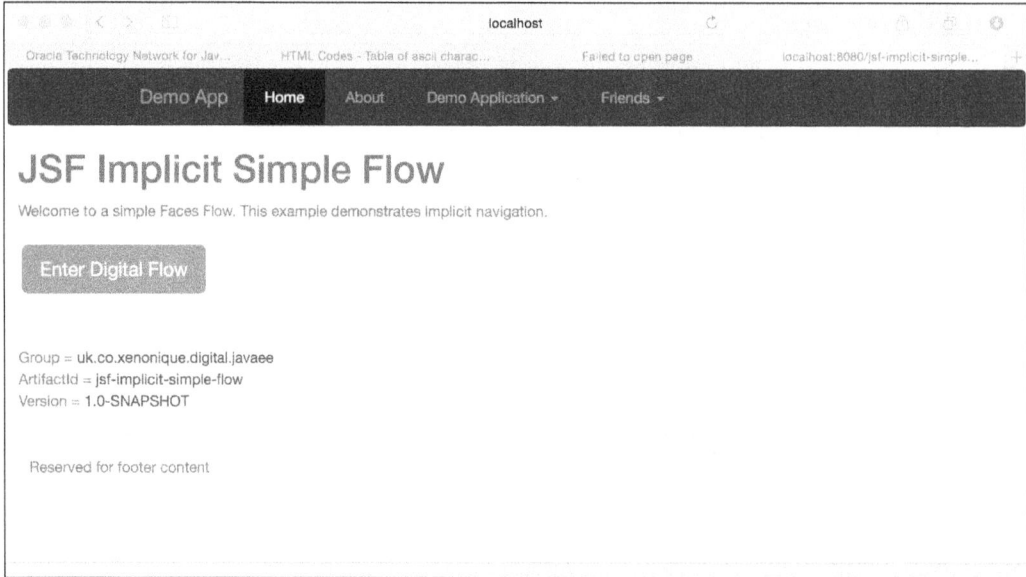

The start page `digital-flow.xhtml` for `DigitalFlow` appears like the following screenshot:

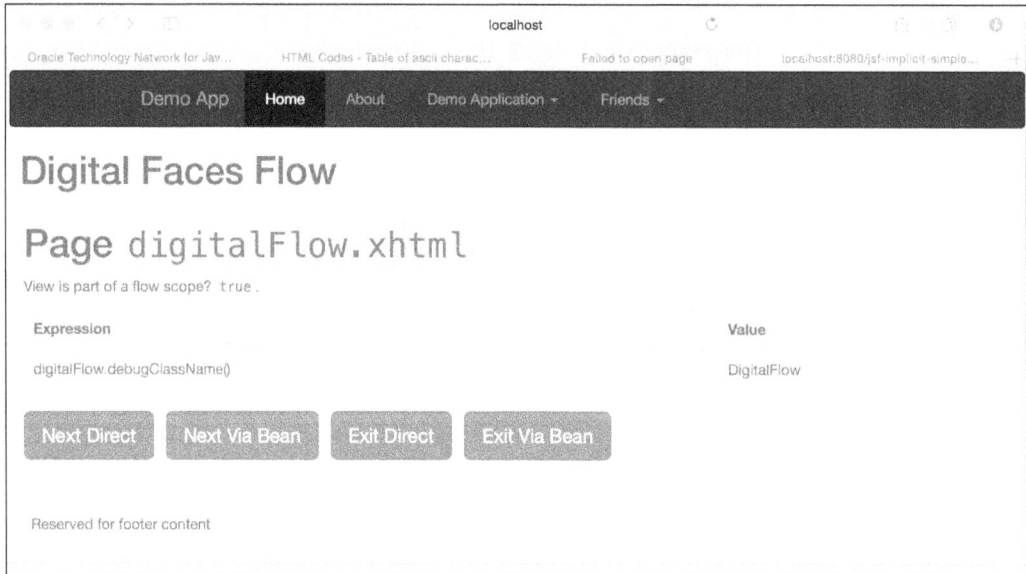

After exiting the flow, the user sees the view /digitalFlow-return.xhtml. The following is a screenshot of this view:

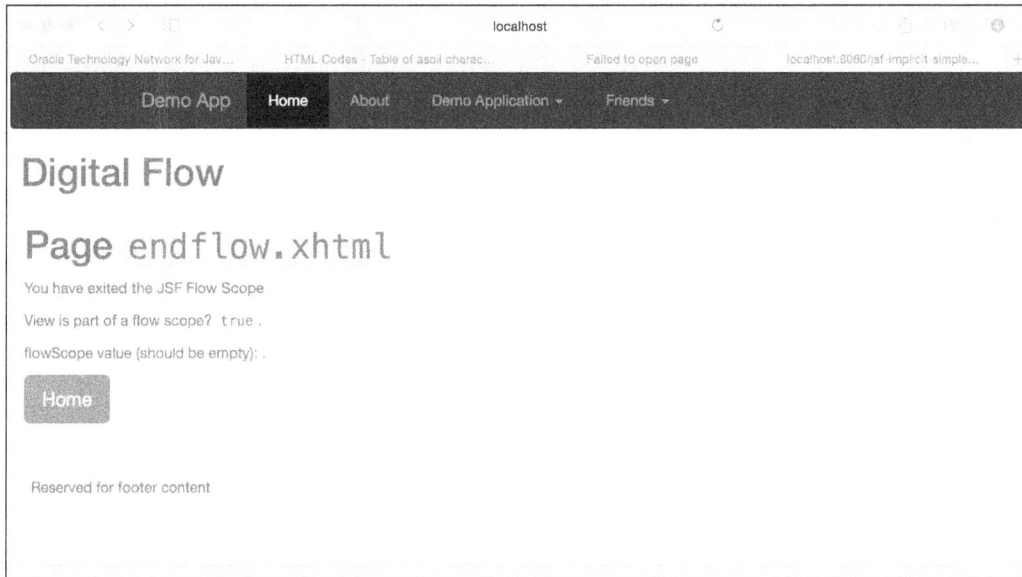

If we attempt to access a Facelet view directly through a known URI /digitalFlow/ digitalFlow.xhtml before entering the flow, the view would be like the following screenshot:

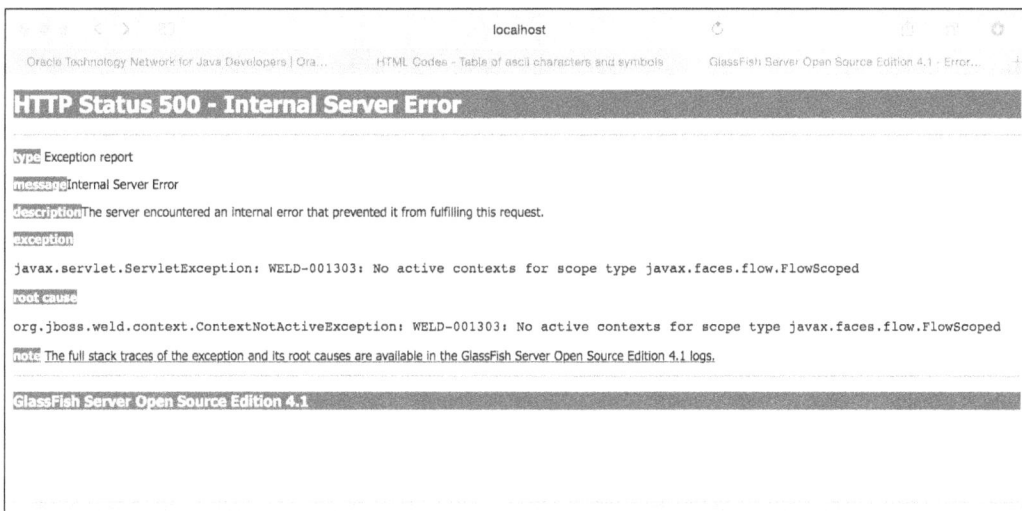

With GlassFish 4.1, we receive an HTTP Response Code of 500, which is an internal server error. Moreover, the CDI container raises an exception that there is no active flow scope.

Handling view expired

I promised you that we would add some finesse to our digital application. If you've worked with JSF for a while, you probably have your fair share of stack traces with `javax.faces.application.ViewExpiredException` as the root cause. This is one of the most notorious exceptions. You could increase the HTTP Session lifetime in order to compensate for an out-of-date request, but how long is break away from the computer for an average person? Meanwhile, the objects would persist in the memory. There is a better way and that is by using the Web XML deployment descriptor.

Inside the applications `web.xml` file, we need to trigger a redirection to a more pleasant error page. The following is an extract of the XML file:

```
<?xml version="1.0" encoding="UTF-8"?>
<web-app xmlns="http://xmlns.jcp.org/xml/ns/javaee" ...>
  <!-- ... -->
  <error-page>
    <exception-type>
    javax.faces.application.ViewExpiredException
    </exception-type>
    <location>/view-expired.xhtml</location>
  </error-page>
  <!-- ... -->
</web-app>
```

The `<error-page>` element specifies an association between an exception type and a page view. Whenever JSF encounters the exception type `ViewExpiredException`, it will progress the response action to the page view `/view-expired.xhtml`. The circumstance of this behavior is illustrated in the following screenshot:

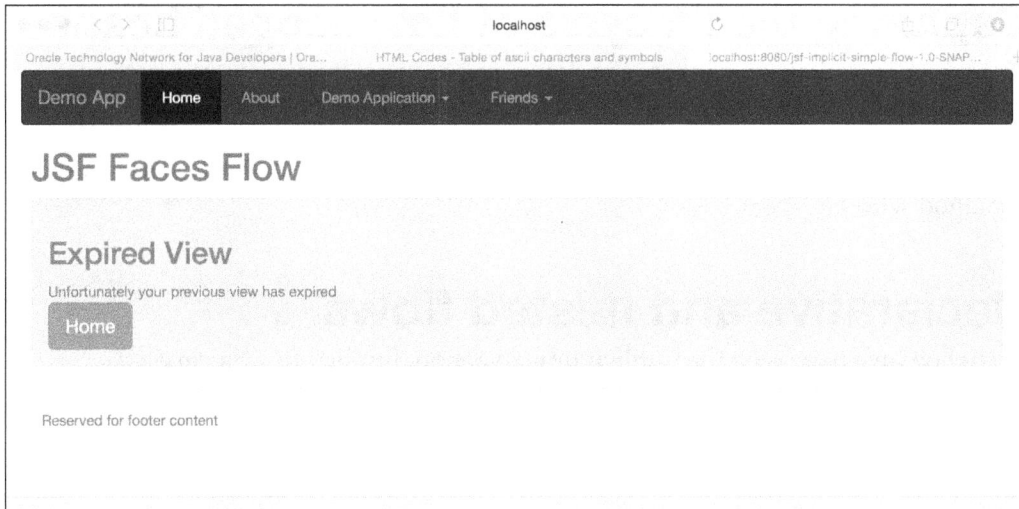

I am sure you'll agree that our public customer will enjoy this improved and dedicated page view rather than being puzzled with a stack trace.

> Flow scoped beans depend on CDI and, therefore, they require a Java EE 7 environment which dictates a CDI 1.1 container such as JBoss Weld. You must also use @Named and not the older style @ManagedBean annotation. If you don't use WildFly 8 or GlassFish 4, then before you dive into the code, please check your container's implementation support for the latest JSF and CDI specifications.

A comparison with conversational scoped beans

If you recall, while using @ConversationScoped beans, we had to explicitly demarcate the state of the conversation. We injected the Conversation instance and from there, at specific points in the digital customer journey, called the begin() and end() methods. With @FlowScoped CDI beans, the scope is automatically started and finished at defined points.

Capturing the lifecycle of flow scoped beans

Since the CDI container manages the flow scoped beans, they can participate normally in the contextual lifecycle. We can annotate a method with `@PostConstruct` in order to initialize the bean, acquire a database resource, or compute cacheable data. Likewise, when the flow goes out of scope, we can annotate a method with `@PreDestroy`.

Declarative and nested flows

Up to now, we have seen the implicit flow in action. Implicit flow is very straightforward for the simplest flow, which performs like a basic web wizard where the user is able to navigate linearly, going forward and backward. It can also use random access to navigate to pages.

If we want to take Faces Flow further, then we must delve into the XML flow definition, but first let us define some terms.

The flow node terminology

The fundamental technology being inspired by workflow and BPM, the Faces Flow specification declares different types of nodes which are given in the following table:

Node Type Name	Description
View	Represents any type of application JSF view
Method Call	Represents a method invocation in the flow graph through **Expression Language** (EL)
Flow Call	Represents an invocation of another flow with outbound (call) and (return) inbound parameters
Flow Return	Represents a return to the calling flow
Switch	Represents navigation selection through logic determined by EL

The following is an illustration of two flows that represent a shopping cart business process. The outside flow invokes the nested flow, which handles the delivery method.

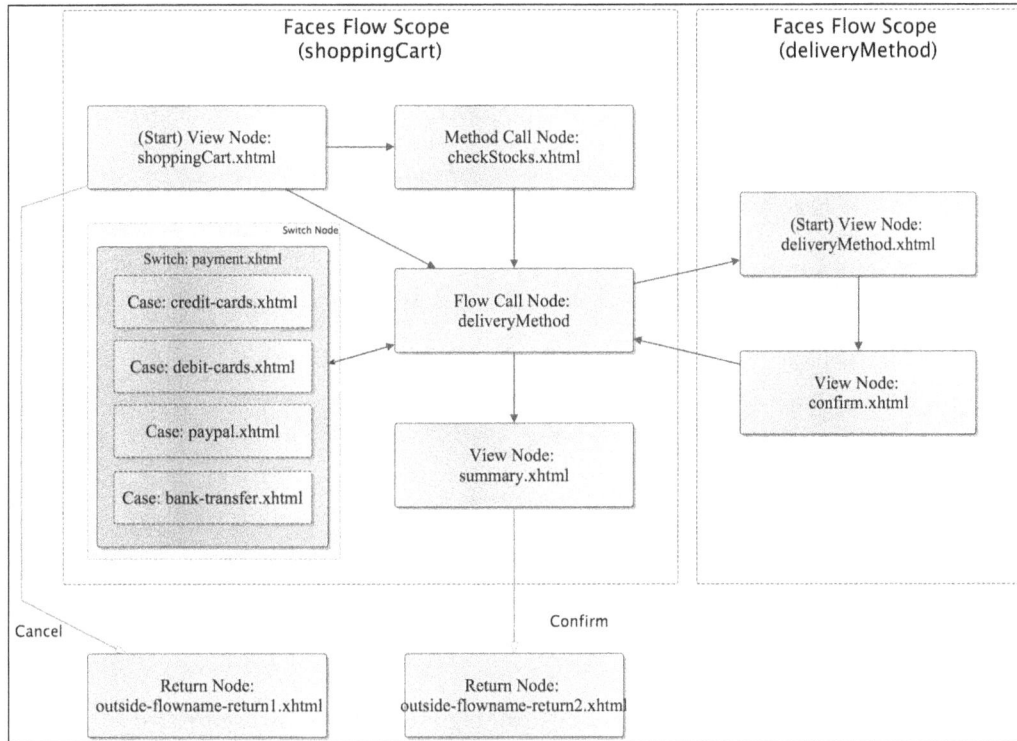

An XML flow definition description file

Given that `<<Flowname>>` is a folder name in the web application, the flow description filename matches the pattern, `<<Flowname>>/<<Flowname>>.xml`. The content of this descriptor file declares to JSF certain characteristics of the flow. It may define an alternative start page, define a set of return outcomes, and map certain outcomes to specific pages. The descriptor can also define the conditional Boolean logic that maps the outcomes to particular pages.

The following is an example of an XML flow definition file:

```
<?xml version='1.0' encoding='UTF-8'?>
<faces-config version="2.2"
  xmlns="http://xmlns.jcp.org/xml/ns/javaee"
  xmlns:xsi="http://www.w3.org/2001/XMLSchema-instance"
  xsi:schemaLocation="
  http://xmlns.jcp.org/xml/ns/javaee
  http://xmlns.jcp.org/xml/ns/javaee/web-facesconfig_2_2.xsd">
  <flow-definition id="flow-id">
```

```
<start-node>startPage</start-node>
<view id="startPage">
  <vdl-document>/flowname/start.xhtml</vdl-document>
</view>

<view id="inside-flow-id-1"> <vdl-document>
  /flowname/inside-flow-id-1.xhtml </vdl-document>
</view>
<view id="inside-flow-id-2"> <vdl-document>
  /flowname/inside-flow-id-2.xhtml </vdl-document>
</view>

<flow-return id="return-from-flow-id-1">
  <from-outcome>/outside-page-1</from-outcome>
</flow-return>
<flow-return id="return-from-flow-id-2">
  <from-outcome>/outside-page-21</from-outcome>
</flow-return>

  </flow-definition>
</faces-config>
```

The root element must be a `<faces-config>` tag with the appropriate XML namespaces. You might be surprised by this choice of root element. This is because a flow definition can be defined globally, across the application, by setting the flow definition in the `/WEB-INF/faces-config.xml` file. However, this practice is an advanced use case and not recommended for modular development.

A flow definition tag

The `<flow-definition>` element establishes the Faces Flow with the defined flow ID. The value of the identifier must match the value for the `@FlowScoped` bean. This element contains a collection of tags to establish the start page, views, flow returns, or the conditional switch statement.

A mandatory flow return tag

A Faces Flow must have at least one return outcome. The `<flow-return>` element establishes a flow return node with an ID. It must contain a `<flow-outcome>` element whose body content specifies the Facelet view.

A view page tag

A flow may optionally define a set of View Nodes (pages) that are useful for direct navigation from one view to another, within the scope. The element `<view>` tag establishes a view description language node through the element `<vdl-document>`. A view requires an identifier. The body content of this tag simply references a Facelet view. Therefore, the view ID does not necessarily have be the same name as the Facelet view.

An optional start page tag

The developer can override the name of the default start page and provide an alternative view. The body content of the element `<start-node>` specifies the view ID and, therefore, references an appropriate flow, a View Node.

Switch, conditional, and case tags

The flow definition offers the developer the capability to define conditional logic through an element tag called `<switch>`. This is the highest of the low-level features in the XML. The `<switch>` tag specifies a Switch Node, which is very similar to the use of the `<if>` tags within a `<navigation-case>` in the `/WEB-INF/faces-config.xml` file, obviously for non-flow navigation. The switch allows a single outcome in the flow to map more than one Facelet view by evaluating an EL expression with conditional logic.

The following is an extended version of the XML flow definition example file:

```
<faces-config version="2.2" ...>
  <flow-definition id="flow-id">
    ...
    <switch id="customerPaymentTab">
      <case>
        <if>
          #{controller.paymentType == 'CreditCard'}
        </if>
        <from-outcome>creditcard</from-outcome>
      </case>
      <case>
        <if>
          #{controller.paymentType == 'DebitCard'}
        </if>
        <from-outcome>debitcard</from-outcome>
      </case>
      <case>
        <if>
```

```
            #{controller.paymentType == 'PayPal'}
          </if>
          <from-outcome>PayPal</from-outcome>
        </case>
        <default-outcome>bacs-direct</default-outcome>
      </switch>
      ...
    </flow-definition>
  </faces-config>
```

The `<switch>` tag contains a number of `<case>` elements and a single `<default-outcome>` element. Each `<case>` element contains a single `<if>` and `<from-outcome>` elements. The body content of the `<if>` defines a conditional logic EL. The `<from-outcome>` maps to the final Facelet view or it references the identifier of a View Node. It is a very good idea to a have a default outcome for a Switch Node. The body content of a `<default-outcome>` establishes this outcome when none of the case conditions happen to evaluate to true.

In the example, we have an imaginary payment controller used in a checkout process on an e-commerce website. When the flow encounters an outcome `customerPaymentTab`, which is the identifier for the Switch Node, JSF processes each of the case conditional logics in order. If one of those condition tests evaluates to true, then JSF chooses that outcome as the result of the switch. Let's say the `#{controller.paymentType == 'DebitCard' }` is true, then debit card is the chosen view. If none of the tests evaluates to true, then the resulting view is `bacs-direct`.

> But shouldn't all logic be defined in a controller instead of a Switch Node? The answer is controversial either way, and it depends. If you are building an application with a complex graph of Faces Flows as a library developer, one can argue for this flexibility for external configurators. If you are building simple applications, then maybe following the practice of YAGNI (You Aren't Going to Need it) will benefit in a minimum viable product.

This covers all that we need to know about the basic flow definition file. Let's move on to the nested declarative flow now.

A nested flow example

It's time to see a practical example of Faces Flow with nested declarative flow definitions. Our application is simple. It allows the customer to record carbon footprint data. So first let's define a data record:

```
package uk.co.xenonique.digital.flows.entity;
```

```
import javax.persistence.*;
import java.io.Serializable;

@Entity
@Table(name = "CARBON_FOOTPRINT")
@NamedQueries({
  @NamedQuery(name="CarbonFootprint.findAll",
    query = "select c from CarbonFootprint c "),
  @NamedQuery(name="CarbonFootprint.findById",
    query = "select c from CarbonFootprint c where c.id = :id"),
})
public class CarbonFootprint implements Serializable {
  @Id
  @GeneratedValue(strategy = GenerationType.AUTO)
  private long id;

  private String applicationId;
  private String industryOrSector;
  // KWh (main source)
  private double electricity;
  // KWh (main source)
  private double naturalGas;
  // Litres (travel commute costs)
  private double diesel;
  // Litres (travel commute costs)
  private double petrol;

  public CarbonFootprint() { }

  // hashCode(), equals() and toString()
  // Getters and setters omited
}
```

The `CarbonFootprint` is a JPA entity bean, which declares a set of properties to store the customer's carbon footprint data. The user can supply their industry or sector, the amount of electricity, natural gas, diesel, and petrol they consume over a time period. The record also has an `applicationId` value, which we shall make use of.

Let's view the file layout for this project:

src/main/java

src/main/webapp

src/main/webapp/WEB-INF/classes/META-INF

src/main/webapp/index.xhtml

```
src/main/webapp/assets/

src/main/webapp/resources/

src/main/webapp/basic-layout.xhtml

src/main/webapp/view-expired.xhtml

src/main/webapp/section-flow/

src/main/webapp/section-flow/section-flow.xml

src/main/webapp/section-flow/section-flow.xhtml

src/main/webapp/section-flow/section-flow-1a.xthml

src/main/webapp/section-flow/section-flow-1b.xthml

src/main/webapp/section-flow/section-flow-1c.xthml

src/main/webapp/footprint-flow/

src/main/webapp/footprint-flow/footprint-flow.xml

src/main/webapp/footprint-flow/footprint-flow.xhtml

src/main/webapp/footprint-flow/footprint-flow-1a.xml

src/main/webapp/endflow.xhtml
```

The project is called `jsf-declarative-flows` and is available as a part of the book's source code. There are two flows: `section-flow` and `digital-flow`. The section flow captures the industry information in this made-up example. The footprint flow captures the energy consumption data. Both flows share a customer detail record, the `CarbonFootprint` entity object, which you will see later in the backing beans.

XML flow definitions

The following is the XML flow definition for the Sector flow, `sector-flow/sector-flow.xhtml`:

```
<faces-config version="2.2" ...>
  <flow-definition id="sector-flow">
    <flow-return id="goHome">
      <from-outcome>/index</from-outcome>
    </flow-return>
    <flow-return id="endFlow">
      <from-outcome>#{sectorFlow.gotoEndFlow()}</from-outcome>
    </flow-return>

    <flow-call id="callFootprintFlow">
      <flow-reference>
```

```
      <flow-id>footprint-flow</flow-id>
    </flow-reference>
    <outbound-parameter>
      <name>param1FromSectorFlow</name>
      <value>param1 sectorFlow value</value>
    </outbound-parameter>
    <outbound-parameter>
      <name>param2FromSectorFlow</name>
      <value>param2 sectorFlow value</value>
    </outbound-parameter>
    <outbound-parameter>
      <name>param3FromSectorFlow</name>
      <value>#{sectorFlow.footprint}</value>
    </outbound-parameter>
    <outbound-parameter>
      <name>param4FromSectorFlow</name>
      <value>#{sectorFlow.footprint.applicationId}</value>
    </outbound-parameter>
  </flow-call>
 </flow-definition>
</faces-config>
```

The identifier for this flow is sector-flow, which matches the folder name. It also establishes the `@FlowScoped` value for the backing bean, the action controller, as we shall see later.

There are two Flow Return nodes, namely `goHome` and `endFlow`. The `goHome` has direct navigation to the home page, whereas `endFlow` invokes an action on the bean through the EL value, `#{sectorFlow.gotoEndFlow()}`. This technique is particularly useful to ensure that a customer has entered correct and validated data before allowing them to complete their digital journey.

The new node `callFootprintFlow` represents a nested flow invocation. The element `<flow-call>` defines a Flow Call node. It must have a `<flow-reference>` tag element with a nested tag, `<flow-id>`. The body content of the latter defines the identifier of the target flow.

The `<outbound-parameter>` elements specify how the parameters and value pairs are passed to the target flow. Each parameter requires a `<name>` and a `<value>` element. The name of the outgoing parameter in the calling flow must match the name of the incoming parameter in the invoked flow.

The `param1FromSectorFlow` and `param2FromSectorFlow` demonstrate how to pass the literal String values from one flow to another. If you are passing numeric values, then you have to encode and decode these values yourself in the target flow. The parameters `param3FromSectorFlow` and `param4FromSectorFlow` also illustrate how EL can be used. Note how we can easily pass the entity record `#{sectorFlow.footprint}` from the Sector Flow to the Footprint Flow. We can also pass an individual property as we have done in the final parameter: `#{sectorFlow.footprint.applicationId}`.

The following is the XML flow definition for the Footprint Flow `footprint-flow/footprint-flow.xml`:

```
<faces-config version="2.2" ...>
  <flow-definition id="footprint-flow">
    <flow-return id="goHome">
      <from-outcome>/index</from-outcome>
    </flow-return>
    <flow-return id="exitFromFootprintFlow">
      <from-outcome>#{footprintFlow.exitFromFootprintFlow}</from-outcome>
    </flow-return>
    <flow-return id="exitToSectionFlow">
      <from-outcome>/section-flow</from-outcome>
    </flow-return>

    <inbound-parameter>
      <name>param1FromSectorFlow</name>
      <value>#{flowScope.param1Value}</value>
    </inbound-parameter>
    <inbound-parameter>
      <name>param2FromSectorFlow</name>
      <value>#{flowScope.param2Value}</value>
    </inbound-parameter>
    <inbound-parameter>
      <name>param3FromSectorFlow</name>
      <value>#{flowScope.param3Value}</value>
    </inbound-parameter>
    <inbound-parameter>
      <name>param4FromSectorFlow</name>
      <value>#{flowScope.param4Value}</value>
    </inbound-parameter>

  </flow-definition>
</faces-config>
```

This flow is identified by the name `footprint-flow.xml`. It has a set of return flow nodes. The `goHome` node actually exits the flows to the calling home, despite the view document value `/index` value. You might think this behavior as odd. However, JSF is correct, because the current flow Footprint is a nested flow and it drives the flow pointer to the state of the calling flow sector. The nodes `exitFromFootprintFlow` and `exitToSectionFlow` represent different navigation strategies, indirect and direct respectively.

The set of `<inbound-parameter>` elements specify the incoming parameter to the flow. The names of the parameters are extremely important, because they must match those in the corresponding `<outbound-parameter>` element in the calling flow. The values define the EL object reference, which say where these values are written. In other words, the passing of parameters in Faces Flow behaves like a mapped property name transfer.

Let's analyze the third parameter from `sector-flow.xml`. It sends a value of the entity record instance `CarbonFootprint` to the nested Footprint Flow:

```
<outbound-parameter>
  <name>param3FromSectorFlow</name>
  <value>#{sectorFlow.footprint}</value>
</outbound-parameter>
```

Inside `footprint-flow.xml`, the inbound parameter name matches the incoming parameter name:

```
<inbound-parameter>
  <name>param3FromSectorFlow</name>
  <value>#{flowScope.param3Value}</value>
</inbound-parameter>
```

The EL specifies the location where JSF sets the value of the parameter to the property of the object. In this case, the `flowScope` map collection has a key and a value set. We can use any existing object that has a lifespan greater or equal to the flow lifecycle. We tend to use the `flowScope`, because it is designed to pass parameters between Face Flows. Because we can reference properties in objects, we also have the ability to return information from the nested flows. The calling flow may retrieve the value after the nested flow ends.

Now that we understand the nested flows from the XML perspective, we can look at the Java source code.

Flow beans

The `sector-flow` backing bean looks as follows:

```
package uk.co.xenonique.digital.flows.control;
import uk.co.xenonique.digital.flows.boundary.*;
import uk.co.xenonique.digital.flows.entity.*;
import uk.co.xenonique.digital.flows.utils.UtilityHelper;
// ...
@Named
@FlowScoped("sector-flow")
public class SectorFlow implements Serializable {
  @Inject UtilityHelper utilityHelper;
  @Inject CarbonFootprintService service;

  private CarbonFootprint footprint
    = new CarbonFootprint();

  public SectorFlow() {}

  @PostConstruct
  public void initialize() {
    footprint.setApplicationId(
      utilityHelper.getNextApplicationId());
  }

  public String gotoEndFlow() {
    return "/endflow.xhtml";
  }

  public String debugClassName() {
    return this.getClass().getSimpleName();
  }

  public String saveFootprintRecord() {
    service.add(footprint);
    return "sector-flow-1c.xhtml";
  }

  // Getters and setters ...
}
```

The class `SectorFlow` is annotated with `@FlowScoped`, and the value matches
the flow definition XML file. We annotate a method `initialize()` with
`@PostConstruct` in order to set a random application ID in the entity record. Note
that we cannot put this logic inside a normal Java constructor here, because our bean
is given life through the CDI container.

We inject a couple of instances into SectorFlow. The UtilityHelper is an @ApplicationScoped CDI POJO class that generates a random application identifier. There is a stateful EJB CarbonFootprintService that handles the JPA persistence.

The gotoEndflow() method is a navigation end to exit the flow. The method, saveFootprintRecord() uses the data service to store the CarbonFootprint entity into a database.

That completes the inner flow, that is, SectorFlow; the code for the nested backing bean FootprintFlow is as follows:

```
@Named
@FlowScoped("footprint-flow")
public class FootprintFlow implements Serializable {
  private CarbonFootprint footprint;
  public FootprintFlow() { }

  @PostConstruct
  public void initialize() {}
    Map<Object,Object> flowMap =
      FacesContext.getCurrentInstance()
        .getApplication().getFlowHandler()
        .getCurrentFlowScope();
    footprint = (CarbonFootprint) flowMap.get("param3Value");
  }

  public String exitFromFootprintFlow() {
    return "/endflow.xhtml";
  }

  public String gotoPage1() {
    return "footprint-flow";
  }

  public String gotoPage2() {
    return "footprint-flow-1a";
  }

  public String debugClassName() {
    return this.getClass().getSimpleName();
  }

  // Getters and setters ...
}
```

We repeat the same trick as before; we annotate the `FootprintFlow` class with `@PostConstruct`. In the `initialize()` method, we retrieve the object from the flow scope programmatically through the `FacesContext` instance. Note that the parameter name `param3Value` must agree with the value inside the XML definition. The value in the flow scope happens to be the `CarbonFootprint` entity.

You must be wondering why we go to the trouble of retrieving an entity from a scope and setting it as a bean property? It is just an example, and allows the page content designer to use a consistent markup in the pages. The EL `#{footprintFlow.footprint.diesel}` is more comprehensible than `#{flowScope.param3Value.diesel}`.

We shall now move on to the markup.

Page views

The content markup for page views is familiar to us by now. Let's study `sector-flow/sector-flow.xhtml`:

```
<h1>Page <code>sector-flow.xhtml</code></h1>
...
<table class="table table-bordered table-striped">
  <tr>
    <th>Expression</th>
    <th>Value</th>
  </tr>
  ...
  <tr>
    <td>sectorFlow.footprint.applicationId</td>
    <td>#{sectorFlow.footprint.applicationId}</td>
  </tr>
  <tr>
    <td>sectorFlow.footprint</td>
    <td>#{sectorFlow.footprint}</td>
  </tr>
</table>

<h:form prependId="false">
  <div class="form-group">
    <label jsf:for="exampleInputEmail1">
    Email address</label>
    <input type="email" class="form-control"
      jsf:id="exampleInputEmail1" placeholder="Enter email"
      jsf:value="#{flowScope.email}"/>
  </div>
```

```
    <div class="form-group">
      <h:outputLabel for="industryOrSector">Industry or Sector</
h:outputLabel>
      <h:inputText type="text" class="form-control"
id="industryOrSector"
        placeholder="Your industry sector"
        value="#{sectorFlow.footprint.industryOrSector}"/>
    </div>

    <h:commandButton id="nextBtn" styleClass="btn btn-primary btn-lg"
value="Next" action="sector-flow-1a" />
     
    <h:commandButton id="exitFlowBtn" styleClass="btn btn-primary btn-
lg" value="Exit Flow" action="endFlow" />
     
    <h:commandButton id="homeBtn" styleClass="btn btn-primary btn-lg"
value="Home" action="goHome" />
     
    <h:commandButton id="callFootPrintFlowBtn" styleClass="btn btn-
primary btn-lg" value="Call Footprint" action="callFootprintFlow" />
     
    <h:commandButton id="saveBtn" styleClass="btn btn-primary btn-lg"
value="Save Record" action="#{sectorFlow.saveFootprintRecord()}" />
     
  </h:form>
```

The view uses a mix of HTML5 friendly markup and the standard JSF tags. The input text field, exampleInputEmail1 and its associated label remind us about the HTML5 friendly markup. This input control is associated with the flow scope map collection, namely #{flowScope.email}. The answer is yes, we are allowed to write this, but we had better store the data value somewhere in the application!

The input element industryOrSector shows us the JSF standard tags and it is directly associated with the CarbonFootprint entity record.

Let me draw your attention to the command button saveBtn that invokes the action method saveFootprintRecord() in the backing bean. Finally, there is a dedicated command button identified by callFootPrintFlowBtn, which invokes the nested flows. The action callFootprintFlow matches the node in the XML flow definition file for sector-flow.xml exactly.

There is a nextBtn command button that directly navigates to the next view in the flow. The homeBtn command button exits the flow and returns the home page.

The rest of the view shows debuggable output in an HTML Bootstrap style table. The `prependId=false` on the JSF `<h:form>` element informs JSF to avoid sugaring the property HTML identifiers for the controls.

> The JSF Form `prependId` specifies whether or not the `<h:form>` should prepend its ID to its descendant's ID during the `clientId` generation process. The flag becomes relevant when importing or inserting composite components that are forms in an outer form. This value defaults to true.

The following is a screenshot of the start page `sector-flow/sector-flow.xhtml`:

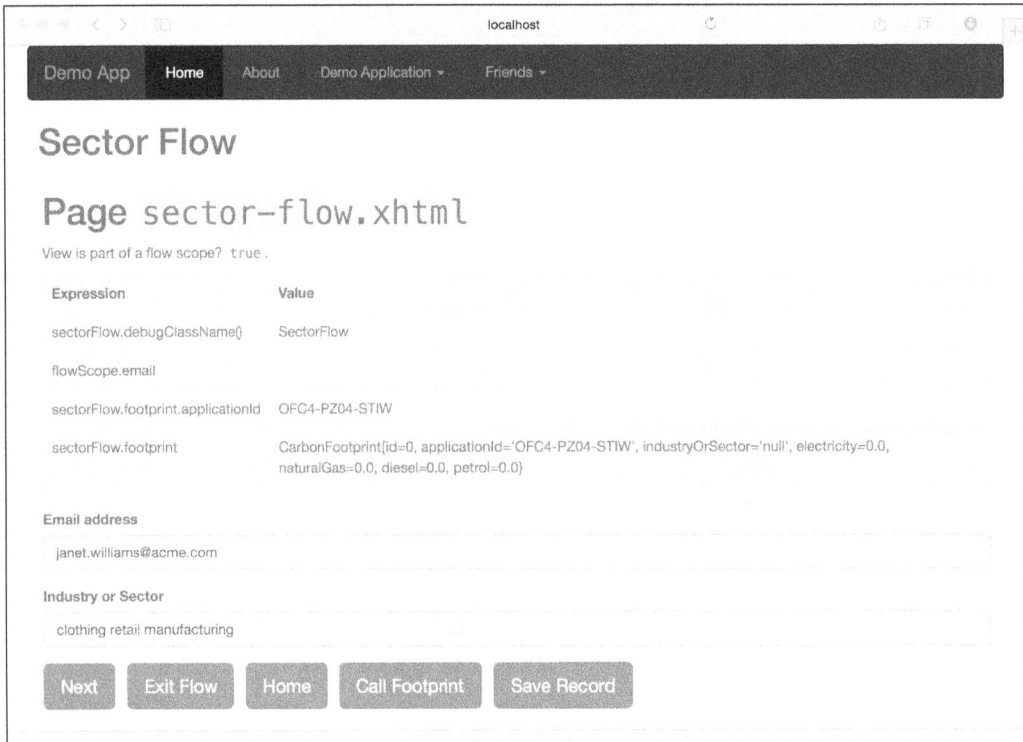

In the source code, we dumped out a set of debuggable values using EL. The project is called `jsf-declarative-form` in the book's source code. You will find a cleaned-out professional version without debuggable output, which is called `jsf-declarative-form-pro`.

The following is a screenshot of the nested flow, `footprint-flow-1a.xhtml`. After navigating to the start page, we hit the **Next** button, entered some data into the form, and save it.

Going back to `SectorFlow`, when we invoke the `SaveBtn` command button, JSF invokes the `saveFootprintRecord()` method. The record is saved to the database and the view `sector-flow-1c.xthml` is displayed as seen in the following screenshot:

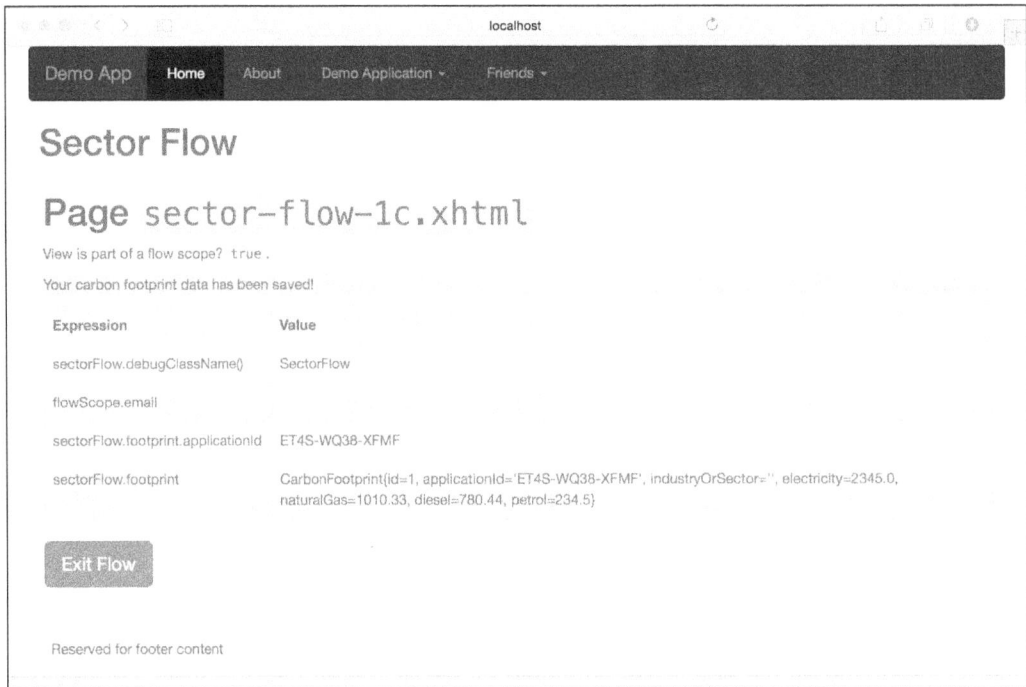

The only parts that remain are the source code for the injected POJO, `UtilityHelper` and the EJB, `CarbonFootprintService`. Unfortunately, we cannot show all the listings in this book.

A real-world example

To wrap up Faces Flows, let's look at adding features to our application. We want our JSF application to have quality and finesse. In the book's source code, you will find these examples under the projects `jsf-product-flow` and `jsf-product-flow-s2`. The first project demonstrates the prototypical design of the concepts. The second project illustrates the improved and cleaned-up digital design with enough quality to present to a business stakeholder.

Ensure the application populates the database

Often, we develop applications that operate against a UAT database for testing. We write code that populates the database with test information, which does not go into production. In a lot of cases, we want to bootstrap our application just to check that the correct schema has been introduced.

Our first thought would be to create an `@ApplicationScoped` POJO with an annotation `@PostConstruct`, and this would solve our bootstrap issue. We can write a `DataPopulator` class with the sole purpose to create data inside a development application. Although we have a firm-wide application instance, we cannot ensure that our bean is invoked after the startup of the web application.

With Java EE, we can use `@javax.ejb.Startup` and `@javax.ejb.Singleton` to start an EJB. The `@Startup` annotation ensures that the EJB container initializes the bean after the application is deployed. The `@Singleton` annotations denotes the session bean that guarantees that there is, at the most, one instance in the application.

The following is the code for the `DataPopulator` bean:

```
package uk.co.xenonique.digital.product.utils;
import javax.annotation.PostConstruct;
import javax.ejb.Singleton;
import javax.ejb.Startup;
import javax.inject.Inject;

@Singleton
@Startup
public class DataPopulator {
  @Inject ExtendedPersistenceLoaderBean loaderBean;

  @PostConstruct
  public void populate() {
    loaderBean.loadData();
  }
}
```

So, in order to populate the application with data, we delegate another bean. The `ExtendedPersistenceLoaderBean` is a CDI bean with a new CDI 1.1 transactional scope. The code for this delegate is as follows:

```
package uk.co.xenonique.digital.product.utils;
import uk.co.xenonique.digital.product.boundary.*;
import uk.co.xenonique.digital.product.entity.*;
```

```
import uk.co.xenonique.digital.product.entity.*;
import javax.annotation.*;
import javax.ejb.*;
import javax.inject.Inject;
import java.io.Serializable;
import java.util.*;

@TransactionAttribute(TransactionAttributeType.REQUIRES_NEW)
@javax.transaction.TransactionScoped
public class ExtendedPersistenceLoaderBean implements Serializable {
  public static final String DEFAULT = "digital";

  @Inject
  UserProfileService service;

  @PostConstruct
  public void init() { /* ... */ }

  @PreDestroy
  public void destroy() { /* ... */ }

  public void loadData() {
    UserRole userRole = new UserRole("user");
    UserRole managerRole = new UserRole("manager");

    List<UserProfile> users = Arrays.asList(
      new UserProfile("user@products.com", DEFAULT, userRole),
      new UserProfile("test@products.com", DEFAULT, userRole),
      new UserProfile("admin@products.com", DEFAULT, managerRole),
    );

    for (UserProfile user: users) {
      service.add(user);
    }
  }
}
```

We annotate the `DataPopulator` bean with `@TransactionScoped`. Whenever we invoke a method on the `@TranscationScoped` bean, the method, the CDI container, will activate a transaction or have one created. A single transaction will be shared amongst many methods on the same bean or shared between other `@TranscactionScoped` beans that may be called. In other words, the transaction context is passed around participating components without requiring the developer to add explicit method arguments to pass around `javax.transaction.TransactionContext` instances.

Going back, we've added another special annotation to our `DataPopulator` bean.

As soon as any method is invoked on this bean, the thread context becomes associated with a brand new transaction, because we annotated the class with `@TransactionAttribute` and pass in an attribute value `TranscationAttributeType.NEW`. This forces the container to create a new transaction, regardless of if there is one existing already. The lifecycle of the transaction scope is the duration of the call to the `loadData()`. The method simply creates a couple of `UserRole` entities in the database, and then it creates user accounts for the login with the `UserProfile` entities.

Finally, the `init()` and `destroy()` methods just print the debug information to the console, and the details are not shown in the extract.

> Even though CDI 1.1 defines a `@javax.inject.Singleton` annotation for CDI beans, this exact launch of a CDI bean is not defined in the specification, because this specification is missing in `@javax.inject.Startup`. Therefore, we must rely on the EJB singleton startup bean. We probably have to wait until CDI 2.0 and Java EE 8 to see this annotation.

Now that we have user profiles and roles, how do we secure a JSF application?

Securing page views and flows

If you want to stay with the standard Java EE libraries, then the specification has the Container Managed Authentication feature. In order to take advantage of this feature, you extend the web deployment descriptor file, `web.xml`, and add a security constraint to your application.

The following is an example of security constraints inside a `web.xml` file:

```
<security-constraint>
  <web-resource-collection>
    <web-resource-name>public</web-resource-name>
    <url-pattern>/products/*</url-pattern>
    <url-pattern>/cart/*</url-pattern>
    <url-pattern>/checkout/*</url-pattern>
    <url-pattern>/promotions/*</url-pattern>
  </web-resource-collection>
  <auth-constraint>
    <role-name>*</role-name>
  </auth-constraint>
  <user-data-constraint>
```

```
      <transport-guarantee>NONE</transport-guarantee>
    </user-data-constraint>
  </security-constraint>

  <security-constraint>
    <web-resource-collection>
      <web-resource-name>admin</web-resource-name>
      <url-pattern>/admin/*</url-pattern>
    </web-resource-collection>
    <auth-constraint>
      <role-name>admin</role-name>
    </auth-constraint>
    <user-data-constraint>
      <transport-guarantee>CONFIDENTIAL</transport-guarantee>
    </user-data-constraint>
  </security-constraint>
```

The first security constraint restricts the products, carts, checkout, and promotion pages of this website to any user. Note the wildcard given as the role name. The second security constraint restricts the admin pages of this website only to users with an admin role.

The <user-data-constraint> element declares whether the page view is accessible with HTTP or HTTPS. It specifies the level of security required. The acceptable values are NONE, INTEGRAL, and CONFIDENTIAL. Setting the transport guarantee to CONFIDENTIAL informs the application server that these pages and resources are only accessible over SSL. The value of INTEGRAL is important in communication when the data sent over the wire from the client or the server should not be changed in any way.

> Tip Java EE 8 Security — a word on the future TODO (note for me to check on updates and progress. See https://javaee8.zeef.com/arjan.tijms). There are not too many alternatives to the standard Java EE security. The other choices are Apache Shiro (http://shiro.apache.org/) or Spring Security (formerly Acegi). It is hoped that Java EE 8 will include a revamp concept and perhaps a separate specification.

Whilst the standard mechanism is fast and easy to add, it is application-server specific. The mechanism applies only to coarse grain resources, and there are no annotations that we can apply to CDI beans. Java EE security requires the configuration of Security Realms, which defines the roles of groups of users. In order to secure a website with fine- grain permission, we have to add multiple roles, which can lead to high complexity.

It is possible to define our own custom security for JSF and the web applications. The advantage of this approach is that we have fine-grained control and it works across the containers. On the other hand, if we ignore the Java EE security standard features, then any home-baked security implementation is unlikely to have been sufficiently proven secure in the wild. Such a component will fail basic penetration testing. At best, custom security works if the requirements are straightforward and there are few demands on complex permissions.

In order to create custom security, we shall define a unique `javax.servlet.ServletFilter`, which protects the access to certain areas of our website. The `LoginAuthenticationFilter` is defined as follows:

```
package uk.co.xenonique.digital.product.security;
import uk.co.xenonique.digital.product.control.LoginController;

import javax.servlet.*;
import javax.servlet.annotation.WebFilter;
import javax.servlet.http.*;
import java.io.IOException;

@WebFilter(urlPatterns={"/protected/*", "/simple/*"})
public class LoginAuthenticationFilter implements Filter {
  private FilterConfig config;

  public void doFilter(ServletRequest req,
    ServletResponse resp, FilterChain chain)
    throws IOException, ServletException
  {
    final HttpServletRequest request =
      (HttpServletRequest)req;
    final HttpServletResponse response =
      (HttpServletResponse)resp;
    if (request.getSession().getAttribute(
      LoginController.LOGIN_KEY) == null) {
      response.sendRedirect(
      request.getContextPath()+LoginController.LOGIN_VIEW);
    } else {
      chain.doFilter(req, resp);
    }
  }

  public void init(FilterConfig config)
  throws ServletException {
    this.config = config;
  }
```

```
    public void destroy() {
        config = null;
    }
}
```

We annotate the class with `@WebFilter` with the URL resources that we want to protect. If a user attempts to access a page under the `/protected/*` and `/simple/*` folder, then the filter, `LoginAuthenticationFilter` is triggered. The servlet container invokes the `doFilter()` method and we check if an HTTP session attribute is defined or not. If the key `LoginController.LOGIN_KEY` does exist, the user is logged into the site, otherwise, the user is redirected to the login page view.

Let's move to the backing bean `LoginController`, which allows a user to log into the website:

```java
package uk.co.xenonique.digital.product.control;
// imports elided...

@Named("loginController") @RequestScoped
public class LoginController {
  public final static String LOGIN_KEY="LOGIN_USERNAME";
  public final static String LOGIN_VIEW="/login.xhtml";

  private String username;
  private String password;

  @Inject UserProfileService userProfileService;

  public boolean isLoggedIn() {
    return FacesContext.getCurrentInstance()
      .getExternalContext().getSessionMap()
      .get(LOGIN_KEY) != null;
  }

  public String login() {
      List<UserProfile> users =
        userProfileService.findById(username);
      if ( users.isEmpty()) {
        throw new IllegalArgumentException("unknown user");
      }
      if ( !users.get(0).getPassword().equals(password)) {
        throw new IllegalArgumentException("invalid password");
      }

      FacesContext.getCurrentInstance().getExternalContext()
```

```
        .getSessionMap().put(LOGIN_KEY, username);
      return "/protected/index?faces-redirect=true";
  }

  public String logout() {
    FacesContext.getCurrentInstance().getExternalContext()
      .getSessionMap().remove(LOGIN_KEY);
    return "/index?faces-redirect=true";
  }

  // Getters and setter omitted ...
}
```

The `LoginController` backing bean accepts two form-based parameters: the username and a password. It relies on the injected `UserProfileService` to find a `UserProfile` record by the username. Inside the `login()` method, a user is allowed to log in if the password parameter matches the entity record. The method adds the username to the HTTP session under the key, `LOGIN_KEY`.

There are a couple of helpful methods. The `logout()` method removes the login key from the HTTP session key. The `isLoggedIn()` method checks if a user has logged in or not.

The servlet filter only handles the direct navigation resources, servlets, filters, and paths. We need another protector for the JSF views, because `LoginAuthenticationFilter` is not enough.

The following is the code for a backing bean controller called `LoginViewAuthenticator`:

```
package uk.co.xenonique.digital.product.security;
import javax.faces.application.NavigationHandler;
// other imports elided...

@Named("loginViewAuthenticator") @ApplicationScoped
public class LoginViewAuthenticator {
  // ...

  public void check() {
    FacesContext facesContext = FacesContext.getCurrentInstance();
    HttpSession session = (HttpSession)
      facesContext.getExternalContext().getSession(true);
    String currentUser = (String)session.getAttribute(
      LoginController.LOGIN_KEY);
    if (currentUser == null || currentUser.length() == 0) {
```

```
        NavigationHandler navigationHandler =
          facesContext.getApplication().getNavigationHandler();
        navigationHandler.handleNavigation(
          facesContext, null, LoginController.LOGIN_VIEW);
      }
    }
  }
```

The class `LoginViewAuthenticator` has a `check()` method that performs a check. We retrieve the known key `LOGIN_KEY` from the HTTP session. Note that we can access parts of the Java Servlet API through a chained call to the `getExternalContext()` method on `FacesContext`. We retrieve the `HttpSession` instance or create one and then check for the associated value. If the user is not logged in, then we change the destination of the current `NavigationHandler`. The navigation handler in JSF is an implementation-defined type that carries the target outcome string during a Faces request-and-response interaction.

We use `LoginViewAuthenticator` in a page view to restrict access:

```
<ui:composition template="/basic_layout.xhtml">
  <ui:define name="mainContent">
    <f:metadata>
      <f:event type="preRenderView"
        listener="#{loginViewAuthenticator.check}" />
    </f:metadata>

    <div class="login-username-box  pull-right">
      <b>#{sessionScope['LOGIN_USERNAME']}</b>
    </div>
    <h1> JSF Protected View </h1>

    <!-- ... -->
</ui:composition>
```

For the page view `/protected/index.html`, we insert a pre-render view event using the `<f:metadata>` section. The `<f:event>` element invokes the `check()` method of the `LoginViewAuthenticator` bean.

In the project, we also secured the Faces Flow by adding the same stanza to the page view `/simple.xhtml`. This view is the start page and, therefore, adding the pre-render view event here effectively restricts access to the flow. The `LoginViewAuthenticator` bean ensures that unknown website users are redirected to the `/login.xhtml` view.

Resource Library Contracts

JSF 2.2, as a part of Java EE 7, introduced the ability to theme and style websites under a facility known as the Resource Library Contracts. The idea of contracts is about reusing Facelets dynamically at runtime. It is possible now with contracts to switch between resources without having to redeploy an application. Contracts can also be declared statically for pages that match a URL pattern.

The specification reserves a specially named folder called `/contracts` as the parent folder for the Resource Library Contracts. This folder is the default one. If you already have a folder named as this view, then you will have to refactor by name, unfortunately.

There is another default location, `META-INF/contracts`, on the classpath for JARs. This location allows the resource library contracts to be packaged as JAR for distribution to the third-party customers.

Inside the `/contracts` folder, a developer can define named contracts (or themes). You can only create folders inside the location folder `/contract` or (`/META-INF/contracts`), and each folder represents a named contract. In the specification, a contract has a declared template. Each contract may define resources such as images, CSS, JavaScript files, and other content files.

There is a project called `jsf-resource-library-contracts` in the book's source distribution, and in there you will see the following files laid out:

```
/src/main/webapp/contracts/
/src/main/webapp/contracts/default/
/src/main/webapp/contracts/default/template.xhtml
/src/main/webapp/contracts/default/styles/app.css
/src/main/webapp/contracts/default/images/
/src/main/webapp/contracts/victoria/
/src/main/webapp/contracts/victoria/template.xhtml
/src/main/webapp/contracts/victoria/styles/app.css
/src/main/webapp/contracts/victoria/images/
```

There are two Resource Library Contracts: `default` and `victoria`. These folders share the same resources although they do not have to. The two `template.xhtml` files are UI composition files that lay out the page view. The two `app.css` files are CSS.

A resource contract must have at least one UI composition template, which is called a declared template in the specification. In each contract folder, the file `template.xhtml` is a declared template. Inside each template file that the specification mentions, any `<ui:insert>` tags are known as declared insertion points. The term declared resources means the collection of images, CSS and JavaScript, and other resources.

Inside the `default/template.xhtml` file, we have an important link to the reference styles sheet:

```
<h:head>
  <!-- ...-->
  <link href="#{request.contextPath}/contracts/default/
    styles/app.css" rel="stylesheet"/>
</h:head>
```

Likewise, in the `victoria/template.xhtml`, we have a link to the alternative style sheet:

```
<link href="#{request.contextPath}/contracts/victoria/
    styles/app.css" rel="stylesheet"/>
```

In each resource contract, we can vary the properties of shared CSS selectors in the CSS files in order to produce alternate themes. The following is an extract of `default/styles/app.css`:

```
.fashion-headline {
    color: #ff4227;
    font-family: Consolas;
    font-style: italic;
    font-size: 22pt;
    margin: 30px 10px;
    padding: 15px 25px;
    border: 2px solid #8b200c;
    border-radius: 15px;
}
```

And this is similar to `victoria/styles/app.css`:

```
.fashion-headline {
    color: #22ff1e;
    font-family: Verdana, sans-serif;
    font-weight: bold;
    font-size: 20pt;
    margin: 30px 10px;
    padding: 15px 25px;
    border: 2px solid #31238b;
    border-radius: 15px;
}
```

There is a difference of color, font family, size, and style.

In order to configure the resource contracts in static usage from the matching URL pattern, we declare the titles in the Faces configuration file, `faces-config.xml`. JSF 2.2 introduces a new `<resource-library-contracts>` element. Each contract is associated with a name and one or more URL patterns.

Static Resource Library Contract references

In our example project, we should have a Faces configuration file that has the following code:

```
<?xml version="1.0" encoding="UTF-8"?>
<faces-config ... version="2.2">
  <application>
    <resource-library-contracts>
      <contract-mapping>
        <url-pattern>/corporate/*</url-pattern>
        <contracts>victoria</contracts>
      </contract-mapping>

      <contract-mapping>
        <url-pattern>*</url-pattern>
        <contracts>default</contracts>
      </contract-mapping>
    </resource-library-contracts>
  </application>
</faces-config>
```

The `<contract-mapping>` element defines two contracts: `default` and `victoria`. The order of the contracts is important for processing. For the entire website, the `default` contract is active whereas the `victoria` contract is active only for the page view underneath the `/corporate/` URL. A contract mapping may have more than one URL pattern.

We can write a page view to trigger this contract statically. The following is an extract of the page view, `/corporate/index.xhtml`:

```
<!DOCTYPE html>
<html... >
  <f:view >
    <ui:composition template="/template.xhtml">
      <ui:define name="mainContent">
        <!-- ... -->
        <p>This is <code>/corporate/index.xhtml</code></p>

        <p class="fashion-headline">
```

```
      This is a fashion statement!</p>

      <a class="btn btn-info"
        href="#{request.contextPath}/index.xhtml">Go Home</a>
      <!-- ... -->
    </ui:define> <!--name="mainContent" -->
  </ui:composition>
 </f:view>
</html>
```

Based on the previous resource library contract definitions in `faces-config.xml`, the paragraph with the CSS class, fashion-headline should be green in color. Notice how JSF searches for and finds the `/template.xhtml` references, which lie in the corporate folder. So defining Resources Library Contracts that can be switched statically is a good feature to have, but what if we wanted to change the contract on the fly? We can achieve this goal and we'll learn how in the next section.

Dynamic Resource Library Contract references

If you surround the UI composition with static reference with an `f:view` element, as we did in the page view, then we can add another new attribute called contracts. This attribute accepts a String expression that references a resource contract by name.

The following is an extract of this home page view `/index.xhtml`:

```
<!DOCTYPE html>
<html ...>
  <f:view contracts="#{fashionSelector.theme}">
    <ui:composition template="/template.xhtml">
      <ui:define name="mainContent">
        <!-- ... -->
        <p> This is <code>/index.xhtml</code>. </p>

        <p class="fashion-headline">
          This is a fashion statement!</p>

        <!-- ... -->
        <div class="content-wrapper">
          <h:form>
            <div class="form-group">
              <label for="theme">Disabled select menu</label>
              <h:selectOneRadio id="theme"
                value="#{fashionSelector.theme}"
```

```
                    styleClass="form-control peter-radio-box"
                    required="true" layout="lineDirection">
                <f:selectItem itemValue="default" itemLabel="Default"/>
                <f:selectItem itemValue="victoria"
itemLabel="Victoria"/>
                </h:selectOneRadio>
              </div>
              <h:commandButton styleClass="btn btn-primary"
                action="#{fashionSelector.changeTheme()}"
                value="Change Theme" />
            </h:form>
          </div>
        </ui:define> <!--name="mainContent" -->
      </ui:composition>
    </f:view>
  </html>
```

The #{fashionSelector.theme} controller references a getter for a backing bean, which we will see in a moment. The value of the expression sets the chosen resource library contract. We make use of the CSS paragraph in order to visually see the contract template in action. In order to change the contract, we employ a form with the radio selection element. The <f:selectItem> tag defines the contract name.

Our backing bean FashionSelector is a controller with one action method:

```
package uk.co.xenonique.digital.flows.control;
import javax.enterprise.context.SessionScoped;
import javax.inject.Named;
import java.io.Serializable;

@Named
@SessionScoped
public class FashionSelector implements Serializable {
  private String theme = "default";

  public String changeTheme() {
    return "/index?faces-redirect=true";
  }

  // Getters and setters omitted
}
```

We annotate the controller as a @SessionScoped bean in order to preserve the contract change across the many request-response cycles.

The resource library contracts also happily function with Faces Flows. The technique of using either static URL patterns or the dynamic selector of the template equals the flows. In the book's source, you will find more demonstrations and source code. In fact, the page view /digitalFlow/digitalFlow.xhtml looks exactly as follows:

```
<html ...>
  <f:view contracts="#{fashionSelector.theme}">
    <ui:composition template="/template.xhtml">
    ... </u:compoition>
  </f:view>
</html>
```

As you can see, in principle, there is no difference at all.

Advice for flows

Faces Flows are a very useful feature in JSF 2.2, because they allow developers and designers to put together components that achieve customer (or user centric) goals. They also allow an architect to define groups of page views and controllers into specific business defined components. If the designer is careful, they can be linked together efficiently and decoupled from dependencies in meaningful strategies. The following points should be kept in mind while using Faces Flows:

- **Start small**: Design a Faces Flow that achieves one responsibility and one goal. Don't try to build the entire process in a single flow.

- **Pass entities and meaning types**: Implement Faces Flows that accept data entities and transfer objects.

- **Compose flows together**: Group together common flows that achieve a similar goal. In a checkout process, you may have a flow dedicated to the shipping address and a flow responsible for payments. These two flows can be invoked by a master flow that handles the entire process.

- **Encapsulate flows**: Encapsulate your flow as much as possible, so that it is self-sufficient.

- **Persist your user's data**: when a customer completes a task, ensure that user data is saved at the determined exit points.

Resist the temptation of building the perfect workflow. Instead, I recommend that you design Faces Flow with change at the back of your mind.

In modern digital teams building websites and applications, the most important person is the UX designer. Often, after several rounds of user-centric testing, you might find the page design and information architecture of the site changing and going back and forth over weeks or even months. By building small, goal-oriented Faces Flow components, you will protect the developer team from the constant changes driven by the UX design team. Design your flows not for reuse, but for replacement.

Summary

In this chapter, we examined the poster child of the JSF 2.2 release: Faces Flows. We learned about flow definitions and lifecycles. We covered ground with implicit navigation and created POJO using the `@FlowScoped` scope. We drilled down into the terminology of flow processes and we studied declarative and nested flows. We saw how we can pass parameters from one flow to another through invocation.

We also learned how to add finesse to our digital application by handling expired views. Then we added security around page views and Resource Library Contracts to our new abilities. We understood how contracts allow the developer to add themes and styles to our JSF application. Another thing that we learned is that the Resource Library Contracts may be driven by static declaration or controlled by backing beans.

In the next chapter, we will step away from JSF and delve into JavaScript programming and library framework.

Exercises

1. Verify that flow-scoped beans are unique with multiple web browsers and tab frames. Modify the `debugClassName()` method in the first flow class, `DigitalFlow` to report the value of `java.lang.System.identityHashCode()` as well as the class name. What is the result?

2. Everyone practically knows how to make a simple breakfast of scrambled eggs; write down the steps for doing so. What processes do you need? What inputs do you need? We know the results of the tasks; are there other outputs?

3. Develop a simple Faces Flow application that takes contact details from a user. Think of the number of properties that you will need. Do you need all of them? (Hint: Name, address, e-mail, and telephone number will do for now.)

4. Take the contact details Faces Flow application from the previous question and now persist that entity record data to a database.

5. Now split the contact detail single flow application into separate flows. Set up the address part as a nested flow. (Hint: You can pass the entity record from one flow to another.)

6. In the contact details application, how can we allow the customer to retrieve entities? Develop the Faces application so that he or she can save the data temporarily. (Hint: maybe the customer requires a temporary application ID, so add one to the contact details entity.)

7. At this point, we will take the contact application and copy it to a new project. We will rebrand the project as `welcome-new-bank-customer`. In the retail banking industry, this business process is called `on-boarding`. You will need one or two nested flows. One flow accepts the person's work status: their salary, their job title, and, obviously, an occupation. If you feel confident, perhaps you can add a work address as another flow, and if you feel even stronger, add the national insurance number and tax records. With a more complicated project, consider, what would happen if it were possible to re-order the flows? How well is your design encapsulated? Can the developers easily rearrange the flows to fit the UX challenges?

8. Given the contact details/banking onboarding application up to now, you should have many database records of contacts. Write another Faces Flow in the same web application that allows a trusted member of staff, a case worker, to amend and delete customer records. In a real business, such an employee sits behind the system and approves each onboarding application request one by one. You will need to write the HTTP login form for security and protect the non-public page views.

7
Progressive JavaScript Frameworks and Modules

"If you're a runner and you run in a race, you might lose. If you don't run, you're guaranteed to lose."

Reverend Jesse Jackson

In the contemporary way of building a website, there is no escape from the language of JavaScript because it is a de facto standard of modern web browsers. JavaScript is either a pleasure or major inconvenience for developers. If you write or intend to build digital web applications for a customer, there is almost no escape from the knowledge of HTML5, CSS, and JavaScript. Fortunately, you do not need to be an expert in JavaScript in order to be productive because there are many frameworks that help you and you can leverage these ideas. Essentially, where JavaScript is concerned, you need to know and catch up with the modern digital best practices.

While JavaScript is a very relevant topic for the digital websites, this chapter cannot teach you everything that you need to know. Instead, I will endeavor to point you in the correct direction and provide you with an oversight, and you should definitely extend your knowledge with further resources.

We will start with the fundamental JavaScript programming and an idea of the language. We will then dive straight into programming with the JavaScript objects. Afterwards, we will look at a few of the major frameworks in the world of JavaScript.

JavaScript essentials

JavaScript is a respected programming language by itself. It has a standard called ECMAScript (http://www.ecmascript.org/) and is accepted as a ratified standard by the W3C. The language is a part of the trinity of the fundamental standard web technologies: HTML5, CSS, and JavaScript. That said, what is JavaScript? It is a prototype dynamically typed scripting language with object types and enclosed scoped function blocks. In JavaScript, every type is strictly an object. The JavaScript support functions as a first-class citizen and rules on a and supports the declaration of functions that are assigned to an associated lexically scoped variable, property, or entity. JavaScript has a support for strings, integers, floating point numbers, and prototypes. JavaScript is essentially a property and prototypical language. It has a lexical support of object-based programming through scopes and closures. The widespread use of the language does not explicitly have reserved keywords and it structures out of the support object-oriented inheritance. Through clever programming and prototypes, developers can replicate the object class inheritance.

> **What is the base level standard JavaScript that I should learn?**
>
> This chapter looks at JavaScript 1.5, which is ECMA Script Edition 3. This version of the language works in all the major web browsers: Firefox, Chrome, Safari, and Internet Explorer. The upcoming JavaScript ECMA 6 will have support for object-oriented programming (http://es6-features.org/).

JavaScript is a popular language on the client side of a normal Java web application. You should be aware that JavaScript can also operate on the server side through an implementation such as Node.js or Nashorn. These topics are, however, out of the scope for this chapter.

Creating objects

Let's wade into JavaScript on the client side. What is JavaScript programming with an object that you, as a digital developer, can write? Here is one answer—an HTML5 web page with an embedded script that creates a contact detail, as follows:

```
<!DOCTYPE html>
<html lang="en">
  <body>
    <script>
      var contact = new Object();
      contact.gender = 'female';
      contact.firstName = 'Anne';
      contact.lastName = 'Jackson';
```

```
      contact.age = 28;
      contact.occupation = 'Software Developer'
      contact.getFullName = function() {
        return contact.firstName + " " + contact.lastName;
      }
      console.log(contact);
    </script>
  </body>
</html>
```

This simple program creates a contact detail with properties. The JavaScript properties may be integer, numerical numbers: number, or Boolean or String types. A JavaScript object may also define the methods as in the case of getFullName(). For a stock blue-collar Classic Java developer, this syntax of defining a property from a function looks peculiar; however, the functions are first-class citizens of many languages. The JavaScript functions that define an object are called methods.

In the modern JavaScript writing practices, you will learn to recognize the functions written similarly in this vein, which is the reverse of the Java notation. Here is a third order polynomial function from mathematics in JavaScript:

```
var polynomial = function(x1,x2,x3) {
    return (2 * x1 * x1 * x1) - ( 3 * x2 * x2 )
        + 4 * x3 + 5;
}

console.log("The answer is: " + polynomial(1.5,2.0,3.75) );
```

This variable defines a JavaScript function called polynomial(), which accepts three number type arguments. It also returns a Number type. JavaScript is a dynamically typed language and thus, there is no static typing.

The console log

The console log is a standard object that is a part of the modern web browsers: Firefox, Chrome, Opera, Safari, and Internet Explorer. It is usually available from the menu that is reserved for the debugging. Formerly, the console object was not completely supported for browsers.

Thankfully, we will not be writing the following conditional code in 2016:

```
if ( window.console && window.console.log ) {
  // console is available
}
```

Let's move to the object constructors. Allow me to provide a final note of advice about writing a console log: use it only in the development code. Developers have been forgotten to remove the console log output from production code, which eventually led to crash in a certain web browser, ruining the digital customer's journey. Take advantage of a JavaScript framework such as jQuery, RequireJS, or Dojo, which abstracts away the console log in a library function.

If you haven't eventually done so, I strongly recommend that you download the Chrome Developer and Web Developer tools for either the Google Chrome or Firefox web browsers.

Writing JavaScript object constructors

The JavaScript language consists of a limited variety of primitive types in comparison. Loosely, these primitives are String, Number, Boolean, Array, and Object. These can be created using native JavaScript object constructors: `String()`, `Number()`, `Boolean()`, `Array()`, and `Object()`.

Here is an illustration of how to use these native constructors:

```
var message = new String('Digital');
var statusFlag = new Boolean(true);
var itemPrice= new Number(1199.95);
var names = new Array();
names[0] = 'Emkala';
names[1] = 'Sharon';
names[2] = 'Timothy';
console.log(message);  // Digital
console.log(statusFlag); // true
console.log(itemPrice); // 1199.95
console.log(names); // Object (Surprise ;-)
```

Obviously, it is rare to assign the String, Boolean, and Number types from the native constructors. However, note the use of the Array native constructor. In JavaScript, arrays are treated as objects. They are enumerated from the index zero like most computer languages. To find the size of the array, invoke the implicit length property (`name.length`).

To establish the JavaScript essentials, we can finesse the earlier example and take advantage of the ability of the functions to introduce their own scope, as follows:

```
var ContactDetail = function(
  gender, firstName, lastName, age, occupation )
{
  this.gender = gender;
```

```
    this.firstName = firstName;
    this.lastName = lastName;
    this.age = age;
    this.occupation = occupation
    this.getFullName = function() {
      return contact.firstName + " " + contact.lastName;
    }
     return this;
  }

  var anne = new ContactDetail(
    'female', 'Anne', 'Jackson', 28, 'Software Developer');

  console.log(anne.female);
  console.log(anne.firstName);
  console.log(anne.lastName);
```

There are a few things going on with this second example. First, we will assign a function type to the `ContactDetail` variable. This function is actually a constructor for a new object type named by the variable name. In this constructor, there is a special `this` reference variable that is associated with the function scope at this level. When the reference is returned, it becomes the object instance. In the function, we are allowed to define the other functions that are associated with the object, such as `getFullName()`. This is how object-based programming works in modern JavaScript.

We will use this new object type constructor to declare a contact detail in the variable called `anne`. For Java regular programmers, this syntax might look very weird at first, but this JavaScript is completely different to Java and is seriously accepted as a programming language in its own right. A scope has practical uses in defining the object modules, which I showed in the first chapter of this book.

The JavaScript property notations

There are two fundamental ways to access the JavaScript properties in a type. The first way is pretty familiar to all Java programmers. It is the dot notation. The second way is called the bracket notation, which looks like a map or dictionary association in the languages other than Java. The bracket notation is equivalent to the dot notation and has its uses.

Examine the following code, which demonstrates another way to create a JavaScript object. Remember that JavaScript is a dynamically typed language.

```
  var product = {
    'title': 'Java EE Developer Handbook',
    'price': 38.75,
```

```
    'author': 'Peter A. Pilgrim'
};

console.log( product.name );
console.log( product['name']);

product.price = 34.50;
product['price'] = 34.50;

product.subject = 'Enterprise Java';
console.log(product['price']);

product.pi = function() { return 3.14159; };
console.log(product.pi());
```

Did you spot the introduction of a new property to the object called subject and also a method function? Of course, I am promoting the title of my first technical book here, but that is beside the point. JavaScript allows programmers to be quite flexible with object internals and properties. The declaration of the object product should ring some bells because it is remarkable how similar this declaration is to the de facto **JavaScript Object Notation (JSON)** standard. The open curly bracket notation is a way to define an object with the property key and values.

Dealing with a null and undefined reference pointer

Professor Charles Antony Richard Hoare (Tony Hoare) developed the classic computer science algorithm called **QuickSort**, but he also regretted when he said that it was also the invention of a billion dollar mistake: the dreaded null reference pointer. Personally, I would have thought that someone else would have stumbled on such an obvious workaround and quick fit for a general problem.

JavaScript deals with a null reference as a sentinel and also features undefined. The following JavaScript extract attempts to print the null reference in a `test` object:

```
var testObject = { item: null };
console.log(testObject.item);   // prints out 'null'.
```

The null value tells you that the object type thing is defined but is not yet available. The undefined value informs the developer that something is missing. Remember that JavaScript is a dynamic language and therefore, it is entirely possible to navigate across the object graph and not find the object type that your team thought was placed there.

In JavaScript, if you need to test for a null value, you must use the triple equal operator (===), as follows:

```
var testbject = null;
console.log(testObject == null);   // Wrong!
console.log(testObject === null);  // Correct.
```

Writing about equivalence, how do we know when two objects are equivalent in JavaScript?

The JavaScript truth

In JavaScript, the conditional expression is false, if it matches one of the Set of Empty Values: `false`, `0`, `-0`, `null`, empty string (`''`), NaN, or `undefined`. A value evaluates to the JavaScript truth in a conditional expression, if and only if the value does not match any of the elements in the Empty Values set. Every other value that does match any of the elements is an empty value set that evaluates to JavaScript true.

The following JavaScript all evaluates to false:

```
console.log(Boolean(0));
console.log(Boolean(-0));
console.log(Boolean(''));
console.log(Boolean(null));
console.log(Boolean(false));
console.log(Boolean(undefined));
console.log(Boolean(Number.NAN));
```

Here, we use the `Boolean` constructor with the new keyword to instantiate a type directly. These statements evaluate to true:

```
console.log(Boolean(1));
console.log(Boolean(-1));
console.log(Boolean('runner'));
console.log(Boolean(true));
console.log(Boolean(1234567);
console.log(Boolean(new Array());
```

Runtime type information

In order to find out the runtime information of the JavaScript values, you can apply the `typeof` operator. This permits the programmer to write a specialist code in order to check the arguments to a function. Here is an example of the `typeof` interrogation:

```
console.log(typeof true); // Prints 'boolean'.
console.log(typeof 'magic'); // Prints 'string'.
console.log(typeof 3.141596527); // Prints 'number'.
```

JavaScript has some other quirks, if you use the native constructors:

```
console.log(typeof new Boolean(true)); // Prints 'object'.
console.log(typeof new String('MAGIC')); // Prints 'object'.
console.log(typeof new Number(3.141596527)); // Prints 'object'.
```

This is surprising! Here is the evidence where you can see why digital web developers are driven mad because of the inconsistency in the language, standards, and implementations of these standards.

The JavaScript functions

In modern JavaScript, you will see a lot of quasi-functional programming in comparison to Classic Java (Java before version 8 and Lambda expressions). The functions are the first-class citizens. You can supply functions as parameters to the functions. You can also return a function type from a function. How does passing a function as a parameter to a method help? In JavaScript, you can write anonymous functions without a name. You can take advantage of passing around the blocks of code to the library functions. This style is the basis of functional programming. Instead of coding imperatively, we can write concise code and inline, which is almost declarative.

Here is an anonymous function example:

```
var outside = function (yourIn) {
  yourIn(); // Invokes the supplied function.
}

outside( function () {
  console.log('inside');
});
```

The `outside()` function accepts an anonymous `yourIn()` function, as a single argument. Now inside the `outside()` function, it immediately invokes the argument `yourIn`, which is the supplied anonymously defined function. This is a powerful technique.

JavaScript has one other trick that lends itself to the declaration of modules, especially when it is combined with the functional object scopes. It is possible to define a function and invoke it inline and directly. Consider this example:

```
var initializeGui = function() {
  console.log("start up the client side GUI...");
} ();
```

In the preceding code, we defined a variable called `initializeGui` and assigned it an anonymous function. The key to the definition is the final round brackets at the end of the method statement. JavaScript immediately invokes the function at the precise location where the definition is parsed. Here, we are pretending to initialize a client side GUI by writing to the console.

You can also pass the parameters to an inlined function, as follows:

```
var initializeGui2 = function(msg,value) {
  console.log("start up GUI..."+msg+","+value);
} ( 'Spirits in the Sky', 1973 );
```

This preceding code demonstrates that the parameters are passed from the outside global scope to the invoked function.

In fact, we can get rid of the variable `initializeGui2` and create a self-invocation anonymous function:

```
(function(msg,value) {
  console.log("start up GUI..."+msg+","+value);
})( 'Spirits in the Sky', 1973 );
```

This kind of code is fairly typical and seen in the popular JavaScript frameworks and applications.

In the function definition, we will take advantage of the JavaScript scope. See *Chapter 1, Digital Java EE 7* for an earlier explanation on the module namespace technique.

I think I will stop here. There is a tremendous variety and a deeper knowledge track to the modern JavaScript programming than I can write about here. I recommend that you invest in other introductory programming books such as Douglas Crockford's excellent *JavaScript: The Good Parts* and also Packt Publishing's *Object-Oriented JavaScript* by authors *Stoyan Stefanov* and *Kumar Chetan Sharma*.

> Steve Kwan has written an excellent example of the Module Pattern in JavaScript; you might want to investigate his best practices at `https://github.com/stevekwan/best-practices/blob/master/javascript/best-practices.md`.

Let's look at a very important programming framework for JavaScript, jQuery.

Introducing the jQuery framework

jQuery (`http://learn.jquery.com/`) is a cross-platform JavaScript framework for client-side web application development. It is a survivor from the original AJAX craze from 2004 and 2005, where it was and still is competing with Prototype (`http://prototypejs.org/`) and Scriptaculous (`http://script.aculo.us/`). jQuery has been called the equivalent of what the Java Collections framework did for the Java programming language. According to Wikipedia, jQuery is 70 percent of the 10,000 most visited websites in the world. In other words, it is the first JavaScript framework that really caught the attention of the developers and caused them to rethink the furthest capabilities of the underlying language. jQuery is free and provided under the MIT open source license.

jQuery was built to make the manipulation of the **Document Object Model** (**DOM**) easier and apply CSS to the HTML elements. In jQuery, there is a secret sauce called Sizzle, which is a selector engine that traverses over the DOM. The engine combines the flexibility of selection, a respect for functional programming, and callback to allow an engineer to comfortably write JavaScript that leverages the underlying HTML and CSS elements in a web page.

Including jQuery in a JSF application

You can include the jQuery JavaScript library in your page view. In JSF, the folder would be under the `src/main/webapp/resources/` folder:

```
<!DOCTYPE html>
<html xmlns="http://www.w3.org/1999/xhtml"... >
  ...
  <script src="#{request.contextPath}
    /resources/javascripts/jquery-2.1.0.min.js"></script>
  <script src="#{request.contextPath}
    /resources/app/main.js"></script>
  ...
</html>
```

We will use the expression language, #{request.contextPath}, in order to provide location independence. Good digital developers will use the minified JavaScript for performance and to improve their business SEO chances!

jQuery ready function callbacks

The jQuery framework repurposes the $ symbol in the global head scope exclusively for our use. (The dollar symbol is an alias for the jQuery object instance and it is obviously short.) Through clever programming, which is out of the scope of this book, jQuery accepts a parameter that represents an HTML DOM object. A jQuery entry point is the ready() method, which accepts a function object type argument.

This argument can be an anonymous or a named function as we will demonstrate here to initialize a fictional website:

```
$( document ).ready(function() {
   // Write your code here.
   console.log("this page view is starting up!");
 MyNamespace.MyModule1.init();
 MyNamespace.MyModule2.init();
});
```

When jQuery invokes the anonymous function, the framework can make certain guarantees that the browser has been initialized, the images have all been downloaded, the event stack is set to go, and the other proprietary features of certain web clients have been finished. In the preceding example, we will initialize the other JavaScript libraries in the module pattern and log to the console:

```
console.log( $ === jQuery );   // true
```

The $(document) expression can be generalized to the following:

```
$( <expression-selector> )
```

The expression-selector stanza can be a CSS selector expression or an HTML DOM element. Here are some example selectors:

```
var divs1 = $('div');
var divs2 = jQuery('div');
var win1  = $( window );

var redBtn  = $( "#redButton" );
var offerSubmitBtn = $( "#offerSubmitBtn" );

var navigationControl  = $( ".navControls" );
var footerArea = $( ".footerArea  div" );
```

The element selectors that start with a hash character (#) are equivalent to the DOM HTML API call, getElementById(), which means that they might return the element or not. The #offerSubmitBtn selector retrieves an element that is specified with the ID attribute:

```
<h:commandButton value="Apply Now!"
    id="offerSubmitButton"
    action="#{longTermProvider.applyForCredit}"/>
```

jQuery offers very powerful class selectors, which retrieve a collection of the HTML elements. The $('div') selector retrieves all of the HTML div elements in the document and page views. Likewise, the $('div') class selector retrieves all the HTML anchor elements. As some might say, knowledge is power! We can combine the CSS class selectors to turn down and fine tune the elements that we want to manipulate. The $(".footerArea div") selector restricts the HTML div elements in the footer area.

Acting on the jQuery selectors

jQuery allows a digital developer to access the HTML DOM elements on the web page. So how do you act on these powerful selectors? The API features many callback methods that accept a function type parameter. Let's take a look at such a method called click(), which fires an event when the particular HTML element is pressed and depressed.

Here is the code for the red button that we saw earlier:

```
$( document ).ready(function() {
  $( "#redButton" ).click(function( event ) {
      alert( "You pressed the red button!" );
  });
});
```

When the user clicks on the red button, jQuery handles the DOM event and invokes the anonymous function that is associated to the jQuery matched selector. The user sees the alert dialog. It does not stop there. Here is some code to make the red button fade out of the view:

```
$( document ).ready(function() {
  $( "#redButton" ).click(function( event ) {
    $( "#redButton").animate(
      {
        'opacity':'0.0'
      }, 250);
  });
}
```

This is an example of the jQuery animation capability. The `animate()` method accepts two arguments: the key and value for the animation properties and a duration time. Here we will specify the opacity of the button but we can set other properties such as the width or height of the element, and even three-dimensional transformations of your target web clients will be served against the CSS3 confirmed web browsers only. The duration time is measured in milliseconds.

If this was a code that is designed to be reused and I wanted a clean modular code for a team of interface developers, here is how I would tidy up the code and avoid embarrassment:

```
var DigitalJavaEE7 = DigitalJavaEE7 || {};

DigitalJavaEE7.RedModule = function($) {
  var init = function() {
    $( document ).ready(function() {
      var redButton = $( "#redButton" )
      redButton.click(function( event ) {
        redButton.animate({'opacity':'0.0'}, 250);
      });
    }
  };

  var performOtherOWork = function() {
    console.log("other animation stuff.")
    /* ... */
  };

  var oPublic = {
      init: init,
      performOtherWork: performOtherWork
  };

  return oPublic;
}(jQuery);
```

Using the popular module pattern, I pushed the initialized code for jQuery into a `RedModule` module with the `DigitalJavaEE7` namespace. In the `init()` function of this module, I optimized the CSS selector in one call to a `redButton` variable. It turns out that jQuery works hard at interpreting the CSS selector to a group of potential HTML DOM elements. So, we will avoid asking the framework to do this search of the DOM twice. Code is essentially the same, but more concise and still comprehensible.

Manipulating the DOM elements

In the previous section, you learned how to select the DOM elements with jQuery. Group elements can be retrieved with the jQuery selectors. Using the manipulation part of the API, we will add and remove the class styles to the elements, insert the elements before and after a component, and replace the content of the elements. There are lots of calls to learn; we will review a small set here.

In order to demonstrate how we can manipulate the DOM elements, let's define two HTML button elements. We will apply a style of the red color and the other will be blue. Here is the code:

```
$( document ).ready(function() {
  var redButton = $( "#redButton" )
  var blueButton = $( "#blueButton" )
  var textArea = $( "#messageArea" )
  redButton.click(function( event ) {
    textArea.addClass('.text-danger');
    textArea.html('Danger Will, watch out!');
  });

  blueButton.click(function( event ) {
    textArea.removeClass('.text-danger');
    textArea.html('Everthing is fine now.');
  });
}
```

We will set up the anonymous functions to add a Bootstrap class, text-danger, to messageArea, which you can rightly assume is a reserved div element for a textual output. The addClass() method appends a style class to the matching elements. We will add the style to the text area with the callback for the redButton element. The second anonymous function for blueButton deletes the class from the element. Both the functions will change the message in the display area.

The html() method is dual purpose. It is overloaded in the jQuery framework. When html() is called with a single argument, it replaces the contents of the element. We will use the html() method to change the text in the message area. If the method is called with no arguments, it returns the element's content. There are several API methods in jQuery that have this duality such as attr() and val(). They are described as follows:

- The attr() method either retrieves or manipulates the attributes for the DOM elements.

- The `val()` method retrieves the current value of the first element in the set of matched elements or it sets the value of every matched element. The `val()` method is particularly useful to access the name and values in a set of HTML select option elements.

Animation

The most sophisticated digital applications on a website incorporate smart animations and hints (obviously approved by the Head of UX) to guide the user on their digital journey. Usually, it is just enough to provide subtle hints on how the user can achieve the best experience with a website and this can make a huge difference in the overall satisfaction. jQuery has a base level animation feature such as sliding up and down the `div` layers and popups, shrinking and expanding the layers, and opacity tricks that can lend a hand.

To see the animation, let's examine how to use jQuery to animate a scroll-to-the-top arrow when the user scrolls down a page for a certain distance. This is a common user interface design pattern. We will not put in a module pattern for obvious space reasons.

Let's assume we have a simple HTML content on our JSF page view:

```
<div id="scrollBackTopArrow">
  <img src="#{request.contextPath}/scroll-back-top-arrow.jpg" >
</div>
```

First, we will need to write a function handler that listens to scroll events when the user is scrolling up or down the page view. In the DOM, there is a standard method, `scroll()`, on the global Window object that accepts a function object as a callback.

With an entry point, we will write a handler function, as follows:

```
$(window).scroll( function(){
  var epsilon    = 0.25;
  var scrollingCount = 0;
     var minOpacity = 0.0, maxOpacity = 0.85;
  var scrollArrow=$('#scrollBackTopArrow');
  scrollArrow.each( function(i) {
    var windowHeight = $(window).height();
    var windowScroll = $(window).scrollTop();
    var opacity = scrollArrow.css("opacity")

    var upper = windowHeight * 0.525;
    var lower = windowHeight * 0.315;
```

```
        if( windowScroll > upper ){
          if ( opacity <= (maxOpacity - epsilon )) {
            if ( scrollingCount == 0 ) {
                scrollArrow.animate({'opacity':'0.75'}, 100);
                scrollingCount = 15;
            }
          }
        }

        if( windowScroll < lower ){
          if ( opacity >= (minOpacity + epsilon)) {
            if ( scrollingCount == 0 ) {
                scrollArrow.animate({'opacity':'0.0'}, 100);
                scrollingCount = 15;
            }
          }
        }

        if ( scrollingCount > 0 ) {
          scrollingCount = scrollingCount - 1;
        }
      });
    }); // end of the scroll function
```

Don't be afraid of the length of this JavaScript function because all will be revealed now. It turns out that attaching a callback as a scroll listener means that the web browser potentially invokes the callback for perhaps 10 or perhaps scores of times per second depending on the user's device. Therefore, we have introduced a dampening factor, scrollingCount, as a countdown variable, which prevents the animation being hyper triggered. The epsilon variable also controls the sensitivity of the animation when it is activated. We can use set minimum and maximum opacity values to bound the animation activations.

As the jQuery selector API, $('#scrollBackTopArrow'), may retrieve zero or more DOM elements, we will invoke the each() method to effectively iterate through the elements. We do so with the anonymous function, which takes a single argument of the element. In this case, we know the selector will only ever return one DOM element, if it exists at all.

We will capture the current window height, $(window).height(), in a variable in the function. Using the windowHeight variable, we will derive some vertical limits where the arrow should fade in and out: lower and upper. The origin coordinate (0,0) sits on the top left-hand corner of the device window. The function call ${window).scrollTop() retrieves an integer position that represents the current scroll position of the page.

Now we will explain the tricky parts. The two conditional statements check if the page view scroll position is above the lowest or highest bounds. If the scroll position exceeds the upper bound, then we will fade in the arrow from view. If the scroll position is less than the lower bound, then we will fade out the arrow from view. We will set up a countdown timer in order to prevent the retriggering of the animation. Note that JavaScript supports access to a lexical scope for the variables that are declared outside the function definition, also known as closures. The minOpacity, maxOpacity, epsilon, and scrollingCount variables are the closure variables.

Here is another example of jQuery that uses the CSS3 three-dimensional transformations to achieve the expanding buttons or icons. This effect is borrowed from the older Mac OS X style user interface where the application icons expand and contract in the dock application bar, as shown in the following code:

```
var selector = $("expando-btn");

selector.mouseenter( function() {
  $(this).each( function(i) {
    css({
        'transition': 'all 0.5s',
        '-webkit-transform': 'scale(1.667)',
        '-moz-transform': 'scale(1.667)',
        '-o-transform': 'scale(1.667)',
        'transform': 'scale(1.667)',
    });
  });
});

selector.mouseexit( function() {
  $(this).each( function(i) {
    css({
        'transition': 'all 0.5s',
        '-webkit-transform': 'scale(1.0)',
        '-moz-transform': 'scale(1.0)',
        '-o-transform': 'scale(1.0)',
        'transform': 'scale(1.0)',
    });
  });
});
```

We will use the `mouseenter()` and `mouseexit()` methods in order to build the effect. These methods respectively capture the desktop mouse entering and leaving the button, if it is displayed and can be seen. The anonymous functions set up the CSS in motion. CSS 3 already has the animation class styles. The transition class declares the length of the total animation, which is 0.5 milliseconds, and we also declare a 2D transform that scales the element up or down. To expand the button element, we will set the scale-factor to `1.667` of the default button size. To contract the button element, we will reset the scale-factor to the default rendering size of `1.0`. Note that we still have to declare the proprietary browser classes such as — webkit-transform for the WebKit browsers such as Apple's Safari and the previous editions of Google Chrome. Ultimately, this example is unhelpful for the touch screen devices because there are no devices available (yet) that can detect fingers hovering very close over a screen! (See the exercise at the end of this chapter.)

Working with HTML, JavaScript, and CSS can be quite involved, and it is a job of an interface developer to figure out the requirements and build frontends. However, a Java developer should also appreciate the work. I hope you see some results.

The RequireJS framework

If you are serious about the organization of lots of JavaScript files and components, then you will be happy that ideas from dependency injection frameworks such as CDI and Spring have also made it in the world. Some professional organizations already rely on a small framework called RequireJS (`http://requirejs.org/`). The RequireJS framework is a JavaScript file and module loader. The framework has a built-in module script loader, which will improve the speed and quality of your code.

RequireJS implements the **Asychronous Module Definition (AMD)** specification for JavaScript (`https://github.com/amdjs/amdjs-api/wiki/AMD`). This specification defines a mechanism that in turn defines the modules and dependencies between modules and how they can be asynchronously loaded.

The AMD specification solves the critical issues where you have many JavaScript modules and define the multiple HTML script elements so as to load them, but then you find that each module had a dependency order.

Let's suppose that we have a JavaScript module A that has a dependency on a module B, then module B has a dependency on modules C and D. You might forget to include the dependency for the module D. Worse, you might get the order of the dependencies wrong:

```
<script src="js/module-b.js" ></script>
<!-- Code failure: we forgot to load the module C -->
<script src="js/module-d.js" ></script>
```

```
<!-- Oops: module B has a dependency on module D -->
<script src="js/module-a.js" ></script>
```

RequireJS helps with these transient dependencies. First, we must understand how RequireJS loads the JavaScript files. The framework has a best practice folder layout.

In terms of a Java web application, let's define some files in a project, as follows:

src/main/webapp/

src/main/webapp/index.xhtml

src/main/webapp/resources/js/

src/main/webapp/resources/js/app.js

src/main/webapp/resources/js/app/

src/main/webapp/resources/js/app/easel.js

src/main/webapp/resources/js/app/nested/sub.js

src/main/webapp/resources/js/lib/

src/main/webapp/resources/js/lib/jquery-2.1.1.js

src/main/webapp/resources/js/lib/bootstrap-3.2.0.js

src/main/webapp/resources/js/require.js

src/main/webapp/resources/js/require-setup.js

In a JSF application, we will place the JavaScript modules in the `resources` folder. This reads differently to the standard JavaScript descriptions because of the indirection required for JSF. The application files are usually saved in the `/js/app` folder. The JavaScript libraries are stored in the `/js/lib` folder. The `/js/require.js` file is the JavaScript file for a RequireJS framework module.

With an HTML5 application, you will first include a reference to the RequireJS file:

```
<!DOCTYPE html>
<h:html>
  <h:head>
    <meta charset="UTF-8">
    <title>Digital Java EE 7 :: Require JS </title>
    <link href="styles/bootstrap.css" rel="stylesheet" />
    <script
      src="#{request.contextPath}/js/lib/require-setup.js" >
      </script>
    <script
```

```
      src="#{request.contextPath}/js/lib/require.js"
      data-main="#{request.contextPath}js/app/app"></script>
    <script
      src="#{request.contextPath}/js/app/main.js" ></script>
  </h:head>

  <h:body>
    <header>RequireJS Application</header>
    <!-- ... -->
  </h:body>
</h:html>
```

The preceding code is a practical use of RequireJS because we are using Bootstrap and jQuery in an application. The most important HTML script element is the second one because it loads RequireJS (require.js). The first script tag is important as it configures the RequireJS framework. We will see this in a moment. The third script tag loads an application JavaScript module.

> Many commercial websites place tags at the bottom of the page content for a best practice convention use and to ease the performance. However, because RequireJS is designed for AMD, then this practice may defeat the purpose to load and execute the scripts asynchronously while the page continues to load. In other words, your mileage may vary and you need to test this out in development work.

A RequireJS configuration

Let's look in reverse order at the loaded JavaScript files, so this is /js/app/app.js. This is the target of the reference data-main attribute in the <script> tag element that includes the RequireJS library:

```
requirejs.config({
  baseUrl: 'js/lib',

  paths: {
      app: '../app'
  }
});
```

This file configures how RequireJS searches and loads the JavaScript files as modules. The requirejs is JavaScript Object type variable that the library defines in a global head scope. The reference object has a method called config() that accepts a JavaScript property object. The baseUrl property defines the default location to load the files. The paths property is a nested property, which lists a collection of the paths that are exceptions to the default loading rule.

By default the previous RequireJS configuration loads any module by ID from the folder js/lib. However if the module ID start with the prefix app, then it is loaded from the js/app directory as specified by the path key.

The paths property configuration is relative to baseUrl and never includes a .js suffix extension as the paths property could stand for a directory folder.

As we will load jQuery and Bootstrap for this example, we will need to shove a square peg in a round hole. In the JavaScript programming world, in order to avoid conflicts with many popular libraries, the authors have adopted the idea of shims.

> **What is a shim?**
> A shim is the idea of a colloquial expression in the JavaScript parlance to force the different frameworks to work together. It is also a term for monkey-patching a JavaScript context to contain all of the EmcaScript 5 methods.

In RequireJS, we must set this up in the first loaded file (require-setup.js):

```
// require-setup.js
var require = {
  shim: {
    "bootstrap" : { "deps" :['jquery'] },
    "jquery": { exports: '$' }
  },
  paths: {
    "jquery" : "jquery-2.1.3",
    "bootstrap" : "bootstrap-3.2.0"
  }
};
```

It is helpful to re-examine the folder layout for our JavaScript files. The require-setup file simply sets up a special named variable called require in the global head scope with an object definition. The nest object referenced by the property name shim defines two changes. First, that a module called bootstrap has a dependency on a module called jquery. Second, the jquery module exports the symbol ($).

The second property key called paths in the configuration defines an association object for the module names. Each module name is mapped to its true name. So, the jquery module is actually associated with a file called jquery-2.1.3. There is a bonus feature with the indirection because now we have an easy way of upgrading the library versions. It's a one line change!

An application module

With the configuration of RequireJS completed, we can now write the default application module for our application, as follows:

```
requirejs(['jquery', 'bootstrap', 'easel', 'nested/sub'],
  function ($, bootstrap, easel, sub) {
    // jquery, easel and the nested/sub module are all
    // loaded and can be used here now.
    console.log("start it up now!");

    var e = new easel();
    console.log("module 1 name = "+e.getName() );

    var s = new sub();
    console.log("module 2 name = "+s.getName() );
    console.log("other name = "+s.getCanvasName() );

    // DOM ready
    $(function(){
      // Programmatically add class to toggles
      $('.btn.danger').button('toggle').addClass('fat');

      console.log("set it off!");

      alert("set it off!");
    });
  }
);
```

The preceding /js/app/main.js script is the common file for our simple client-side application. The global requirejs() function is the pathway to the library's feature of a dependency injection. The following is the format of this function:

```
requirejs( <MODULE-ARRAY-LIST>, <CALLBACK> )
```

Here, < MODULE-ARRAY-LIST> is the list collection of the module name dependencies and <CALLBACK> is the single function argument.

Therefore, the code example asks RequireJS to initialize the modules: `jquery`, `bootstrap`, `easel`, and `nested/sub`. Pay particular attention to the last module because `sub.js` is in a subdirectory of the `app` folder; therefore, the name uses the path separator. Remember, with RequireJS, you do not need to add the suffix (`.js`).

By the time RequireJS invokes the callback function, the modules are loaded. Hence, we will write to the console log, and if we are using jQuery, we will make another anonymous function declaration in order to do some fancy selector manipulation on the toggle buttons. It should start to make sense as to why we will explicitly export the dollar symbol in the preceding shim configuration. Also note that we are able to access the reference dependencies through the function arguments.

So, how will we define the module patterns with RequireJS? Read the next section.

Defining modules

In order to define our own custom modules with RequireJS, we will make use of another global scope method from the framework. Following the AMD specification, the framework provides a method called `define()`. The format for this method is as follows:

```
define( <MODULE-ARRAY-LIST>, <FUNCTION-OBJECT> )
```

This is almost the same as the `requirejs()` call. The `define()` method accepts a list of the module names as a dependency. The `<FUNCTION-OBJECT>` second argument means that the function must explicitly return a JavaScript object. In other words, it can't return a void or nothing result.

Let's look at the definition for the canvas module:

```
// js/app/easel.js
define([], function () {
  console.log("initializing the `easel' module");
  var returnedModule = function () {
    var _name = 'easel';
    this.getName = function () {
      return _name;
    }
  };

  return returnedModule;
});
```

The module list can be an empty array, which means that the module has no required dependencies. The file path is /js/app/easel.js. In the anonymous function, we will instantiate our JavaScript constructor object with methods and properties and then return it to RequireJS. The module just defines a method called getName(), which returns the value of a private accessible variable. Following the module pattern in JavaScript, it is possible to declare the private scope variables and functions such as _name in the example, which are not accessible outside of the function definition.

Here is the listing of the other module with a file path of /js/app/nested/sub.js, which has a dependency on the easel module:

```
// js/app/nested/sub.js
define(['easel'], function (easel) {
  var easel = new easel();
  console.log("initializing the `nested' module");
  var returnedModule = function () {
    this.getCanvasName = function () {
      return easel.getName();
    }
    this.getName = function () {
      return "sub";
    }
  };

  return returnedModule;
});
```

The nested/sub module defines a function object that contains two methods: getName() and getCanvasName(). We will create an object variable called easel. RequireJS supplies the module reference as an argument during the invocation of the function. The getCanvasName() method uses this private reference to invoke the getName() method on the dependent module, easel.

Here is a screenshot of RequireJS in action, loading the modules. The Chrome Developer Tools has a network view that allows us to inspect the JavaScript files being loaded over the wire:

A screenshot of the RequireJS example application

If you find this terse at first, please bear in mind that it takes a little while to get your head around the functions and object scopes. The advantages are clear to the professional interface developers to get around the severe drawbacks of JavaScript's original design. We covered enough of RequireJS for the digital development to continue far and wide. We will move on to another framework.

UnderscoreJS

I will introduce you to one more JavaScript framework that can be helpful in development. UnderscoreJS (http://underscorejs.org/) is a framework that brings functional programming constructs and techniques to the language. The library contains over 100 methods that add functional support to JavaScript.

UnderscoreJS is a single JavaScript file downloaded just like jQuery and RequireJS. If you add the requisite versioned `underscore.js` file to the `/js/lib` folder, then you already have the means to inject it into your application. Here is the additional configuration in the file, `require-setup.js`:

```
var require = {
  shim: {
    "bootstrap" : { "deps" :['jquery'] },
    "jquery": { exports: '$' },
    "underscore": { exports: '_'}
  },
  paths: {
    "jquery" : "jquery-2.1.3",
    "bootstrap" : "bootstrap-3.2.0",
    "underscore" : "underscore-1.8.2"
  }
};
```

UnderscoreJS exports the symbol underscore (_) for its library to a developer and its function methods are accessible through the symbol. We will review a small subset of these methods.

Functional programmers tend to be interested in the following five primary concerns:

- How to internally iterate through a collection of elements?
- How to filter the elements in a collection?
- How to map the elements in a collection from one type to another?
- How to flatten a collection of elements into just a collection?
- Finally, how to collect or reduce the elements in a collection to a single element or value?

You may recognize these concerns as standard ideas in the alternative programming languages in JVM such as Scala, Clojure, or even Java 8 with Lambdas.

The for-each operations

In UnderscoreJS, we can take an array object and simply iterate over it.

The `each()` function allows you to iterate over the list collections, as follows:

```
// /js/app/underscore-demo.js
requirejs(['underscore'],
  function (_) {
```

```
    console.log("inside underscore-demo module");

    _.each( [1, 2, 3], function(n) { console.log(n); });
  }
);
```

Here, we used RequireJS as an AMD loader in a module called `underscore-demo.`
`js`. The `each()` function iterates over the elements of the array object and invokes the
supplied function, which is called the **iteratee** with the element as a single argument.
The `each()` function replaces the typically `foreach` or `for-do` compound statements
in imperative programming languages.

The filter operations

Filtering can be achieved in several ways. Let's take a basic example of filtering a list:

```
var r1 = _.filter(['Anne','Mike','Pauline','Steve'],
  function(name){ return name.startsWith('P'); });
console.log(r1);    // ['Pauline']
```

This code searches through each value in the list, returning an array of all the values
that pass a truth test (predicate). The second argument to `filter()` is known as the
predicate, which is a function callback that returns a Boolean value if the element
that is supplied meets the condition test or not. Here, we are filtering the names in
the list if they begin with the letter `P`.

UnderscoreJS also provides a more sophisticated filtering method. The `where()`
method searches a list and returns an array of all the values that contain all of the
key-value pairs listed in the properties:

```
var contacts = [
  new ContactDetail( 'F', 'Anne', 'Jackson', 28, 'Developer' ),
  new ContactDetail( 'M', 'William', 'Benson', 29, 'Developer' ),
  new ContactDetail( 'M', 'Micheal', 'Philips', 33, 'Tester' ),
  new ContactDetail( 'M', 'Ian', 'Charles', 45, 'Sales' ),
  new ContactDetail( 'F', 'Sarah', 'Hart', 55, 'CEO' ),
];

var r2 = _.where(contacts, {occupation: 'Developer', age: 28 });
console.log(r2);
```

The preceding code uses the `ContactDetail` JavaScript object that we defined earlier in this chapter. We will invoke the `where()` method with the list of contacts and supplied key-value objects with the properties that we want to filter. The result is `ContactDetail` that matches Anne Jackson because she has a matching occupation (software developer) and age (28).

The map operations

The `map()` function produces a new array object by mapping each element in the list, with the user supplied function:

```
console.log(
  _.map( [1, 2, 3],
    function(n){ return n * 3; } )
);
// [3, 6, 9]

console.log(
  _.map( [ 1, 2, 3, 4], function(x){ return x * x; } )
);
// [1, 4. 9, 16]

console.log(
  _.map( [ 1, 2, 3, 4],
    function(x){ return "A" + x; } )
);
// [ 'A1', 'A2', 'A3', 'A4']
```

The user-supplied function accepts the current element parameter and is responsible for returning the new element type. In these examples, we will create a new array list of triples of the number element, and next, we will create a new array list of the squares of the number element. Finally, we will create an array list of the string elements.

The flatten operations

Now that we know how to iterate, filter, and map a collection with UnderscoreJS, we should also learn how to flatten the collections of elements. There is a method called `flatten()` that accepts a collection of elements and flattens it if one or more of these elements is itself a collection.

Let's examine the following two examples:

```
var Sector = function( name, value ) {
  this.name = name;
  this.value = value;
};

var salesSectorData = [
  [
    [
      new Sector("New York", 3724.23),
      new Sector("Boston", 8091.79)
    ],
    [
      new Sector("Houston", 9631.54)
    ],
  ],
  [
    new Sector("London", 2745.23),
    new Sector("Glasgow", 4286.36)
  ]
];

var f3 = _.flatten(salesSectorData);
console.log("f3 = "+f3);
// [Sector, Sector, Sector, Sector, Sector ]
var f4 = _.flatten(salesSectorData, true );
console.log("f4 = "+f4);
// [ [Sector, Sector], [Sector], Sector, Sector ]
```

Here, we defined an object called Sector that represents, say, the sales and marketing data. We created a nested collection, salesSectorData, which is actually an array of two elements but each element is a further collection. In short, salesSectorData is a level two ordered data structure.

The first flatten() call completely flattens the data structure in an array list. So we will end up with an array of five items. We will pass a second argument to the second flatten() call, which is a boolean argument that specifies whether the flatten operation should operate also on the elements of the collection or not. The result of f4 is an array of four items. The first element is an array list of two items, the second element is an array list of one item, and then the remaining elements will follow.

It should be clear why a JavaScript interface developer raves about UnderscoreJS. We will move on to the final operation in this firebrand review.

The reduction operations

What good are all of these functional operations if we cannot reduce them to a single scalar value or object? Thankfully, RequireJS provides us with several varieties of methods such as `reduce()`, `reduceRight()`, `min()`, and `max()`.

We will just look at the `reduce()` operation for now. If we wanted to discover the total sale value for all of the previous sector objects, how will we do it? Here is the answer:

```
var totalValue= _.reduce(
  f3,
  function(acc, sector) {
    return acc + sector.value;
  },
  0 );
console.log("totalValue = " + totalValue)
```

The `reduce()` operation accepts three arguments: the collection, an iteratee function, and initial value. In order to reduce the collection to a single scalar value, the `reduce()` operation calls the iteratee on each element. The iteratee function accepts the scalar value argument and element. The anonymous function adds the sale sector value to the accumulator.

The `reduce()` operator is left-associative in respect to the collection, whereas `reduceRight()` is right-associative. This completes our journey in UnderscoreJS. A more interested reader can delve further into this framework online and through other resources of information.

GruntJS

Before we conclude this chapter on progressive JavaScript programming, we will quickly take a look at a tool to launch actions. This tool is GruntJS (`http://gruntjs.com/`), and the people behind it describe it as the JavaScript task runner. GruntJS is a Node.js tool and works in this ecosystem. Therefore, developers must install Node.js before they can work with GruntJS.

The tool is currently a favorite with many in the digital community. The following are some of the reasons why GruntJS is seen as a bonus:

- The configuration is in one place and can be shared among other developers, testers, and operators across your digital team.
- GruntJS is built with a plugin system.
- The tool compresses your CSS and minimizes your JavaScript files for performance and delivery to the product site.

- GruntJS allows teams of dedicated interface developers to work separately or together on the client-side bits of a website. The tools then concatenate their JavaScript and CSS components together for a production delivery.

- It can optimize your images to reduce the overall file size and yet still retain the quality, which is perfect to deliver the massive *hero* style retina display graphics and also create mobile-friendly images.

- Developers can take advantage of Sass and Less for CSS authoring.

There are GruntJS plugins for Less, Sass, RequireJS, CoffeeScript, and others.

Node.js is a JavaScript runtime platform and therefore, it is absolutely different from the Java platform. If you happen to use Gradle, there are two open source plugins available that help to bridge the gap between them. They are called Gradle-GruntJS Plugin (`https://github.com/srs/gradle-grunt-plugin`) and Gradle-Node Plugin (`https://github.com/srs/gradle-node-plugin`). Node.js also has its own package manager called npm, which handles the installation, updating, and removing of the libraries. Npm permits the Node.js and JavaScript open source libraries to be shared with the community.

Every GruntJS project requires the following two files in the root folder:

- `package.json`: This file specifies the metadata for an npm project and contains JavaScript tool and library dependencies that your project requires, including GruntJS.

- `gruntfile.js`: This file configures and defines the build tasks for your project. It is the file where you can also add dependencies for the GruntJS plugins.

For a JSF project, you will place `package.json` in the project root folder. Here is a code for the file:

```
{
  "name": "my-digital-project",
  "version": "1.0-SNAPSHOT",
  "devDependencies": {
    "grunt": "~0.4.5"
  }
}
```

You will notice that the file looks almost like a JSON file. The critical `devDependencies` property declares a set of npm tools and frameworks. We want to definitely load GruntJS from version 0.4.5 or better.

Now, we will dive straight into a real-world case of GruntJS. In a digital project, we want to optimize the performance and ensure our SEO ranking with the search engines. We are required to merge together the third-party JavaScript libraries and minimize the JavaScript files. The interface developers prefer to keep using the Sass tool for the flexibility management of the CSS files. We have an agreement with our management to keep the developed JavaScript files untouched for now.

Here is the `gruntfile.js` file that achieves this ambition:

```
module.exports = function(grunt) {
  grunt.initConfig({
    pkg: grunt.file.readJSON('package.json'),

    concat: {  /* ... */ }

    uglify: { /* ... */ }

    sass: { /* ... */ }
  });

  grunt.loadNpmTasks('grunt-contrib-concat');
  grunt.loadNpmTasks('grunt-contrib-uglify');
  grunt.loadNpmTasks('grunt-contrib-sass');
  grunt.registerTask('default', ['concat', 'uglify', 'sass']);
};
```

The preceding `gruntfile.js` file defines a single module in the Node.js system. It sounds confusing to have a module system in another module; however, all we have to know is that modules are a form of encapsulation that permits sharing through reuse. The `module.exports` definition allows grunt to participate in the Node.js system. Therefore, it is possible to share this grunt module with the other node modules.

The `grunt.initConfig()` stanza is required to initialize the GruntJS tool. The most important part specifies the name of the metadata file, `package.json`. Afterwards, we have an area reserved for the plugin configuration. Each GruntJS plugin has a separate configuration of properties. There are three plugins: `grunt-contrib-concat`, `grunt-contrib-uglify`, and `grunt-contrib-sass`. Each plugin declares a configuration property name: `concat`, `uglify`, and `sass`.

To configure the concatenation plugin, we have the following stanza:

```
concat: {
  dist: {
    src: [
      'src/main/webapp/resources/js/libs/*.js',
```

```
        'src/main/webapp/resources/js/global.js'
    ],
    dest: 'build/webapp/js/build/thirdparty.js',
  }
}
```

The `grunt-contrib-concat` plugin requires a source of files and a destination file. It takes whatever JavaScript library files that are there and then generates a single file called `thirdparty.js`. In our Gradle (or Maven project), let's assume that we have a WAR task that will eventually bundle the final destination file.

We must be aware of the de facto Gradle and Maven directory layout configuration for the web projects. Therefore, we will add `src/main/webapp` to the file paths.

To configure the minimization plugin, we will execute the following code:

```
uglify: {
  build: {
    src: 'src/main/webapp/thirdparty.js',
    dest: 'src/main/webapp/thirdparty.min.js'
  }
}
```

This configuration is very easy to understand; we will just point the `grunt-uglify-contrib` plugin to a source and target the file path.

Finally, we will configure the Sass CSS build plugin as follows:

```
sass: {
  dist: {
    options: {
      style: 'compressed'
    },
    files: {
      'src/main/webapp/resources/js/styles/build/mysite.css':
      'build/webapp/resources/styles/mysite.scss'
    }
  }
}
```

We will need slightly more instructions for the `grunt-contrib-sass` plugin. This plugin requires the key-value properties of files. The target file is the key property and the SASS source file is the value.

> Installing SASS additionally requires the installation of a valid Ruby installation and the corresponding RubyGem.

GruntJS is an exciting and powerful tool for the client-side digital developers. There is no doubt about this. The plugin system is still quite immature and I recommend that you check the documentation for the configuration changes.

Summary

This chapter was a whirlwind tour of the modern digital JavaScript programming. If you have not worked with the JavaScript language at all or left it far behind for several years, then I do hope that you have been invigorated to learn this essential skill. We looked at the programming of the JavaScript objects. We saw how to construct the objects. We learned about the property notations and dealt with the JavaScript truth.

We paid a particular respectable visit to jQuery — the grandmother or granddaddy of the JavaScript programming. If you learned nothing else, then you can now understand jQuery. We saw how the selectors can search HTML DOM for the elements, which can then be manipulated for effect. We made a brief foray into animation, which opened the door to the creation of more sophisticated experiences for the customers and business owners.

We ventured into dependency management of the modules with RequireJS. We learned how this framework can help a digital developer to organize the modules and leave the order of retrieving them to the framework.

At the end of the chapter, we crossed the bridge to a non-Java platform called Node. js and, in particular, learned the basic details about GruntJS. We studied an example of a GruntJS definition that bundled the JavaScript library files together, generated CSS from Sass, and optimized the size of the JavaScript files.

In the next chapters, we will look at AngularJS and the up-and-coming Java EE MVC framework.

Exercises

The following are the exercises and questions for this chapter:

1. What does the following JavaScript code define? What else is similar to it?

```javascript
var hospital = {
  name: "St Stephen's Hospital",
  location: "Kensington & Chelsea",
  patients: 1250,
  doctors: ['Patel', 'Radeksky', 'Brown', 'Shockley']
};
```

2. From the preceding code, explain what is the main difference between the `hospital.patients` and `hospital['patients']` property accessors?

3. Write a JavaScript object that constructs a participant to a Java User Group member. Let's say you call your object `JUGParticipant`. You will need to capture their first and last names, their telephone contact numbers, their e-mail addresses (optional), and also their specific interests (optional).

4. Modify `JUGParticipant` to accept the interests as another object. Write a JavaScript Tag object so that you build an array of skills such as Java EE, Android, or HTML. Demonstrate that you can build this object graph of the `JUGParticipants` and Tag objects.

5. Adapt your JavaScript object graph by creating a `JUGEvent` meeting object. Your object will need to hold properties such as the event title, its description, location, presentation speaker (optional), and willing `JUGParticipants`.

6. Find out the nine native object constructors in JavaScript 1.5 (or ECMAScript edition 3). To start you off, here are four: `Number()`, `String()`, `Boolean()`, and `Object()`.

7. With the following HTML, use jQuery to change the background color of the `div` element, `messageArea`. There are three buttons in the code to denote the convention of a traffic light. (You are allowed to make the content pretty!)

```html
<div class="traffic-light">
  <div id="messageArea" class="message-area">
    <p class="lead">
      This is it!
    </p>
  </div>
  <div>
    <a id="#redBtn" href="#" class="button" >Red</a>
    <a id="#yellowBtn" href="#" class="button" >Yellow</a>
    <a id="#greenBtn" href="#" class="button" >Green</a>
  </div>
</div>
```

8. Explain the difference between the following two jQuery statements:

```
$('hero-image').attr('alt');
$('hero-image').attr('alt', 'Voted best by Carworld 2015!');
```

9. With the following HTML5 code, which displays a Bootstrap alert box, we want the user to make the warning disappear when they click on the close icon. Write JavaScript and jQuery to animate the critical notice, fade it out, and then remove the content from HTML.

```
<div>
  <p class="lead">
    Here is something I desperately want you
    to know right here, right now.
  </p>

  <div class="critical-notice  alert-danger">
    <button type="button" class="close  pull-right"
      aria-label="Close">
      <span aria-hidden="true">&times;</span>
    </button>

    <span class="glyphicon glyphicon-warning-sign"
      aria-hidden="true" id="closeNotch" ></span>
    <strong>Danger!</strong> I'm very annoyed.
  </div>
</div>
```

10. Look at the book's source code and get started with RequireJS. Study the code. Your task is to modify the code and add your module, which you may call /js/app/oxygen.js. You will need to use the AMD specification define() method call.

11. Now that you have written the new RequireJS module, oxygen.js, how do you know that it works as expected? Did you write a test web page? You will probably need to write a /js/app/oxygendemo.js JavaScript file.

12. Define two modules called /js/app/hydrogen.js and /js/app/water. js. Set up the water module such that it depends on the other two modules: hydrogen and oxygen.

13. Working with UnderscoreJS and assuming that you have set up the dependencies, exercise the following JavaScript example:

```
var arr = [1, 2, 3, 4, 5];
var newArr = _.map(arr, function (x) {
  return (x + 3) * (x - 2) * (x + 1);
});
```

14. Look at the following JavaScript code, which defines a percentage and an array of product prices. Using UnderscoreJS, calculate the grand total price and also the grand total price when each price is increased by the percentage:

```
var Product = function(name, price, type ) {
  this.name = name;
  this.price = price;
  this.type = type;
}

var percentage = 3.25,
var productPrices = [
  new Product("Secutars", 27.99, "Garden"),
  new Product("Chair", 99.99, "Home" ),
  new Product("Luxury Red Wines", 79.99, "Food" ),
  new Product("Microwave", 49.99, "Home" ),
  new Product("Mower", 169.99, "Garden" )
];
```

15. Note that we have different types of products. Using UnderscoreJS, work out the grand total of the original prices and then work out the grand total with an increase of 5.35 percent.

8
AngularJS and Java RESTful Services

"Slow – Anything faster than 50ms is imperceptible to humans and thus can be considered 'instant'.

Misko Hevery, co-creator of AngularJS

For this chapter, we shall move out of the comfort zone of JSF and explore a different mode of web application. Most of you will be familiar with popular social media like Google Mail, Facebook, and Twitter and their web-user interfaces. These web applications have a special user experience and information architecture that gives the illusion of the interaction taking place on one single web page. However, behind the scenes, these applications depend on standard technologies: HTML5, CSS, and client-side JavaScript. They all use AJAX calls to communicate over HTTP to a back-end server. When the server side application sends data to the web client, only a partial part of the page is updated. In contemporary use, many digital sites take advantage of the RESTful service endpoints on the application backend. Some sophisticated enterprise applications may deliver notices to the working multiple users using **Server Sent Events** (**SSE**), and the more leading-edge ones lean on the newly minted HTML5 WebSocket specification to deliver a full-duplex communication between the client and the server. Incidentally, the full Java EE 7 specification from the Java Community Process supports JAX-RS, SSE, and WebSocket.

Single-page applications

The design philosophy behind building an application on a single page such that it resembles a desktop application is in marked contrast to the JavaServer Faces' original design of navigation links between pages. JSF 1.0 was created in the early noughties, long before the rediscovery of the `XMLHttpRequest` JavaScript object and Google Maps in 2005, so that historical note should not be a surprise (`http://en.wikipedia.org/wiki/JavaServer_Faces`). It is entirely possible to write JSF as a single-page application, but I would not recommend the effort of forcing a square peg into a round hole! JSF lends itself to applications that are extremely stateful in nature and design, where the customer journey is based on page-to-page navigation. In the previous chapters, we have already covered a great deal about stateful web applications with JSF, flow scopes, conversations, and view-scoped beans. If you are not thorough with those concepts, then I strongly recommend you revise the material again. We shall press on now with the alternate design mode.

Let's list the beneficial characteristics of single-page applications:

- SPAs often feature a website or web application that fits on a single page.
- They rely on the modern digital JavaScript techniques including AJAX, HTML5, and CSS.
- Instead of loading whole pages during navigation, this type of application manipulates the **Document Object Model** (**DOM**) in order to provide page updates.
- These applications typically employ an HTML-templating engine to render the content locally on the client side. There is a separation of concerns between the presentation logic on the client and the business logic on the server side.
- SPAs communicate dynamically with a web server, usually with RESTful services, with JSON as a popular payload type.

There are some drawbacks for single-page applications that the content strategists, technical lead developers, and, obviously, the stakeholder businessperson should be aware of:

- It may be hard to apply Search Engine Optimization to an SPA.
- Using the back button in the browser may cause lost data entries; SPAs do not play well with web browser history.
- SPA requires a higher degree of application development knowledge to deal with reactive programming and concepts. Notably, engineers should be aware of factors concerning trade-off round scalability, resilience, event-driven handling, and notifications, and be responsive.

Finally, allow me to offer you a word of advice. Digital interface developers in the industry have JavaScript, HTML5, and CSS skills. In this chapter, you will learn to acknowledge that the JavaScript programming capability is equally as important as the Java server-side requirement. In other words, working with AngularJS and similar client-side frameworks tends to be a full-stack engagement.

The caseworker application

For this chapter, we are going to look at one particular type of single-page application for international governments called a caseworker system. The business users of the caseworkers will sit on desks, and for the majority of their day, process applicants through stages of applying for a product.

The following is a screenshot of the application:

Screenshot of the caseworker application, xen national force

The application is called **xen-national-force**, and it is designed to process passports through a miniature workflow. It is far from serving the requirements of a true business application. For example, there is no user input security implemented in order to keep things as simple as possible. It works very well for only one caseworker and there is a very obvious design flaw from the user-experience side. However, the xen-national-force application demonstrates how to build a system having master-detail records with CRUD operations using AngularJS, and it features a basic Finite State Machine implementation.

We shall now move on to learning about the popular AngularJS framework.

AngularJS

In recent years, one particular JavaScript client-side framework has emerged as a strong contender for building single page applications for enterprise business. It is called AngularJS (`http://angularjs.org`) and is supported and licensed by Google. The software repository can be found on GitHub at `https://github.com/angular/angular.js`. I should say that it is not the only framework to provide DOM two-way binding, Model-View Controller, templating, modules, services, and factories.

In this book, we are only concerned with AngularJS, but you should be aware of two major competitors in the JavaScript client-side world, namely `Backbone.js` and `Ember.js`. Due to the scope of the task, we hit the ground with the AngularJS framework, and in this chapter there is beginner's introduction to the framework. We will cover the AngularJS version 1.3.15 running against Java EE 7.

> For a thorough discussion on AngularJS and client-side JavaScript from the ground up, we recommend reading another Packt Publishing book, *Mastering Single Application Development with AngularJS* by *Kozlowski and Darwin*.

Programming with AngularJS means that you very rarely need to delve into the low-level W3C HTML DOM API. In fact, operations that took tens-of-lines of JavaScript custom binding code to sanity check, now become one-liners.

Let's suppose we have a simple HTML form that implements the classic `Hello, World!` snippet. We want the user to type his/her name in a text field and have that name in a greeting in the real world. Our HTML content might appear like this:

```
<form id="helloForm">
  <input class="greeting-name" type="text" ></input>
  <div class="greeting-name">message </div>
</form>
```

How would we wire up the text input with the message area in the `div` element with jQuery? One plausible approach would be to write event handlers and callback functions like the following fragment of a JavaScript module:

```
$('#helloForm input.greeting-name').on('value', function() {
  $('#helloForm div.greeting-name').text('Hello ' + this.val() + '!');
});
```

The preceding code snippet, without the boilerplate of the JavaScript object modules and dependency injection, will do the trick. When the user types into the text field identified by the CSS class selector `input.greeting-name`, then jQuery invokes the callback function, which updates the inner HTML in the `div` element layer, identified with the CSS class `div.greeting.name`. We could extend this code and write a generic solution with parameters, especially if we have more cases like this in our application, but sooner rather than later, programming at this low-level introduces complexities and bugs.

The designers of AngularJS realized that there was an opportunity for improvement. The same example can be re-written using AngularJS, as follows:

```
<!DOCTYPE HTML>
<html>
<head>
  <script
    src="http://ajax.googleapis.com/ajax/lib/angularjs/1.3.15/angular.
      js"></script>
</head>
<body ng-app ng-init="greeting-name = 'Mr. Anderson'">
  <form>
    <input ng-model="customer-name" type="text" />
    <div class="greeting-name">Hello {{customer-name}}!</div>
  </form>
</body>
</html>
```

The preceding fragment is entirely in HTML. It includes the AngularJS framework from a remote server, **Content Delivery Network (CDN)**. The body HTML element is annotated with a non-standard attribute, `ng-app`, in order to declare that this DOM node is part of the overall template. The other attribute, `ng-init`, declares a data model before the template is rendered on the client side. AngularJS needs to know where to start templating or modifying the DOM dynamically; therefore, every page starts with the `ng-app` attribute. Usually, the `ng-app` attribute is applied to the HTML `body` element. An AngularJS template would be useless without access to a data model, and this is the purpose of the `ng-init` attribute. It sets up a scoped variable called `greeting-name` and assigns it the String literal value, `Mr. Anderson`.

Note the additional attribute type `ng-model` and the special, double curly bracket syntax: `{{customer-name}}`. The attribute is a special extension provided by the AngularJS framework that identifies the data model inline, and the curly brackets represent a special HTML templating syntax called directive. Here we applied the `ng-model` attribute to the input field element. When the page is loaded, the input text field is shown with the text `Mr Anderson`. The code also allows the user to enter text in the input field and simultaneously updates the message area. There is no programming required for this simple case; in fact it is declarative. So what is the secret sauce? The following code shows one form of two-way binding. Let's extend it to demonstrate the complete two-way binding:

```
<form>
  <input ng-model="customer-name" type="text" />
  <div class="greeting-name">Hello {{customer-name}}!</div>
  <p>
   <button class="btn-large" ng-click="user-model = 'Karen'">
   Karen </button> </p>
  <p>
   <button class="btn-large" ng-click="user-model = 'Albert'">
   Albert </button> </p>
</form>
```

We introduced the HTML `button` elements with a new attribute, `ng-click`. The value of the attribute is an AngularJS JavaScript expression. Each button updates the data model with a new name. Effectively, they reset the name in the input field and the message area. How cool is that? There is no jQuery programming in there at all. AngularJS has many special custom attributes such as `ng-repeat`, `ng-switch`, and `ng-option`, which we will encounter later in this chapter.

You might be wondering about these bindings and templates being very clever; so how does it work on the client side?

How does AngularJS work?

AngularJS is loaded in a web browser as part of the HTML page content. The strongest part of the framework is that it encourages the separation of concerns. The presentation view should be mixed deliberately with business logic and the data model. There are a couple of reasons for this. When the Angular JS framework is loaded a page is triggered, the framework marches up and down the DOM and looks for certain non-standard attributes called directives. It parses and processes this markup with the compiler. Effectively, AngularJS transforms the statically loaded DOM and produces a rendered view. The framework takes these directives and creates associations, binding, and extra behavior.

The ng-app attribute is linked to a directive that initializes the application. The ng-init is linked to a directive that allows the programmer to set up a data model. It can be used to assign values to the variables. The ng-model is associated with directive access or stores the value that is associated with an HTML Input element. AngularJS allows the developers to write custom directives. You may want to write one in the future to get access to the DOM.

AngularJS works on the idea of nested scopes within a template view. A scope is an execution context for expressions. Scopes can be organized in an hierarchical fashion such that they mimic the DOM model.

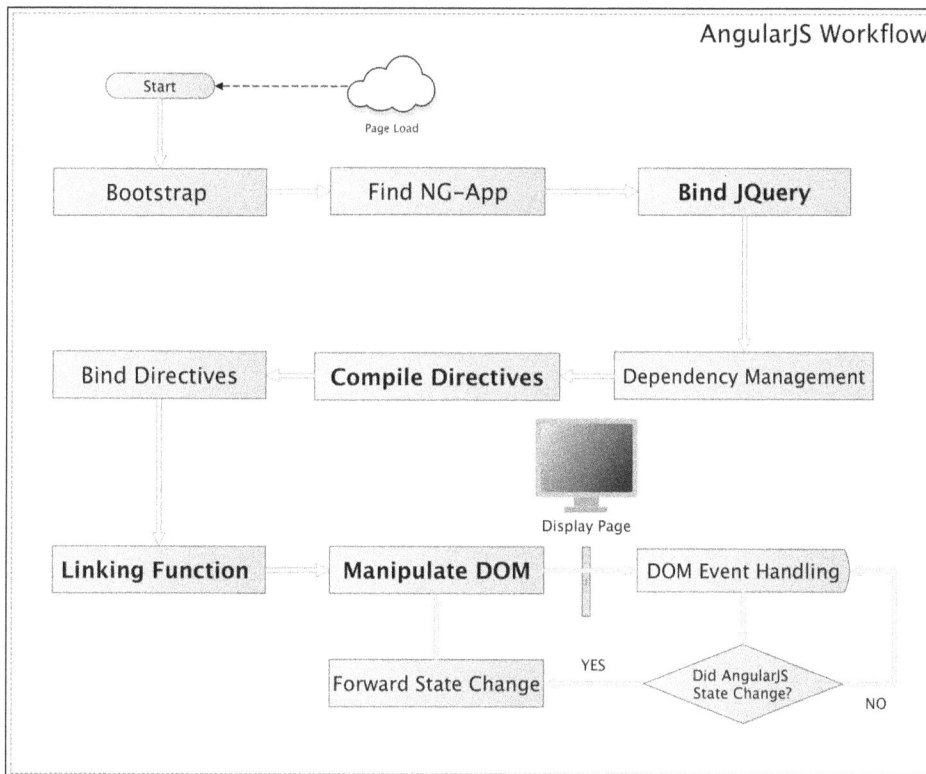

How AngularJS works in principle

AngularJS relies on the JavaScript modules that define controllers and other logic. Modules can be dependent on other modules; however, unlike RequireJS, modules that are a part of disparate JavaScript files are not automatically loaded in the application. A scope is the glue that binds the presentation and the data model. A scope is the place in the AngularJS where watchers and listeners are defined. Most of the time, the framework will automatically handle expression handling and data binding, and handle the notifications between JavaScript modules and DOM element components. After the compilation phase, AngularJS moves on to the linking phase and associates expressions to the module controller methods and other resources.

Let's summarize these steps:

1. AngularJS framework bootstraps itself. In particular, it searches the DOM for an HTML element with the ng-app attribute. This is the trigger point for the framework.

2. Once the ng-app element is found, AngularJS creates a dependency injector.

3. It then compiles the static DOM into rendering an intermediate view, collecting directives as it goes.

4. AngularJS then starts to link and compose the directives with their associated scope. This is an algorithmic and hierarchical operation. The framework creates an initial scope called the root scope before executing the linking phase.

5. Finally, AngularJS invokes an apply call using the root scope, and during this stage, the view is rendered.

Let's look at the view of the caseworker. In the book's source code, you will find the Gradle project called **xen-force-angularjs**. It follows the Maven convention for Java EE projects. Our discussion will be split into two sections. We will look at the frontend code that consists of HTML5, JavaScript, and some CSS. Afterwards, we will delve into the Java server-side backend. Let's have a look at the following figure:

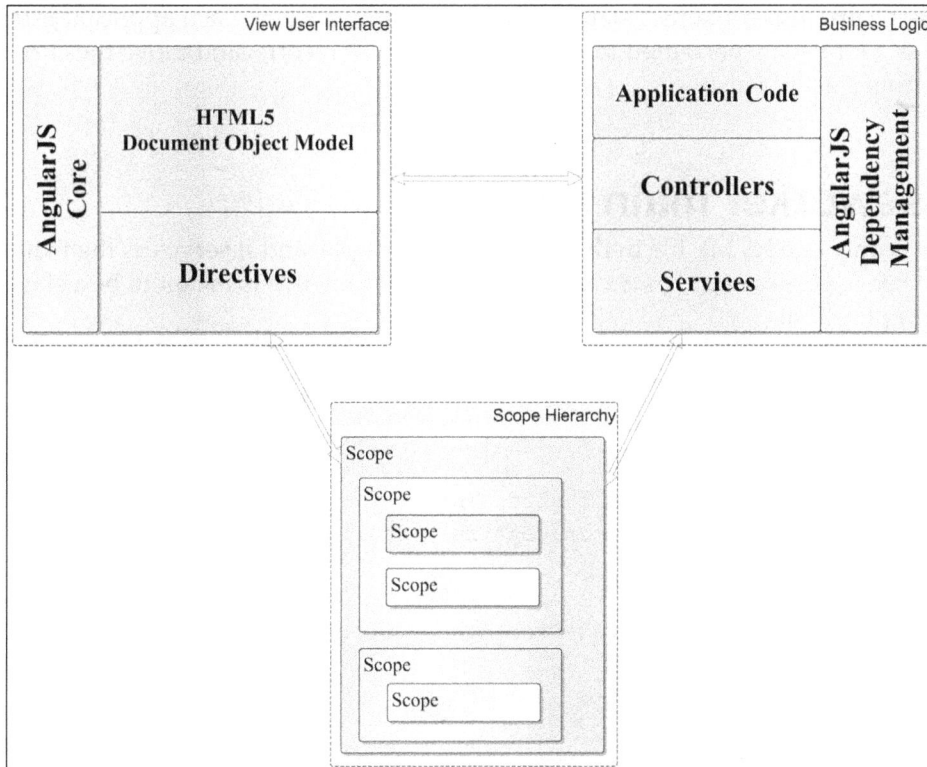

Th relationship of directives to business logic in AngularJS

Caseworker overview

The caseworker project shows a master-detail application. Our worker starts the application and sees a list of case records, which contains the names and the passport details for each applicant. This is the master record. Each case record may have a zero or more task records attached. Those are the details records of the master. Each master record also contains a state property that shows where each applicant is in the process. Our user is permitted to access all of the case records and move the current state from start to finish.

Caseworker main view

There is only one HTML file in the caseworker example, and it serves as the template in the `src/main/webapp/index.xhtml` file. Remember, this is meant to be a single-page application!

```
<!DOCTYPE html>
<html ng-app="app">
  <head>
    ...
    <link href="styles/bootstrap.css" rel="stylesheet">
    <link href="styles/main.css" rel="stylesheet">
  </head>

  <body ng-controller="CaseRecordController">
    ...
    <div id="mainContent">
      ...
      <div class="case-record-view" >
        ...
        <div class="actionBar"
          ng-controller="NewCaseRecordModalController" >
          <button class="btn btn-primary" ng-
            click="openCreateCaseRecordDialog()" >Add New Case
              Record</button>
          <div ng-show="selected">Selection from a modal: {{
            selected }}</div>
        </div>

        <h2 class="case-record-headline">Case Records</h2>
        <table class="table table-bordered" >
          <tr>
```

```
          <th>Id</th>
          <th>Last Name</th>
          <th>First Name</th>
          <th>Sex</th>
          <th>Country</th>
          <th>Passport No</th>
          <th>D.o.B</th>
          <th>Expiration Date</th>
          <th>Status</th>
        </tr>
        ...
      </table>
    </div>
  </div>
 </body>
</html>
```

The HTML tag element is attributed with an AngularJS directive, `ng-app`, which specifies the name of the scoped value that serves as the application. We have the usual `head` and `body` elements. We include the CSS files Bootstrap (`bootstrap.css`) and the application's style file, `main.css`. There is not much difference until we arrive at the `Body` tag, which is declared with the `ng-controller` attribute. The `ng-controller` directive attaches a controller to the view. The controller is the JavaScript object that is part of the MVC pattern. So the entire `body` tag element in the DOM is bound to the JavaScript object called `CaseRecordController`. We will see the code for it later, but first, let's dive just a little bit deeper.

As you examine the code further, you will notice another controller directive on the `div` element with the CSS selector named `action-bar`. This element is associated with a different controller called `NewCaseRecordModalController`. Every time an `ng-controller` directive is attributed, AngularJS creates a brand new scope. So scopes can be nested with one another. This is the key concept in the AngularJS framework. The scope exists on the element that is associated with and enclosing other nested scopes, should they exist.

The main view renders a table of the case records. The preceding code renders the first and last names of the applicant, their sex, their date of birth, their ISO country code, their passport number, and their passport's expiration date.

The following is the next part of the content that renders the master table row:

```
<tr ng-repeat-start="caseRecord in caseRecords">
  <td>
    <div ng-controller="NewCaseRecordModalController"
      style="display: inline;">
      <a class="btn" href="#" ng-
        click="showOrHideTasks($parent.caseRecord)">
        <i class="glyphicon" ng-
          class="getIconClass($parent.caseRecord)" ></i>
      </a>
    </div>
  </td>
  <td>{{caseRecord.lastName}}</td>
  <td>{{caseRecord.firstName}}</td>
  <td>{{caseRecord.sex}}</td>
  <td>{{caseRecord.country}}</td>
  <td>{{caseRecord.passportNo}}</td>
  <td>{{caseRecord.dateOfBirth}}</td>
  <td>{{caseRecord.expirationDate}}</td>
  <td>{{caseRecord.currentState}}</td>
</tr>
```

There are several parts to this code content. The ng-repeat-start is a special directive that allows the content to be iterated using an expression. The expression is a form selection query that AngularJS evaluates dynamically. So, the <"caseRecord in caseRecords"> expression means an overall iteration of the objects in the scope named caseRecords, and assigning each element as an object called caseRecord. We use the AngularJS binding directive expressions to render the information for each case record in the appropriate table cell element. We do this for the cell {{caseRecord.lastName}}, then rinse and repeat.

The first data cell is special, because it renders an embedded div element. It illustrates how to associate a Boolean value and provides an expanding and collapsing association to the case record. We must create a scope on the div and associate the appropriate controller NewCaseRecordModalController with the ng-controller attribute. We take advantage of the ng-click directive to invoke a method on the controller called showOrHideTasks(). Notice that we pass the parent of the scope, which contains the current CaseRecord as the table is being rendered. There is another directive, ng-class, that associates the icon element with the appropriate glyph icon from Bootstrap by setting the CSS selector. This code opens and closes a secondary row in the table view, which renders a task view. It also updates the glyph icon correctly based on whether the task view is open or closed.

The third part of this table view content now follows:

```
<tr ng-repeat-end  ng-if="caseRecord.showTasks" >
  <td colspan="9">
    <div class="case-record-task-view">
      <div ng-controller="NewCaseRecordModalController">
        <button class="btn btn-info"
        ng-click="openEditCaseRecordDialog($parent.caseRecord)" >Edit
Case Record Details</button>
        <button class="btn btn-info"
        ng-click="changeStateCaseRecordDialog($parent.caseRecord)"
>Change State</button>
      </div>
      <br />

      <div ng-controller="NewTaskModalController">
        <p>
          <button class="btn btn-primary"
            ng-click="openNewTaskDialog(caseRecord.id)">Add New Task</
button>
        </p>
      </div>

      <table class="case-record-task-table">
        <tr>
          <td> Item </td>
          <td> Description </td>
          <td> Completed </td>
          <td> Due Date </td>
          <td> Control </td>
        </tr>

        <tr ng-repeat="task in caseRecord.tasks">
          ...
        </tr><!-- ng-repeat-end ## tasks in caseRecords.tasks -->
      </table>
    </div>
  </td>
</tr><!-- ng-repeat-end ## caseRecord in caseRecords -->
```

The secondary row in the master table has an ng-repeat-end directive, which
informs AngularJS which DOM element finishes the loop iteration for each
CaseRecord element. There is actually another directive called ng-repeat that
combines ng-repeat-start and ng-repeat-end for a single DOM element. That
directive is usually for rendering the simple rows in a table.

The `ng-if` directive conditionally adds or removes content from the DOM. We use this `ng-if` to show and hide the task view area for each case record element. AngularJS provides other similar directives called `ng-show` and `ng-hide`, but those do not dynamically add or remove content from the DOM.

> Why would we choose `ng-if` over `ng-show`? Suppose you have hundreds of case record elements in your database, would we want to render all of those cases and their task history on the web frontend?

We have a `div-layer` element dedicated for showing the tasks associated with a case record. Look at the CSS selector, `case-record-task-view`. We add content to display each `task` element as a table. There is an example for using the `ng-repeat` that has an expression task, in `caseRecord.tasks`.

There are two other inner `div` layers. The first element is bound to the logic to edit the current case record and references the controller called `NewCaseRecordModalController`. The second element allows the user to create a new task, and it references a new controller called `NewTaskModalController`. We will see the JavaScript code for these controllers later on.

The following screenshot illustrates the expansion and contraction for show tasks:

Case Records

Id	Last Name	First Name	Sex	Country	Passport No	D.o.B	Expiration Date	Status
+	Bingham	Connor	M	ZAR	16992425557	1960-09-21	2015-05-24	STATE:[Start]
–	Cassidy	Muhammad	M	MWI	15877026362	1984-03-22	2015-05-21	STATE:[Reviewing]

Edit Case Record Details   Change State

Add New Task

Item	Description	Completed	Due Date	Control
266	~~Allocate~~	✓ Done	2015-05-22	
267	Review case	Done	2015-05-30	

This screenshot depicts the expansion and contraction of the secondary row element with `ng-if`.

To complete the content for the table view, we write table data rows to show the properties of the `task` element:

```
<tr ng-repeat="task in caseRecord.tasks">
  <td> {{task.id}} </td>
  <td>
    <span class="done-{{task.completed}}"> {{task.name}} </span>
  </td>
  <td>
    <label class="checkbox">
      <input type="checkbox" ng-model="task.completed"
        ng-change="updateProjectTaskCompleted(task)">
      Done
    </label>
  </td>
  <td>
    {{task.targetDate}}
  </td>
  <td>
    <div ng-controller="NewTaskModalController">
      <a class="btn" href="#"ng-
        click="openEditTaskDialog($parent.task)" >
        <i class="glyphicon glyphicon-edit"></i></a>
      <a class="btn" href="#"ng-
        click="openDeleteTaskDialog($parent.task)" >
        <i class="glyphicon glyphicon-trash"></i></a>
    </div>
  </td>
</tr><!-- ng-repeat-end ## tasks in caseRecords.tasks -->
```

In the fourth part of the view, we take full advantage of the AngularJS two-way binding to render an HTML `checkbox` element and associate it with the Boolean property, `caseRecord.completed`. Using the CSS selector, we dynamically change the text of the task name with the class selector expression, `class="done-{{task.completed}}"`. When the user changes the checkbox, the following CSS is chosen:

```
.done-true {
  text-decoration: line-through; color: #52101d;
}
```

When the task is completed, the text is struck through! We added an `ng-change` directive to the checkbox element, which AngularJS associates with a change event. AngularJS invokes the method, `updateProjectTaskCompleted()` on the controller `NewTaskModalController`. This method invokes a `WebSocket` call. We will explain the code behind it soon! Notice that the method call passes the current `task` element, because we are still in the rendering scope.

In order to complete the task view, we have a `div` layer associated with the controller `NewTaskModalController` with glyph icon buttons to edit and remove a task. As you can see, we need to pass in `$parent.task` in order to reference the element loop variable.

It's time to look at the project organization and then the individual JavaScript modules, controllers, and factories.

Project organization

The project is organized into a Java EE web application. We put all our JavaScript code into the folders that follow the convention for AngularJS, because it is likely that we are professionally working in a full-stack environment and sharing the code base with mixed skills. The AngularJS controllers are placed under `app/controllers`, while the factories and services are placed under `app/service`, as shown in the following structure:

```
src/main/webapp/app/controllers

src/main/webapp/app/controllers/main.js

src/main/webapp/app/controllers/newcaserecord-modal.js

src/main/webapp/app/controllers/newtask-modal.js

src/main/webapp/app/services

src/main/webapp/app/services/iso-countries.js

src/main/webapp/app/services/shared-services.js
```

Next, we put the third-party JavaScript libraries into their designated area:

```
src/main/webapp/javascripts

src/main/webapp/javascripts/angular.js

src/main/webapp/javascripts/bootstrap.js

src/main/webapp/javascripts/jquery-2.1.3.js

src/main/webapp/javascripts/ui-bootstrap-0.12.1.js

src/main/webapp/javascripts/ui-bootstrap-tpl-0.12.1.js
```

Note that our caseworker application also depends on Bootstrap, jQuery, and the extension library, Bootstrap UI for AngularJS. We include all these libraries explicitly in the last part of the content for the main view index.html, which is as follows:

```
<html ng-app="app">  ...
  <body> ...
    <script src="javascripts/jquery-2.1.3.js"></script>
    <script src="javascripts/angular.js"></script>
    <script src="javascripts/bootstrap.js"></script>
    <script src="javascripts/ui-bootstrap-tpls-
      0.12.1.js"></script>
    <script src="app/controllers/main.js"></script>
    <script src="app/controllers/newcaserecord-modal.js"></script>
    <script src="app/controllers/newtask-modal.js"></script>
    <script src="app/services/shared-service.js"></script>
    <script src="app/services/iso-countries.js"></script>
  </body>
</html>
```

As I said earlier, we've kept the code base simpler for the purpose of demonstration, but we could have used RequireJS to handle the dependency loading.

> If you don't explicitly load jQuery before AngularJS, then it will load its own smaller version of jQuery called **jq-lite**. So if your application depends on the full version of the jQuery library, please ensure it is loaded before AngularJS.

The final step is to put the CSS in their own special area:

src/main/webapp/styles

src/main/webapp/styles/bootstrap.css

src/main/webapp/styles/bootstrap-theme.css

src/main/webapp/styles/main.css

The preceding files are loaded at the top of the main view, inside the usual head HTML element.

Application main controller

The first module in our AngularJS application declares the name of the application. The following is the declaration in the file: `src/main/webapp/app/controllers/main.js`:

```
var myApp = angular.module('app', ['ui.bootstrap',
'newcaserecord','newtask', 'sharedService', 'isoCountries']);
```

The framework exports a function object called `angular`, and it has a method called `module` that defines a module. The first argument is the name of the module and the second argument is an array of the dependent module names. The `module()` method returns an AngularJS module object to the caller. From there, we declare the initial controller.

The module `ui.bootstrap` contains AngularJS and Bootstrap integrations. The module `newcaserecord` is part of the caseworker application and defines a controller, which inserts and amends the master records. The module `newtask` defines a controller, which inserts, amends, and removes the details records. The `sharedService` defines a factory provider that performs utility functions for the application, and, finally, `isoCountries` defines another provider that holds a list of the ISO passport countries.

AngularJS framework has a fluent API for defining modules, controllers, and providers; therefore, we could write an almost declarative JavaScript like the following code extract shows:

```
angular.module('myApp', [ 'depend1', 'depend2'])
  .controller( 'controller1', function( depend1, depend2 ) {
      /* ... */
  })
  .controller( 'controller2', function( depend1 ) {
      /* ... */
  })
  .filter('greet', function() {
   return function(name) {
      return 'Hello, ' + name + '!';
    };
  })
  .service( 'our-factory', function( ... ) {
      /* ... */
  })
  .directive( 'my-directive', function( ... ) {
      /* ... */
  });
```

The preceding coding style is a matter of taste and the disadvantage is that all your modules are lumped together. A lot of professional developers prefer to assign the actual Angular module objects to global module variables.

The body tag element in the view defines a controller:

```
<body ng-controller="CaseRecordController">
```

The following extract shows the controller `CaseRecordController` that binds the user interface to a client-side data model:

```
myApp.controller('CaseRecordController', function ($scope, $http,
  $log, UpdateTaskStatusFactory, sharedService, isoCountries ) {
var self = this;
$scope.caseRecords =
  [{sex: "F", firstName: "Angela", lastName: "Devonshire",
    dateOfBirth: "1982-04-15", expirationDate: "2018-11-21",
      country: "Australia", passportNo: "123456789012",
        currentState: "Start"},];

$scope.isoCountries = isoCountries;

$scope.getCaseRecords = function () {
  $http.get('rest/caseworker/list').success(function(data) {
    $scope.caseRecords = data;
  });
}

$scope.$on('handleBroadcastMessage', function() {
  var message = sharedService.getBroadcastMessage();
  if ( message !== "showTasksCaseRecord")  {
    $scope.getCaseRecords();
  }
})

// Retrieve the initial list of case records
$scope.getCaseRecords();

$scope.connect = function() {
  UpdateTaskStatusFactory.connect();
}

$scope.send = function( msg ) {
```

```
      UpdateTaskStatusFactory.send(msg);
    }

    $scope.updateProjectTaskCompleted = function( task ) {
      var message = { 'caseRecordId': task.caseRecordId, 'taskId':
        task.id, 'completed': task.completed }
      $scope.connect()
      var jsonMessage = JSON.stringify(message)
      $scope.send(jsonMessage)
    }
  });
```

The controller method in the AngularJS object accepts the first parameter as the name. The second argument is the function object and as conventional wisdom, we pass in an anonymous JavaScript function with arguments.

```
function ($scope, $http, $log, UpdateTaskStatusFactory, sharedService,
isoCountries ) { /* ... */ }
```

The parameters are all object modules that AngularJS injects to the controller. AngularJS defines standard modules beginning with the dollar character ($). The module $scope is a special parameter that denotes the current scope. The module $http represents a core AngularJS service with methods that communicate with a remote HTTP server. The module $log is another core service for logging to the console. The other parameters UpdateTaskStatusFactory, sharedService, and isoCountries are factories and services that our application provides. AngularJS, like many JavaScript modern digital frameworks, encourages modular programming and avoids polluting the global scope as much as possible.

So what does this controller do? First, for demonstration purposes, the controller initializes a dummy JSON record, $scope.caseRecord, just in case the server is not available by the time the page view loads. Next, we define a property for the list of records, $scope.caseRecords. Yes, adding custom properties to the AngularJS $scope is the way to communicate from the data model to the user interface.

We define properties for the controller, $scope.isoCountries.

We define our first function, getCaseRecords(), which is as follows:

```
$scope.getCaseRecords = function () {
  $http.get('rest/caseworker/list').success(function(data) {
    $scope.caseRecords = data;
  });
}
```

This function makes a RESTful GET request to the remote server from the same host that serves the page view. The URL would be something like this: `http://localhost:8080/xen-national-force/rest/caseworker/list`.

We leverage the fluent API to perform an action once the server returns a JSON result. The anonymous function overwrites the `$scope.caseRecords` property with the latest data.

Incidentally, as we construct the function object `CaseRecordController`, we invoke the method `getCaseRecords()` in order to kick start the application.

In AngularJS, we can pass information from one controller to another using a factory service that our application creates or by making an HTTP request to the server. It is also possible to listen to the events that AngularJS publishes on a broadcast channel.

The following code in `CaseRecordController` demonstrates how to update the user interface on all messages but one:

```
$scope.$on('handleBroadcastMessage', function() {
  var message = sharedService.getBroadcastMessage();
  if ( message !== "showTasksCaseRecord")  {
    $scope.getCaseRecords();
  }
})
```

Here, we register an event handler on the AngularJS scope in order to retrieve a notification from our `SharedService` provider. The `$on()` method registers a listener on a specific event type. The first parameter is the message type, and the second parameter is the callback. Inside the function callback, we make an HTTP request to retrieve the entire set of case records from the server side if the message, and therefore the custom event, is not `showTasksCaseRecord`.

> Inside the handler callback, we read the entire the dataset, which could be thousands of case records in a real enterprise application. Therefore, we can improve the performance of the REST call-and-response code. We should, however, resist the urge to descend down the path of too early optimization. You should prefer to just get the user story working.

The other methods in the controller, `connect()` and `send()`, establish a WebSocket channel to the server and send a JSON message down to the server respectively. We will examine the `UpdateTaskStatusFactory` module, and the final method, `updateProjectTaskCompleted()`, in a later section.

If you've never developed, professionally, any JavaScript before, then this chapter might appear very daunting initially. However, please persevere as it is really only about having enough patience to succeed. In this regard, I have prepared a simplistic diagram of the AngularJS scopes as they appear in our caseworker application.

AngularJS scopes in the caseworker application

This preceding diagram charts the journey of the progress and helps us understand where we are going. It also establishes the concept of how AngularJS binds scopes in an hierarchical fashion resembling the DOM itself. Behind the scenes, AngularJS creates internal scopes to handle the repeatable DOM elements that render the HTML `table` element, which is the list of the case records. Developers cannot access these internal data except by programming with expressions, and we should treat them as opaque objects.

> At the time of writing, there is a Google Chrome plugin called Batarang (`https://chrome.google.com/webstore/detail/angularjs-batarang-stable/`), which I would have strongly recommended to examine the AngularJS scope inside the browser. Sadly, it seems that the tool is no longer maintained. It is still worth checking if someone has adopted it.

New case record controller

We have placed the code to create and edit the case records in a separate file called `newcaserecord-modal.js`, which contains the user-defined AngularJS module `newcaserecord`. This module has dependencies on other modules, some of them mentioned before. The `ui.bootstrap.modal` is a special module from the AngularJS UI Bootstrap third-party framework. The module defines the Bootstrap components written by the AngularJS team. In particular, it has a helpful modal dialog extension, which we use throughout the caseworker application.

The following is the shortened code for the `newcaserecord` module and the `NewCaseRecordModalController`:

```
var newcaserecord = angular.module('newcaserecord',
  ['ui.bootstrap.modal', 'sharedService','isoCountries'])


newcaserecord.controller('NewCaseRecordModalController',
  function($scope, $modal, $http, $log, sharedService,
    isoCountries ) {
  $scope.caseRecord = {
    sex: "F", firstName: "", lastName: "", country: "",
      passportNo: "", dateOfBirth: "", expirationDate: "",
        country: "", currentState: "", showTasks: false};
  $scope.returnedData = null;
  $scope.isoCountries = isoCountries;

  $scope.openCreateCaseRecordDialog = function () {
    var modalInstance = $modal.open({
      templateUrl: 'newCaseRecordContent.html',
        controller: newCaseRecordModalInstanceController,
          isoCountries: isoCountries, resolve: {
            caseRecord: function () {
              return $scope.caseRecord;
            }
        }
    });

    modalInstance.result.then(function (data) {
      $scope.selected = data;
      $http.post('rest/caseworker/item',
        $scope.caseRecord).success(function(data) {
        $scope.returnedData = data;
        sharedService.setBroadcastMessage("newCaseRecord");
      });

    }, function () {
```

```
            $log.info('Modal dismissed at: ' + new Date());
        });
    };
    // . . .
);
```

The controller function object accepts injected parameters such as $http, $log, and sharedService. We also inject the $modal instance, which allows us to open modal dialogs in the controller.

Since each controller has its own scope injected into it, we need to provide elements of the data model in order to be accessible to the view. So we create an empty case record in the scope as $scope.caseRecord. We also set up return data and the ISO countries list.

The function $scope.openCreateCaseRecordDialog() generates a modal dialog, so the user is allowed to enter a master case record.

> Allowing a user to create arbitrary application passport records would be probably forbidden and restricted to any employee except to the administrators and managers. Our demonstration application has no concept of roles and permissions at all. Developers should be careful to avoid introducing zero-day exploits into their digital applications.

The UI Bootstrap extension accepts several parameters. The first parameter is a reference to the HTML template directive. The second parameter refers to another controller called newCaseRecordModalInstanceController, which is responsible for handling the interaction with the dialog. The third argument is a resolver and it permits the library code to find the reference data in the user's modal inside the enclosing scope:

```
var modalInstance = $modal.open({
    templateUrl: 'newCaseRecordContent.html',
      controller: newCaseRecordModalInstanceController,
        resolve: {
          caseRecord: function () {
            return $scope.caseRecord;
          }
        }
});
```

The next part of the controller, `NewCaseRecordModalController` handles the callback after the modal dialog completes successfully, because the user entered the data and pressed the confirm button. We register two function objects as parameters on the object called `then`.

```
modalInstance.result.then(function (data) {...},
    function () { /* modal dismissed */ });
```

The first function is the callback handler that contains the code to make a REST POST request to the server with the case record data. The second function is reserved for when the dialog is dismissed. You will notice that AngularJS employs fluent interfaces. The code should be fairly understandable even if you don't happen to know everything about JavaScript and the framework.

So let's look at the code for the modal dialog instance, namely the object `newCaseRecordModalInstanceController`:

```
var newCaseRecordModalInstanceController = function ($scope,
$modalInstance, caseRecord ) {
  caseRecord.showTasks = true; // Convenience for the user
  $scope.caseRecord = caseRecord;

  $scope.ok = function () {
    $modalInstance.close(true);
  };

  $scope.cancel = function () {
    $modalInstance.dismiss('cancel');
  };
};
```

If you notice, this variable is not quite an encapsulated module in JavaScript; rather, the `newCaseRecordModalInstanceController` function is declared in the global scope. I suppose there are always exceptions to the rule. The UI Bootstrap code invokes this controller function through the `$modalInstance.open()` call. The framework supplies the three arguments, the scope `$scope`, the modal instance `$modalInstance`, and the case record `caseRecord` to the function. We assign the case record to the supplied scope in order to write-back the data from the modal dialog. There, the function object implements two methods, `ok()` and `cancel()`, that handle the confirmation and cancellation of the dialog respectively.

We only need to write the HTML directive for the dialog.

The case record modal view template

As we know, all the content for the site is inside a single page application. HTML directives are also found in the view, index.html. How do you write a directive into the page content without it appearing in the view? Is the secret sauce something to do with CSS?

Although styling is a good idea, it is not the correct answer. The AngularJS designers take advantage of the formal definition for the HTML Script tag, which is the element that embeds or references the executable script.

The following is the HTML directive for inserting a new case record into the application:

```html
<script type="text/ng-template" id="newCaseRecordContent.html">
  <div class="modal-header">
    <h3>New Case Record </h3>
  </div>
  <div class="modal-body">
    <form name="newCaseRecordForm" class="css-form" novalidate>
      Sex:<br />
      <select ng-model="caseRecord.sex" required>
        <option value="F" ng-option="selected caseRecord.sex ===
          'F'">Female</option>
        <option value="M" ng-option="selected caseRecord.sex ===
          'M'">Male</option>
      </select>
      <br/>
      First Name:<br />
      <input type="text" ng-model="caseRecord.firstName"
        required /><br />
      Last Name:<br />
      <input type="text" ng-model="caseRecord.lastName"
        required /><br />
      Date of Birth:<br />
      <input type="text" ng-model="caseRecord.dateOfBirth"
        datepicker-popup="yyyy-MM-dd" required /><br />
      Country:<br />
      <select ng-model="caseRecord.country" required
        ng-options="item.code as item.country for item in
          isoCountries.countryToCodeArrayMap">
      </select>
      <br />
      Passport Number:<br />
      <input type="text" ng-model="caseRecord.passportNo"
        required /><br />
```

```
    Expiration Date:<br />
    <input type="text" ng-model="caseRecord.expirationDate"
      datepicker-popup="yyyy-MM-dd" required /><br />
  </form>
</div>
<div class="modal-footer">
  <button class="btn btn-primary" ng-click="ok()"
    ng-disabled="newCaseRecordForm.$invalid" >OK</button>
  <button class="btn btn-warning"
    ng-click="cancel()">Cancel</button>
</div>
</script>
```

The preceding HTML directive defines a UI Bootstrap modal dialog, because the HTML `script` tag is denoted with the type attribute of `text/ng-template`. All AngularJS directives require an identifier. This directive contains a header, footer, and main as we can see from the CSS. The main `div` layer is an HTML form.

Each input field in the form is bound to the data model in the instance of `newCaseRecordModalInstanceController`. The case record was assigned to the scope as soon as the UI Bootstrap invoked the function object. Hence, the `ng-model` data model, `$scope.caseRecord.firstName` is available to the HTML text input element reserved for first names.

AngularJS has an elegant additional markup for validating the form input elements. You can see the additional required attribute on almost all of the inputs. Unfortunately, as this book cannot delve into deeper details of validation checking, I want to draw your attention to two subtle validation checks.

The data input exploits the UI Bootstrap date picker component to allow the case worker to easily enter dates;

```
<input type="text" ng-model="caseRecord.dateOfBirth" datepicker-
popup="yyyy-MM-dd" required />
```

The format of the date is defined by the attribute, `datepicker-popup`.

Lastly, we display a drop-down list of the ISO passport country names in an HTML `select` element. The code for this part is as follows:

```
<select ng-model="caseRecord.country" required
  ng-options="item.code as item.country for item in
    isoCountries.countryToCodeArrayMap">
</select>
```

The `isoCountries` is a service instance, which we will see later. Since that module was injected into the `NewCaseRecordModalController` module and the scope of the latter happens to enclose the modal instance scope, AngularJS allow us to access the service. The `isoCountries` instance contains a list of the passport countries in a key and value dictionary. The code allows us to associate the ISO code `AUS` with the country name Australia. The `ng-option` attribute accepts an expression, which resembles an SQL query. We declaratively inform AngularJS how to derive the display name (`item.country`) and the input form value (`item.code`) for each HTML `option` element.

The following is a screenshot of the create case record modal dialog with the date picker:

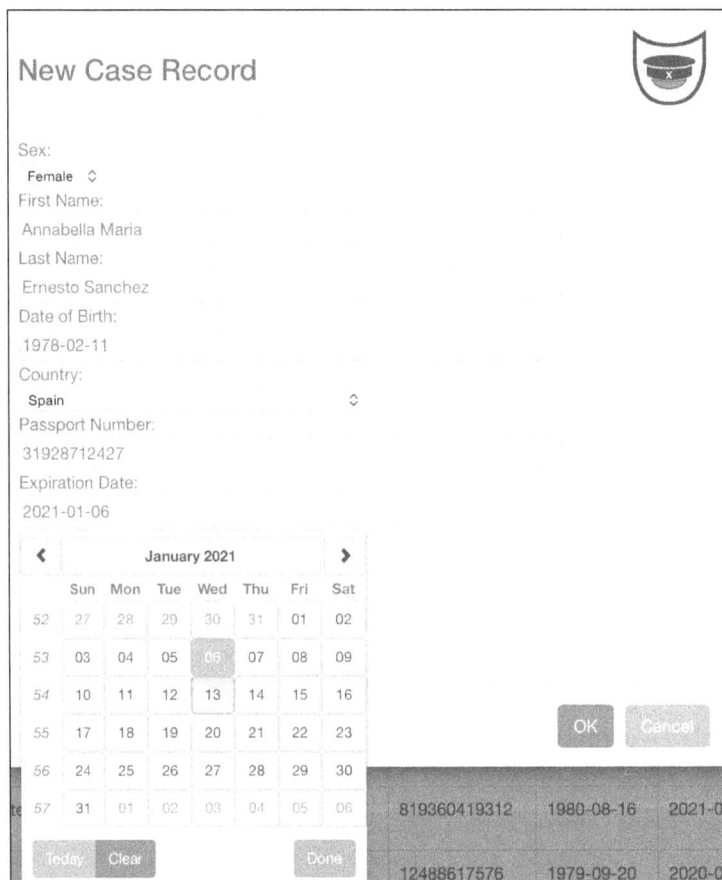

A screenshot of the create case record modal dialog with date picker in full effect

Let's move onto the task record controller that is similar to the case record controller.

New task record controller

As a caseworker uses the system, he or she is able to expand and collapse the task record associated with the case record. The user can create, edit, and amend tasks, and can also change the state of the case.

The AngularJS module `newtask` is defined thus:

```
var newtask = angular.module('newtask', ['ui.bootstrap.modal',
'sharedService'])
newtask.config(function($httpProvider) {
  $httpProvider.defaults.headers["delete"] = {
    'Content-Type': 'application/json;charset=utf-8'
  };
})
```

We add a configuration change to AngularJS around the HTTP remoting. There is a subtle bug with the HTTP DELETE request. The JAX-RS reference implementation, Jersey, which is present in the GlassFish and Payara application server, raises an HTTP error with a response code 415: Unsupported Media Type. This forces AngularJS to send the MIME type, as JSON on the DELETE requests solves the issue.

Since the code for the task controller is so similar, only the create part of CRUD will be revealed in this book. Refer to the source for the other methods. The following is the source code for `NewTaskModalController`:

```
newtask.controller('NewTaskModalController', function($scope, $modal,
$http, $log, sharedService ) {
  $scope.selected = false;
  $scope.task = {
      id: 0, name: '', targetDate: null, completed: false,
caseRecordId: 0
  };
  $scope.returnedData = null;
  $scope.openNewTaskDialog = function(caseRecordId) {
    var modalInstance = $modal.open({
      templateUrl: 'newTaskContent.html',
      controller: newTaskModalInstanceController,
      resolve: {
        task: function () {
          return $scope.task;
        }
      }
    });

    modalInstance.result.then(function (data) {
```

```
        $scope.selected = data;
        $http.post('rest/caseworker/item/'+caseRecordId+'/task',
          $scope.task).success(function(data) {
          $scope.returnedData = data;
          sharedService.setBroadcastMessage("newTask");
          // Reset Task in this scope for better UX affordance.
          $scope.task = {
            id: 0, name: '', targetDate: null, completed: false,
              caseRecordId: 0
          };
        });
      }, function () {
          $log.info('Modal dismissed at: ' + new Date());
      });
    };

    $scope.openEditTaskDialog = function(taskItem) {
      // ...
    };

    $scope.openDeleteTaskDialog = function(taskItem) {
      // ...
    };
  });
```

In this controller, instead of $scope.caseRecord, we have an empty, default
$scope.task object. Every Task object has a reference to the parent through the
property, caseRecordId.

The function, openNewTaskDialog() opens a UI Bootstrap modal dialog that
allows the user to enter a brand task. The method wires up the modal dialog with
the AngularJS scope of the current Task object. The big difference is the REST URL
endpoint, which is in the form of rest/caseworker/item/'+caseRecordId+'/task.

We use the UI Bootstrap $modal object and create a modal dialog instance as before,
except that we now pass different arguments. The arguments are the HTML directive
ID, which is newTaskContent.html; the controller is called newTaskModalInstan
ceController,and the resolver function. AngularJS invokes the resolver function,
which is defined as an anonymous function, in order to reference the enclosing Task
object.

In the callback function for the modalInstance object, we conveniently reset the
Task object so that the user is not surprised by stale form data when the dialog is
raised again. We set the broadcast message in sharedService.

The code to handle the modal instance in the task dialog is almost the same:

```
var newTaskModalInstanceController = function ($scope, $modalInstance,
task) {
  $scope.task = task;

  $scope.ok = function () {
      $modalInstance.close(true);
  };

  $scope.cancel = function () {
    $modalInstance.dismiss('cancel');
  };
};
```

The function `newTaskModalInstanceController` accepts three arguments: the `$scope` that binds the modal instance dialog, `$modalInstance` itself, and the `Task` object. The last argument, the `Task` object, is resolved and we set it as a property on the scope in order to easily render the view in the template.

The task modal view template

The AngularJS directive `newTaskContent.html` renders the view for the modal dialog that lets the user enter a new task. There are only four properties, so this view is shorter than the case record.

The definition for this view is as follows:

```
<script type="text/ng-template" id="newTaskContent.html">
  <div class="modal-header">
    <h3>New Task</h3>
  </div>
  <div class="modal-body">
    <form name="newTaskForm" class="css-form" novalidate>
      Task Name:<br />
      <textarea ng-model="task.name" rows="3" required /><br />
      Target Date:  <br />
      <input type="text" datepicker-popup="yyyy-MM-dd"
        ng-model="task.targetDate" required /><br />
      Task Completed: <br />
      Done <input type="checkbox" ng-model="task.completed" />
        <br />
    </form>
  </div>
  <div class="modal-footer">
```

```
        <button class="btn btn-primary" ng-click="ok()"
          ng-disabled="newTaskForm.$invalid" >OK</button>
        <button class="btn btn-warning"
          ng-click="cancel()">Cancel</button>
     </div>
   </script>
```

This view also follows the UI Bootstrap CSS style for modal dialogs. We demonstrate an HTML `text area` element associated with a data model, which is the `Task` object. Each form field has an `ng-model` association. For the target date, we reuse the date picker and we illustrate how to use the HTML `checkbox` element.

The code for editing and deleting task records looks roughly the same. However, for editing, we don't reset the task record after the user confirms the modal dialog, and for deletion, we show only a read-only view of the task record; the modal dialog is simply a confirmation.

Let's see how we handle the change of state.

State change

A case record exists in the following states:

State	Description
Start	Every new applicant in the system begins at this initial state
End	At the end of the process, the applicant's case finishes in this end state
Reviewing	The case worker is reviewing the applicant's record
Decision	The case has been reviewed and the business is taking a decision
Accepted	The case has been accepted and the applicant is being notified
Rejected	The case has been rejected and the applicant is being rejected

All these business requirements are captured in Finite State Machine.

Controller code

By now the code should be familiar to you. The controller method
`changeStateCaseRecordDialog()` in `NewTaskModalController` is as follows:

```
$scope.changeStateCaseRecordDialog = function (caseRecordItem) {
    /* Copy */
  $scope.caseRecord = {
    id: caseRecordItem.id,
    firstName: caseRecordItem.firstName,
    lastName: caseRecordItem.lastName,
    dateOfBirth: caseRecordItem.dateOfBirth,
    country: caseRecordItem.country,
    passportNo: caseRecordItem.passportNo,
    expirationDate: caseRecordItem.expirationDate,
    currentState: caseRecordItem.currentState,
    nextStates: caseRecordItem.nextStates,
    showTask: caseRecordItem.showTasks
  };

  $scope.caseRecord.nextStates.push( caseRecordItem.currentState );
  $scope.saveCurrentState = caseRecordItem.currentState;

  var modalInstance = $modal.open({
    templateUrl: 'changeStateCaseRecordContent.html',
      controller: moveStateRecordModalInstanceController,
        resolve: {
          caseRecord: function () {
            return $scope.caseRecord;
          }
      }
  });

  modalInstance.result.then(function (data) {
      $scope.selected = data;
      if ( $scope.saveCurrentState !==
        $scope.caseRecord.currentState ) {
          $http.put('rest/caseworker/state/'+$scope.caseRecord.id,
            $scope.caseRecord).success(function(data) {
            $scope.returnedData = data;
            sharedService.setBroadcastMessage("editCaseRecord");
          });
      }
  }, function () { $log.info('Modal dismissed.'); } );
};
```

Since we are just editing an existing case record, we copy the properties of CaseRecord from the enclosing scope into the controller scope. Remember, the outside scope is the main module.

Every JSON case record sent by the server (as we will see later) has a property called nextStates, which is a list of the next possible states that the user can move a record to. To take an example, the Start state has only one possible next state, which is called Reviewing.

Each case record object has a currentState property. We push the current state on to the list of subsequent states stored in the current scope. This array $scope. nextStates allows the dialog HTML directive to render a drop-down menu in the view.

You can see that this function, changeStateCaseRecordDialog(), opens a UI Bootstrap modal dialog.

The template view code

So let's inspect the HTML directive for the state change:

```
<script type="text/ng-template" id="changeStateCaseRecordContent.
html">
  <div class="modal-header">
    <h3>Change State of Case Record</h3>
  </div>
  <div class="modal-body">
    <p>
      <table class="table table-bordered">
        <tr>
          <th> Field </th> <th> Value </th>
        </tr>
        <tr>

          <td> Case Record Id</td> <td> {{caseRecord.id }}</td>
        </tr>
          ...
      </table>
    </p>
      <form name="moveStateCaseRecordForm" class="css-form"
        novalidate>
      Next States:<br />
      <select ng-model="caseRecord.currentState"
        ng-options="state for state in caseRecord.nextStates">
      </select>
```

```
        </form>
    </div>
    <div class="modal-footer">
      <button class="btn btn-primary" ng-click="ok()"
        ng-disabled="moveStateCaseRecordForm.$invalid" >OK</button>
      <button class="btn btn-warning"
        ng-click="cancel()">Cancel</button>
    </div>
  </script>
```

The preceding directive, identified as `changeStateCaseRecordContent.html`, is essentially a read-only view of the entire case record. The only modifiable part is the HTML `select` element that displays the next possible states for the case record. In order to generate the HTML `option` element, there is a different form of expression for the attribute `ng-options`, which is declared as `state for state in caseRecord.nextStates`. This expression implies that the option name and the value are the same for the array String, which is as follows:

Change state for a case record

The modal instance code is essentially the same. The corresponding function associated with the dialog is called `moveStateRecordModalInstanceController()`.

```
var moveStateRecordModalInstanceController = function ($scope,
$modalInstance, caseRecord) {
  $scope.caseRecord = caseRecord;
  $scope.ok = function () { $modalInstance.close(true); };
  $scope.cancel = function () { $modalInstance.dismiss('cancel');
    };
};
```

Before we finish off this long example of AngularJS and the client side, we shall cover a couple of more functions. These functions are part of the module that defines `NewCaseRecordModalController`.

Toggling the task display state

The first function `showOrHideTasks()`, toggles the display property `showTasks` in the case record. It also invokes an HTTP PUT request with the case record JSON data to the server. The code is as follows:

```
$scope.showOrHideTasks = function(caseRecord) {
  caseRecord.showTasks = !caseRecord.showTasks;
  $http.put('rest/caseworker/showtasks/'+caseRecord.id,
    caseRecord).success(function(data) {
    sharedService.setBroadcastMessage("showTasksCaseRecord");
  });
}
```

The second function `getIconClass()` is a bit of cheat mode. It returns the Bootstrap CSS glyph selector depending on the display state. AngularJS does have a conditional expression for `ng-class`; however, at the time of writing, the author could not get it to work for the array of case record elements. Therefore, this function exists in the code base as a work around.

```
$scope.getIconClass = function(caseRecord) {
  if ( caseRecord.showTasks)
    return "glyphicon-minus"
  else
    return "glyphicon-plus"
}
```

If you are interested, the correct code for the client-side that should work is the following:

```
<i class="glyphicon"
  ng-class="{true: 'glyphicon-minus',
    false: 'glyphicon-plus'}[caseRecord.showTasks]">
```

We will jump over to the server-side now.

Server-side Java

Our Java EE application for the caseworker system is built around RESTful services, Java WebSocket, JSON-P, and Java Persistence.

> This section of the book relies on a prior understanding of Java EE development from the elementary level. I recommend that you read the sister book *Java EE 7 Development Handbook*, especially if you find some of these topics difficult to follow.

Entity objects

The server-side would be nothing without a couple of domain objects. It should not be surprising that these are called `CaseRecord` and `Task`.

The following is the extracted `CaseRecord` entity object with full annotations:

```
@NamedQueries({
  @NamedQuery(name="CaseRecord.findAllCases",
    query = "select c from CaseRecord c order by c.lastName,
c.firstName"),
    /* ... */
})
@Entity
@Table(name = "CASE_RECORD")
public class CaseRecord {
  @Id @GeneratedValue(strategy = GenerationType.AUTO)
  private Integer id;
  @NotEmpty @Size(max=64) private String lastName;
  @NotEmpty @Size(max=64) private String firstName;
  @NotEmpty @Size(max=1) private String sex;
  @NotEmpty @Size(max=16) private String passportNo;
  @NotEmpty @Size(max=32) private String country;
```

```
@Past @NotNull @Temporal(TemporalType.DATE) private Date
  dateOfBirth;
@Future @NotNull @Temporal(TemporalType.DATE) private Date
  expirationDate;
@NotEmpty private String currentState;
private boolean showTasks;
@OneToMany(cascade = CascadeType.ALL, mappedBy = "caseRecord",
  fetch = FetchType.EAGER)
private List<Task> tasks = new ArrayList<>();

// Required by JPA
public CaseRecord() {}
/*  ... */
}
```

For these entities, we leverage the popular Hibernate Validator annotations to ensure that the information is correctly saved into the database. The detailed entity `Task` is as follows:

```
@Entity
public class Task {
  @Id @GeneratedValue(strategy = GenerationType.AUTO)
  @Column(name="TASK_ID") private Integer id;
  @NotEmpty @Size(max=256) private String name;
  @Temporal(TemporalType.DATE)
  @Column(name="TARGET_NAME") @Future
  private Date targetDate;
  private boolean completed;
  @ManyToOne(cascade = CascadeType.ALL)
  @JoinColumn(name="CASE_RECORD_ID")
  private CaseRecord caseRecord;

  public Task() { /* Required by JPA */ }
  /*  ... */
}
```

The entities map very closely to the JavaScript objects that we have seen on the client side. In practice, a business application in a different domain might choose an alternative design such as a facade, aggregation, or projection of the data model.

Of course, these entities have a persistence layer in order to retrieve and store information into the database. In the source code, there is a `CaseRecordTaskService` that has the responsibility to persist the `CaseRecord` and `Task` records.

RESTful communication

The stateless session EJB class `CaseWorkerRESTServerEndpoint` serves as our RESTful endpoint:

```
package uk.co.xenonique.nationalforce.control;
/* ... */
import javax.json.*;
import javax.json.stream.*;
import javax.ws.rs.*;
import javax.ws.rs.container.*;
import javax.ws.rs.core.*;
import static javax.ws.rs.core.MediaType.*;

@Path("/caseworker/")
@Stateless
public class CaseWorkerRESTServerEndpoint {
  static JsonGeneratorFactory jsonGeneratorFactory =
    Json.createGeneratorFactory(
      new HashMap<String, Object>() {{
        put(JsonGenerator.PRETTY_PRINTING, true);
      }});

  @Inject
  CaseRecordTaskService service;
/* ... */
}
```

This class is annotated with `@Path` with the initial URI for this endpoint. This relative URI `/caseworker/` matches the AngularJS client side. We inject the persistent stateful session EJB `CaseRecordTaskService` into this endpoint, and we also set up a JSON generator factory that will print the JSON output. We use the standard Java EE 7 JSON generator factory throughout.

Retrieval of case records

To handle the retrieval of caseworker records, I shall demonstrate how to handle an asynchronous operation with JAX-RS. We need a managed executor from the application server and also to ensure that the web application supports the `async` operations after deployment.

For Java EE 7, it is crucially important to enable the asynchronous support in the Web XML deployment descriptor (`src/main/web-app/WEB/web.xml`). This file is as follows:

```xml
<?xml version="1.0" encoding="UTF-8"?>
<web-app xmlns="http://xmlns.jcp.org/xml/ns/javaee" ...
         version="3.1" ... >
  <servlet>
    <servlet-name>javax.ws.rs.core.Application</servlet-name>
    <load-on-startup>1</load-on-startup>
    <async-supported>true</async-supported>
  </servlet>
  <servlet-mapping>
    <servlet-name>javax.ws.rs.core.Application</servlet-name>
    <url-pattern>/rest/*</url-pattern>
  </servlet-mapping>
  <resource-env-ref>
    <resource-env-ref-name>
      concurrent/LongRunningTasksExecutor
    </resource-env-ref-name>
    <resource-env-ref-type>
      javax.enterprise.concurrent.ManagedExecutorService
    </resource-env-ref-type>
  </resource-env-ref>
</web-app>
```

The important XML element is `<async-supported>` and we set its body content to true. We also set the URI for receiving the REST queries for the entire application, as `/rest`. So taking the class `CaseWorkerRESTServerEndpoint` together, the full relative URI, so far, is `/rest/caseworker`. Finally, we declare to the Java EE 7 application server that our application requires a managed executor with the addition of XML elements around `<resource-env-ref>`. This managed executor is referred to by the name, `concurrent/LongRunningTasksExecutor` (the JNDI lookup name).

We shall use it now in the first REST query method:

```java
@Resource(name="concurrent/LongRunningTasksExecutor")
ManagedExecutorService executor;

@GET
@Produces(MediaType.APPLICATION_JSON)
@Path("/list")
public void getCaseRecordList(
  @Suspended final AsyncResponse asyncResponse) {
```

```
      executor.submit(new Runnable() {
        @Override
        public void run() {
          final List<CaseRecord> caseRecords =
            service.findAllCases();
          final StringWriter swriter = new StringWriter();
          final JsonGenerator generator =
            jsonGeneratorFactory.createGenerator(swriter);
            CaseRecordHelper.generateCaseRecordAsJson(generator,
              caseRecords).close();
          final Response response =
            Response.ok(swriter.toString()).build();
          asyncResponse.resume(response);
      }
    });
  }
```

We annotate the method `getCaseRecordList()` with `@GET` to handle the HTTP GET request from the full relative URI, `/rest/caseworker/list`. This method works asynchronously. It relies on the injected `ManagedExecutorService` instance, which is a thread pool executor that Java EE 7 manages. In order to participate in the service, we supplied a method argument, the `AsyncResponse` object, that is annotated with `@Suspended`.

The body of our `getCaseRecordList()` method submits a worker instance (`java.lang.Runnable`) to the managed executor service. The worker retrieves a list of case records from the persistence service and turns them into a JSON output. The output is converted into a String and we ask the `AsyncResponse` instance, through its `resume()` method, to start sending data down the output channel to the client. We annotate the method `getCaseRecordList()` with the JAX RS `@Produces` to declare the MIME type `application.json` of the output content.

> Incidentally, there are two `@Produces` annotations in Java EE 7. One is a part of JAX-RS and the other is a CDI.

We also have a REST endpoint for the retrieval of a specific case record by its ID. Let's take a look at how we can achieve this:

```
@GET
@Path("/item/{id}")
@Produces(APPLICATION_JSON)
public String retrieveCase(
    @PathParam("id") int caseId ) {
  List<CaseRecord> caseRecords = service.findCaseById( caseId );
```

```
        StringWriter swriter = new StringWriter();
        JsonGenerator generator =
          jsonGeneratorFactory.createGenerator(swriter);
        CaseRecordHelper.writeCaseRecordAsJson(generator,
          caseRecords.get(0)).close();
        return swriter.toString();
    }
```

The method `retrieveCase()` is annotated with @GET for an HTTP GET request. It has the relative URI of `/rest/caseworker/item/{id}`. The method searches for the case record by ID and creates a JSON representation of it. It sends the output to the client synchronously. Just a quick note: we removed the sanity checking code in these extracts in order to save space.

Creating a case record

We've covered the retrieval side and now we move onto creational REST endpoints. In our system, a web client may create a case record using REST calls. The following code inserts a new case record into the application. The relative URI for creating a new case record is `/rest/caseworker/item`.

```
@POST
@Path("/item")
@Consumes(APPLICATION_JSON)
@Produces(APPLICATION_JSON)
public String createCase( JsonObject json )
  throws Exception {
  CaseRecord caseRecord = new CaseRecord();
  caseRecord.setSex(json.getString("sex"));
  caseRecord.setFirstName(json.getString("firstName"));
  caseRecord.setLastName(json.getString("lastName"));
  caseRecord.setCountry(json.getString("country"));
  caseRecord.setPassportNo(json.getString("passportNo"));
  caseRecord.setDateOfBirth(
    CaseRecordHelper.FMT2.parse(json.getString("dateOfBirth")));
  caseRecord.setExpirationDate(
    CaseRecordHelper.FMT2.parse(json.getString("expirationDate")));
  caseRecord.setCurrentState(
    BasicStateMachine.FSM_START.toString());
  caseRecord.setShowTasks(json.getBoolean("showTasks", false));

  JsonArray tasksArray = json.getJsonArray("tasks");
  if ( tasksArray != null ) {
    for ( int j=0; j<tasksArray.size(); ++j ) {
```

```
        JsonObject taskObject = tasksArray.getJsonObject(j);
        Task task = new Task(
          taskObject.getString("name"),
            ( taskObject.containsKey("targetDate") ?
              CaseRecordHelper.FMT.parse(taskObject.
getString("targetDate"))
                : null ), taskObject.getBoolean("completed"));
          caseRecord.addTask(task);
          task.setCaseRecord(caseRecord);
        }
    }

    service.saveCaseRecord(caseRecord);
    StringWriter swriter = new StringWriter();
    JsonGenerator generator =
      jsonGeneratorFactory.createGenerator(swriter);
    CaseRecordHelper.writeCaseRecordAsJson(generator,
      caseRecord).close();
    return swriter.toString();
  }
```

The method `createCase()` is longer, because it transfers the data inside the JSON-P object instance to a `CaseRecord` entity. We annotate the method with `@POST` to denote that this endpoint handles HTTP POST requests. This is a long-winded boilerplate, which is solved through data-type binding on other non-Java EE 7 frameworks like GSON (`https://code.google.com/p/google-gson/`) or Faster Jackson Processing API for JSON (`http://wiki.fasterxml.com/JacksonInFiveMinutes`), but I must demonstrate the standard approach here. We will have to wait until the specification body delivers JSON-B (Java JSON Binding API) before we can streamline this code.

Updating a case record

Updating a case record, is very similar to creating a new record, except that we first search for a record by its ID and then update the record field by field from the JSON input.

The method `updateCase()` is as follows:

```
@PUT
@Path("/item/{caseId}")
@Consumes(APPLICATION_JSON)
@Produces(APPLICATION_JSON)
public String updateCase(
  @PathParam("caseId") int caseId, JsonObject json ) throws
    Exception {
```

```
final List<CaseRecord> caseRecords = service.findCaseById(caseId);
CaseRecord caseRecord = caseRecords.get(0);
caseRecord.setSex(json.getString("sex"));
/* ... omitted */
caseRecord.setDateOfBirth(
  FMT2.parse( json.getString("dateOfBirth")));
caseRecord.setExpirationDate(
  FMT2.parse(json.getString("expirationDate")));
caseRecord.setCurrentState(
  BasicStateMachine.retrieveCurrentState(
    json.getString("currentState",
      BasicStateMachine.FSM_START.toString())).toString());
caseRecord.setShowTasks(json.getBoolean("showTasks", false));
service.saveCaseRecord(caseRecord);
final StringWriter swriter = new StringWriter();
final JsonGenerator generator =
  jsonGeneratorFactory.createGenerator(swriter);
CaseRecordHelper.writeCaseRecordAsJson(
  generator, caseRecord).close();
return swriter.toString();
}
```

This RESTful endpoint is annotated with @PUT in order to handle an HTTP PUT request. This time, the relative URI is /rest/caseworker/item/{id} that denotes that the client must supply a case record ID. Again, we copy the values from the JSON object and overwrite the properties in the CaseRecord that was retrieved from persistence; then we save the record. We generate a JSON representation of the record and set that as a response that JAX-RS will send back to the client.

The static instance FMT2 is a java.text.SimpleDateFormat, which translates between the expiration date and date-of-birth String and the java.util.Date instances. The pattern format is yyyy-MM-dd. The BasicStateMachine instance is the implementation of the finite state machine. The FSM_START is a singleton instance of one of the possible states. Refer to the book's source code in order to see how it is implemented.

Creating a task record

We shall now examine the create, update, and delete endpoints for the task record in quick succession. Retrieval has already been settled because every CaseRecord instance has a collection of zero or more Task entities, which fulfilled the master detail arrangement.

Creating and updating a task record are very similar operations. So let's study the create method first:

```
@POST
@Path("/item/{caseId}/task")
@Consumes(APPLICATION_JSON)
@Produces(APPLICATION_JSON)
public String createNewTaskOnCase(
  @PathParam("caseId") int caseId, JsonObject taskObject ) throws
    Exception
{
  final List<CaseRecord> caseRecords =
    service.findCaseById(caseId);
  final CaseRecord caseRecord = caseRecords.get(0);
  final Task task = new Task(
    taskObject.getString("name"),
    ( taskObject.containsKey("targetDate") ?
      CaseRecordHelper.convertToDate(
      taskObject.getString("targetDate")) :
      null ),
    ( taskObject.containsKey("completed")) ?
        taskObject.getBoolean("completed") : false );
  caseRecord.addTask(task);
  service.saveCaseRecord(caseRecord);
  final StringWriter swriter = new StringWriter();
  JsonGenerator generator =
    jsonGeneratorFactory.createGenerator(swriter);
  CaseRecordHelper.writeCaseRecordAsJson(
    generator, caseRecord).close();
  return swriter.toString();
}
```

We annotate the method `createNewTaskOnCase()` with `@POST`. The relative URI is `/rest/caseworker/item/{caseId}/task`. The client submits the parent case record and the method uses this ID to retrieve the appropriate `CaseRecord`. It's probably a good idea to cross-reference with the AngularJS client side from the new task record controller. Inside the `createNewTaskOnCase()`, we removed the sanity checking code again in order to concentrate on the substance. The next part of the code is mapping JSON to the Java entity. Afterwards, we add the `Task` entity to `CaseRecord` and then persist the master record. The method is complete once we write the response.

Updating a task record

The method `updateTaskOnCase()` performs an update of the task. We annotate this method with @PUT and with two RESTful arguments. The relative URI is `/rest/caseworker/item/{caseId}/task/{taskId}`. The code for updating a task record is as follows:

```
@PUT
@Path("/item/{caseRecordId}/task/{taskId}")
@Consumes(APPLICATION_JSON)
@Produces(APPLICATION_JSON)
public String updateTaskOnCase(
  @PathParam("caseRecordId") int caseRecordId,
  @PathParam("taskId") int taskId,
  JsonObject taskObject ) throws Exception
{
  final List<CaseRecord> caseRecords =
    service.findCaseById(caseRecordId);
  final CaseRecord caseRecord = caseRecords.get(0);
  caseRecord.getTasks().stream().filter(
    task -> task.getId().equals(taskId)).forEach(
      task -> {
        task.setName( taskObject.getString("name") );
        task.setTargetDate(
          taskObject.containsKey("targetDate") ?
          CaseRecordHelper.convertToDate(
            taskObject.getString("targetDate")) : null );
        task.setCompleted(
          taskObject.containsKey("completed") ?
            taskObject.getBoolean("completed") : false );
    });
  service.saveCaseRecord(caseRecord);
  final StringWriter swriter = new StringWriter();
  final JsonGenerator generator =
    jsonGeneratorFactory.createGenerator(swriter);
  CaseRecordHelper.writeCaseRecordAsJson(
    generator, caseRecord).close();
  return swriter.toString();
}
```

With our two coordinates `caseRecordId` and `TaskId`, we locate the appropriate `Task` entity and then update the properties from the JSON input. Here, we take advantage of the Java 8 Lambdas and Stream API for a functional approach. We save the entity and render the JSON response from the current `CaseRecord` entity.

Deleting a task record

Last, but not the least, we provide the client side frontend a means to removing the task records from the case records. The code it as follows:

```
@DELETE
@Path("/item/{caseRecordId}/task/{taskId}")
@Consumes( { APPLICATION_JSON, APPLICATION_XML, TEXT_PLAIN })
@Produces(APPLICATION_JSON)
public String removeTaskFromCase(
  @PathParam("caseRecordId") int caseRecordId,
  @PathParam("taskId") int taskId,
  JsonObject taskObject )
  throws Exception
{
  final List<CaseRecord> caseRecords =
    service.findCaseById(caseRecordId);
  final CaseRecord caseRecord = caseRecords.get(0);
  caseRecord.getTasks().stream().filter(
    task -> task.getId().equals(taskId))
    .forEach( task -> caseRecord.removeTask(task) );
  service.saveCaseRecord(caseRecord);
  final StringWriter swriter = new StringWriter();
  final JsonGenerator generator =
        jsonGeneratorFactory.createGenerator(swriter);
  CaseRecordHelper.writeCaseRecordAsJson(generator, caseRecord).
close();
  return swriter.toString();
}
```

For an HTTP DELETE request, we annotate the method `deleteTaskFromCase()` with `@DELETE`. The relative URI for this method is the strictly RESTful service endpoint of `/rest/caseworker/item/{caseId}/task/{taskId}`.

In this method, the tricky part is to search for the actual `Task` record. Here, Java 8 Lambda and the stream functions make this a very comprehensive and pleasant task. With the `Task` entity correctly identified, we remove it from the parent `CaseRecord` and then save the master record with persistence. At the end of the message, we send a JSON response of `CaseRecord`.

This covers the JAX-RS side of the application; we shall now move on to the Java EE WebSocket support.

WebSocket communication

WebSocket is an HTML protocol extension that allows a client and server to participate in full duplex asynchronous communication across a network. It works by an initial handshake between two endpoints across backwards-compatible HTTP before switching to the faster TCP/IP streams. The WebSocket specification (RFC 6455) is part of the conglomerate of the HTML5 technologies driven by **Web Hypertext Application Technology Working Group (WHATWG)** (https://whatwg.org) and **Internet Engineering Task Force (IETF)** (https://www.ietf.org).

WebSocket support has been available since the Java EE 7 release, and the related JSCP specification is JSR 356 (https://jcp.org/en/jsr/detail?id=356). We can develop JavaEE WebSocket with either annotations or directly against the API. It is easier to write with annotations, as we will see.

AngularJS client side

It is helpful to review again the AngularJS client side around the new task record controller and the application main controller. Let's examine the method `updateProjectTaskCompleted()` in the controller `CaseRecordController`. Whenever the user decides the task is complete by selecting or deselecting the HTML `checkbox` element, we wire up the frontend to send a WebSocket message via the `send()` method:

```
$scope.updateProjectTaskCompleted = function( task ) {
    var message = { 'caseRecordId': task.caseRecordId, 'taskId':
task.id, 'completed': task.completed }
    $scope.connect()
    var jsonMessage = JSON.stringify(message)
    $scope.send(jsonMessage)
}
```

The entire local JavaScript task record is sent over as JSON.

In order to provide the WebSocket communication generally across to other modules on the client side, AngularJS recommends that we define a factory or service. A factory is usually initialized only once. A service, on the other hand, adds functionality and returns different instances depending on the calling context.

The following is the missing factory:

```
myApp.factory('UpdateTaskStatusFactory', function( $log ) {
  var service = {};

  service.connect = function() {
    if (service.ws) { return; }
```

```
    var ws = new WebSocket("ws://localhost:8080/
      xen-force-angularjs-1.0-SNAPSHOT/update-task-status");
    ws.onopen = function() {
      $log.log("WebSocket connect was opened"); };
    ws.onclose = function() {
      $log.log("WebSocket connection was closed"); }
    ws.onerror = function() {
      $log.log("WebSocket connection failure"); }
    ws.onmessage = function(message) {
      $log.log("message received ["+message+"]"); };
    service.ws = ws;
  }

  service.send = function(message) {
      service.ws.send(message);
  }

  return service;
});
```

The idiom for defining an AngularJS factory resembles the defining of a controller or a module, strongly. With the main module myApp, we invoke the library factory() method with two arguments: the name of the factory and the function callback that defines the service. The factory has only one dependency on the default logging module, $log.

This connect() method initializes an HTML5 WebSocket with the URL by instantiating a WebSocket instance. With the handle, we register optional callbacks to deal with events: when the WebSocket is opened, closed, receives a message, or there is an error. Each callback dumps a message to the web browser's console log.

We define a couple of send() methods that send the message body content down the WebSocket to the peer. In WebSocket parlance, the remote endpoint is known as the peer, because there is no distinction between the client and server endpoints. Both sides can start a connection to the other and begin communicating; hence the term full duplex.

Server-side WebSocket endpoints

As mentioned earlier, in Java EE 7 we can quickly develop WebSocket endpoints using the standard annotations. The Java WebSocket API closely follows the IETF specification, and you will recognize the similarities with the many JavaScript implementations inside a web browser. There is far too much to the configuration and to the different approaches of annotation and programming directly to the library that can be reasonably squeezed in this digital Java EE book.

Nevertheless, the essential Java class is actually annotated as a stateless session EJB as well as a WebSocket. This should not be surprising, because the Java EE specification allows this mixture of annotations in certain cases.

The following is the endpoint in `CaseRecordUpdateTaskWebSocketEndpoint`:

```java
package uk.co.xenonique.nationalforce.control;
/* ... */
import javax.websocket.*;
import javax.websocket.server.ServerEndpoint;

@ServerEndpoint("/update-task-status")
@Stateless
public class CaseRecordUpdateTaskWebSocketEndpoint {
  @Inject
  CaseRecordTaskService service;

  static JsonGeneratorFactory jsonGeneratorFactory =
    Json.createGeneratorFactory(...);

  @OnMessage
  public String updateTaskStatus(String message) {
    final StringReader stringReader = new StringReader(message);
    final JsonReader reader = Json.createReader(stringReader);
    final JsonObject obj = reader.readObject();
    final int projectId = obj.getInt("caseRecordId");
    final int taskId = obj.getInt("taskId");
    final boolean completed = obj.getBoolean("completed");
    final List<CaseRecord> projects =
      service.findCaseById(projectId);
    if ( !projects.isEmpty()) {
      projects.get(0).getTasks().stream()
        .filter(task -> task.getId() == taskId).
        forEach(task -> {
            task.setCompleted(completed);
            service.saveCaseRecord(task.getCaseRecord());
```

```
        });
      return "OK";
    }
    return "NOT FOUND";
  }

  @OnOpen
  public void open( Session session ) { ... }
  @OnClose
  public void close( Session session ) { ... }
  @OnError
  public void error( Session session, Throwable err ){
      err.printStackTrace(System.err);
  }
}
```

We annotate the bean with @ServerEndpoint to denote a server-side endpoint. The notion of *server-side* is essentially a Java EE nomenclature to declare an intention that this endpoint lives on an application server. There are also such things as @ClientEndpoint connections.

Instead of callbacks, Java EE uses annotated methods to handle the opening, closing, and failure events around the WebSocket with @OnOpen, @OnClose, and @OnError respectively.

To handle the receiving of a message on WebSocket correctly, a POJO or bean must only have one method annotated with @Message. Behind the scenes, the library framework transforms the message into a String for the simplest case as we have here. It is possible to send binary and complex data types down and across the wire.

Inside the updateTaskStatus() method, we leverage the JSON-P API to parse the text into the salient properties of a task. From the input text message, we require the case record ID, the task ID and the completion properties of the task. We retrieve the matching CaseRecord entity from persistence and filter the collection of the Task objects for the correct item. Once we have it, we set the completed property and persist the entire record back to persistence.

WebSockets are permitted to return a response back to the peer. We send the response synchronously, as we do here, with a text message like OK or NOT FOUND. Readers should be aware that it also possible to send responses asynchronously.

We have reached the end of the server-side discussion.

Consider your design requirements

AngularJS is a powerful JavaScript MVC framework for the client side. Developers, designers, and digital managers are always looking at the next exciting technology. People often tend to gauge the impact of a new framework. It is fair to say that AngularJS is a game changer because of the ease of the developing components that are bound to the model. The effort for not implementing such potential error-prone code with jQuery, by default, is huge!

We know that AngularJS is suited for single-page applications. Does that mean that your next enterprise application must be a SPA? Well, the practicing consultant's answer is that it always depends on your goals. SPA is suited to limited customer journeys and in cases where the experience happens mostly in one place. The caseworker application is of this type, because the person is assessing the passport applicants on a case-by-case basis, and therefore, they stay in and work on one web page most of the time during their working day.

The caseworker application demonstrates a master-detail relationship. Your next enterprise application may probably require the involvement of a more complicated set of use stories. Your domain might require an extensive set of entities. A single SPA might not cover all the areas. For one thing, you will need many more JavaScript modules, controllers and factories, and HTML directives to fully surround the bounded context of the system.

So what to do with these complicated requirements? One approach is to bundle all of the JavaScript logic on the client script into one download. Tools for this such as GruntJS, which we briefly covered in the last chapter, can then merge, compress, and optimize files. We can take advantage of the Java EE strengths with more than one web page and navigation.

Array collection of single-page applications

We can structure an SPA into a linear sequence so that the customer journey of the system almost follows a workflow. There are domains such as warehouse order management, engineering, and financial trading where such an approach might make sense. In such domains, the business user works in a series of complex steps in order to process bulk units of work from A to B. The advantages of an array of SPAs are won if they have a short linear sequence consisting of, perhaps, three or four steps, but will be lost if the length of the chain is greater than or equal to seven.

Hierarchical collection of single-page applications

The other approach is to descend fully from a linear sequence into the hierarchical tree structure of SPA. This approach is extremely specialized, and it is advisable to seek some architectural assurance that this path is sustainable for your business. Why would a business want to organize SPA in this fashion? Your stakeholder may want to sustain the organizational function in a way that mirrors the domain exactly. The design approach is a risky procedure because it introduces inflexibility in the overall model, and in my humble opinion, appears to be authority power led by the management rather than being organic. If the hierarchy tree is organized in a length by breadth manner rather than length by depth, ask yourself why?

In these times, where engineers and architects are looking at micro-services in order to scale and have a single business function in an elegant box, an HSPA might indeed be useful. The tree structure size should be around 10 nodes.

Summary

In this long chapter, we covered client-side AngularJS development with a caseworker application. We learned how the AngularJS framework manipulates the DOM and how it provides the binding between the data and the rendering of the elements using the MVC. We also learned some AngularJS concepts like scopes, modules, controllers, and factories.

Using the study example, we illustrated how AngularJS communicates to a remote server using RESTful service invocations from the client side. We also studied the WebSocket interaction briefly. On the client side of JavaScript, we went through the entire CRUD idiom in the caseworker application.

On the server side, we saw the implementation of the RESTful services with JAX-RS, which covered the four standard HTTP method requests. We also learnt about the Java WebSocket implementation.

AngularJS fits the mode of applications that single page applications need. However, this may or may not be appropriate to your business requirements. Adopting AngularJS requires full stack knowledge of both JavaScript programming and Java EE development. Moving to a framework like AngularJS exposes your business to the risk of hiring, retaining, and learning more technologies.

There is also another side of the triangle to consider: organizational dynamics. Apple Inc., USA famously divided their then agile teams that worked on the online shopping store into a pure server and client division. The only communication allowed between them was an agreed upon programming interface. This division happened when the iPhone was being developed (circa 2005-2007), which obviously predates AngularJS. Your team might operate differently, but the concept of design-by-contract is still relevant, because it showed what can be achieved, especially in terms of RESTful services.

I will leave you with a second quote from Misko Hevery, co-creator of AngularJS. He said:

> *"Limited – You can't really show more than 2000 pieces of information to a human on a single page. Anything more than that is really bad UI, and humans can't process this anyway."*

Exercises

1. Download the source code for the xen-national-force caseworker application and study the implementation for a few hours. What do you notice? Compile the code and deploy the resultant WAR to your application server of choice.

2. With the material from this chapter, create your CRUD AngularJS application with just one simple entity, EMPLOYEE. This entity should have an employee ID, name, and social security number. Build the client side with AngularJS and the server side with JAX-RS. (In the book's source code, there is a blank project that will help you get started.)

3. While building the EMPLOYEE CRUD from the previous question in AngularJS and JavaEE, did you use the modal dialog from UI Bootstrap? If not, investigate other means of rendering the view to insert, update, and delete records. (Hint: One possible way is dynamically showing and hiding different DIV elements.)

4. There is an obvious design flaw with the caseworker application. Did you find it? When the caseworker shows and hides a task view, it updates the persistence database; explain why is this a problem?

5. Imagine that from today, you have become the project lead for the entire xen-national-force team, and suddenly, the business decides that they want instant notifications to be broadcast to other caseworkers once a state has been changed. Explain at a technical level how this user story might be achieved. Think about the challenges on the AngularJS client side. How might you build the Java EE server side?

6. Study the factory module (`iso-countries.js`) in xen-national-force that is responsible for the maintaining a collection of the ISO passport country names and their codes. How is this module used in the frontend? Where does it get used?

7. Instead of using a dedicated Boolean property in the `CaseRecord` JPA entity to denote if the task view is shown or not, write an AngularJS factory module that stores this information for all the case records locally on the client side.

8. The sample caseworker application retrieves every record in the database and returns it to the user. Suppose the real system had 1,000 case records. What could be an issue with this functionality? How would you solve it? If the caseworker is not able to see all the records, explain how do you ensure that they get to see relevant cases? What do you need to implement on both the AngularJS client and the Java EE server side?

Java EE MVC Framework

9

"Compared even to the development of the phone or TV, the Web developed very quickly."

Sir Tim Berners-Lee, inventor of the World Wide Web

In the past couple of chapters, we reviewed the web application service from the perspective of the client side. For this last chapter, we will return to the digital application written mainly on the server-side. We will examine a brand new specification under the Java EE umbrella. It is called **Model-View-Controller** (**MVC**) and falls under the Java EE 8 release (March 2017) with JSR 371 (`https://jcp.org/en/jsr/detail?id=371`). At the time of writing this book, there was already an Early Draft Release of Java EE MVC that demonstrates the working of the reference implementation called Ozark (`https://ozark.java.net/index.html`).

The MVC framework is based on a design pattern that was invented in the Smalltalk programming language and environment, which was particularly common in the early user interface applications. The idea is that the Model refers to the component that stores the application data such as a value object or data transfer objects. The View is the component that renders or is responsible for the delivery of a representation of the application's data to the user and the Controller is the component that contains the logic to process the input and output between the two former components: the View and Model. The design pattern is extremely popular because it embraces the separation of concerns, which is a key concept in a good pragmatic object-oriented design.

In 2014, Oracle issued a public open survey to the wider Java EE community and collected the results (`https://java.net/downloads/javaee-spec/JavaEE8_Community_Survey_Results.pdf`). Thousands of technologists responded to this survey. One key question in the survey was, *Should Java EE provide support for MVC, along with JSF?* The correspondence was 60.8 percent in favor with a yes vote, 20 percent with a no vote, and 19.2 percent were unsure. This was enough to sanction the MVC 1.0 specification to be a part of Java EE 8.

Java EE 8 MVC

Before we continue on to the programming, I should warn you that the information here is subject to change, because MVC is evolving right in front of our eyes. As an avid reader, you should certainly verify, at least, that the API is with the current or final specification.

With all this said, the MVC framework certainly — even at this early stage — will be a leading specification for the future digital web development framework for many years to come, and not just because it is now officially part of the Java EE umbrella drivetrain. MVC leverages the JAX-RS (Java for RESTful Services) API and currently integrates with the other Java EE technologies including CDI and Bean Validation.

The expert group made the decision to layer on top of JAX-RS rather than the older Java servlet API, because JAX-RS fits the modern programming practice to use full semantics of the HTTP mapping capabilities. They also felt that adopting servlet would expose the developer to the lower-level programming interfaces that are already duplicated in the JAX-RS specification.

From a digital developer's and modern web practices' points of view, the layering of MVC on top of JAX-RS is really a good adoption. The servlet specification has been criticized severely by the likes of the Play framework and others as being a wide and thick Context Map abstraction (Eric Evans' Domain-Driven Design) and a blocker to the natural design of the web and HTTP utilization.

We will be working with the Java EE 8 MVC reference implementation called Ozark. At the time of writing, Ozark is still a work in progress. However, the milestone release contains the essential components and interfaces of the MVC applications.

MVC controllers

There is a new package structure reserved for MVC under `javax.mvc`. The `@javac.mvc.Controller` annotation declares a class type or method as a controller component. Here is an example of its use in a method:

```
@Controller
public String greet()
{
    return "Greetings, Earthling";
}
```

This controller method is missing the HTTP semantics and this is where the JAX-RS annotations help. It is also useless from an MVC perspective because there are associations with either a Model or View component.

So, first let's turn the method into a proper RESTful resource, starting with the model object:

```
package uk.co.xenonique.basic.mvc;
import javax.enterprise.context.RequestScoped;
import javax.inject.Named;
@Named(value="user")
@RequestScoped
public class User {
    private String name;
    public User() {}
    public String getName() {return name; }
    public void setName(String name) {this.name = name; }
}
```

The User component serves as our Model component. It has one property: the name of the person whom we are greeting politely. We can, therefore, write an MVC resource endpoint and inject this model instance into it.

Here is the initial version of our controller:

```
package uk.co.xenonique.basic.mvc;
/* ... */
import javax.mvc.Controller;
import javax.mvc.Viewable;
import javax.ws.rs.*;

@Path("/hello")
@Stateless
```

```
public class AlienGreetings {
  @Inject User user;

  @GET
  @Controller
  @Path("simple1")
  @Produces("text/html")
  public String simple1( @QueryParam("name") String name )
  {
    user.setName(name);
    return "/hello.jsp";
  }
}
```

We will annotate a JAX RS @Path element to our AlienGreetings class in order to declare that it is a resource endpoint. Although our type is defined as an EJB stateless session bean, MVC is expected to work with the CDI scopes such as @ApplicationScoped and @SessionScoped. The reference implementation is changing as I write this.

We will annotate the simple1() method as an MVC @Controller annotation. This method accepts one argument name as @QueryParam. We will add the other JAX-RS annotations in order to define the HTTP method protocol @GET, relative URI @Path, and MIME content type @Produces. The method sets the name property in the User instance and returns a reference string, which is the name of the view: /hello.jsp.

An MVC controller method can return a string, which means that the servlet container takes over the rendering of the final view. However, MVC can also render different views due to an extendible implementation. We will see more on this later. Behind the scenes, MVC converts the string to a view type. The Java interface javax.mvc.Viewable represents the abstraction of a view technology. The Viewable is an association between javax.mvc.ViewEngine and javax.mvc.Models.

The abstract class type javax.mvc.Engine has the responsibility to render a model to a technology choice. Engineers can develop or add this engine to render the views. At the moment, Ozark supports many rendering styles, from Apache Velocity to AsciiDoc.

The Java interface javax.mvc.Models represents a key value store that is passed from the view to the rendering engine. The model's type is a request-scoped map collection.

So, let's extend the `AlienGreeting` controller with a few more methods. The following `simple2()` method returns a `Viewable` instance:

```
@GET
@Controller
@Path("simple2")
@Produces("text/html")
public Viewable simple2( @QueryParam("name") String name )
{
   user.setName(name);
   return new Viewable("/hello.jsp");
}
```

As you can see, the `simple2()` method is a variation on `simple1()`, and MVC is rather flexible. It even supports the void methods that do not return types. We will annotate the subsequent `simple3()` method with `@javax.mvc.View` in order to declare the next view:

```
@GET
@Controller
@Path("simple3")
@Produces("text/html")
@View("/hello.jsp")
public void simple3( @QueryParam("name") String name )
{
   user.setName(name);
}
```

All of the three methods are HTTP GET requests so far. As MVC is layered on top of JAX-RS, we can utilize other protocol methods too. It is straightforward to write an HTML form handler that handles an HTTP POST request.

Here is the code extract for the `helloWebForm()` method:

```
@POST
@Controller
@Path("webform")
@Produces("text/html")
public Viewable helloWebForm( @FormParam("name") String name )
{
   user.setName(name);
   return new Viewable("/hello.jsp");
}
```

The preceding controller method, `helloWebForm()`, accepts an HTML form named parameter. It sets the model object and returns a view instance. In the HTML5 standard, the form element officially supports the HTTP GET and POST requests. The popular web browsers tend to have access only to the HTTP PUT and DELETE protocol requests through JavaScript. This limitation does not, however, prevent the MVC controllers being annotated with @PUT or @DELETE.

The MVC controllers have access to a full gamut of the URI space that is available to the JAX-RS endpoints. The following example illustrates the path parameter:

```
@GET
@Controller
@Path("view/{name}")
@Produces("text/html")
public Viewable helloWebPath( @PathParam("name") String name )
{
  user.setName(name);
  return new Viewable("/hello.jsp");
}
```

The preceding controller method, `helloWebPath()`, accepts a path parameter as the user's name. The `@PathParam` annotation establishes the parameter token used in the relative URI. The URI is defined by the `@Path` annotation. The full URL will be `http://localhost:8080/javaee-basic-mvc/rest/hello/view/Curtis`.

MVC page views and templates

Under the MVC specification, a `view` instance can be treated as a templating technology reference. We have seen only JavaServer Page views up until now. A view can be anything that a developer can imagine, as long as there is a corresponding `ViewEngine` instance that knows exactly how to process (render) a view from the associated model and the other results from a controller.

Let's look at the first basic JSP view, `index.jsp`, in the sample source code project from this book (`ch09/basic-javaee-mvc`):

```
<%@ page import="uk.co.xenonique.basic.mvc.AlienGreetings" %>
<!DOCTYPE html>
<html>
<head> ...
  <link href="${pageContext.request.contextPath}/styles/bootstrap.css"
rel="stylesheet">
  <link href="${pageContext.request.contextPath}/styles/main.css"
rel="stylesheet">
</head>
```

```
<body>
  <div class="main-content"> ...
    <div class="other-content">
      <h2>Simple MVC Controller</h2>
      <p>
        HTTP GET Request with query parameter and invocation of
        <code><%= AlienGreetings.class.getSimpleName() %>
        </code> with HTML Form:<br>
        <a href="${pageContext.request.contextPath}
          /rest/hello/simple1?name=James"
          class="btn btn-primary"> Person called James
        </a>
      </p>
      <p>...
        <a href="${pageContext.request.contextPath}
          /rest/hello/simple2?name=Patricia"
          class="btn btn-primary"> Person called Patricia
        </a>
      </p>
      <p>...
        <a href="${pageContext.request.contextPath}
          /rest/hello/simple3?name=Aliiyah"
          class="btn btn-primary"> Person called Aliiyah
        </a>
      </p>
      <p>
        <form action="${pageContext.request.contextPath}
          /rest/hello/webform"method="POST" >
          <div class="form-group">
            <label for="elementName">Name</label>
            <input type="text" class="form-control"
              id="elementName" name="name" placeholder="Jane Doe">
          </div>
        </form>
      </p>
      ...
    </div>
  </body>
</html>
```

In this JSP view, we will take advantage of an EL to generate a URL with the context path for the web application, namely `pageContext.request.contextPath`. There are three HTML anchor elements that invoke the `AlienGreeting` controller methods: `simple1()`, `simple2()`, and `simple3()`. The HTML form invokes the `helloWebForm()` method.

The page extract JSP view called `hello.jsp` looks as follows:

```
<div class="main-content">
  <div class="page-header">
    <h1> Java EE 8 MVC - Hello</h1>
    <p> Model View Controller </p>
  </div>
  <div class="other-content">
    <div class="jumbotron">
      <p> Hello ${user.name} </p>
    </div>
    <p> How are you?</p>
  </div>
</div>
```

The view template is very straightforward; we will use the request-scoped user instance to supply the name.

At the time of writing this, Ozark supported the following view rendition technologies in the beta reference implementation, as shown in the following table:

Template name	Description
AsciiDoc	This a text document format to write notes, documents, articles, books, e-books, slideshows, man pages, and blogs.
	`https://github.com/asciidoctor/asciidoctorj`
Freemarker	This is a Java template engine that generates HTML, RTF, and source code.
	`http://freemarker.org/`
Handlebars	This is a multiple language and platform extension to the original Mustache templating specification with helpful utilities tokens.
	JavaScript version: `http://handlebarsjs.com/` and Java port: `https://github.com/jknack/handlebars.java/`
JSR 223	This is an extension of the MVC framework that supports JSR 223 for a dynamic scripting language such as Groovy and Jython.
	`https://www.jcp.org/en/jsr/detail?id=223`

Template name	Description
Mustache	This is a simple web template language that separates the presentation from the business view logic. It is available on multiple platforms and languages. `https://github.com/spullara/mustache.java`
Thymeleaf	This is a Java-based HTML5 template library that works in the web and non-web environments. It is associated strongly with the string framework. `http://www.thymeleaf.org/`
Velocity	Apache Velocity is a suite of the templating tools. The Velocity engine is the component library that provides templating. It was one of the first web template frameworks that was written for server-side Java. `http://velocity.apache.org/`

> MVC is a server-side template solution. Don't confuse the world of client-side templating with the backend variety.

MVC models

The MVC specification supports two forms of models. The first is based on the `javax.mvc.Models` instance and the second form leverages the CDI `@Named` beans. The `Models` interface types map the key names to the values in a map collection. All the view engines must mandatorily support `Models`. A view engine may optionally support CDI. The specification recommends that the view engine implementers provide the CDI beans support.

The default implementation of the `Models` interface is a request-scoped bean: `com.oracle.ozark.core.ModelsImpl`. This class delegates to a `java.util.Map` collection. Developers normally never instantiate this type but prefer to inject the `Models` type. As you will see later, it is sometimes necessary to create an instance for a particular view engine.

Let's demonstrate the practical use of the `Models` interface in a second version of our controller class:

```
@Path("/hello2")
@Stateless
public class PhobosGreetings {
  @Inject
```

```
    Models models;

    @GET
    @Controller
    @Path("simple2")
    @Produces("text/html")
    public Viewable simple1(  @QueryParam("name") String name )
    {
      models.put("users", new User(name));
      return new Viewable("/hello2.jsp");
    }
}
```

In `PhobosGreetings`, we will replace the CDI injection of the `User` type with a `Models` instance. We will create a `User` instance and store this under the property key, `user`. After the method returns, the framework will retrieve all of the properties in the `Models` instance and place them in the attributes collection of `HttpServlerResponse`. Therefore, a JSP template view has access to the data through an EL or inline scripting.

Response and redirects

MVC also supports the controller that returns an instance of the JAX RS Response type. This is especially useful to the sites that shove the Grunt work of rendering to the client side. A highly scalable web application may choose to send the megabytes of a JSON response rather than render on the server through a template.

We will now inspect another MVC controller called `RedirectController`:

```
@Path("redirect")
@Stateless
@Controller
public class RedirectController {
  @GET
  @Path("string")
  public String getString() {
      return "redirect:redirect/here";
  }

  @GET
  @Path("response1")
  public Response getResponse1() {
    return Response.seeOther(
      URI.create("redirect/here")).build();
```

```
    }

    @GET
    @Path("deliberateError1")
    public Response getErrorResponse1() {
      return Response.status(Response.Status.BAD_REQUEST)
        .entity("/error.jsp").build();
    }

    @GET
    @Path("here")
    @Produces("text/html")
    public String getRedirectedView() {
      return "redirected.jsp";
    }
  }
```

We will annotate `RedirectController` with JAX-RS `@Path` and we must pay particular attention to the base value, `redirect`.

The `getString()` method performs a URI redirection using the special prefix operator, redirect. This method has a unique relative URI of `redirect/string`. MVC detects the prefix internally and builds a JAX-RS Response as a redirect request. The URI that is returned is a reference to the `getRedirectedView()` controller, which has a relative path URI of `redirect/here`.

We can directly build the response ourselves as seen in the `getResponse()` method. Invoking the static `Response.seeOther()` method with a URI is the equivalent of achieving an HTTP redirect response. This method has its own unique relative URI of `redirect/response1`.

The `getRedirectedView()` method simply navigates to the view template, `redirected.jsp`. This controller method is the eventual target of the other controller methods: `getString()` and `getResponse()`.

> At the time of writing this, the MVC specification was designing the HTTP redirect approach. There was a question about providing a Flash scope or an equivalent of a JSF View scope bean for the MVC applications in order to save the data among the multiple request scopes. I strongly recommend you to check for updates on the specification.

Finally, an MVC controller can also return HTTP error responses. The `getErrorResponse()` method has a relative URI of `redirect/deliberateError1` and returns a Response instance with an HTTP Bad Request error code (401). The controller also informs the MVC framework to serve the view template under the view ID `error.jsp`. `RedirectController` represents the simplest form of an MVC controller. We can enrich it with the injection of `Models` or other CDI beans. We can also use the Viewable instances instead of the dumb strings as entities in a Response builder.

Let's move on to the different templating technologies, and this is the unique selling point of MVC so far.

Reconfiguring the view root

In the working MVC early draft release, the view root is set by default to `WEB-INF/views`. Programmatically, this is found in the static property of `ViewEngine.DEFAULT_VIEW_ENGINE`.

This may be inconvenient for the digital engineers with relative URI, especially in the redirection of the page views. Luckily, the Ozark implementation can be reconfigured from the web XML descriptor (`web.xml`), as follows:

```
<?xml version="1.0" encoding="UTF-8"?>
<web-app xmlns="http://xmlns.jcp.org/xml/ns/javaee" ...>
  ...
  <servlet>
    <servlet-name>javax.ws.rs.core.Application</servlet-name>
    <init-param>
      <param-name>javax.mvc.engine.ViewEngine.viewFolder</param-name>
      <param-value>/</param-value>
    </init-param>
    <load-on-startup>1</load-on-startup>
    <async-supported>true</async-supported>
  </servlet>...
</web-app>
```

We will override the `javax.mvc.engine.ViewEngine.viewFolder` property in the web page root in order to achieve the behavior that we want.

Handlebars Java

The Handlebars framework is a templating library for a developing web application. In its JavaScript incantation (`http://handlebarsjs.com/`), you might already have heard the digital interface developers raving about it. We will use the Handlebars Java port for the rest of this chapter.

The Handlebars framework permits the developers along with designers to write semantic templates. It is based on a slightly older templating framework called Mustache (`https://mustache.github.io/`). Both of these refer to the masculine facial hair that can be seen if you squint your eyes and look at a curly bracket rotated by 90 degrees.

Templating frameworks drive home the separation of concerns and reduction of mixing the business logic in the rendered page view as much as possible. The Handlebars framework borrows the double curly bracket notation from Mustache. For our masculine readers, this is a deliberate play on words and an idiosyncrasy of computer programming. The Handlebars framework has a clear advantage of leveraging the same template engine on the server side that also works on the client side.

A compiled-inline template servlet

We will start with a servlet example as an introduction. We will create a Java servlet with just one dependency, which is the Handlebars Java implementation. We are not considering the MVC framework just yet. Our servlet will instantiate the templating framework, invoke an inline template script, and then return the output as a straightforward direct response.

Here is our servlet:

```
package uk.co.xenonique.basic.mvc;
import com.github.jknack.handlebars.*;
import javax.servlet.*;
/* ... other imports omitted */

@WebServlet("/compiled")
public class CompileInlineServlet extends HttpServlet {
  @Override
  protected void doGet(HttpServletRequest request, HttpServletResponse response)
    throws ServletException, IOException
  {
    final Handlebars handlebars = new Handlebars();
    final Template template = handlebars.compileInline(
        "Hello {{this}}!");
    final String text = template.apply("Handlebars.java");
    response.setContentType("text/plain");
    response.getOutputStream().println(text);
  }
}
```

The `CompileInlineServlet` class illustrates how to compile a basic Handlers template example in the Java code. We will instantiate a Handlebars engine template and then compile the template inline, as shown in the following text:

```
Hello {{this}}!
```

After compilation, we will obtain a `Template` instance that contains the content. We will then call the `apply()` method with a simple string and this will serve as the context for the template. The `{{this}}` placeholder refers to the context object. We will then retrieve the text representation and send the response back to the web browser. We will see the following plain text output:

```
Hello Handlebars.java!
```

There are no dependencies in Handlebars Java that tie the framework to Java EE. Therefore, it can also be used in Java SE as a standalone Java executable.

Template expressions in Handlebars

Here is another example of a Handlebars template with a different context:

```
<div class="trade-entry">
  <h1>{{title}}</h1>
  <div class="trade-detail">
    {{detail}}
  </div>
</div>
```

The template renders in a DIV layer with a token name substitution with an embedded expression. An expression is reserved and activated between the double curly brackets. It renders an output for the domain of the trading system. In both Handlebars and Mustache notation, the double curly bracket surrounding a variable name denotes a placeholder entry. A placeholder entry in a template means that it can be replaced with a dynamic content. Therefore, during the template rendering process, the `{{title}}` placeholder is replaced with the trade entry headline and the `{{detail}}` is replaced with the trade detail. The expression value may be literal strings or they could be an embedded HTML5 markup.

Let's write another Java servlet that renders this view using the Handlebars framework:

```
package uk.co.xenonique.basic.mvc;
import com.github.jknack.handlebars.*;
import com.github.jknack.handlebars.io.*;
```

```
/* ... imports omitted */

@WebServlet("/tradeinfo")
public class TradeInfoServlet extends HttpServlet {
  @Override
  protected void doGet(HttpServletRequest request,
    HttpServletResponse response)
      throws ServletException, IOException
  {
    final TemplateLoader loader =
      new ServletContextTemplateLoader(
        request.getServletContext());
    final Handlebars handlebars = new Handlebars(loader);
    final Template template = handlebars.compile("trade");
    final Map<String,String> context =
        new HashMap<String,String>() {{
      put("title", "12345FUND-EURO-FUTURE6789");
      put("detail", "Nominal 1.950250M EUR");
      put("trade-date", "23-07-2015");
      put("maturity-date", "23-07-2018");
    }};
    final String text = template.apply(context);
    response.setContentType("text/html");
    response.getOutputStream().println(text);
  }
}
```

This `TradeInfoServlet` servlet is almost the same as the previous one, `CompileInlineServlet`; but this time, we will utilize the `ServletContextTemplateLoader` class. This is a loader class that retrieves the view templates from the Java EE web context via the servlet engine. We will create the loader and pass this as an argument during the construction of a Handlebar instance. We will then compile a template using a reference name, trade. The framework invokes the loader to retrieve the view template, which by default is suffixed as `trade.hbs`.

We built a literal map collection of the keys and values. They will serve as our collection of placeholders in the view, and we will apply them to the template. Navigating to the web browser with `http://localhost:8080/handlebars-javaee-mvc-1.0-SNAPSHOT/tradeinfo` should display the following screenshot:

Screenshot of the TradeInfoServlet

In addition to straightforward replacements, Handlebars supports the `Block`, `Partials`, and `Helper` expressions. The Handlebars framework provides the standard building blocks; however, engineers can register custom helpers. In the JavaScript implementation, developers usually define the compiled script templates in the page in order to reuse the content. `Handlebars.js` tends to be used with one or the other JavaScript framework such as RequireJS or EmberJS in order to deliver reusable content.

We will proceed to write a CRUD example with Handlebars Java. Our application will allow the user to manipulate a basic product catalog. We will need a welcome page, so let's create it with the template framework.

The welcome controller

In the Java port, we do not have to register or compile the templates because the page content is delivered from the server side. The project for this is called `handlebars-javaee-mvc`. The first thing to do is cause an HTTP redirect in an initial JSP, as follows:

```
<%@ page contentType="text/html;charset=UTF-8" language="java" %>
<html>
<body>
<meta http-equiv="refresh" content="0;
  url=${pageContext.request.contextPath}/rest/welcome" />
</body>
</html>
```

The preceding code will immediately redirect the web browser to send an HTTP GET request to the URI, `handler-javeee-mvc-1.0/rest/welcome`. In this URI path, we already have an MVC controller waiting for this invocation:

```
@Path("/welcome")
@Stateless
public class WelcomeController {
  @Inject Models models;

  @GET
  @Controller
  @Produces("text/html")
  public Viewable welcome()
  {
    models.put("pageTitle", "Handlebars.java Java EE 8 MVC" );
    models.put("title", "Welcome");
    return new Viewable("/welcome.hbs");
  }
}
```

After populating a couple properties in the model instance, the `WelcomeController` progresses the response to the Handlebars Java template `/welcomee.hbs`. The absolute URI with the forward slash character ensures that the MVC framework searches for the page template from the web context root. The suffix extension `*.hbs` is generally reserved for the Handlebars view templates in both the client and server editions.

Let's look at the following Handlebars template (`welcome.hbs`):

```
<!DOCTYPE html>
<html>
{{> header }}
<body>
  {{> navbar }}

  <div class="main-content">
    ...
  </div>

  {{> footer}}
</body>
{{> bottom }}
</html>
```

Handlebars support the concept of Partials. A partial is a template that is used in another template. They are extremely useful for page composition. The syntax begins with {{> NAME }}, where NAME refers to another template. In a JavaScript stack, the partials must be registered beforehand; however, the Java port knows how to find the partial template by loading them from the servlet container. Therefore, the partial template reference, {{> header }}, instructs Handlebars to load the `header.hbs` view.

There are four partial templates in the `welcome.hbs` view: `header.hbs`, `navbar.hbs`, `footer.hbs`, and `bottom.hbs`. You can examine the source code for these templates in this book's code distribution.

The custom view engine

Handlebars Java ships with several template view engines. The default extension view engine, unfortunately, does not provide all of the features that we would like to use. For one, Handlebars does not render the decimal numbers readily, and so, we must register our own function. Luckily, it is reasonable to write a view engine extension with CDI, as follows:

```
package uk.co.xenonique.basic.mvc;
import com.github.jknack.handlebars.*;
import com.github.jknack.handlebars.io.*;
import com.oracle.ozark.engine.ViewEngineBase;
// ... other imports ommitted

@ApplicationScoped
public class MyHandlebarsViewEngine extends ViewEngineBase {
  @Inject private ServletContext servletContext;

  @Override
  public boolean supports(String view) {
    return view.endsWith(".hbs") || view.endsWith(".handlebars");
  }

  @Override
  public void processView(ViewEngineContext context) throws
ViewEngineException {
    final Models models = context.getModels();
    final String viewName = context.getView();

    try (PrintWriter writer = context.getResponse().getWriter();
         InputStream resourceAsStream =
         servletContext.getResourceAsStream(resolveView(context));
```

```
            InputStreamReader in =
                new InputStreamReader(resourceAsStream, "UTF-8");
        BufferedReader buffer = new BufferedReader(in);) {
        final String viewContent = buffer.lines()
          .collect(Collectors.joining());
        final TemplateLoader loader =
          new ServletContextTemplateLoader(servletContext);
        final Handlebars handlebars = new Handlebars(loader);
        models.put("webContextPath",
            context.getRequest().getContextPath());
        models.put("page", context.getRequest().getRequestURI());
        models.put("viewName", viewName);
        models.put("request", context.getRequest());
        models.put("response", context.getResponse());
        handlebars.registerHelper("formatDecimal", new
    Helper<BigDecimal>() {
            @Override
            public CharSequence apply(BigDecimal number, Options
    options) throws IOException {
                final DecimalFormat formatter =
                    new DecimalFormat("###0.##");
                return formatter.format(number.doubleValue());
            }
        });
        Template template = handlebars.compileInline(viewContent);
        template.apply(models, writer);
    } catch (IOException e) {
        throw new ViewEngineException(e);
    }
  }
}
```

We will annotate our `MyHandlebarsViewEngine` class as an application-scoped bean and also ensure that it subclasses `ViewEngineBase` from Ozark. We will inject `ServletContext` into this class because we need to retrieve certain properties from it such as the web context path.

We will override the `supports()` method so as to establish the support for the Handlebars files. The MVC View type is passed as a single argument.

The real work happens in the `processView()` method, and we are totally responsible for rendering the Handlebars View template. The MVC framework supplies `javax.mvc.engine.ViewEngineContext`, which provides access to the current `View` and `Models` instances. We can establish the name of the View template that we need to retrieve. From here on, we can create the `ServletContextTemplateLoader` and `Handlebars` instances to load a view as we saw in the earlier `TradeInfoServlet` class. Then we have to navigate some tricky waters a little bit by reading the contents of the current view in a buffer. `ViewEngineBase` provides a `resolve()` method that helps us immensely and returns `InputStream`. By the way, the Java 7 acquire/resource syntax for the try-catch statements reduces the boilerplate code. At the end of the method, we can compile the view inline because we have the content in a buffer.

We will add a couple of useful features in `MyHandlebarsViewEngine`. First, we will add extra properties to the `Models` instance. We will add the web context path and request and response objects to the `Models` instance. Second, we will register a Handlebars helper in order to better render the BigDecimal types.

When our application is deployed, Ozark relies on CDI to find the `ViewEngineBase` types. Ozark scans the classpath of JAR files and classes to find types of `ViewEengineBase` objects. It builds an internal list of available renders. `MyHandlebarsViewEngine` is the place presently where you can add additional helpers and utilities in the rendering phase. Keep a watch on the MVC specification to see if any of these interfaces are exposed in a meaningful public accessible API.

We will move on to our controller and the product list view.

The product controller

Our domain object is the humble `Product` entity, which has an outline that resembles the following form:

```
@Entity
@NamedQueries({
  @NamedQuery(name="Product.findAll",
    query = "select p from Product p order by p.name"),
  @NamedQuery(name="Product.findById",
    query = "select p from Product p where p.id = :id"),
})
public class Product {
  @Id
  @GeneratedValue(strategy = GenerationType.AUTO)
  private Integer id;
  @NotEmpty @Size(max=64) private String name;
  @NotEmpty @Size(max=256) private String description;
```

```
@NotNull @DecimalMin("0.010") private BigDecimal price;

public Product() { this(null, null, null); }

public Product(String name, String description, BigDecimal
  price) {
  this.name = name;
  this.description = description;
  this.price = price;
}
/* ... */
}
```

Note that `Product` takes full advantage of the Bean Validation annotations. In particular, it uses a BigDecimal type for the accurate prices and the `@DecimalMin` annotation prevents storage negative and zero prices at the bounded context.

Given our entity object, we will need `ProductController` to interface the domain to the presentation view:

```
@Path("/products")
@Stateless
public class ProductController {
  @Inject Models models;
  @Inject ValidatorFactory validatorFactory;
  @Inject FormErrorMessage formError;
  @EJB ProductService productService;

  private void defineCommonModelProperties(String title ) {
    models.put("pageTitle", "Handlebars.java Java EE 8 MVC" );
    models.put("title", title);
  }

  private void retrieveAll() {
    final List<Product> products = productService.findAll();
    models.put("products", products );
    models.put("title", "Products");
  }

  @GET
  @Controller
  @Path("list")
  @Produces("text/html")
  public Viewable listProducts()
  {
```

```
        retrieveAll();
        defineCommonModelProperties("Products");
        return new Viewable("/products.hbs");
    }
    /* ... */
}
```

As usual, we will annotate `ProductController` with the JAX-RS annotations in order to bring in the RESTful service space. We will be using Bean Validation to verify the state of our input objects, and therefore, we will inject `ValidatorFactory` from the Java EE container. We will inject the `Models` instance for the MVC operations. We also have a custom `FormErrorBean` POJO to capture the error messages, and finally, there is an EJB, `ProductService`, to persist the records to a database.

The `listProducts()` controller method delegates to the shared methods: `retrieveAll()` and `defineCommonModelProperties()`. The `retreieveAll()` method pulls all the products from the database using the EJB. It saves the list collection in `Models` under a known property key. The `defineCommonModelProperties()` method saves a title as a key in the same `Models` instance. It turns out that many controller methods need the same functionality and so we refactored it. We will place the retrieved product collection in a `Models` key property called products. Finally, `listProducts()` forwards it to the Handlebars Java view template, `product.hbs`. After our controller method is returned, Ozark will eventually delegate to our custom view engine: `MyHandlebarsViewEngine`.

Block expressions

We can take a look at the view and learn about the useful block expressions. The following is the extract of the view template, `/products.hbs`:

```
<div class="other-content">
  <div class="jumbotron">
      <p> {{title}} </p>
  </div>

  <p>
    <a href="{{webContextPath}}/rest/products/preview-create"
      class="btn-primary btn">Add New Product</a>
  </p>

  <table class="product-container-table table table-bordered table-
responsive table-striped">
    <tr>
      <th> Product Name </th>
```

```
            <th> Description </th>
            <th> Unit Price </th>
            <th> Action </th>
        </tr>

    {{#each products}}
        <tr>
          <td> {{this.name}} </td>
          <td> {{this.description}} </td>
          <td> {{formatDecimal this.price}} </td>
          <td>
            <a class="btn" href="{{webContextPath}}/rest/products/view/
{{this.id}}" ><i class="glyphicon glyphicon-edit"></i></a>
            <a class="btn" href="{{webContextPath}}/rest/products/
preview-delete/{{this.id}}" ><i class="glyphicon glyphicon-trash"></
i></a>
          </td>
        </tr>
    {{/each}}
    </table>
</div>
```

As you can see, we actually used the {{title}} expression in this view template, which was set in the defineCommonModelProperties() method. The value for the {{webContextPath}} placeholder is set in our extension class, MyHandlebarsViewEngine.

There are two new expressions: {{#each}} and {{/each}}. These are the built-in block expressions that allow us to loop over a context element. In this case, we will iterate over the products. The product element at the heart of the loop becomes accessible under the {{this}} placeholder.

In order to print the BigDecimal price correctly, we will invoke the {{formatDecimal}} helper function that was defined in our custom view engine. A helper function can accept more than one parameter. The result is a rendered table of the products with their names, descriptions, and prices with the anchor links to edit or delete an item.

Here is the screenshot for the view template, `products.jsp`:

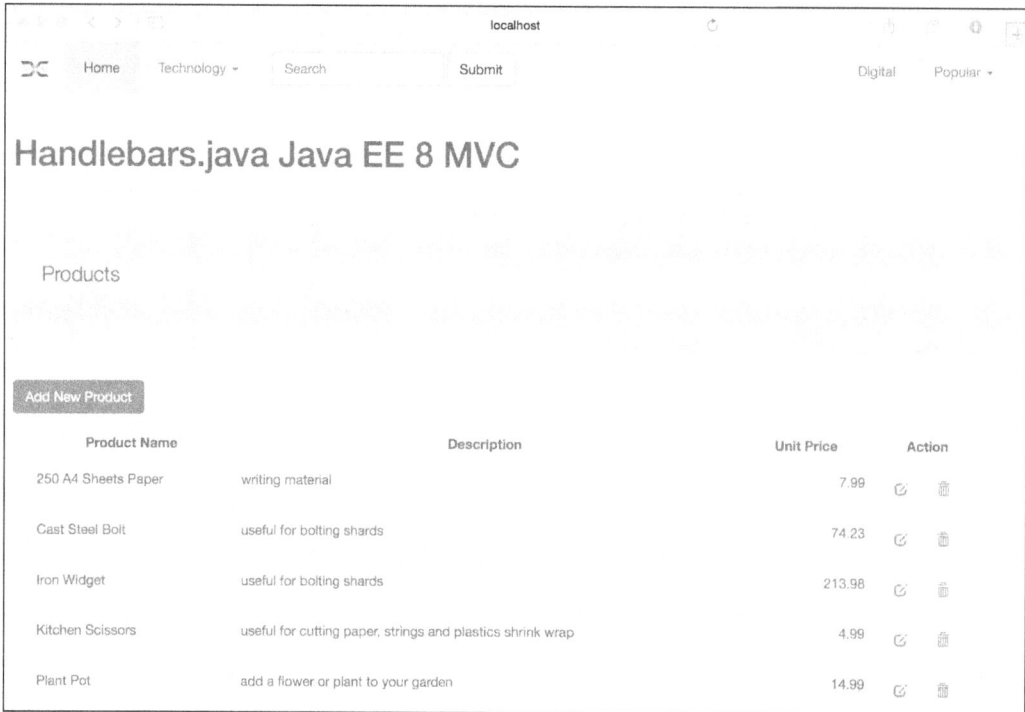

A product listing view template rendered by Handlebars

The retrieve and edit operations

Once a customer selects a product to edit, then we will need to retrieve the data from the database and push them to a different view template. This is the purpose of the preview edit method in the controller, as follows:

```
@GET
@Controller
@Path("view/{id}")
@Produces("text/html")
public Viewable retrieveProduct( @PathParam("id") int id )
{
    final List<Product> products = productService.findById(id);
    models.put("product", products.get(0) );
    defineCommonModelProperties("Product");
    return new Viewable("/edit-product.hbs");
}
```

We will annotate this controller method, `retrieveProduct()`, with `@PathParam` in order to retrieve the product ID. With the identifier, we will simply look up the `Product` entity and put the result in the request-scoped `Models` property. Obviously, for a production application, we would probably be really defensive-minded in checking whether the identifier is valid or not. The method progresses the final delivery of the response to the view template, `/edit-products.hbs`. The source code for the view template is available with this book's source distribution.

We will move on to the next part when the user has submitted the HTML form on this page view template. If the customer submits the form, then their journey will invoke the next controller method in `ProductController`, which is called `editProduct()`:

```
@POST
@Controller
@Path("edit/{id}")
@Produces("text/html")
public Response editProduct(
  @PathParam("id") int id,
  @FormParam("action") String action,
  @FormParam("name") String name,
  @FormParam("description") String description,
  @FormParam("price") BigDecimal price)
{
  defineCommonModelProperties("Edit Product");
  if ("Save".equalsIgnoreCase(action)) {
    final List<Product> products =
      productService.findById(id);
    final Product product2 = new Product(
      name, description, price );
    final Set<ConstraintViolation<Product>> set =
      validatorFactory.getValidator().validate(product2);
    if (!set.isEmpty()) {
      final ConstraintViolation<?> cv = set.iterator().next();
      final String property = cv.getPropertyPath().toString();
      formError.setProperty(
        property.substring(property.lastIndexOf('.') + 1));
      formError.setValue(cv.getInvalidValue());
      formError.setMessage(cv.getMessage());
      models.put("formError",formError);
      return Response.status(BAD_REQUEST).
        entity("error.hbs").build();
    }
    final Product product = products.get(0);
```

```
        product.setName(name);
        product.setDescription(description);
        product.setPrice(price);
        productService.saveProduct(product);
        models.put("product", product);
    }
    retrieveAll();
    return Response.status(OK).entity("/products.hbs").build();
}
```

Our controller method is invoked on the submission of the HTML form and so we will annotate it with the necessary @PathParam and @FormParam declarations in order to receive the product ID and properties. Our controller expects a form parameter with the name, action. The customer may cancel the operation and if so the action does not match the Save operation. Therefore nothing occurs and the method progress the response to the product list view.

With the Save action, our method will utilize the injected ValidatorFactory instance so as to manually validate the form parameters. As the entity product has the validation annotations, we will construct a temporary instance with the form parameter and then create a validator to check it. We do not directly change a persisted entity at this juncture because the data may be invalid. If this is the case, then the Java EE container will raise javax.persistence.RollbackException after the controller method exits because the thread of control passes through a transaction barrier. After validating the temporary instance, a collection of the ConstraintViolation elements is returned.

Let's assume that the form data is invalid. We will retrieve the information from the first violation and populate the details in a request scope FormErrorMessage bean. The form errors are accessible in the view template from the property key, formError. The controller method then builds a response with the HTTP Bad Request error code and then forwards to a view template, /error.hbs.

On the other hand, if the form is valid according to the Bean Validation check, then we will proceed to retrieve the Product entity from the database by the product ID. We will update the Product entity from the form properties and then save it in the database. As we have already checked the data manually, there should not be an error in saving the data. We will build an HTTP OK response and forward to the view template, /products.hbs.

At the time of writing this, the MVC specification leads were still developing the validation and binding of the parameters post the Early Draft Release of MVC. Notably, if a controller injected the `javax.mvc.BindingResult` instance, then it would be possible to handle the form validation in a precise and narrow user story instead of globally, as in the case of a straight JAX-RS API.

To complete the picture, here is the compact version of the `FormErrorMessage` bean:

```
@Named("error")
@RequestScoped
public class FormErrorMessage {
  private String property;
  private Object value;
  private String message;

  /* ... getters and setters omitted */
}
```

This is a request-scoped bean and we will render the information in a Handlebars view template, `error.hbs`:

```
<div class="page-header">
  <h1> {{pageTitle}} </h1>
</div>
<div class="other-content"> ...
  <div class="main-content" >
    <table class="table table-stripped table-bordered table-
responsive">
      <tr>
        <th>Name</th><th>Value</th>
      </tr>
      <tr>
        <td>Property</td> <td>{{formError.property}}</td>
      </tr>
      <tr>
        <td>Message</td> <td>{{formError.message}}</td>
      </tr>
      <tr>
        <td>Value</td> <td>{{formError.value}}</td>
      </tr>
    </table>
  </div> ...
</div>
```

This view renders the error message in the `FormErrorMessage` bean. You might be wondering why we are sending the form validation errors to a separate view. The answer is simple: baby steps. In a professional digital application, we would take advantage of an AJAX validation and a JavaScript framework such as jQuery on the client side. Our client-side JavaScript module would invoke an HTTP POST request to an MVC controller method in order to validate the property information. This method called, say `validateCheck()`, would check on a temporary instance and report with a JSON response containing the constraint violations, if any. Perhaps the members of the JSR-371 expert group will ease this part of the development for Digital.

The JAX-RS global validation

The problem with the `editProduct()` method is that we are forced to use manual validation steps. The only alternative at the moment is to fall back on the JAX-RS validation.

So, let's inspect a new version of the controller method called `altEditProduct()`:

```
@POST
@Controller
@Path("alt-edit/{id}")
@Produces("text/html")
public Response altEditProduct(
  @PathParam("id") int id,
  @FormParam("action") String action,
  @NotNull @NotEmpty @FormParam("name") String name,
  @NotNull @NotEmpty @FormParam("description") String description,
  @NotNull @DecimalMin("0.0") @FormParam("price") BigDecimal price )
{
  defineCommonModelProperties("Edit Product");
  if ("Save".equalsIgnoreCase(action)) {
    final List<Product> products = productService.findById(id);
    final Product product = products.get(0);
    product.setName(name);
    product.setDescription(description);
    product.setPrice(price);
    productService.saveProduct(product);
    models.put("product", product);
  }
  retrieveAll();
  return Response.status(OK).entity("/products.hbs").build();
}
```

This time, we will inscribe the Bean Validation annotations directly on the controller method, `altEditProduct()`. You might be concerned that this is duplication, with the annotation already on the Entity bean. You would be correct, but let's continue. The `altEditMethod()` method is shorter, which is great. There is a problem now with this approach in that the validation is delegated globally to JAX-RS. If the customer submits an HTML form to `altEditMethod()`, then they will send an HTTP Bad Request error response and a user-unfriendly error message direct from the application server. Obviously, the UX team would be throwing a fit! What can we do?

The JAX-RS specification permits an application to provide a handler for an error response. The way to achieve this goal is to configure a provider through CDI, as follows:

```
package uk.co.xenonique.basic.mvc;
import javax.annotation.Priority;
import javax.mvc.*;
import javax.ws.rs.*;
/* ... other import omitted ... */
import static javax.ws.rs.core.Response.Status.*;

@Provider
@Priority(Priorities.USER)
public class ConstraintViolationExceptionMapper
  implements ExceptionMapper<ConstraintViolationException> {
  @Context HttpServletRequest request;

  @Override
  public Response toResponse(
    final ConstraintViolationException exception) {
    final Models models = new com.oracle.ozark.core.ModelsImpl();
    final ConstraintViolation<?> cv =
      exception.getConstraintViolations().iterator().next();
    final String property = cv.getPropertyPath().toString();
    final FormErrorMessage formError = new FormErrorMessage();
    formError.setProperty(
      property.substring(property.lastIndexOf('.') + 1));
    formError.setValue(cv.getInvalidValue());
    formError.setMessage(cv.getMessage());
    models.put("formError",formError);
    request.setAttribute("formError", formError);
    final Viewable viewable = new Viewable("error.hbs", models);
    return Response.status(BAD_REQUEST).entity(viewable).build();
  }
}
```

This `ConstraintViolationExceptionMapper` class is a JAX-RS provider because we annotated it with `@javax.ws.rs.ext.Provider`. The class is generically typed to `ConstraintViolationException` and therefore, it handles all the failures in the web application! There is no leeway here. We will inject into the `HttpServletRequest` POJO in order to get access to the web context. The `toResponse()` method transforms the constraint violation into a new response. We will need an implementation of the `Models` instance, so we will instantiate the class in the Ozark framework. We will build a `FormErrorMessage` POJO directly and populate it from the first instance of a `javax.validation.ConstraintViolation` type. We will set a key property in the `Models` instance and servlet request scope. From here, we will create a `Viewable` instance with the view template reference, `error.hbs`, and the `Models` instance and then build and return a response.

It is worth looking at some of the internals of the reference implementation, Ozark. We have always seen `ViewEngineBase` and `ViewEngineContext`. Here is a diagram of some of the important internal classes and their packages:

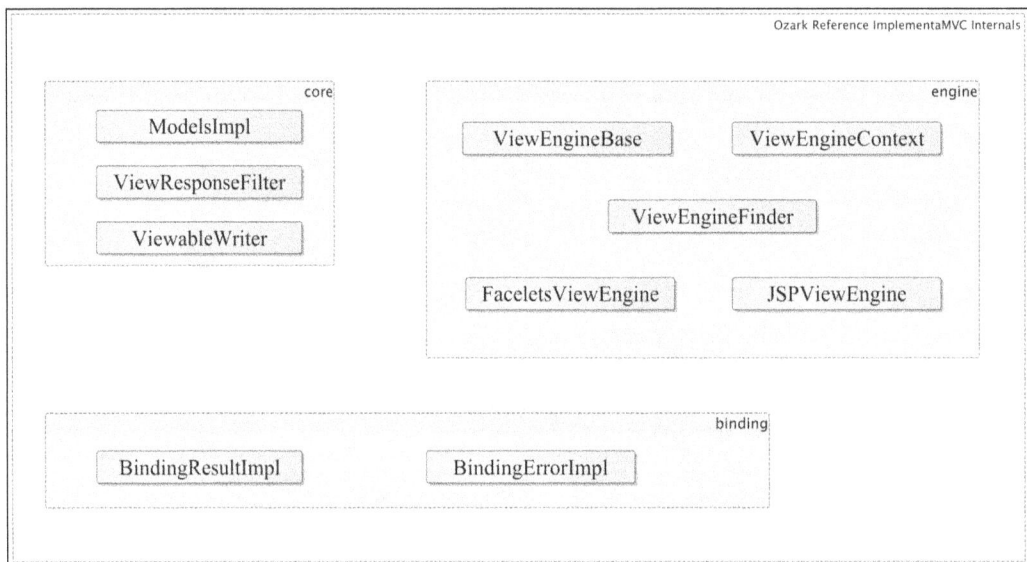

An MVC binding result validation

The MVC specification has an API for fine grain validation, which is still being decided on. There are two interface types—`BindingResult` and `BindingError`—in the `javax.mvc.binding` package.

`BindingResult` captures the constraint violations during an attempt to validate the input arguments of an MVC controller method, which is annotated with `@FormParam`. The specification describes the term binding to reflect the association between the form parameter and actual type of the property that is being validated and the possible constraint violations that could occur. Therefore, an integer property cannot be bound if the HTML form parameter, which is a string, cannot be converted to a number in a meaningful manner. The interface for `BindingResult` is as follows:

```
package javax.mvc.binding;
public interface BindingResult {
  boolean isFailed();
  List<String> getAllMessages();
  Set<BindingError> getAllBindingErrors();
  BindingError getBindingError(String param);
  Set<ConstraintViolation<?>> getViolations(String param);
  ConstraintViolation<?> getViolation(String param);
}
```

The interesting members of `BindingResult` are `isFailed()`, `getAllViolations()`, and `getAllBindingErrors()`.

The `BindingError` type is designed to represent a single error that occurs while binding a parameter to a controller method. Here is the condensed interface API for this type:

```
package javax.mvc.binding;
public interface BindingError {
  String getMessage();
  String getMessageTemplate();
  String getParamName();
}
```

The `BindingError` type works similarly to the Bean Validation specification for an interpolated message. Therefore, it is helpful for internationalization because the messages may be retrieved from `java.util.ResourceBundle`.

For our final example, we will use `BindingResult` to validate our new `editMethod()` method:

```java
@Path("/products")
@Stateless
public class ProductController {
  @Inject BindingResult br;

  /* ... */

  @POST
  @Controller
  @Path("edit/{id}")
  @Produces("text/html")
  @ValidateOnExecution(type = ExecutableType.NONE)
  public Response editProduct(
    @PathParam("id") int id,
    @FormParam("action") String action,
    @Valid @BeanParam Product incomingProduct)
  {
    defineCommonModelProperties("Edit Product");
    if ("Save".equalsIgnoreCase(action)) {
      Set<ConstraintViolation<?>> set = vr.getAllViolations();
      if (!set.isEmpty()) {
        final ConstraintViolation<?> cv = set.iterator().next();
        final String property = cv.getPropertyPath().toString();
        formError.setProperty(
            property.substring(property.lastIndexOf('.') + 1));
        formError.setValue(cv.getInvalidValue());
        formError.setMessage(cv.getMessage());
        models.put("formError",formError);
        return Response.status(BAD_REQUEST).
          entity("error.hbs").build();
      }
      final List<Product> products = productService.findById(id);
      final Product product = products.get(0);
      product.setName(incomingProduct.getName());
      product.setDescription(incomingProduct.getDescription());
      product.setPrice(incomingProduct.getPrice());
      productService.saveProduct(product);
      models.put("product", product);
    }
    retrieveAll();
    return Response.status(OK).entity("/products.hbs").build();
  }
}
```

In order to get the benefit of fine grain validation, we will inject @BindingResult as a property into ProductController. We will change the annotations around the editProduct() method. In order to ensure that JAX-RS performs the validation and the CDI and Bean Validation do not abort the process, we will annotate @ValidateOnExecution and set the type parameter to ExecutableType.NONE. According to the Bean Validation specification, the @ValidateOnExecution annotation is used to selectively enable and disable the violation. Switching off the validation allows JAX RS to take over our controller method, editProduct(). We will also use @Valid and @BeanParam to direct the MVC provider to validate the Product entity bean.

MVC takes over the validation when it notices that the controller class has injected the BindingResult instance or has a JavaBean setter method that accepts BindingResult. In the editProduct() method, we will check the Boolean status of the validation by calling the isFailed() method. If the input failed to get validated, we will grab the first constraint violation from the BindResult result and then populate the FormErrorMessage bean as before. We will then send an HTTP response with a Bad Request error code that forwards to the error.hbs view template.

Note that we will write the editProduct() method with a separate named variable argument, incomingProduct, in order to keep a temporary holder of the HTML form data. We will copy the properties of this variable over the product entity that is retrieved from the database and save it. By the time we reach the end of the controller method, the entity bean must be valid. We will retrieve a list of the products and return an OK response. With BindingResult, it is clear to the developers that this validation is easier to program with. There is less code to deliberate over.

Design considerations

MVC is a very promising specification, and at the moment, the view technology solution is usual for digital developers. There is still a story to be developed regarding the handling of an HTTP redirects response and especially a way to hold over a form state. Many digital web developers are already familiar with the design pattern, HTTP POST– REDIRECT–GET (https://en.wikipedia.org/wiki/Post/Redirect/Get), and therefore, they would be looking for an equivalent and safe option in the MVC specification.

On the other side of the equation lies the question about an HTML form validation; however, there may be breaking news on this front. The story on form validation shares much of the ground as HTTP redirect requests. Developers want to take advantage of the Bean Validation on an entity but they also want to seamlessly invoke the validation in a controller and introspect the validation result. The fact is that JAX-RS allows the validation through a global provider. However, this approach does not provide fine-grain validation handling and it cannot map constraint violation instances to individual HTML form input elements. Nevertheless, the post Early Draft Release snapshots have shown early promise in this regard.

As we have seen in the Handlebars Java code examples, there is a design consideration and trade-off for many digital architects. How much of the presentation logic resides in the client against the server side?

Majority server-side templating

Considering the option of mostly server-side templating, why would a technical architect choose this mode? There are a lot of reasons for this approach. One reason may be that the team is slightly intimidated by JavaScript programming and wants minimum dependencies and time-to-market. This is a skill, training, and maintenance trade-off. Another reason might be that the final end client devices are sufficiently underpowered, such as an Internet of Things device. It is unlikely that a digital thermostat would have to render retina edition images. Yet another reason could be an easier migration for a very old legacy application in order to bring it up to date: this is digital transformation. MVC can help here with the extensive view templates support.

Majority client-side templating

This design choice implies that the client side renders much of the content on a device. It has been said that smartphones with JavaScript and HTML5 have orders of magnitude of computing power over the rocket ship computers that took humankind to the moon. One reason that a technical architect might want to delegate the load to a client is to reduce the load on a server application. This is a trade-off in scalability on the server. Handlebars.js is a JavaScript view templating implementation that is perfectly adequate for this requirement among the other competing JavaScript frameworks out there on the Internet. The MVC controllers in this mode become thin layers of architecture that truly bind the view to the model. This mode may also be appropriate if your team features very strong interface designers and developers or if they have a lack of experience with the modern Java EE development. On the UI front, there may be a valid reason to have customer journeys that map to a page-by-page navigation. Therefore, the architecture avoids single page applications and this might rule out frameworks such as AngularJS.

Shared templating

The final design choice is to combine both the client-side and server-side templating and share the responsibility of the presentation view. This may be a favored strategy for the digital technical architects working across cross-functional teams. If there is a strong interface development team and server-side Java EE team and they communicate well, then this is a reasonable approach. Apart from human resource considerations in an agile team, this approach technically favors an architecture where there is a shared template and vision to organize the digital assets. Let's say the architecture is decided on Handlebars Java on the server and Handlebars.js on the client-side; the team is immediately faced with the organization of the view templates. Which templates are compiled on the JavaScript frontend and which templates matter on the server side? The resolution to this design choice will result in the construction of the MVC controllers on the server side.

Let me leave you with one note of warning about these three design considerations. If you are worth your salt, you will consider the effect of the UX changes and sudden surprises. Therefore, a digital technical architect must factor the effect of design changes into his or her calculations.

Summary

In this final chapter of the book, we covered the burgeoning MVC specification from the ground up. We covered the essential elements of the models, views, and controllers. We saw that MVC is a layering on top of JAX-RS and it reuses the same annotations, including `@GET`, `@FormParam`, `@Path`, `@FormParam`, and `@POST`.

In order to establish a method as an MVC controller, we annotated them with `@Controller`. We wrote controllers that generate either the response instance or, if they returned a void type, we would annotate the method with `@View`.

You learned about the various view technologies that are supported by the MVC reference specification, Ozark. We used the Handlebars Java view template to build the elements of a CRUD example. We also understood that the MVC specification might change in respect to the redirection and validation APIs.

Exercises

Here are the questions and exercises for this chapter:

1. What are the constituent components of the Java EE MVC framework? What does MVC attempt to solve?

2. What is the difference between `@Controller`, `@Model`, and `@View`?

3. What is the difference between the Response and Viewable types?

4. Given that the standard HTML form element does not send an HTTP PUT or DELETE request, just how would you handle the removing of a record from the database using MVC? What does this mean for the businesses that already have full RESTful interfaces?

5. By the time this book is published, the MVC framework will be further along and there is likely to be many milestone releases. Update your knowledge. What has changed? Look especially at the redirection and validation.

6. Download the `handlebars-javaee-mvc-validation` project from the book's source code repository and adapt the product instance in order to include the `description` (`string`), `manufacturer` (`string`), and `manufacturedDate` (`java.util.Date`) properties. What needs to happen in order to display a formatted date correctly (say, MMM-dd-yyyy or dd-MMM-yyyy)?

7. Working from the previous exercise, ensure that the proper validation techniques are in place using MVC. How would you validate the user input?

8. If you are reasonably comfortable with the JavaScript programming, write a module to invoke validation over AJAX. (Hint: you will probably need to understand the JQuery REST requests and responses.)

9. In this exercise, take the `Product` entity and `ProductController` controller classes and use them as a basis to experiment with another view template technology with the Ozark reference implementation. There are plenty of choices. Adapt a new templating framework to the product CRUD application—try Thymeleaf or even AsciiDoc. What is the difference between the templating choices? What are the benefits? What are the disadvantages?

10. Write a short essay that proposes the MVC framework to your current team for a particular project. What are the design considerations of the MVC approach? Does your target audience suit a single page navigation or page-by-page navigation or a mixture of both the ideas? (Hint: personas might be useful; you can write a proposal aimed to convince the technical leader in your team or you might be a technical leader aiming to convince the members in your team.)

A

JSF with HTML5, Resources, and Faces Flows

This appendix contains a quick reference to the JSF library in two parts. The first part covers the reference material on the library, architecture resource library contracts, and internationalization configuration. The second part is dedicated to writing Faces Flows using the Java API.

An HTML5 friendly markup

After Java EE 7 and the release of JSF 2.2, the framework always renders the HTML5 document type: `<DOCTYPE html>`. This is the default behavior for the modern digital websites. With the HTML5 support, developers can just write the content in a Facelets view (a `*.xhtml` file) that is compatible with the rendering engines in a modern web browser.

JSF 2.2 provides two types of attributes for the HTML elements: `pass-through` attributes and `pass-through` elements.

The pass-through attributes

The `pass-through` attributes enable JSF to seamlessly support the new and extended attributes that are defined by the HTML5. These attributes are applicable to the JSF HTML render kit custom tags such as `<h:inputText>`. In order to use the `pass-through` attributes, we will define a JSF namespace at the top of the Facelets view that references the URL `http://xmlns.jcp.org/jsf/passthrough`.

Let's take an example that uses the HTML5 attributes for a placeholder text:

```
<html xmlns="http://www.w3.org/1999/xhtml"
      xmlns:h="http://xmlns.jcp.org/jsf/html"
      xmlns:p="http://xmlns.jcp.org/jsf/passthrough">
...
  <div class="form-group">
    <label for="birthday" class="col-sm-3 control-label">
    Birthday </label>
    <div class="col-sm-9">
      <h:inputText p:type="date"
       class="form-control" id="birthday"
       value="#{customerController.birthday}"
       p:placeholder="1977-10-25"/>
    </div>
  </div>
  <div class="form-group">
    <label for="email" class="col-sm-3 control-label">
    Email </label>
    <div class="col-sm-9">
      <h:inputText p:type="email"
       class="form-control" id="email"
       value="#{customerController.email}"
       p:placeholder="yourname@yourserverhost.com"/>
    </div>
  </div>
```

The `pass-through` attribute in the preceding example is demarcated with the full namespace, `p:placeholder` and `p:type`. One input field annotates for the date format and the other for the e-mail address. The value of placeholder provides the customer/user with a visual hint about how to fill in the field. The JSF render kit will pass this attribute minus the XML namespace to the rendered tag output. The value of type overrides the default render kit setting.

Some JavaScript frameworks also rely on extended attributes such as AngularJS or certain JQuery plugins. JSF allows page content writers and interface developers to pass these values as attributes. The value of the pass-through attribute may be dynamic and can also be derived from an EL. We can thus write the following markup to validate for a secured loan amount:

```
<h:inputText p:type="range"
 class="form-control" id="loanAmount"
 value="#{customerController.loanAmount}"
 p:min="#{loanHelper.min}"
 p:max="#{loanHelper.max}" p:step="#{loanHelper.step}"
```

```
    p:placeholder="Decimal number between {loanHelper.min} and
{loanHelper.max}"/>
```

With the preceding code extract, the `pass-through` attribute `p:type` as a range value causes the modern browsers to render a slider control instead of a text control. There is a backing bean named `loanHelper` that dynamically supplies the minimum, maximum, and step unit values to the control.

The pass-through elements

The drawback of the `pass-through` attributes is that they do not look at the standard HTML5 attributes that are available in a modern web browser. An input field that is defined with a rapid UX markup such as `<h:inputText>` is not directly viewable by a stakeholder client without a microservice already running in the background process.

To enable the `pass-through` elements in our Facelets view, we must first define the JSF namespace `http://xmns.jcp.org/jsf`. In order to trigger a `pass-through` element, at least one of the attributes of an HTML element must be in the namespace.

Let's see how this works in practice with a Facelets view:

```
<html xmlns="http://www.w3.org/1999/xhtml"
      xmlns:jsf="http://xmlns.jcp.org/jsf">
  <head jsf:id="head"> ... </head>
  <body jsf:id="body">
    ...
    <form jsf:id="vacationForm">
      ...
      <input type="text" jsf:id="companyId"
         placeholder="Your company identity number"
         jsf:value="#{vacationController.companyNo}"/>
      <input type="text" jsf:id="lastName"
         placeholder="Enter last name"
         jsf:value="#{vacationController.name}"/>
      ...
      <button class="btn btn-primary"
        jsf:action="#{vacationController.makeRequest}">
        Make Vacation Request</button>
    </form>
  </body>
</html>
```

The HTML elements—head, body, form, input, and button—have at least one JSF namespace attribute. JSF detects the attribute and adds a component to its rendering tree. The name of the element determines the type of the component that is added. So, the head element is in fact rendered by the equivalent of the <h:head> custom tag, and the body element is also rendered by the equivalent JSF <h:body> custom tag. The HTML input type is treated specially and rendered with <h:inputText>. The id and value attribute are passed with the JSF namespace. The placeholder attributes are passed as normal attributes without the JSF namespace. They are surprisingly supplied and treated like pass-through attributes!

We can add validation to what looks like normal HTML5 elements. Here is the code to ensure that the user enters at least six characters:

```
<input type="text" jsf:id="companyId"
    placeholder="Your company identity number"
    jsf:value="#{vacationController.companyNo}"/>
  <f:validateLength minimum="6" />
</input>
```

We will insert <f:validateLength> as the direct body content of the HTML input element. The HTML5 support ensures that the tag is translated as a JSF input component. The support also extends to the AJAX tags and library functions.

Resource identifiers

In JSF 2.0, a resource is an image, document, or some other digital asset. They are placed under the resources folder at the web context folder. In a Gradle or Maven project, a particular resource lives on the path, as shown:

```
src/main/webapp/resources/<RESOURCE-IDENTIFIER>
```

A resource may also be stored in a JAR file under the WEB-INF/lib folder:

```
src/main/webapp/WEB-INF/lib/<SOME>.jar
```

If the resource is stored in a JAR file, it must be located in the META-INF folder such that it can be located with the path:

```
META-INF/resources/<RESOURCE-IDENTIFIER>
```

RESOURCE-IDENTIFIER can be further divided into separate paths. The widest case supports full internalization. The constituent parts are as follows:

```
<RESOURCE-IDENTIFIER> :=
  [ <LOCALE-PREFIX> / ] [ <LIBRARY-NAME> / ]
  [ <LIBRARY-VERSION> / ]
  <RESOURCE-NAME> [ / <RESOURCE-VERSION> ]
```

The subterms allow the resource identifiers to be easily identified and separated out.

The optional LOCALE-PREFIX term represents a locale such as en_gb (British English) or de (Germany).

The optional LIBRARY-NAME term specifies a library name. You can define the library name and use it in the JSF custom tags, as follows:

```
<h:outputStylesheet library="default" name="styles/app.css" />
<h:outputStylesheet library="admin" name="styles/app.css" />
```

The preceding example retrieves an application style sheet that is appropriate to the library. This helps to distinguish the different parts of your digital application. The resource lookup may resolve to the following:

```
<WEB-CONTEXT>/resources/en/default/1_0/styles/app.css
<WEB-CONTEXT>src/main/webapp/resources/en/admin/1_0/styles/app.css
```

These URLs map to the following source file assets in a conventional project:

```
src/main/webapp/resources/en/default/1_0/styles/app.css
src/main/webapp/resources/en/admin/1_0/styles/app.css
```

Developers do not specify the library version. Instead, the JSF Resource Lookup mechanism searches for the highest version files of the respective resources. The version number of the folder name must match the regex: \d_\d. Therefore, the version folder name 2_0 is greater than 1_5, which in turn, is higher than 1_0.

Resource Library Contracts

JSF 2.2 introduces the concept of Resource Library Contracts, which allows a digital developer to organize a library of assets and templates in a reusable set of resources. A resource library contract must reside in the contracts directory folder in the application's web context root. In the standard Maven or Gradle build convention, this folder is src/main/webapp/contracts. Each subfolder in the contracts folder represents a named resource contract.

The setup for the *Chapter 6, JSF Flows and Finesse* used a layout for the Resource Library Contracts, as follows:

```
/src/main/webapp/contracts/

/src/main/webapp/contracts/default/

/src/main/webapp/contracts/default/template.xhtml

/src/main/webapp/contracts/default/styles/app.css
```

```
/src/main/webapp/contracts/default/images/
```

```
/src/main/webapp/contracts/victoria/
```

```
/src/main/webapp/contracts/victoria/template.xhtml
```

```
/src/main/webapp/contracts/victoria/styles/app.css
```

```
/src/main/webapp/contracts/victoria/images/
```

Every contract must have at least one declared `template.xhtml` file. A contract may have more than one template for its own customization. The declared template has at least one declared insertion point, which is defined as the `<ui:insert>` tag. A template usually relies on the digital assets, and these are known as declared resources.

Contracts can be packaged in the JAR files for a customer's use. A resource library contract must be placed in the `META-INF/contracts` folder of the JAR file. So, we could repackage the flow examples in the following layout:

```
META-INF/contracts/
```

```
META-INF/contracts/default/javax.faces.contract.xml
```

```
META-INF/contracts/default/template.xhtml
```

```
META-INF/contracts/default/styles/app.css
```

```
META-INF/contracts/default/images/
```

```
META-INF/contracts/victoria/
```

```
META-INF/contracts/victoria/javax.faces.contract.xml
```

```
META-INF/contracts/victoria/template.xhtml
```

```
META-INF/contracts/victoria/styles/app.css
```

```
META-INF/contracts/victoria/images/
```

We will need to add an empty marker file to each contract, `javax.faces.contract.xml`. The reference for this filename is found in the static `string: javax.faces.application.ResourceHandler.RESOURCE_CONTRACT_XML`.

A Faces servlet

In JSF, FacesServlet acts as the front controller, is the conduit for all the requests, and also sends the response back to the client. This servlet is a subclass of `javax.servlet.Servlet`.

A web browser client sends an HTTP request to the servlet container. If it is a Faces request, then the servlet container invokes the `service()` method of FacesServlet. The method hands over the processing of the request to a member instance `javax.faces.lifecycle.LifeCycle` object. The method also creates a FacesContext instance. The `LifeCycle` instance is responsible for the processing of a request to all of the JSF phases described in *Chapter 2, JavaServer Faces Lifecycle* and the rendering of the response.

Reconfiguration of the resource paths

It is possible to change the path name of the resource lookup and contract folders as well by configuring the web XML deployment descriptor. The constants are defined in the `javax.faces.application.ResourceHandler` class. The `WEBAPP_RESOURCES_DIRECTORY_PARAM_NAME` string constant defines the resource directory property's name and `WEBAPP_CONTRACTS_DIRECTORY_PARAM_NAME` defines the contract directory property.

We can redefine the JSF web application defaults with the following `web.xml` settings:

```
<web-app xmlns="http://xmlns.jcp.org/xml/ns/javaee" ...>
  <servlet>
    <servlet-name>Faces Servlet</servlet-name>
    <servlet-class>javax.faces.webapp.FacesServlet</servlet-class>
    <init-param>
      <param-name>javax.faces.WEBAPP_RESOURCES_DIRECTORY</param-name>
      <param-value>/myresources</param-value>
    </init-param>
    <init-param>
      <param-name>javax.faces.WEBAPP_CONTRACTS_DIRECTORY</param-name>
      <param-value>/mycontracts</param-value>
    </init-param>
  </servlet> ...
</web-app>
```

We can specify the initial parameters on the Faces servlet in overriding the default configuration.

A JSF-specific configuration

The Faces servlet understands several other configuration parameters. Here is a table of the possible parameter names. These are prefixed with `javax.faces`:

Parameter name	Description
CONFIG_FILES	This specifies a comma-delimited list of the additional context related resource paths that are loaded automatically with `WEB-INF/faces-config.xml`.
DEFAULT_SUFFIX	This sets the suffix for the JSF files; the default is `*.xhtml`. If you change this configuration, then I recommend that you also change welcome-file-list in `web.xml`.
DISABLE_FACELET_JSF_VIEW_HANDLER	If this parameter is set to `true`, then it disables Facelets as the default page declaration language. The default is `false`.
FACELETS_BUFFER_SIZE	This specifies the buffer size for a JSF response. The default size is `-1`, which means an unlimited size.
FACELETS_REFRESH_PERIOD	This sets the interval time in seconds that the JSF compiler should check for changes. In the production mode, this value is set to `-1`, which means that the JSF compiler should not check; otherwise, the default is set to `2` in the reference implementation.
FACELETS_SKIP_COMMENT	This is a Boolean value that determines if the XML comments in a Facelets view is included in a response. The default value is `true`.
FACELETS_LIBRARIES	This specifies a semicolon delimited list collection of the Facelets tag libraries by a path.
LIFECYCLE_ID	This overrides the default implementation of the JSF `javax.faces.lifecycle.Lifecycle` instance.
PROJECT_STAGE	This specifies the development project stage. The acceptable values are `Development`, `UnitTest`, `SystemTest`, or `Production`.
STATE_SAVING_METHOD	This specifies the location where a state is saved in a JSF application. The acceptable values are `client` and `server`.
WEBAPP_CONTRACTS_DIRECTORY	This overrides the default location of the JSF resource contracts. The default is `<web-context>/contracts`.
WEBAPP_RESOURCES_DIRECTORY	This overrides the default location of the JSF resources reserved for the digital assets. The default is `<web-context>/resources`.

These settings are best configured in the web deployment descriptor file (`web.xml`).

Internationalization

A JSF application can be internationalized with standard resource bundles (java.util.ResourceBundle) and messages. Resource bundles are suitable to internationalize the text on the components, controls, and digital assets; whereas message files are meant to internationalize the JSF validation errors.

In a Gradle or Maven project, we will add a resource bundle or message file to the src/main/resources project location with the necessary Java package as folders.

Resource bundles

We will configure the resource bundles in the Faces configuration file, /WEB-INF/faces-config.xml, for the web application.

For the contact details application in *Chapter 4, JSF Validation and AJAX*, we have two resource bundle files in English and German: appMessages.properties and appMessage_de.properties respectively.

Here is the English language bundle:

```
// uk/co/xenonique/digital/appMessages.properties
contactForm.firstName=First Name
contactForm.lastName=Last Name
contactForm.houseOrFlatNumber=House or Flat Number
contactForm.street1=Street 1
contactForm.street2=Street 2
contactForm.townOrCity=Town or City
contactForm.region=Region
contactForm.postCode=Post Code
```

Here is the German language bundle:

```
// uk/co/xenonique/digital/appMessages_de.properties
contactForm.firstName=Vornamen
contactForm.lastName=Nachnamen
contactForm.houseOrFlatNumber=Haus oder Wohnung Nummer
contactForm.street1=Strasse 1
contactForm.street2=Strasse 2
contactForm.townOrCity=Stadt oder Gemeinde
contactForm.region=Lande
contactForm.postCode=PLZ
```

In order to use these bundles in our JSF bundle, we will configure the Faces configuration as follows:

```
<?xml version="1.0"?>
<faces-config version="2.2"
  xmlns="http://xmlns.jcp.org/xml/ns/javaee"
  xmlns:xsi="http://www.w3.org/2001/XMLSchema-instance"
  xsi:schemaLocation="http://xmlns.jcp.org/xml/ns/javaee
  http://xmlns.jcp.org/xml/ns/javaee/web-facesconfig_2_2.xsd">
  <application>
    <resource-bundle>
        <base-name>uk.co.xenonique.digital.appMessages</base-name>
        <var>appMessages</var>
    </resource-bundle>
  </application>
</faces-config>
```

We will define a resource bundle configuration in `/WEB-INF/faces-config.xml` for our application messages. In this file, we can define an application scope variable for our bundle, namely `appMessages`.

From here, we can use the bundle with an EL syntax. Here is the code for the house number in the application:

```
<h:form id="yourAddressForm"
        styleClass="form-horizontal" p:role="form">
  <div class="form-group">
    <h:outputLabel for="houseOrFlatNumber"
      class="col-sm-3 control-label">
        #{appMessages['contactForm.houseOrFlatNumber']}
    </h:outputLabel>...
  </div> ...
</h:form>
```

As we use dots (.) in our property name, we must use the map EL syntax so as to obtain the required message: `#{appMessages['contactForm.houseOrFlatNumber']}`.

Resource bundles may also contain parameterized message properties with formatted token arguments. The token arguments are expanded during message resolution by the JSF framework or through application custom code. Here is an example of parameterized message property:

```
contactForm.specialNote = proctor records {0}, {1} and {2}
```

Then, we will use the `<h:outputFormat>` tag to render the output, as follows:

```
<h:outputFormat value="#{appMessages['contactForm.specialNote']}">
  <f:param value="first argument" />
  <f:param value="second argument" />
  <f:param value="third argument" />
</h:outputFormat>
```

Message bundles

The backing code in the JSF applications in general may generate messages for the output that can also be internationalized. The messages are stored in the FacesContext object. We will need to ensure that a user can see all or some of these messages. We will do this with the `<h:messages>` or `<h:message>` JSF tags.

In *Chapter 4, JSF Validation and AJAX*, we already looked at `faces-config.xml` for the message bundles.

A browser configured locale

For many digital sites, the user's browser determines the locale of the website. Developers can inform JSF about the languages that are supported in an application in the `/WEB/faces-config.xml` file.

Here is the setting for the contact details application:

```
<faces-config>
  <application>
    <locale-config>
        <default-locale>en</default-locale>
        <supported-locale>fr</supported-locale>
        <supported-locale>de</supported-locale>
    </locale-config>
  </application>
</faces-config>
```

In this file, we will specify that our default locale is English and the supported locales are French and German.

An application controlled locale

There are certain digital sites where the requirement is to allow the user to switch between two or more locales. So, we must programmatically achieve this goal. For each rendered view in JSF, we will need to set the locale in the controller method. We will use FacesContext to gain access to the root view UI in the Faces response and set the locale here.

Suppose that we are working for a sports automotive manufacturer with their offices in London, UK, and Heidelberg, Southern Germany; then, we can write the following code:

```
final UIViewRoot viewRoot = FacesContext
  .getCurrentInstance().getViewRoot();
viewRoot.setLocale(new Locale("de"));
```

The view will be set to the German locale.

An individual page controlled locale

If the stakeholder wants a digital site where each individual page may have its own configured locale, then JSF can achieve this goal. Developers can use the `<f:view>` view tag to override the locale for a page. Before the JSF 2.0 standard, the view tag wrapped the content and acted as a container element. In JSF 2.0 and later versions, this is now unnecessary and the view tag can set the locale.

Here is a code extract that retrieves the locale from a user profile bean with a property called `primaryLocale`:

```
<f:view locale="#{userProfile.primaryLocale}"/>
```

Here is the session-scoped bean that goes with the page view:

```
@SessionScoped
class UserProfile {
  private Locale primaryLocale = Locale.ENGLISH;
  public Locale getPrimaryLocale() {
    return primaryLocale;
  }
}
```

A web deployment descriptor

This is to go to a separate appendix.

Here is a reference development XML deployment descriptor for JSF 2.2 and Java EE 7:

```xml
<?xml version="1.0" encoding="UTF-8"?>
<web-app xmlns="http://xmlns.jcp.org/xml/ns/javaee"
 xmlns:xsi="http://www.w3.org/2001/XMLSchema-instance"
 xsi:schemaLocation="http://xmlns.jcp.org/xml/ns/javaee
 http://xmlns.jcp.org/xml/ns/javaee/web-app_3_1.xsd"
 version="3.1">
  <context-param>
    <param-name>javax.faces.PROJECT_STAGE</param-name>
    <param-value>Development</param-value>
  </context-param>
  <servlet>
    <servlet-name>Faces Servlet</servlet-name>
    <servlet-class>javax.faces.webapp.FacesServlet</servlet-class>
    <load-on-startup>1</load-on-startup>
  </servlet>
  <servlet-mapping>
    <servlet-name>Faces Servlet</servlet-name>
    <url-pattern>*.jsf</url-pattern>
  </servlet-mapping>
  <session-config>
    <session-timeout> 30 </session-timeout>
  </session-config>
  <welcome-file-list>
    <welcome-file>index.jsf</welcome-file>
  </welcome-file-list>
</web-app>
```

Programmatic Faces Flows

In this appendix, we will provide a quick reference to the JavaServer Faces Flow. A flow is as per user and per web application finite state machine is with nodes. There is a default entry node and at least one exit node.

View types

In *Chapter 6, JSF Flows and Finesse*, we discussed the building of the flow navigation from the Faces configuration XML file. The JSF 2.2 specification describes the convention to store and set up the flows with a directory structure.

There are several types of nodes. They are tabulated in the following table:

Node type	Description
View Node	This node represents a view. The JSF provider renders the view, the flow is still active.
Return Node	This node represents an exit point from the flow to the outside of this flow. The current flow terminates on the invocation of this node.
Flow Call Node	This node represents an invocation to another nested flow.
Method Call Node	This node represents an invocation to a method call in a flow-scoped bean. After leaving this method call, the current flow is still active.
Switch Node	This node represents a selectable conditional state. Depending on the state, the flow may move to one or more alternative states and there is a default outcome. The current flow is still active.
Navigation Case Node	This node represents a generalized conditional state with navigation. Depending on the state, the flow may move to a new outcome or execute an HTTP redirect out of the flow.

> By comparing the Faces Flows with the other flows or business process technology, it should be acknowledged that there is no so-called initial node.

The Faces Flows programmatic interface

The Faces Flows are powered by CDI. It is possible to write programmatic flows by declaring a POJO that produces a Faces Flow. In order to generate a flow dynamically, we must annotate a bean as a CDI producer and generate a flow instance.

Here is a basic `SimpleFlowFactory` class that supplies a Faces Flow:

```
import javax.faces.flow.builder.*;

public class SimpleFlowFactory implements Serializable {
  @Inject DocumentIdGenerator generator;

  @Produces @FlowDefinition
  public Flow createFlow(
    @FlowBuilderParameter FlowBuilder flowBuilder)
  {
    final String documentId = generator.generate();
    flowBuilder.id(documentId, "simpleFlow");
    flowBuilder.viewNode("simpleFlow",
```

```
        "/simpleFlow/simpleFlow.xhtml")
        .markAsStartNode();
    return flowBuilder.getFlow();
  }
}
```

We will annotate the `createFlow()` method as a CDI producer with the special qualifier, `@FlowDefinition`. We will also supply this method with a single argument, `FlowBuilder`, which is also annotated with `@FlowBuilderParameter`. These definitions, by the way, are found in the reserved imported package: `javax.faces.flow.builder`. We use an injected `FlowBuilder` to generate a specific flow. The actual node types are found in the `javax.faces.flow` package.

A Faces Flow requires a flow identifier, which is `simpleFlow`. We can optionally also define a specific document ID. We will use a dependent generator instance to demonstrate how this works. If there is no need for a document ID, then supply an empty string.

A Faces Flow requires at least one view, which is usually the default name in the XML configuration. In order to complete the first view node, we will define a ViewNode and the URI for the flow's view template: `/simpleFlow/simpleFlow.xhtml`. We will also need to set the flow's start node with the call set to `markAsStartNode()`, because a Faces Flow requires an initial node. The API for `FlowBuilder` is taken from the fluent builder pattern. At the end of the `createFlow()` method, we will generate a flow instance and return it. The JSF provider takes over the flow definition from this point onwards.

Remember that as we are building the flow ourselves, we don't have to follow all the rules of the XML configuration exactly. However, all the view templates for a flow definition must fall under one single folder in the root context of the web application.

Just because we defined a flow definition producer, we will still require the actually flow-scoped bean, namely:

```
@Named("simpleFlowController")
@FlowScoped("simple")
public class SimpleFlow implements Serializable {
  /* ... */
}
```

We will look at the specifics of each node type in the following sections.

The following UML class diagram illustrates the key types in the API:

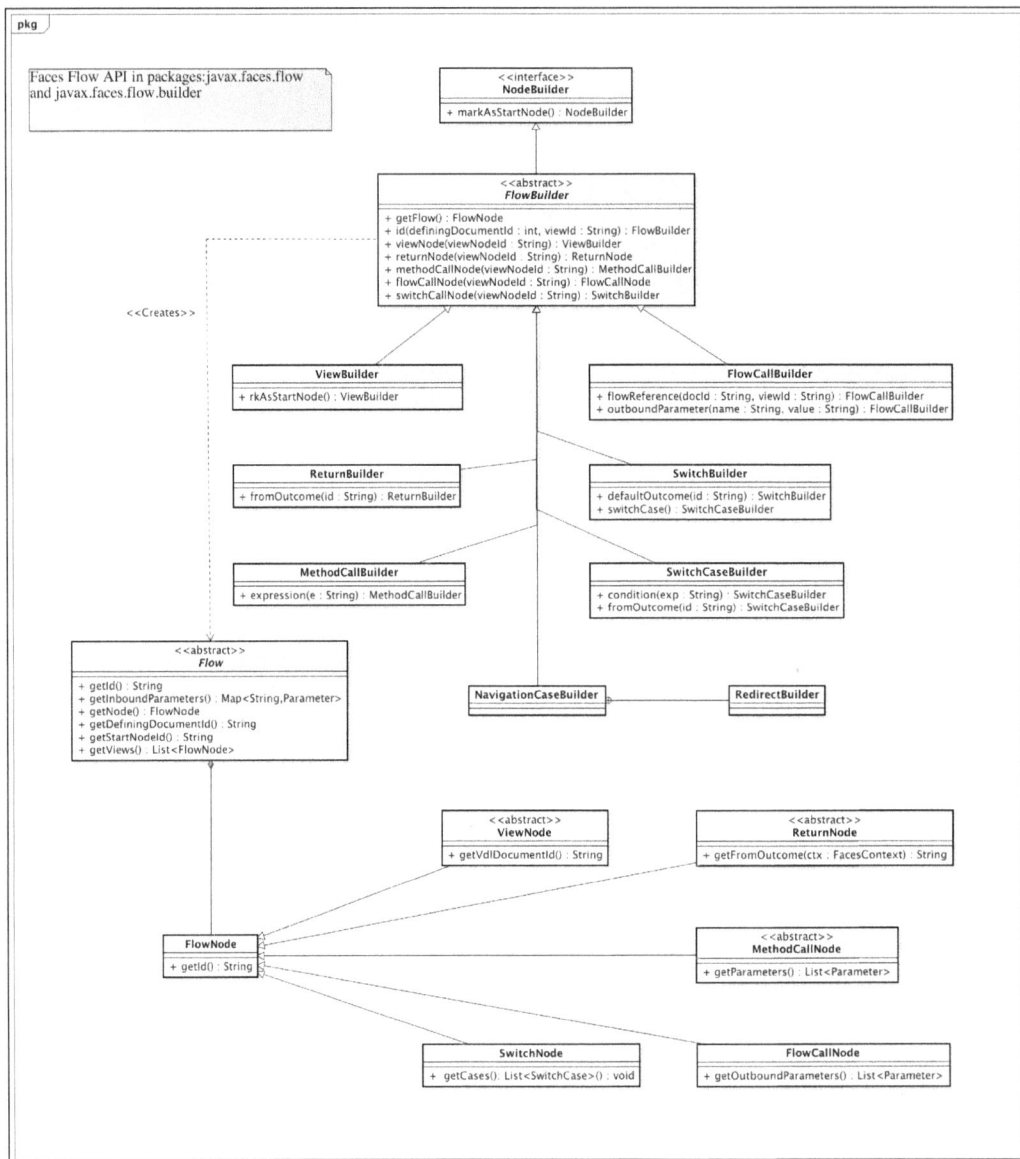

UML class diagram for the Faces Flow API

ViewNode

With `FlowBuilder`, we can define the ViewNode instances. The actual type is a subclass of `javax.faces.faces.ViewNode`.

The following example of a code extends the last flow instance and provides additional view nodes:

```
@Produces @FlowDefinition
public Flow createFlow(
  @FlowBuilderParameter FlowBuilder flowBuilder)
{
  final String documentId = generator.generate();
  flowBuilder.id(documentId, "simpleFlow");
  /* ... */
  flowBuilder.viewNode("page1", "/simpleFlow/page1.xhtml")
  flowBuilder.viewNode("page2", "/simpleFlow/page2.xhtml")
  flowBuilder.viewNode("page3", "/simpleFlow/page3.xhtml")
  return flowBuilder.getFlow();
}
```

The `viewNode()` method accepts two arguments. The first argument is the view node ID, which we will write in and refer to in the view content. The second argument is the view description language document identifier, which translates to the URI of the Facelets view.

The path of the URI can also be a relative URL. This means the eventual path is relative to the flow URI path. Otherwise, the URI must be absolute in terms of the web context root path, as we can see in the preceding code extract.

The `viewNode()` method returns a `ViewBuilder` type, which has only one additional `markAsStartNode()` method.

ReturnNode

We can also generate a ReturnNode instance from `FlowBuilder`. This is straightforward with the `returnNode()` method. The actual type is a subclass of `javax.faces.faces.ReturnNode`.

This is an extract of the `createFlow()` method that specifies a return node:

```
@Produces @FlowDefinition
public Flow createFlow(
  @FlowBuilderParameter FlowBuilder flowBuilder)
{
  final String documentId = generator.generate();
  flowBuilder.id(documentId, "simpleFlow");
  /* ... */
  flowBuilder.returnNode("return-backup").fromOutcome("welcome");
  return flowBuilder.getFlow();
}
```

The `returnNode()` method accepts a single argument the view node ID and returns an instance of `ReturnBuilder`. The `fromOutcome()` method call specifies the view name of the outcome that we navigate to after returning from the current flow.

MethodCall

With the `FlowBuilder` instance, we can also create a method call node and add it to the Faces Flow. The actual type is a subclass of `javax.faces.faces.MethodCallNode`. Here is the POJO class:

```
@Produces @FlowDefinition
public Flow createFlow(
  @FlowBuilderParameter FlowBuilder flowBuilder)
{
  /* ... */
  flowBuilder.methodCallNode("check-funds")
    .expression(
      "#{loanController.verifyCustomer(customer.account)}",
      new Class[]{String.class});
    .defaultOutcome("no-funds-available")
  return flowBuilder.getFlow();
}
```

The `methodCallNode()` call accepts a view node ID and creates a `MethodCallBuilder` instance. This node requires an expression that informs JSF about the name of the bean and the method to invoke. Here, the method is `verifyCustomer()` on an accessible backing bean controller `loanController`. We can also pass the account record in the customer's details using an expression language. In case the target method invocation returns null or an empty string, we can specify a default outcome view identifier.

I recommend that you should reduce the coupling in a layered architecture as much as possible. Be careful about mixing too much presentation tier information with the business logic.

FlowCall

We will create a flow call node using the same abstract class type `FlowBuilder`. This node type invokes a nested Faces Flow. The `flowCallNode()` method accepts a single argument in the view node ID and returns a `FlowCallBuilder` instance. The actual type is a subclass of `javax.faces.faces.FlowCallNode`.

In this code extract, which is based on the *Industrial sector carbon footprint* discussion from *Chapter 6, JSF Flows and Finesse*, we will rewrite the flow definition XML file called `footprint-flow.xml` as the following `SectorFlowFactory` POJO class:

```
class SectorFlowFactory implements Serializable {
  /* ... */
  @Produces @FlowDefinition
  public Flow createFlow(
    @FlowBuilderParameter FlowBuilder flowBuilder)
  {
    flowBuilder.id("", "sector-flow");
    /* ... */
    flowBuilder.flowCallNode("callFootprintFlow")
      .flowReference("", "footprint-flow)
      .outboundParameter("param1FromSectorFlow",
        "param1 sectorFlow value")
      .outboundParameter("param2FromSectorFlow",
        "param2 sectorFlow value")
      .outboundParameter("param3FromSectorFlow",
        "#{sectorFlow.footprint}");
    return flowBuilder.getFlow();
  }
}
```

In the preceding code, the node is identified as `callFootprintFlow`. We must provide the node ID of the nest flow through a `flowReference()` method. The first argument of `flowReference()` is the flow document ID, which is an empty string here. The nested flow is identified as footprint-flow by the second argument.

We will use the `outboundParameter()` method on `FlowCallBuilder` in order to declare the outbound parameters that pass the data from the calling sector-flow to the nested footprint-flow. The first argument to `outboundParameter()` is the parameter name and the second argument is a literal string or an expression.

We can also rewrite the flow definition XML file from the nested flow programmatically. Here is an extract of the `FootprintFlowFactory` class:

```
class FootprintFlowFactory implements Serializable {
  /* ... */
  @Produces @FlowDefinition
  public Flow createFlow(
    @FlowBuilderParameter FlowBuilder flowBuilder)
  {
    flowBuilder.id("", "footprint-flow");
    flowBuilder.inboundParameter("param1FromSectorFlow",
```

```
        "#{flowScope.param1Value}");
      flowBuilder.inboundParameter("param2FromSectorFlow",
        "#{flowScope.param2Value}");
      flowBuilder.inboundParameter("param3FromSectorFlow",
        "#{flowScope.param3Value}");
      /* ... */
      return flowBuilder.getFlow();
    }
  }
```

In this code, we notice that the footprint-flow ID must match the caller reference ID. For this Faces Flow, we will declare the inbound parameters with the `inboundParameter()` method call. The first argument is the parameter name and the second is an expression language reference that defines where the value is stored.

SwitchNode

We can use `FlowBuilder` to create the declaration of a switch node. These node types are composed of an association between a conditional statement and the outcome. The outcome is the view ID. A switch node has one or more conditional statements. It may also have a default outcome. During the processing of the flow, JSF executes each conditional statement in turn. If it evaluates to true (or rather, `Boolean.TRUE`), then the associated outcome is the chosen one. The actual type is a subclass of `javax.faces.faces.SwitchNode`.

Let 's see an example of the switch node in action in a POJO. Here is another class for a monetary loan decision maker called `LoanDecisionFlowFactory`:

```
class LoanDecisionFlowFactory implements Serializable {
  /* ... */
  @Produces @FlowDefinition
  public Flow createFlow(
    @FlowBuilderParameter FlowBuilder flowBuilder)
  {
    flowBuilder.id("", "loan-application");
    /* ... */
    flowBuilder.switchNode("loan-decision")
      .defaultOutcome("home")
      .switchCase()
        .condition("#{loanMaker.decision=='Agreed'}")
        .fromOutcome("loan-agreement")
      .switchCase()
        .condition("#{loanMaker.decision=='Declined'}")
        .fromOutcome("loan-declined")
```

```
            .switchCase()
              .condition("#{loanMaker.decision=='Pending'}")
              .fromOutcome("loan-pending")
         /* ... */
         return flowBuilder.getFlow();
       }
    }
```

In the `createFlow()` method, we will create a Faces Flow identified as loan-application. We will then create a switch node declaration with `switchNode()` and identified as loan-decision. This method returns a `SwitchBuilder` type. This builder type has `switchCase()` that returns `SwitchCaseBuilder`. The other overloaded methods included are called `defaultCome()`.

It is recommended that you also declare a default outcome with the `defaultOutcome()` method, which accepts a view ID. In this way, the flow always moves to the next viable location.

Given the `SwitchBuilder` builder type, we will declare the individual cases with the `condition()` and `fromOutCome()` methods. The `condition()` call accepts an expression string and it returns `SwitchCaseBuilder`. The only property on this builder is a valid outcome, which is a view identifier.

NavigationCase node

The final builder type in the API relates to a general abstract class type `NavigationCaseBuilder`. We can create a navigation case node with `FlowBuilder`. The actual type is a subclass of `javax.faces.faces.FlowNode`.

Here is a POJO from the financial services domain that is designed to allow the back office staff in an investment bank to post the process trades in a workflow:

```
class PostProcessTradeFlowFactory implements Serializable {
  /* ... */
  @Produces @FlowDefinition
  public Flow createFlow(
    @FlowBuilderParameter FlowBuilder flowBuilder)
  {
    flowBuilder.id("", "post-process-trade-flow"); /* ... */
    flowBuilder.navigationCase()
      .fromOutcome("trade-check")
      .condition("#{trade.amount > global.risk.limit}")
      .toViewId("exceptional");

    flowBuilder.navigationCase()
```

```
            .fromOutcome("trade-check")
            .condition("#{trade.settlementCcy != 'USD'")
            .redirect().includeViewParams()
            .parameter("deskCodeNotice", "OUT_OF_CURRENCY_DEAL");
        /* ... */
        return flowBuilder.getFlow();
    }
}
```

In this `PostProcessTradeFlowFactory` POJO, we again have a `createFlow()` method, but this time we will call `navigationCase()` twice. This method has no arguments and returns a `NavigationCaseBuilder` type that creates the specified Faces Flow. A navigation case flow requires a trigger point, a conditional expression, and an outcome or redirection response.

In the first flow, we will call the `fromOutcome()` method on `NavigationCaseBuilder` in order to declare the JSF view ID that triggers the check. The `condition()` method defines the expression that must return a Boolean value. The `toViewId()` method defines the outcome view ID to navigate if the conditional expression evaluates as `Boolean.TRUE`. So, therefore, if the trade value exceeds the firm-wide exposure limit (`trade.amount > global.risk.limit`), then the flow navigates to the exceptional view.

With the second flow declaration, we will define a navigation case to handle an out-of-currency deal, which might be a Swap, Bond, or some other derivative. With the same trigger outcome trade check, we will trap on the expression for the currencies that settles in non-US dollars: `trade.settlementCcy != 'USD'`. With this navigation case node, we will execute an HTTP redirect that causes the customer to exit the entire flow. We will invoke `redirect()` and it will return `NavigationCaseBuilder.RedirectBuilder`. This nested abstract class has two methods: `includeViewParams()` and `parameter()`. The `includeViewParams()` method adds all of the view parameters to the redirect URL. The `parameter()` method adds the name and value pairs to the redirect URL. Remember that after the flow is completed, from a security digital developer's point of view, these parameters will be highly visible in the URL of the eventual HTTP GET request!

Builder types

The builder types—`ViewBuilder`, `ReturnBuilder`, `MethodCallBuilder`, `FlowCallBuilder`, `SwitchBuilder`, `SwitchCaseBuilder`, and `NavigationCaseBuilder` are abstract classes. They are implementations of the `javax.faces.flow.builder.NodeBuilder` interface. The Faces Flow API is an example of an embedded Domain Specific Language.

B

From Request to Response

During the job interviews for a software developer role, many people are frequently asked to describe how the web actually works behind the scenes. A candidate that can explain well the architectural layers of a software application to an interviewer may give the impression of a so-called full stack developer. However, it can be surprising how many candidates have just plausible knowledge of this topic, especially if they purport to work professionally in the digital domain. This appendix provides a concise and definitive description of the modern issues. The digital developers ought to be able to sketch and effectively document their current working architecture. So let's start with HTTP.

HTTP

HTTP is a fundamental stateless protocol designed to transport hypermedia between a server and client. HTTP 1.1 supports the fine-grained caching of resources and the ability to retain persistent connections and chunked transfer encoding. HTTP 1.1 was created in 1999 (refer to the superseded RFC `https://tools.ietf.org/html/rfc2068`). To cope with the modern demand and usage patterns, the HTTP now supports the WebSocket handshaking and upgrade requests (`https://tools.ietf.org/html/rfc6455`). The next HTTP 2.0 standard will provide the multiplexing of streams over a single client server channel. There are exciting possibilities for Java EE 8 (expected by May/June 2017) and the HTTP 2.0 support in the Java Servlet 4.0 specification. For more details, see RFC 7540 (`http://www.rfc-editor.org/rfc/rfc7540.txt`) and JSR 369 (`https://www.jcp.org/en/jsr/detail?id=369`).

An HTTP request

An HTTP request consists of a payload with a header and then body content. The header information contains the URI request, HTTP method, agent information, request parameters, and cookies. For the POST and PUT requests, it may also contain the form encoded properties with names and values.

The four basic HTTP methods that every digital engineer ought to understand are GET, POST, PUT, and DELETE. They are described in the following list:

- **GET**: This request fetches the contents of the resources associated with a given URL
- **POST**: This creates a brand new resource with a payload (body content) that specifies the data for the new resource
- **PUT**: This updates an existing resource with a payload that specifies some or all of the data that is being replaced
- **DELETE**: This is a request to delete the specified resource association with the URL

The following are the rare HTTP methods that are also used in special circumstances:

- **HEAD**: This performs an acknowledgement of the resources associated with a given URL by just retrieving the headers. This request is similar to the GET request but without the body content.
- **OPTION**: This retrieves the application server features or web container capabilities.
- **TRACE**: This request allows the infrastructure to find out the network hops between the client and servers and therefore validates the latency, availability, and performance.

An HTTP response

The HTTP response consists of the header information and payload data (the body content). The header contains the HTTP status code, MIME type, data length, last modified date, character set encoding, cookie parameters, and cache information of the resource. The header may also contain the authentication data. The body content is the data returned that is the client's request.

The HTTP Status codes are defined by the W3C. These are integer codes with ranges. Generally, the status codes 100-199 are informational messages, 200-299 represent the successful outcomes, 300-399 represent the redirection requests, 400-499 are server side errors, and the 500-599 status codes represent the authentication failures. Hence, the HTTP OK 200 and 404 NOT FOUND status codes are well-known to developers outside the digital domain. You can find all of them listed in the RFC at `http://www.w3.org/Protocols/rfc2616/rfc2616-sec10.html`.

Java Enterprise Architectures

Applications in the digital domain share a common thread of architecture across multiple industrial sector domains. Obviously, they share and rely on the Java EE 7 standard platform and JVM in order to piggy-bank the development, various nonfunctional attributes, and enterprise application infrastructure. There are subtle differences in the building of the applications.

Standard Java EE web architecture

The standard Java EE web architecture is derived from the client-server models of the 1990s. The application server is the key component as it is responsible for three containers in the full Java EE 7 specification: Servlet, CDI, and EJB. Generally, we map these containers to the layer tier architecture for a monolithic web application. The idea of this architecture is to enhance the best practice from the point of view of solid software engineering. We want to maintain a separation of the concerns in the layers in order to avoid rigid coupling between layers and have a strong cohesion in the layers. The three layers are as follows:

- Presentation layer is strongly associated with code that depends and requires the Servlet container. FacesServlet is supplied as a part of the JSF. Alternative web application frameworks also have the idea of Front Controller that dispatches a request to the separate controllers. The presentation tier also contains the controllers and view templates.

- Domain layer is associated with code that holds the business logic and projections of the persistence objects. It contains the application rules, business logic, and business process management. Domain objects may or may not be a part of a dependency injection. In most of the modern web applications, almost all the domain layer components and objects are a part of a dependency injection container. Therefore, domain layer is associated with the CDI container.

- Integration layer is associated with the transportation of data from the application to the durable persistence or service areas of the system. This layer maps to a POJO that is a part of the EJB container. Usually, these objects handle the service calls from the application. As EJBs, they are transactional and not necessarily contextual, which is why they are not a part of the CDI container. These objects communicate with an external system like database through JPA and/or JDBC asynchronously to the other systems through a message over JMS or they can also synchronously (or asynchronously) invoke the remote web service endpoints through the REST or SOAP calls.

The following diagram illustrates the architecture:

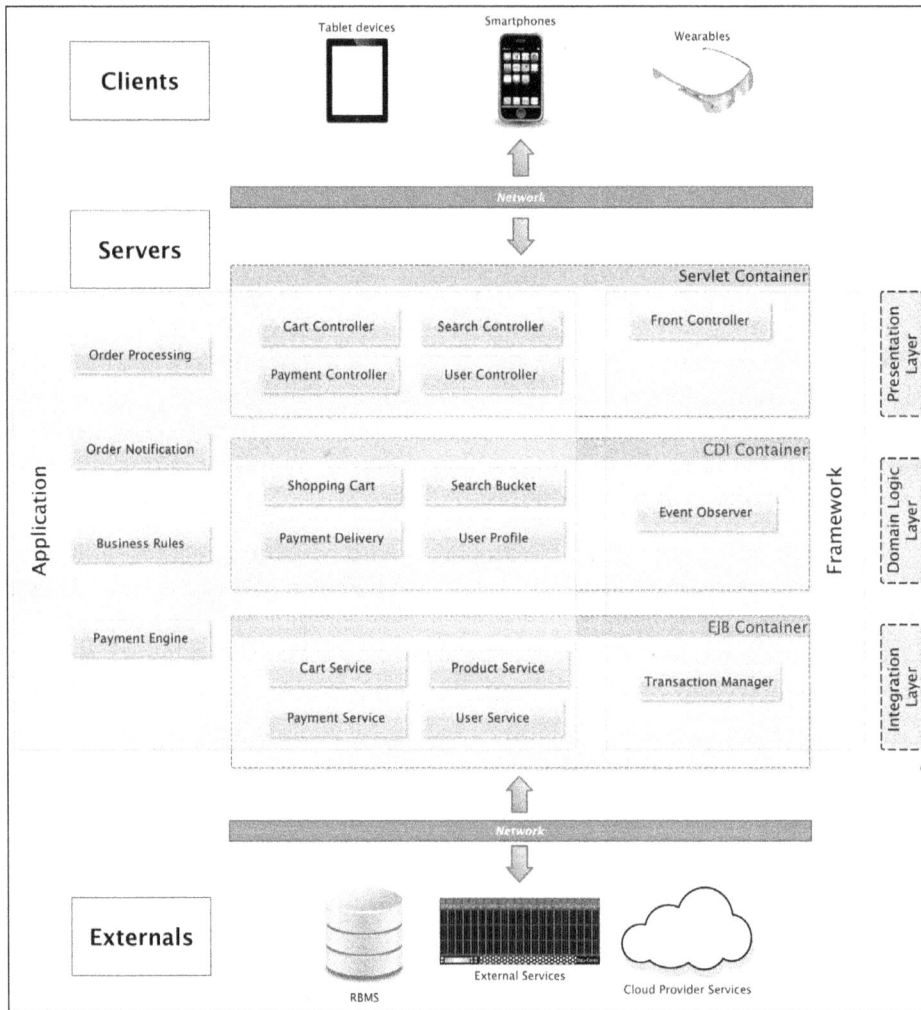

The standard Java EE web architecture

Extended architectures

From the standard Java web architecture, there are several adaptations. Organizations may choose to optimize their architecture in order to suit a particular trade-off. A trade-off might be performance versus scalability, which may mean restructuring the integration layer in order to use a NoSQL database over a particular RDMS solution.

In this section, we will examine availability versus performance for a particular customer. Availability is the degree of a system to be accessible. If the system is down, then it is not available. Performance is the ability of the system to carry out the required functionality in a target timeframe. So, this customer is truly interested in the uptime of the system because the downtime will cost money, but they also want a fixed quantum of throughput.

Which items can degrade the performance? If the application has too much sanity checking in the code (check pointing), then it will degrade the performance. If the performance is degraded, then it may also reduce availability. However, if you do not perform a sanity check for enough parameters, then a system will be culpable to errors. If a hacker finds a weakness in your security or your caseworkers enter the wrong data too often, then your availability is compromised because your business will suffer downtime to fix issues.

One solution is to split the architecture in two computation bunkers. We can take advantage of the modern power in smartphones, tablets, and desktop computers to render the content on the client side. Therefore, this architecture, suits rich clients and other suitable devices with enough GPU power.

The code that has been sanity-checked and rendered is removed from the server side to a large degree. Depending on the architecture, we can use the JavaScript framework technologies that rely on **Model View ViewModel** (**MVVM**), which is supported by AngularJS. Based on the technology choice, we can use an alternative to JSF such as the upcoming Java EE 8 MVC or directly the JAX-RS endpoints. We must ensure that correct validation takes places on both the client and server sides. We must also design the REST API or other remote invocation between client and server to be secure, safe, and idempotent. Note that we still have the features such as CDI, EJB, JMS, and JPA available to us on the server side.

There are benefits in this extended Java EE 7 architecture that help in the performance versus scalability trade-off. If we introduce a caching layer of data, we will gain the ability to return the data that is mostly derived from static references or changes very infrequently or is requested most often. The key benefit of caching requests from the smart clients means that response times are minimized.

Just after Java EE 7 was released in 2013, JCache temporary caching 1.0 final JSR 107 (`https://jcp.org/en/jsr/detail?id=107`) was released, which is now supported by brands such as HazelCast and Terracota.

This architecture suits a hybrid form that extends Java EE and goes beyond and outside the box of specifications. The Java EE 7 umbrella specification does not specify the orchestration of the servers, monitoring of servers or systems, deep authorization, and cloud provisioning. Let's take a look at the following figure:

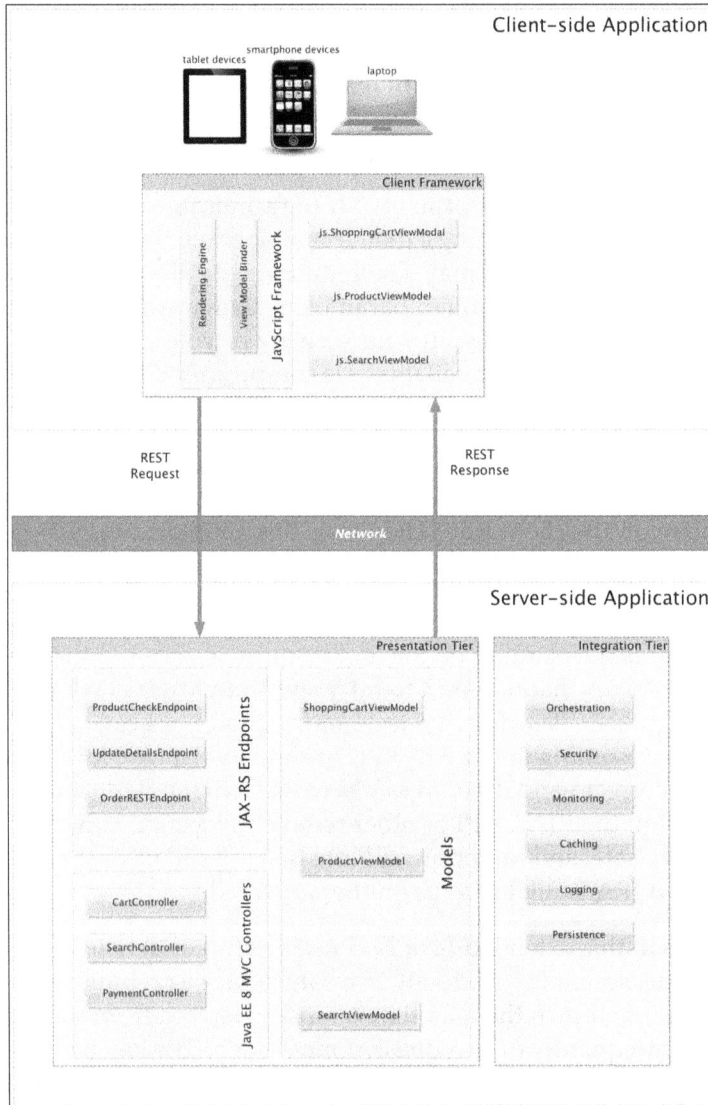

An extended hybrid Java EE architecture that remedies performance versus availability

Containerless systems

There is another architecture that is popular with the leading edge businesses that favor continuous deployment and guerilla engineering. This is called containerless application, which is actually a misnomer. If we think about it, every entity system is contained in some abstract component from the highest level container and down to the hardware CPU. The operating system is constrained by the CPU, the JVM process is constrained by the operating system, and the application server contains the deployed Java EE application.

Technical architects make trade-offs all the time. They may consider agility like time-to-market versus cost, innovation versus affordability, and politically, the integration of legacy systems with new technology, such as a containerless system. The proper name for the containerless application ought to be embedded application controlled server, which accurately describes the architecture. There are several Java EE application server providers that allow a standalone Java application to spin a fully embedded server from the `static void main()` entry point. Vendors such as JBoss's WildFly, Tomitribe's Tom EE, and of course, Oracle's GlassFish have nonstandard APIs for embedded execution. Some of the proprietary vendor solutions even allow the modular selection of the Java EE abilities in the runtime of the embedded server. An architect may thus pick and choose the provisioning of the JAX-RS, JSF, CDI, EJB, and JMS modules. A well-balanced and proficient developed team is able to circumvent the change management. The team operates *under the radar* by writing a Containerless solution instead of being told for the 100th time that they are not permitted to upgrade the IBM WebSphere 7 application server.

Therefore, embedded servers are popular for the beginning of building the microservices architecture across several concerns. Allowing the application to control the start up and halting of the embedded servers means that these archetypes play well with the modern DevOps movement (Developers/Operations team) and the concepts around the automatic configuration management control.

The clear disadvantage of the containerless solution is that the building of the development tools for the traditional WAR deployment does not understand this mode. So, a digital engineer may lose the interactive and fast turnaround of increment engineering using a Java EE solution. However, it might be a short-term issue as the Java IDE makers are fairly good at picking up trends in engineering. We can hope that the Java EE technical leaders, architects, and the wider community voice their support for the specification to include a containerless API.

With an embedded server, engineering teams have the responsibility to ensure that the infrastructure is correctly set up. The technical architects gain the benefit of precisely controlling the external integration points and this is useful for the security, authorization and authentication, monitoring and logging, and persistent access. However, going from request to the response is exactly the same as in the standard Java web architecture. Let's have a look at the following screenshot:

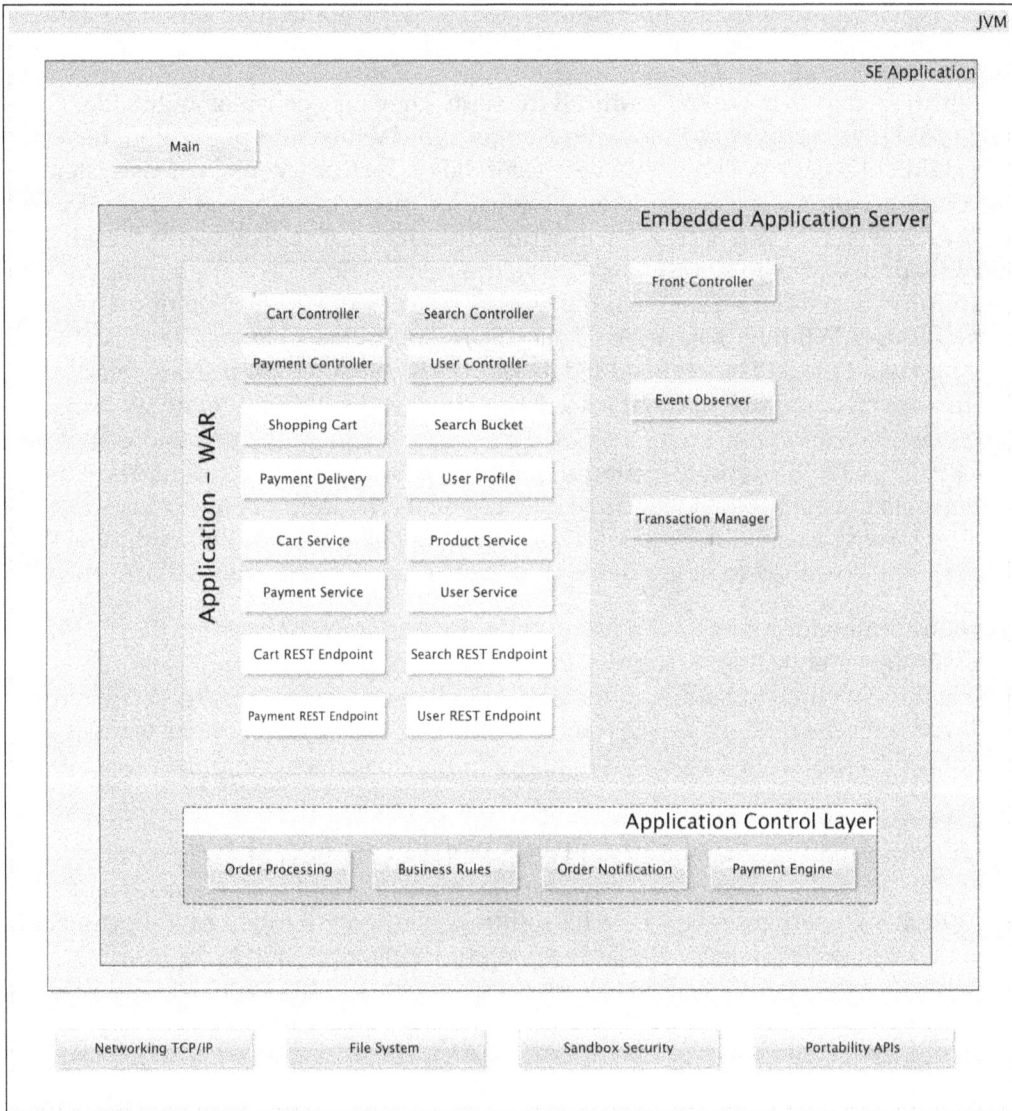

Containerless Java EE architecture diagram

Although there is no standardization on Java EE 8 for the embedded server application architecture, other developers have at least precipitated some innovations in order to move the community in this direction. There is the Apache Delta Spike CDI Container Control (`https://deltaspike.apache.org/documentation/container-control.html`) that currently provides a cross server library to start and stop the CDI container in a standalone Java SE environment. Delta Spike is an award-winning open source project that has specialist modules for Bean Validation, CDI, Data, Security, and Servlets as well as container management. It is worth keeping an eye on this project because some of their innovations have made it to the Java EE 8 standard. The `@javax.transactional.Transational` annotation that allows CDI managed beans take part in Container Managed Transactions (Java EE 7 and JTA 1.2) was first proposed and developed in project Delta Spike.

Microservices

The embedded application controlled server is a gateway to the Java-based microservices architecture. These microservices are a style of designing an enterprise architecture where each component solves and operates one requirement of the overall system. These key drivers are the nonfunctional requirements and can be any combination of Availability, Flexibility, Maintainability, Networkability, Performance, Robustness and Scalability. Of these, the original requirements for businesses to choose this style over the traditional monolithic architecture were Availability and Scalability.

Architects see certain advantages in microservices: these components follow the UNIX architectural principle of *do one thing and do it well* and the ability to chop and change the component at will. The microservices style enables the language agnostic communications; therefore, the implementer has the freedom to write a component in Java, Groovy, or Scala or even in a non-JVM language such as C++. This architecture strongly favors JSON or XML over REST; however, there is nothing to stop a software shop from using SOAP and XML. Technically, microservices are some of the most exciting digital projects on the planet today; because of these investments, some businesses have clear distinct commercial advantages.

The cost of microservices is the networking complexity that includes payload sizes, monitoring (heart-beating), logging, and fault tolerance with redundancy management and service routing. There are ancillary costs that business managers and stakeholders should be aware of, namely time-to-marketing, training, information silos, and of course, change culture.

As with many movements, there is also a spectrum of effort, ability, and feasibility. A business may not necessarily have to give up on the monolith architecture completely, especially if scalability and high availability are not a high priority. There is certainly a route for the componentized services architecture for the majority of the digital business, which takes the best of the monolith — transactions, persistence, and configuration — and radically employs as much of the styles of the microservices as possible. Therefore, an embedded server dedicated for order management should not have code that is relevant to the payment processing in it. Rather, the order management component should invoke the payment processing component externally. Let's have a look at the following figure:

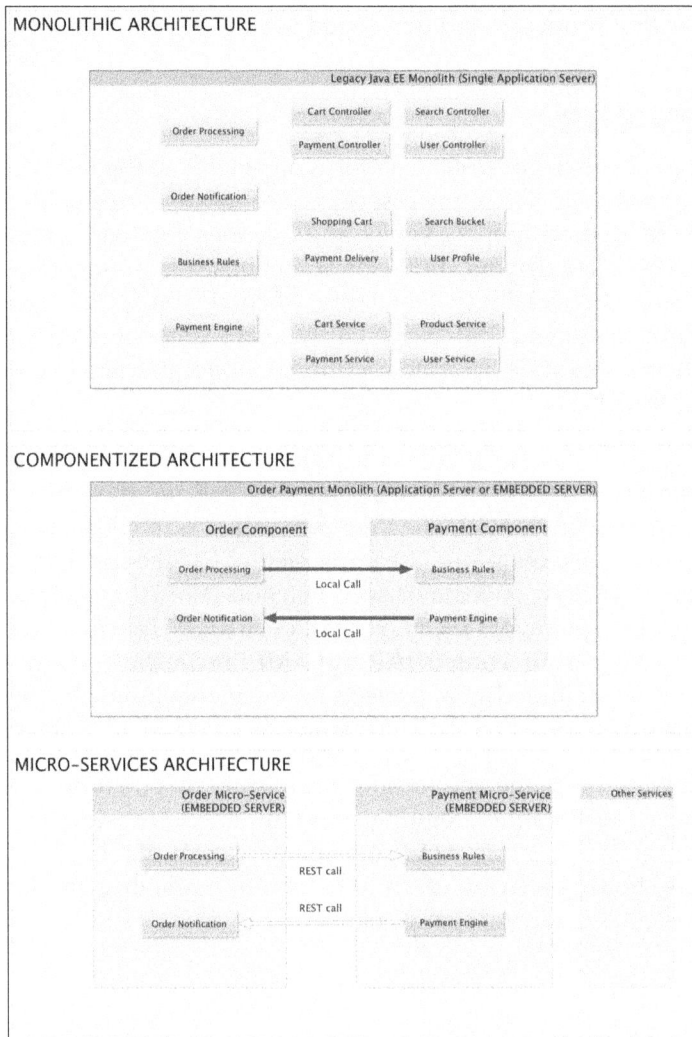

An evolution of a Java EE monolith to a microservices architecture

The preceding illustration shows a decomposition of the standard Java EE web architecture into a hybrid component architecture and then an evolution to a full microservice.

There are many ways to go from the request and then back to the response. In addition to where do we go as a team in order to get there? We must ask ourselves the key questions: how do we get there? Why do we want to get there?

To be full stack or not

Is it important to be known as a full stack developer? The consultant's typical answer is that it always depends on the context. Some cynics might say that the term full stack is a loaded marketing term, but then these same people may also suggest that digital is likewise. Obviously, there is more meaning to the term than the thoughts that are recurring through some poor recruitment consultant's brain. There is a lot to be desired for large organizations that claim and advertise that they want to recruit only full stack developers. Are they cutting corners? Or are they genuinely interested in getting the best programming talent?

That said, from the discussion in this appendix, it is important to know the architecture of a project to a certain degree. For a couple of decades already, it has been impossible to be a jack of all trades in the software business and therefore, an engineer will specialize in a certain environment, field, role, or system. It is no longer possible to live completely closeted in an underground silo and resolutely say, *all I want to know is Java on the server side because it is the only skill that I care about and it will always be that way*. Decent professional engineers must be sympathetic to the other staff members including front-end developers, back-end developers, interface and UX designers, testers, stakeholders, and management. Everyone has an ultimate stakeholder and therefore they share the ultimate responsibility with accountability. Whether this means full stack or not depends largely on your attitude towards working life and knowing about and respecting the modern web architecture around you.

Agile Performance – Working inside Digital Teams

We are in the digital age. This is great for those of us who work in digital teams; but the practice of software development, design, and architecture is never a free ride. There is a real tangible cost to the building of good quality engineered solutions. We are the cost. It costs us our time, resources, and energy, and there is a never-ending demand for better performance, profit margins, and user friendliness. The performance in digital teams as in any other line of business depends heavily on good communication and the ability to play nice with others in our workplace.

Digital teams and adaptation

As a part of a digital team, we are in the business of helping to adapt to the old world of commerce and move it onwards online and optimistically towards a better future.

The other side of digital is the work performance. If your team is responsible for a high-profile business or customer, you might find yourself under severe scrutiny so as to ensure that the project goes according to the plan. Meeting customer targets sometimes is at odds with an agile laissez-faire development. There are crucial times where the team has to pull together in order to deliver a product quickly and yet be well-balanced enough to allow technical decisions with their user stories to be self-organized by the team. Often digital teams can race ahead with little thought to the overall technical architecture, leading to an end state and final delivery that leaves the stakeholder frustrated and concerned. Agile is not a guarantee of the quality of a product, but it helps.

So what can we do to improve these concerns? As readers of this book, you are probably a Java EE 7 developer and involved in both the aspects of programming and testing. We have to be clear in our engineering role in a digital team and moreover, understand the roles and preoccupations of the other members in our respective teams. Due diligence and returns on investment, reduction of the technical debt, and time-to-market really point the way to greater transparency, integrity, and respect for others. This is the prime directive for modern digital teams and thereby drives our performance to go forward. Let's have a look at the following screenshot:

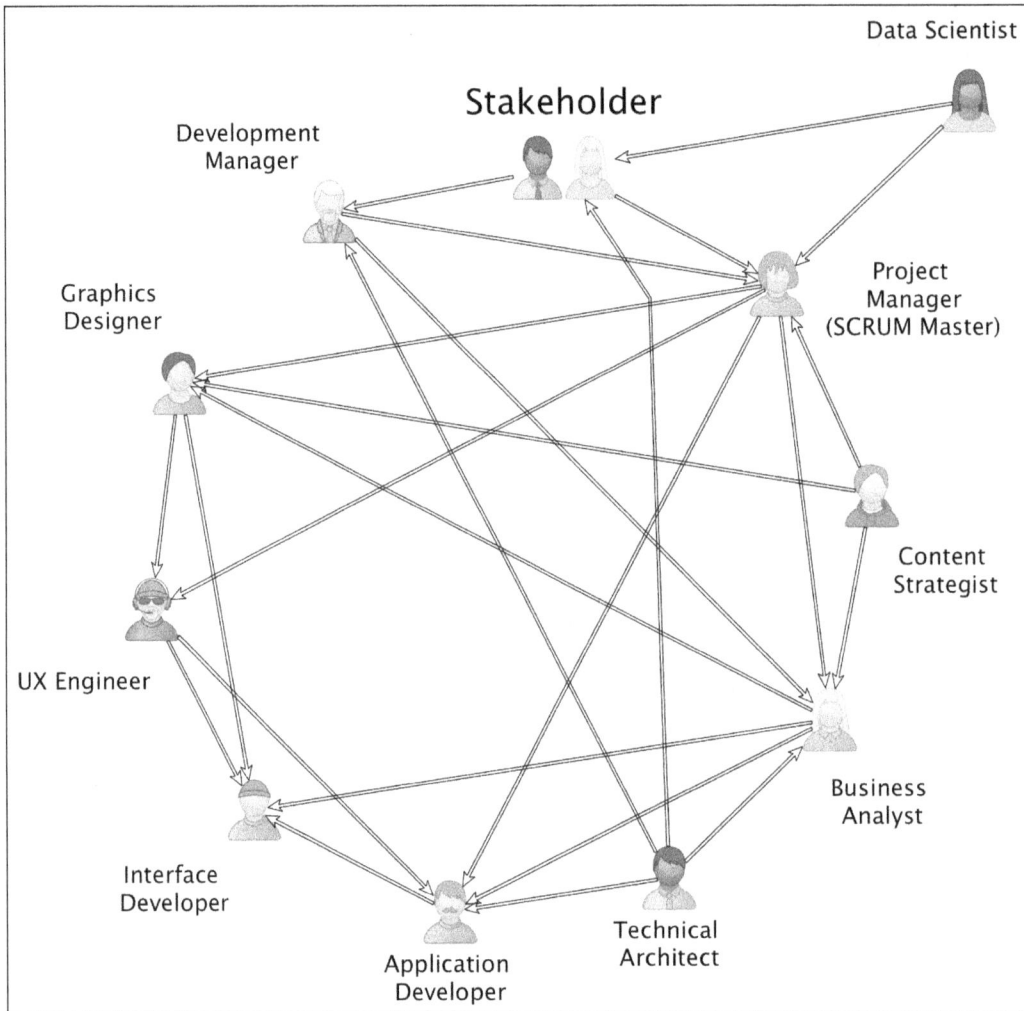

The organization people and their roles in the modern digital team

Roles

Let's look at the roles in the next sections. We will divide the roles into distinct perspectives: development, design, architectural, and management.

The development perspective

There are many roles in the digital team that require viable software construction skills and the ability to solve problems with a programming logic along with hints of creativity.

A Java engineer

Because you are reading this book, you are mostly likely to be already acquainted with the role of Java engineer. You role as a software developer means you have responsibility to write the implementation of the product code for a digital application. I will go further that this role includes writing unit tests, functional tests and integration tests. Modern developers follow agile practices for proficiency. They are involved with the business and domain logic, the presentation tier, domain tier, and integration tier. A Java engineer will be in close communication with testers, interface developers, and sometimes a business analyst.

An interface developer engineer

An interface developer is responsible for writing the client side JavaScript code for the frontend of a digital application. This title is also amenable to the smartphone developers that write code with iOS, Android, and other platforms. Interface developers tend to be involved with the HTML5, CSS, and JavaScript coding. Invariably, they are also knowledgeable about modern practices and the latest frontend testing, debugging, and testing.

Interface developers will work almost exclusively on the presentation tier. They may also help design and supply input and ideas to the domain tier architect. It was Apple USA that divided, reputedly, their web team between user interface engineering and server-side engineering while sharing a domain model.

An interface developer will communicate with the tester, Java engineers, and business analysts. They will definitely be in close proximity with the user experience designers, creative designers, and content strategists because a part of an interface developer's job is to translate the designs into a frontend product code.

Quality assurance tester

This role ranges from a traditional dedicated tester in a separate team that finds the breakages in the product team in a non-agile environment to those testers that are part of an agile team and involved in all the aspects of the software development life cycle. A tester in a digital environment may be responsible for asserting the quality of the production code in a variety of different devices: smartphones, tablets, and desktops and also throw in modern wearable computers. A tester may also write the specifications that have to be heavily involved in a behavioral-driven design specification so that the quality of the eventual system is high and fits the targets of the entire team.

The testers will communicate and talk to everyone in the team including the designers. Often, in proficient agile teams, they are the people that everyone has to impress because they write the definition of done.

Software in developer test

A software developer in a test is a variation of the quality assurance tester, which is a controversial role according to the different points of view. At best, this role is a migratory and contentious role that ensures that the other software developers in the team are writing enough production code that is testable and verifiable. Therefore, this role requires an ability to develop the Java code; it may also require the JavaScript ability and automated tests. Due to the ramifications of the political outcome, whether Java and interface developers are writing enough quality tests such as unit tests, functional tests, and integration tests, it remains a loosely defined role. The role probably includes testing advocacy.

A wider role beyond software in a developer test might include the responsibility to maintain and solve issues in the build environment and also include the aspects of continuous integration and continuous deployment.

The design perspective

If you get invited to a party and you meet another professional there and you happen to ask them, what do they do for a living? The other person then says that they also work in the digital field, but as a designer. It is often not clear what they do as a daily job. There are many types of designers under the umbrella term. Here we are talking about a digital and creative designer for a software application as opposed to a software architect and designer. This role is also different to the designers in the other industries such as automotive (cars and automobiles), aviation (airplanes), electronics, and industrial products (vacuum cleaners and iPods) because they work with tangible products. There is one common aspect of a designer: they design a solution to a problem where there is no right or clear answer.

In the next sections, we will look at the designers in the digital domain.

A creative designer

A creative designer has a role to illustrate or render the digital concepts to client and stakeholder requirements. This role is about artistic ability and using the knowledge around graphic design, typography, and modern standards.

Usually, a creative designer works in a team and it is important that they support others and communicate in a group environment in order to explore different ideas. It is okay to be different and individualistic; however, the key design of the project must take priority, ensuring that only the best graphic designs are released to the stakeholder.

A creative designer has knowledge of the popular professional software packages including Adobe PhotoShop, Fireworks, InDesign, Illustrator, and Xara Design.

Designers, especially those that work in the digital agencies, have a great deal of communication. Therefore, this role requires the ability to meet deadlines and deliver clever concepts to differentiate from the client's competition and there is pressure to perform with meticulous attention to details as well. Often there might be long hours of work compared to the rest of the team in order to deliver a new digital industrial concept. Designers work closely with the usability engineers, interface designers, and content strategists.

A usability experience engineer

The role of a usability engineer is to design and develop engaging user experiences for a digital application. The role is about enhancing the kinesthetic emotion and feel for a product. A usability engineer is responsible for field testing the visual compositions of the design. This may mean working in and with an external usability testing laboratory and building the wireframes of the interaction design.

The **User Interface** (**UI**) and **User Experience** (**UX**) engineer/designers' roles are relatively recent in the workplace because businesses have concentrated their efforts in building human interaction across many device screens. The roles have become a specialism on their merits and split off from the general purpose creative designer. The UX role is about identifying the human level interfaces, elements and core functions, the visual language of the language so that it helps the customer progress quickly and proficiently so as to achieve their end goal. The UX engineers generate mockups, wireframes, and give presentations of the customer's journey to the stakeholders and team. As a key feature of this role is completely about user testing, they also facilitate AB testing and they perform a lot of research in the behavior and design language.

A UX engineer typically communicates frequently with the creative designers, interface developers, and quality assurance. For core development, they also communicate with the Java developers. A UX engineer will also directly discuss issues with the content strategists to clarify the overall design language of the project.

A content strategist

A content strategist is a person who writes the design of the content. This role is about looking at the language of an interaction for a project. It is about planning the copy writing, the style of the writing, how to control the process of language delivery, and being a source of governance. A content strategist's role may be likened to that of a museum curator, winemaker, or master taster. The content strategist has an excellent command of the written language, which may include media content, video, filmmaking, and photography, if this is required.

A very common role for a content strategist is the foundation of the business term knowledge for the entire project. The role requires delivering the key messages and themes for a digital business (or government department). They are also responsible for the content that determines the optimization for search engines. A strategist will work with the metadata, content purpose, and web writing as well.

During the day-to-day activities, the content strategist works very closely with the business analysts and stakeholders to identify the design language.

The architectural perspective

In digital, there are also some roles that are about the architecture of the application and are more than the creative or software design.

A data scientist

In recent times, digital has seen the emergence of another role for the express purpose of analyzing data statistically, modeling data, and information design. This is the duty of a dedicated data scientist, which is an emerging area to do with the so-called big data. A data scientist is responsible for extracting the information and knowledge from large data sets that may be structured or unstructured. Simply, they can make sense of the signals in what may appear to the casual reader as just noise. The results are data visualizations and models that are presented to the key business stakeholders and management.

Data scientists analyze the immense swathe of data by applying scientific and mathematical techniques. They might use some particular computer algorithms in order to gain insights into the patterns of the data set. Some data scientists can write computer programs, although many are familiar with statistical analysis packages. They usually have post-university degrees such as an MSc or a PhD so as to practice in their role.

A data scientist may work independently of the digital team. They might work for several different teams. They generally communicate with the Java engineers, business, and the management.

A technical architect

A digital team may have a specific technical architect in order to ensure that the application meets certain **non-functional requirements**. A **non-functional** requirement is an aspect or feature of the target software that does not reflect on its functional operation. A functional operation for a caseworker is that the staff are allowed to process the cases in real time. **Non-functional requirements (NFRs)** are features or criteria that specify and describe the operation of a system's architecture. The operational features are known as adaptability, availability, flexibility, maintainability, performance, reusability, robustness, scalability, security, and testability. Usually, an architect has to trade off these non-functional requirements. For example, they consider availability versus performance and ask the business stakeholder which feature is more important or strike a compromise with the architecture.

The architect is responsible for ensuring that the final application is on track and meets the non-functional requirements. There tends to be a lot of software design and analysis of the domain model. An experience of the common design patterns in software might be helpful, but a good architect will examine the root requirements in great detail before deciding on a particular strategy.

The technical architects communicate directly with the core platform team: the Java engineers and interface developers, especially in the design process. They will facilitate the team discussions about which programming language to use and whether an open source library framework should be used. Architects are also in touch with the business stakeholders and management. They may also talk to a data scientist in order to help with the process of retrieving or capturing information for statistical analysis. Finally, the hands-on architects are expected to develop software and need to be able to coach and mentor the other technical engineers on all the levels.

The management perspective

A project needs a good quality management. Your manager is a key members of staff that sits between the business stakeholder and the rest of the team of engineers, testers, and designers. He is effectively the buffer between the senior management and the software developer team.

A business analyst and liaison officer

Some digital teams will have a dedicated business analyst for the purpose of looking at the business requirements of the project. This type of role depends on the agility of the project. Some projects and companies dispense with the role of the business analyst and rely on the agile process of a scrum to gain knowledge of the requirements. Other types of enterprises, especially those that practice the aspects of Waterfall software development, still have a separate person that bridges the gap between the engineers and designers and helps to establish the deeper domain knowledge in the team: the analyst.

A business analyst assesses the change proposals. They define the scope and definition of user stories that are unclear and in early progress. They gather the information and evidence to assess the benefits, costs, and risks to a project. The analyst dives into the business domain knowledge to clarify the legal and commercial terms and policies that ultimately affect the project. Therefore, a business analyst is the key to establishing the ubiquitous language with the stakeholders. This is the discourse for the software team to understand the requirements of the business stakeholders and vice versa. An analyst communicates widely with the stakeholder, project manager, development manager, and the other technical staff when necessary.

A project manager/scrum master

The project manager is responsible for delivering the product to the stakeholder and business. Sometimes a project manager is also known as the product owner. In other organizations, the role is split between two persons: the developer manager and project manager. Often, the project manager is a certified scrum master or has some idea of the agile process.

The project manager leads the software team to deliver the product on time and within the budget. They liaise closely with the stakeholders to define the product delivery. In an agile project, they record and set up the background stories by running various activities. The project manager then assumes the role of a scrum master by organizing sprint planning sessions, retrospectives, daily stand-ups, and running the iterations. At the end of the sprint, they set up the show and sense meeting where the stakeholder gets a chance to see the current progress, demonstrations, and work delivered.

This role requires lots of communication in order to be continuously kept abreast of the project details because the project manager has to track the progress of the product. Project managers essentially rely on the information during the daily stand-up. Therefore, project managers talk to every person on their project regularly. The members of the team notify the scrum master if there is a user story that cannot be reasonably progressed. These user stories are known as blockers. The best project managers focus on the updates on the user stories rather than the actual work and pressurizing individuals.

A digital development manager

A development manager is responsible for the delivery projects and functioning of the development team. In this role, the manager has a close collaboration with the other departments or divisions. He or she will be involved with the sales and marketing, retail, consumer finance, insurance, and human resources personnel. Therefore, this person has responsibilities for the strategies and operations of the business. A manager running the in-house projects delivers ultimately to the other functions in a corporation, whereas a customer-facing project involves in-depth conversations and interactions with the customers and stakeholders.

With this manager role, the individual will work with financial planning; if not involved in the finance, they will be making decisions and modeling the business. Therefore, development managers require budget, organizational planning, and numeration skills.

Although the development manager has an overall authoritative leadership over the direct reports, he or she may delegate the day-to-day responsibilities to the team leaders, especially if there are multiple development projects going on concurrently. In flat hierarchical organizations, the development manager may delegate to the effective project managers and scrum masters, especially if the individual projects are working as viable self-organized teams. The best development managers encourage organic growth for individuals and the team as a whole.

Software quality

In digital teams, the key deliverable ought to be all about the quality. It is hard to write software at a high quality level without management, discipline, and people. The team must be careful to avoid going down the insular route known as design by committee, otherwise anecdotally known in the business as Conway's law (Melvin Conway's sociological observation, which can be found at `https://en.wikipedia.org/wiki/Conway%27s_law`).

In order to avoid dysfunction in the final deliverable of the software, the digital team should practice the behavior with the following characteristics:

- They should be programmatic when they architect, design, and construct software.

- They should aim to develop plans that are wholly manageable.

- The team should have very clear ideas on the end state of the software delivery. Does everyone know who they are writing for? How are they achieving it? Why is the project in existence?

- Everyone on the team must understand the customer's journey and therefore, prioritize on the customer's needs over the business processes and tools.

- They should ensure the digital software delivery makes the best possible use of the technology while reducing the technical debt.

If the team is using an old version of Java 6 or Java EE 5 or Java EE 6, then fight hard to get this upgraded in a new project. The quality will be worse if you allow a digital team to build new software with a legacy technology without a force of change. If you have any issues, consider the bounded context concept (Eric Evan's domain-driven design at `http://martinfowler.com/bliki/BoundedContext.html`).

Class versus form

If you are sports fan, then you probably heard of the phrase, *class is permanent, form is temporary*. If you want a digital team to deliver a fast, proficient, and accurate code, then you need to hire the best people and just as in sports, finding these talented individuals is expensive and difficult. If you are in a digital team with these souls, then congratulations! You are a part of the elite and already working in an environment that delivers at pace. Most of us are not so lucky, especially if you are working in the provinces outside the megacities. Elite development, design, and architecture are an unaffordable luxury.

So, do ensure that a digital team works, especially if you are just a developer, keep the following things in mind:

- Recognize that digital teams are people and they have ups and downs from families, friends, and life in general.

- Don't be a workaholic. Give your brain and your team a rest. Take your annual holiday allocation.

- The best creative, design, and architectural ideas sometimes come from the left field: the gym shower, walking the dog, and an afternoon nap.

- Technical leaders, managers, and stakeholders, heads up! Organize the projects to include slack time. Don't bunch the tasks and project one after another.

- Team members at the bottom of the corporate hierarchy, heads up! Don't be a shrinking violet. If the projects are difficult and challenging, then communicate! Let the other people in the team know the issues and push back to the senior management at the earliest opportunity.

- Don't multitask. It doesn't work. Concentrate on one thing at a time.

- Allow individuals to rise to future role models in order to foster growth: organic technical leadership.

- Allow you and your team a chance to learn, go to conferences, meet other industry folk, and take extra training.

Remember if you want to get good at playing rock as a lead guitarist, then you need to practice, practice, and practice. It is the same for the high achievers who build some of the best software applications on the planet.

D
Curated References

This is an appendix of the curated set of references around the digital software development. They are divided into concepts and themes.

Service delivery

- US Digital Service Playbook, services standard for the United States government's interactions with its citizens, 2014 `https://playbook.cio.gov/`

- Inside Obama's Stealth Startup, by John Gertner, FastCompany, 2015 `http://www.fastcompany.com/3046756/obama-and-his-geeks`

- The White House announces the US Digital Services Playbook, 2014 `https://www.whitehouse.gov/blog/2014/08/11/delivering-customer-focused-government-through-smarter-it`

- UK GOV.UK Service Manual describes the Agile service delivery policies of the United Kingdom Government `https://www.gov.uk/service-manual/agile`

- UK Government Digital Service (GDS) Blog `https://gdsengagement.blog.gov.uk/`

- Digital Transformation definition on Wikipedia `https://en.wikipedia.org/wiki/Digital_transformation`

- 18F, building 21st century digital government, US General Services Administration `https://18f.gsa.gov/`

- Government as a Platform, concept form UK GDS 400 days delivery `https://gds.blog.gov.uk/2015/02/10/that-was-400-days-of-delivery/`

- Re-imagining the bank: why financial services need digital transformation, Ben Rossi, Information Age `https://shar.es/1tuJ4D`

- Australia announces a Digital Service, Prime Minister Tony Abbot MP, `http://www.pm.gov.au/media/2015-01-23/establishment-digital-transformation-office`

Agile and leadership

- Agile Coaching blog, Rachel Davies `http://rachelcdavies.github.io/archive/`

- Who's afraid of Conway's Law by Rachel Davies, 2015 `http://rachelcdavies.github.io/2015/04/20/afraid-conways-law.html`

- Organic Technical Leadership—Gerald Weinberg, Becoming a Technical Leader, `https://leanpub.com/becomingatechnicalleader`

- Continuous Integration article by Martin Fowler, 2006 `http://www.martinfowler.com/articles/continuousIntegration.html`

- Continuous Delivery article from the NetFlix technical blog `http://techblog.netflix.com/2013/08/deploying-netflix-api.html`

- Continuous Delivery, JavaPosse Round-up episode 459 podcast, 2014 `http://javaposse.com/java-posse-459`

- Team Organizational Structure, JavaPosse Round-up episode, 2013 `http://javaposse.com/java-posse-446`

- The Importance of Tribe for Agile Sustainability by Thomas Meloche and Geri Scheidner, 2013 `http://www.tomandgeriscrum.com/2013/05/24/the-importance-of-tribe-for-agile-sustainability/`

- Reinventing Organizations blog by Bruce Eckel, fellow Java Champion, 2015 `http://www.reinventing-business.com/2015/01/reinventing-organizations.html`

- Confidence article by Lisa Crispin, agile coach, blog, 2015 `http://lisacrispin.com/2015/08/04/confidence/`

- Test-Driven Development by Kent Beck, Ward Cunningham et al `http://c2.com/cgi/wiki?TestDrivenDevelopment`

- Java Test-Driven Development book by Viktor Farcic, Alex Garcia, Packt Publishing, 2015 `https://www.packtpub.com/application-development/java-test-driven-development`
- Behavior-Driven Development with Java in Mind by John Ferguson, 2013 `https://weblogs.java.net/blog/manningpubs/archive/2013/06/10/introducing-behavior-driven-development`

Architecture

- Microservices blog article by Martin Fowler, 2013 `http://martinfowler.com/articles/microservices.html`
- The Great Micro Services versus Monolithic Architecture debate, High Scalability, 2014 `http://highscalability.com/blog/2014/7/28/the-great-microservices-vs-monolithic-apps-twitter-melee.html`
- Micro Services – A Reality Check(Point) by Andrew Hamel-Law, Cap Gemini, 2014 `http://capgemini.github.io/architecture/microservices-reality-check/`
- Building Scalable Web Architecture and Distributed Systems by Kate Matsudaira, Dr Dobbs Journal, 2012 `http://www.drdobbs.com/web-development/building-scalable-web-architecture-and-d/240142422`
- API Best Practice Blog by Apigee, 2013-, RESTful design of interface `https://blog.apigee.com/taglist/restful`
- RESTful Web Services: The Basics by Alex Rodriguez, IBM, 2014 `http://www.ibm.com/developerworks/library/ws-restful/`
- Representation State Transfer (REST) by Roy Fielding, 2000 `http://www.ics.uci.edu/~fielding/pubs/dissertation/rest_arch_style.htm`
- Best Practices for Horizontal Application Scaling by Shekhar Gulati, 2013 `https://blog.openshift.com/best-practices-for-horizontal-application-scaling/`
- High Performance Browser Networking book by Ilya Grigorik, Publ: O'Reilly, 2014, sponsored by Chimera `http://www.liquibase.org/`

User interface

- 10 Tips for Working with Web Designers by Paul Boag; Boagworld website; 2013 `https://boagworld.com/design/working-with-web-designers/`
- A Good User Interface from the Good UI blog, 2015, `https://www.goodui.org/`

- UI Do's and Don't from Apple Corporation, 2015, it is focused on iOS and mobile development but has wide appeal `https://developer.apple.com/design/tips/`

- User Centered Design, Wikipedia definition `https://en.wikipedia.org/wiki/User-centered_design`

- Improving the User Experience from US Department of Health and Human Services, 2015 `http://www.usability.gov/`

- User Centered Design, GOV.UK, 2014 `https://www.gov.uk/service-manual/user-centred-design`

- Content Strategy by, Kristina Halvorsson, Melissa Rach, 2nd Edition, 2015 `http://contentstrategy.com/`

- The Premier JavaScript blog by Brendan Eich, inventor of JavaScript and co-founder of the Mozilla project `https://brendaneich.com/`

- Smashing Magazine, relevant news and articles on HTML, CSS and JavaScript developer `http://www.smashingmagazine.com/`

- Josh on Design, blog opinions from fellow Java Champion Joshua Marinacci ex-HP Palm tablet Java and web UI designer `http://joshondesign.com/`

- Six Revisions is a new site for interface designers and developers `http://sixrevisions.com/`

- Jasmine Behavior-Driven JavaScript 2.3 Tests `http://jasmine.github.io/`

- JavaScript: The Good Parts by Douglas Crockford, O'Reilly books, Published in May 2008 `http://javascript.crockford.com/`

- Object Oriented JavaScript programming by Stoyan Stefanov, Packt Publishing, Published in 2013 `https://www.packtpub.com/web-development/object-oriented-javascript-second-edition`

- UI Bootstrap, Bootstrap components written in pure AngularJS Framework `http://angular-ui.github.io/bootstrap/`

- Foundation, a layered UI framework for responsive designed web application `http://foundation.zurb.com/`

- Grunt JS, JavaScript task runner `http://gruntjs.com/`

- Ionic Framework, open source JDK for developing hybrid HTML5 mobile applications `http://ionicframework.com/`

- Backbone JavaScript client side framework `http://backbonejs.org/`

- Ember JS, open source `https://en.wikipedia.org/wiki/Ember.js`

- Dojo Toolkit JavaScript client side `https://dojotoolkit.org/`

- Polymer Project from Google, HTML5 web components `https://www.polymer-project.org/1.0/`

- JSLint, the oldest JavaScript Lint checker by Douglas Crockford `http://www.jslint.com/`

- ESLint, the newest JavaScript Lint checker with advanced customizable features `http://eslint.org/`

Java EE and JVM technology

- Reactive Java EE – Let Me Count Ways by Reza Rahman, Oracle , 2014 `http://www.slideshare.net/reza_rahman/reactive-javaee`

- Going Asynchronous with CompletableFutures and JavaEE 7 screencast by Adam Bien, 2015 `https://www.youtube.com/watch?v=KUISpHbWib0`

- Reactive Programming Patterns by Josh Sureth, Typesafe, JavaOne 2014 `https://www.youtube.com/watch?v=tiJEL3oiHIY`

- RX Java, Java implementation of Reactive Extensions Framework, 2015 `https://github.com/ReactiveX/RxJava/wiki`

- Drop Wizard Metrics Library from Code Hale, capturing JVM and application metrics 2014 `https://github.com/dropwizard/metrics`

- Faster XML Jackson Data Processor and Annotations, open source project for JSON `https://github.com/FasterXML/jackson-annotations`

- Jackson JAX-RS Provider for JSON, XML and YAML data formats `https://github.com/FasterXML/jackson-jaxrs-providers`

- JAX-RS Reference Implementation Jersey now prefers MOXy for JSON marshaling and unmarshalling POJOs `https://jersey.java.net/documentation/latest/media.html`

- Embedded Container and modules WildFly Swarm (Alpha-ware in 2015) `http://wildfly.org/swarm/`

- Apache TomEE 7.0.0-SNAPSHOT `http://tomee.apache.org/download/tomee-2.0.0-snapshot.html`

- Jersey the reference implementation of JAX-RS 2.0 specification in Java EE 7 `https://jersey.java.net/`

- RESTeasy, a JBoss Red Hat implementation of the JAX-RS 2.0 specification in Java EE 7 `http://resteasy.jboss.org/`

- Payara, professionally supported open source GlassFish 4.1 compatible application server `http://www.payara.co.uk/home`

- Apache MyFaces CODI, portable extensions for CDI `http://myfaces.apache.org/extensions/cdi/`

- Spring Web Flow `http://projects.spring.io/spring-webflow/`

- Arquillian Integration Test Framework `http://arquillian.org/`

- Selenium Web Driver, integration testing `http://www.seleniumhq.org/projects/webdriver/`

- Cucumber JVM, port of the functional testing suite Cucumber `https://github.com/cucumber/cucumber-jvm`

- The Cucumber for Java book by Seb Rose, Matt Wynne & Aslak Hellesoy, published by Pragmatic Bookshelf Press, 2014 `https://pragprog.com/book/srjcuc/the-cucumber-for-java-book`

- Java Performance by Charlie Hunt, Binu John, publ: Addison Wesley, 2011 `http://www.amazon.co.uk/Java-Performance-Addison-Wesley-Charlie-Hunt/dp/0137142528`

- Vanilla Java, blog by Peter Lawrey, about performance core Java `http://vanillajava.blogspot.co.uk/`

- Java 8 Lambdas: Functional Programming for the Masses by Richard Warburton, publ: O'Reilly, 2014 `http://www.amazon.com/Java-Lambdas-Functional-Programming-Masses/dp/1449370772`

- Maurice Naftalin's Lambda FAQ by Maurice Naftalin, blog `http://www.lambdafaq.org/`

- Nashorn: JavaScript for the JVM `http://openjdk.java.net/projects/nashorn/`

- Apache JMeter for testing load performance on application servers `http://jmeter.apache.org/`

- Java EE 7 Developer Handbook by Peter Pilgrim, Packt Pub, 2013 `https://www.packtpub.com/application-development/java-ee-7-developer-handbook`

- Iron-Clad Java: Building Secure Web Applications by Jim Manico, publ: Oracle Press, 2014 `http://www.amazon.co.uk/Iron-Clad-Java-Building-Secure-Applications/dp/0071835881`

- Salted Password Hashing - Doing it Right by Defuse Security, 2014 `https://crackstation.net/hashing-security.htm`

- Swagger, open source framework to model and render descriptive RESTful API `http://swagger.io/`

- Apache Shiro, an open source framework for Java Security for authentication, authorization and realms `http://shiro.apache.org/`

- LiquiBase, a source control delta package for updating schema and information inside databases `http://www.liquibase.org/`

- NetFlix Hystrix, latency and fault tolerance open source library designed to isolate remote invocation `https://github.com/Netflix/Hystrix`

- IBM WebSphere WAS Liberty application server for Java EE 7 `https://developer.ibm.com/wasdev/websphere-liberty/`

- Apache Kafka, a high-throughput distributed messaging system `http://kafka.apache.org/`

- REST-Assured, a Java domain specific language for testing and validation of RESTful services `https://github.com/jayway/rest-assured`.

Index

Symbols

@FacesComponent annotation
  createTag attribute 208
  namespace attribute 208
  tagName attribute 208
  value attribute 208
<ui:debug> tag
  about 158
  hotkey attribute 159
  rendered attribute 159

A

Action Event listener
  invoking 156, 157
address page view 193
advanced libraries, JavaScript 9-11
agile and leadership
  references 438, 439
Ajax custom tag
  about 149
  attribute values 149, 150
  delay attribute 149
  disabled attribute 149
  event attribute 149
  execute attribute 149
  immediate attribute 149
  listener attribute 149
  onerror attribute 149
  onevent attribute 149
  render attribute 149
AngularJS
  about 9, 11, 302
  programming with 302-304
  URL 9, 302
  working 304-306
Apache Delta Spike CDI Container Control
  URL 421
Apache Shiro
  URL 248
application controlled locale 402
Application Development
      Framework (ADF) 216
application module, RequireJS 282, 283
application servers 21, 22
Apply Request Values phase 34
architectural perspective role
  about 430
  data scientist 430, 431
  technical architect 431
arithmetic expressions 52
AsciiDoc
  about 362
  URL 362
Asychronous Module Definition (AMD)
  URL 278
Asynchronous JavaScript and XML (AJAX)
  used, for validation 142-145

B

Backbone JS
  about 10
  URL 10
backing bean controller
  using 71-73
Batarang
  URL 320
Bean scopes 102, 103

Bean Validation
  @DecimalMax annotation 113
  @DecimalMin annotation 113
  @Future annotation 113
  @Max annotation 113
  @Min annotation 113
  @NotNull annotation 113
  @Null annotation 113
  @Past annotation 113
  @Pattern annotation 113
  @Size annotation 113
  form content, constraining 111-117
best practices, JavaScript
  reference link 270
Bootstrap CSS
  about 20
  URL 20
bounded context concept
  reference link 434
browser configured locale 401
business analyst 432

C

case tag 231, 232
caseworker application
  about 301, 302
  case record modal view template,
    inserting 324-326
  main controller 316-320
  main view 308-313
  new case record controller, creating 321-323
  new task record controller, creating 327-329
  overview 308
  server-side Java 335
  states, modifying 330
  task modal view template,
    inserting 329, 330
class
  versus form 434, 435
client-side validation 108
compiled-inline template servlet
  creating 367, 368
completion page view 197
component-oriented framework 61
composite custom components
  about 200

  composite components 206, 207
  custom components 206, 207
  URL 204
  with self-generating tag 208-211
  with XHTML 201-205
conditional navigation 56
conditional tag 231, 232
confirmation page view 194-196
console log 263
contact details form
  backing bean controller, using 71-73
  creating 63-67
  data, editing 91-96
  data, removing 97-101
  data service 74-77
  date time entry, enhancing 85-90
  JSF HTML command button 70, 71
  JSF HTML input text 68
  JSF HTML output label 67
  JSF HTML select Boolean checkbox 69
  JSF HTML select one menu 68, 69
  list collection of objects, displaying 83, 84
container-less systems 419-421
Content Delivery Network (CDN) 303
content strategist 430
Context and Dependency Injection (CDI)
  about 5, 163
  bean scopes 102, 103
  Context 163
  Dependency Injection 163
  scope 101, 163, 164
controller methods
  Action Event listener, invoking 156, 157
  invoking 151
  parameterized method invocations 151-153
  parameters, passing 154, 155
conversational scope
  about 165
  lifecycle 167
  serialization 167
  timeout 167
conversational scoped beans
  view expired, comparing 227
conversation scope controller
  about 168
  customer journey, revealing 170-172
  data service 175, 176

entity classes 173-175
Entity-Control-Boundary
 design pattern 170
implementation 168-170
converters
 about 136
 example 136-142
core JSF custom tags
 <f:actionListener> 79
 <f:attribute> 79
 <f:convertDateTime> 79
 <f:converter> 80
 <f:convertNumber> 79
 <f:facet> 80
 <f:loadBundle> 80
 <f:metadata> 80
 <f:param> 80
 <f:phaseListener> 80
 <f:selectItem> 80
 <f:selectItems> 80
 <f:setProperty-ActionListener> 80
 <f:subview> 80
 <f:validateDoubleRange> 80
 <f:validateLength> 80
 <f:validateLongRange> 80
 <f:validateRegex> 80
 <f:validateRequired> 80
 <f:validator> 80
 <f:valueChangeListener> 80
 <f:verbatim> 80
 <f:view> 80
 <f:viewParam> 80
 about 79
 URL 79
Create, Retrieve, Update, and
 Delete (CRUD)
 about 62, 63
 contact details form, creating 63-67
creative designer 429
custom tags
 about 77
 binding attribute 82
 core JSF custom tags 79-81
 HTML render kit custom tags 77-79
 id attribute 82
 Immediate attribute 82
 rendered attribute 82

required attribute 82
styleClass attribute 82
stylestyle attribute 82
template composition custom tags 81, 82
valuevalue attribute 82
custom view engine
 writing 372-374

D

data scientist 430, 431
declarative flow 228
deferred expression 46, 47
design consideration
 about 388
 majority client-side templating 388
 majority server-side templating 388
 shared templating 389
design perspective role
 about 428, 429
 content strategist 430
 creative designer 429
 usability experience engineer 429, 430
development perspective role
 about 427
 interface developer engineer 427
 quality assurance tester 428
 software in developer test 428
digital application
 database, populating 245-247
 enhancing 244
 flows, securing 247-252
 page views, securing 247-252
digital development manager 433
digital domain 2
digital e-commerce applications 165
digital Java developer
 requisites 2, 3
digital teams
 about 425, 426
 adaptation 425, 426
 characteristics 434
Document Object Model
 (DOM) 145, 270, 300
Dojo Toolkit
 about 10
 URL 10

dynamic Resource Library Contract
references 256, 257

E

ECMAScript
URL 262
Ember JS
about 10
URL 10
Enterprise Java Bean (EJB) 73
Entity-Control-Boundary design pattern 170
event handling 36
execute and render lifecycle
about 33
Apply Request Values phase 34
Invoke Application phase 35
Process Validation phase 35
Render Response phase 36
Restore View phase 33, 34
Update Model Values phase 35
expression language
about 46
arithmetic expressions 52
deferred expression 46, 47
immediate expression 46, 47
method expressions 51
predefined object instances 50
value expression 47, 48
Expression Language (EL) 38, 228
extended architectures 417, 418
Extensible Mark-up Language (XML) 64

F

Facelets 31
Faces Flows
about 216
builder types 412
considerations 258
definitions 216, 217
FlowCall node, creating 408-410
lifecycle 216, 217
messages, adding 109-111
MethodCall node, creating 408
NavigationCase node, creating 411, 412
programmatic interface 404, 405

ReturnNode, generating 407, 408
SwitchNode, creating 410, 411
terminology 228
ViewNode, defining 406, 407
XML flow definition
description file 229, 230
Faces servlet
about 397
JSF-specific configuration 398
resource paths, reconfiguration 397
Faces servlet, parameters
CONFIG_FILES 398
DEFAULT_SUFFIX 398
DISABLE_FACELET_JSF_
VIEW_HANDLER 398
FACELETS_BUFFER_SIZE 398
FACELETS_LIBRARIES 398
FACELETS_REFRESH_PERIOD 398
FACELETS_SKIP_COMMENT 398
LIFECYCLE_ID 398
PROJECT_STAGE 398
STATE_SAVING_METHOD 398
WEBAPP_CONTRACTS_DIRECTORY 398
WEBAPP_RESOURCES_DIRECTORY 398
Faster Jackson Processing API
URL 341
filter operations 287
flatten operations 288, 289
flow definition tag 230
flow return tag 230
flow scoped beans
lifecycle, capturing 228
for-each operations 286, 287
form
versus class 434, 435
form content
constraining, with Bean validation 111-117
Foundation
URL 65
Freemarker
about 362
URL 362
full stack developer 423
functions, JavaScript 268, 269

G

getting started page view 180, 181
GlassFish 4.1
  about 21
  URL 21
Gradle-GruntJS Plugin
  URL 291
Gradle-Node Plugin
  URL 291
GruntJS
  about 9, 290
  benefits 290
  gruntfile.js file 291, 292
  package.json file 291
  plugins 291-294
  URL 9, 290
GSON
  URL 341

H

Handlebars Java
  compiled-inline template servlet 367, 368
  custom view engine 372-374
  product controller 374-376
  template expressions 368-370
  using 366
  welcome controller 370-372
Handlebars JS
  about 10, 362, 366
  URL 10
Hierarchical model-view-controller
      (HMVC) 30
HTML render kit custom tags
  <h:column> 78
  <h:commandButton> 78
  <h:commandLink> 78
  <h:dataTable> 78
  <h:form> 78
  <h:graphicImage> 78
  <h:inputFile> 78
  <h:inputHidden> 78
  <h:inputSecret> 78
  <h:inputTextarea> 78
  <h:link> 78
  <h:message> 78
  <h:messages> 78

  <h:outputFormat> 78
  <h:outputLabel> 78
  <h:outputLink> 78
  <h:outputText> 78
  <h:panelGrid> 79
  <h:panelGroup> 79
  <h:selectBooleanCheckbox> 79
  <h:selectManyCheckbox> 79
  <h:selectManyListbox> 79
  <h:selectManyMenu> 79
  <h:selectOneListbox> 79
  <h:selectOneMenu> 79
  <h:selectOneRadio> 79
  about 77
  reference link 77
HTML tags 103
HTTP
  about 413
  HTTP request 414
  HTTP response 414, 415
HTTP methods
  DELETE 414
  GET 414
  HEAD 414
  OPTION 414
  POST 414
  PUT 414
  TRACE 414
HTTP POST- REDIRECT-GET
  reference link 387
HTTP Status codes
  about 414
  URL 415

I

immediate expression 46
Implicit Faces Flows
  creating 217, 218
  Facelet views, defining 220-226
  flow scoped bean, defining 219
  implicit navigation 218
individual page controlled locale 402
Information Architecture (IA) 11-13
InfoSecurityComponent 208
initial page view 177-179
interface developer engineer 427

internationalization
 about 399
 application controlled locale 402
 browser configured locale 401
 individual page controlled locale 402
 message bundles 401
 resource bundles 399, 400
Internet Engineering Task Force (IETF)
 URL 346
Invoke Application phase 35
iteratee 287

J

Java
 about 3
 history 3-6
Java Community Process (JCP) 25
Java EE 7
 API 14-16
 architecture 13
 references 441-443
 standard platform components 14-16
Java EE 8
 MVC 356
 reference link 248
Java Enterprise Architectures
 about 415
 container-less systems 419-421
 extended architectures 417, 418
 microservices 421-423
 standard Java EE web architecture 415, 416
Java Persistence API (JPA) 75
Java Persistence Query Language (JPQL) 75
JavaScript
 about 262
 advanced libraries 9-11
 example 7, 8
 functions 268, 269
 growth 7
 module pattern 8
 object constructors, writing 264, 265
 property notations 265, 266
 runtime type information 268
 truth value 267
JavaScript ECMA 6
 URL 262

JavaScript Object Notation (JSON) 266
Java SE 8
 about 4
 reference link 6
Java Server Faces. *See* **JSF**
JavaServer Pages Tag Library (JSTL) 204
Java Specification Request (JSR)
 about 25
 URL 25
Java Transaction API (JTA) 77
jq-lite 315
jQuery
 about 9
 including, in JSF application 270
 ready function callbacks 271, 272
 URL 9, 270
jQuery selectors
 about 272, 273
 animation 275-278
 DOM elements, manipulating 274
jQuery UI
 about 9
 URL 9
JSF
 about 25, 26
 benefits 28, 29
 Composition example 41-44
 content, debugging 158, 159
 example 36-38
 JSF XML namespaces 40, 41
 lifecycle 150, 151
 Model-View-Controller (MVC) 30
 reference link 300
 resources, serving 44, 45
 scopes 101
 web deployment descriptor 39, 40
 XML namespaces 40, 41
JSF 1.0
 history 27
JSF 2.0
 history 27
JSF 2.2
 features 27, 28
 HTML5 friendly markup 391
 pass-through attributes 391-393
 pass-through elements 393, 394

JSF tags
  attributes 109
JSF validation
  conversionMessage attribute 122
  customizing 122-125
  custom validation methods,
     adding 125, 126
  custom validators, defining 127, 128
  for user input 117-120
  groups of properties, validating 130-135
  requiredMessage attribute 122
  validatorMessage attribute 122
JSR 107
  URL 418
JSR 223
  about 362
  URL 362
JSR 356
  URL 346
JSR 369
  URL 413
JSR 371
  URL 355
JVM
  about 4
  references 441-443

L

lambda expression 6
LESS
  about 9
  URL 9
liaison officer 432
list expressions 49

M

majority client-side templating 388
majority server-side templating 388
management perspective role
  about 432
  business analyst 432
  digital development manager 433
  liaison officer 432
  project manager/scrum master 432, 433
map expressions 49
map operations 288

message bundles 401
method binding expression 51
method expressions
  about 51
  parameterized method expressions 51, 52
microservices 421-423
Model-View-Controller (MVC)
  about 9, 25, 355
  controller 30
  design pattern 29, 30
  in JSF 30
  model 30
  view 30
Model-view-presenter (MVP) 30
Model View ViewModel (MVVM) 30, 417
module pattern, JavaScript 8
modules
  defining, with RequireJS 283-285
Mojarra 2.2
  about 27
  URL 27
Mustache
  about 363, 367
  URL 363
MVC, Java EE 8
  about 356
  controllers 357-359
  models 363, 364
  page views 360-363
  redirects 364-366
  response 364-366
  templates 360-363
  view root, reconfiguring 366

N

Nashorn
  about 10
  URL 10
nested flow
  about 228
  example 232-234
  flow beans 238-240
  page views 240-244
  XML flow definition 234-237
New Input Output (NIO) 15
Node.js 291

nodes, Faces Flows
 Flow Call Node 404
 Method Call Node 404
 Navigation Case Node 404
 Return Node 404
 Switch Node 404
 View Node 404
npm 291
null reference pointer
 dealing with 266

O

object constructors, JavaScript
 writing 264, 265
objects
 creating 262, 263
optional start page tag 231
Ozark
 URL 355

P

Page Description Language (PDL) 18
page navigation
 about 53
 conditional navigation 56
 rules 53-55
 static navigation 57
 wildcards 55, 56
page views
 about 176, 177
 address page view 193
 completion page view 197
 confirmation page view 194-196
 contact details page view 181, 182
 getting started page view 180, 181
 initial page view 177-179
 utility classes 198-200
 your rate page view 183, 184
parameterized method expressions 51, 52
parameterized method invocations 151-153
pass-through attributes
 about 391-393
 URL 391
pass-through elements
 about 393, 394
 URL 393

Payara Server
 about 22
 URL 22
Phase Listeners 36
Plain Old Java Object (POJO) 5
predefined object instances
 application 50
 applicationScope 50
 cookie 50
 facesContext 50
 header 50
 headerValues 50
 initParam 51
 param 51
 paramValue 51
 request 51
 requestScope 51
 session 51
 sessionScope 51
 View 51
Prime Faces
 URL 89
Process Validation phase 35
product controller
 block expressions, using 376, 377
 JAX-RS global validation 382-384
 MVC binding result validation 384-387
 retrieve edit operations, using 378-381
 writing 374-376
programmatic Faces flows
 about 403
 view types 403, 404
project manager/scrum master 432, 433
project organization 314, 315
Project Rave 27
property notations, JavaScript 265, 266
Prototype
 about 7
 URL 270

Q

quality assurance tester 428
QuickSort 266

R

Read-Evaluate-Print-Loop (REPL) 4

ready function callbacks, jQuery 271, 272
reduction operations 290
Render Response phase 36
request context path expression 65
request-oriented framework 61
request processing lifecycle
    about 31, 32
    execute and render lifecycle 33
RequireJS
    about 10, 278-280
    application module 282, 283
    configuring 280, 281
    modules, defining with 283-285
    URL 10, 278
resource bundles
    configuring 399, 400
resource identifiers 394, 395
Resource Library Contracts
    about 253, 254, 395, 396
    dynamic Resource Library
        Contract references 256, 257
    static Resource Library
        Contract references 255
RESTful communication, caseworker
        application
    about 337
    case records, creating 340, 341
    case records, retrieving 337-339
    case records, updating 341, 342
    task record, creating 342, 343
    task record, deleting 345
    task record, updating 344
Restore View phase 33, 34
RFC 7540
    URL 413
Rich Faces
    URL 89
roles
    architectural perspective 430
    design perspective 428
    development perspective 427
    management perspective 432
runtime type information, JavaScript 268

S

Sass
    about 9
    URL 9
Script.aculo.us
    about 7
    URL 270
Selenium Web Driver framework
    URL 223
self-generating tag
    used, for composite component 208-211
Server Sent Events (SSE) 299
server-side Java, caseworker application
    about 335
    entity objects 335, 336
    RESTful communication 337
    WebSocket communication 346
server-side validation 108
service delivery
    references 437, 438
shared templating 389
shim 281
single-page applications
    about 300
    array collection 350
    characteristics 300
    design considerations 350
    hierarchical collection 351
Small & Medium Enterprises (SME) 21
software in developer test 428
software quality 433
standard Java EE web architecture
    about 415, 416
    domain layer 415
    integration layer 416
    presentation layer 415
states, caseworker application
    controller code 331, 332
    modifying 330
    task display state, toggling 334
    template view code 332-334
static Resource Library Contract
        references 255
superseded RFC
    URL 413
switch tag 231, 232

T

technical architect 431
template composition custom tags
  <ui:component> 81
  <ui:composition> 81
  <ui:debug> 81
  <ui:decorate> 81
  <ui:define> 81
  <ui:fragment> 81
  <ui:include> 81
  <ui:insert> 81
  <ui:param> 81
  <ui:remove> 81
  <ui:repeat> 81
  about 81
  URL 81
template expressions 368-370
Test Compatibility Kit
  about 21
  URL 21
Thymeleaf
  about 363
  URL 363
Tom EE
  about 22
  URL 22
Tomi Tribe
  URL 22
truth value, JavaScript 267

U

undefined reference pointer
  dealing with 266
UnderscoreJS
  about 10, 285, 286
  filter operations 287
  flatten operations 288, 289
  for-each operations 286, 287
  map operations 288
  reduction operations 290
  URL 285
Undertow
  about 21
  URL 21

Update Model Values phase 35
usability experience engineer 429, 430
user experience 11-13
user input
  validating, with JSF 117-120
user interface
  references 439-441
UserProfile instances 164
utility classes 198-200

V

validation
  about 111
  Bean Validation 111-117
  client-side validation 108
  converters 136-142
  methods 107
  on groups of input field 146, 147
  server-side validation 108
  user input, validating with JSF 117-120
  with Asynchronous JavaScript
    and XML (AJAX) 142-145
value expression
  about 47, 48
  initial term, resolving 50
  list expressions 49
  map expressions 49
Velocity
  about 363
  URL 363
View Declaration Language (VDL) 31
view expired
  comparing, with conversational
    scoped beans 227
  handling 226, 227
  lifecycle of flow scoped beans,
    capturing 228
view page tag 231
views
  controller methods, invoking 151
  handling 151
  JSF content, debugging 158, 159
  page redirection, setting 157, 158

W

web deployment descriptor
  about 402
  using 39, 40
Web Hypertext Application Technology
    Working Group (WHATWG)
  URL 346
WebSocket communication,
    caseworker application
  about 346
  AngularJS client side 347
  server-side WebSocket endpoint 348, 349
welcome controller 370-372
wildcards 55, 56
WildFly 9
  about 21
  URL 21
Wireless Application Protocol (WAP) 26
World Wide Web Consortium (W3C) 18, 142

X

xen-force-angularjs 307
xen-national-force 302
xenonique 8
XenTracker
  Java Server Faces (JSF) example 16-20
XHTML
  with composite custom
      components 201-205
XML flow definition description file
  about 229, 230
  case tag 231, 232
  conditional tag 231, 232
  flow definition tag 230
  flow return tag 230
  optional start page tag 231
  switch tag 231, 232
  view page tag 231

Y

your rate page view
  about 183, 184
  AJAX, using for partial update 185
  components, binding 185-189
  HTML5 friendly support 184, 185
  updating, with AJAX partial
      updates 189-192

[PACKT] PUBLISHING enterprise
professional expertise distilled

Thank you for buying
Digital Java EE 7 Web
Application Development

About Packt Publishing

Packt, pronounced 'packed', published its first book, *Mastering phpMyAdmin for Effective MySQL Management*, in April 2004, and subsequently continued to specialize in publishing highly focused books on specific technologies and solutions.

Our books and publications share the experiences of your fellow IT professionals in adapting and customizing today's systems, applications, and frameworks. Our solution-based books give you the knowledge and power to customize the software and technologies you're using to get the job done. Packt books are more specific and less general than the IT books you have seen in the past. Our unique business model allows us to bring you more focused information, giving you more of what you need to know, and less of what you don't.

Packt is a modern yet unique publishing company that focuses on producing quality, cutting-edge books for communities of developers, administrators, and newbies alike. For more information, please visit our website at www.packtpub.com.

About Packt Enterprise

In 2010, Packt launched two new brands, Packt Enterprise and Packt Open Source, in order to continue its focus on specialization. This book is part of the Packt Enterprise brand, home to books published on enterprise software – software created by major vendors, including (but not limited to) IBM, Microsoft, and Oracle, often for use in other corporations. Its titles will offer information relevant to a range of users of this software, including administrators, developers, architects, and end users.

Writing for Packt

We welcome all inquiries from people who are interested in authoring. Book proposals should be sent to author@packtpub.com. If your book idea is still at an early stage and you would like to discuss it first before writing a formal book proposal, then please contact us; one of our commissioning editors will get in touch with you.

We're not just looking for published authors; if you have strong technical skills but no writing experience, our experienced editors can help you develop a writing career, or simply get some additional reward for your expertise.

[PACKT] enterprise
professional expertise distilled

PUBLISHING

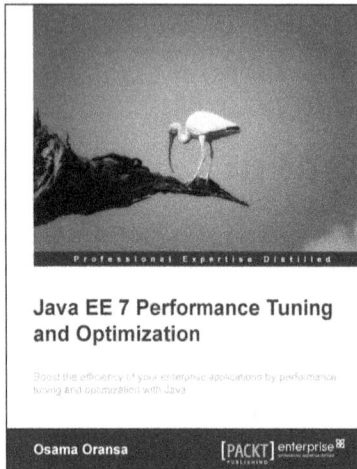

Java EE 7 Performance Tuning and Optimization

ISBN: 978-1-78217-642-8   Paperback: 478 pages

Boost the efficiency of your enterprise applications by performance tuning and optimization with Java

1. Learn to plan a performance investigation in enterprise applications.

2. Build a performance troubleshooting strategy.

3. Design and implement high performing Java enterprise applications.

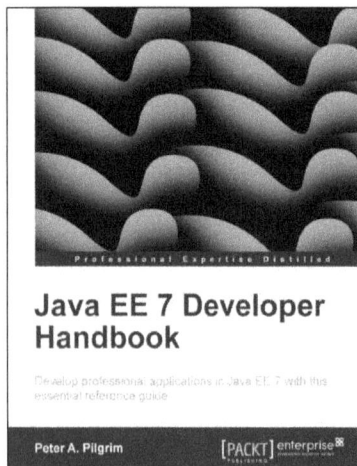

Java EE 7 Performance Tuning and Optimization

Boost the efficiency of your enterprise applications by performance tuning and optimization with Java

Osama Oransa   [PACKT] enterprise
PUBLISHING

Java EE 7 Developer Handbook

ISBN: 978-1-84968-794-2   Paperback: 634 pages

Develop professional applications in Java EE 7 with this essential reference guide

1. Learn about local and remote service endpoints, containers, architecture, synchronous and asynchronous invocations, and remote communications in a concise reference.

2. Understand the architecture of the Java EE platform and then apply the new Java EE 7 enhancements to benefit your own business-critical applications.

3. Learn about integration test development on Java EE with the Arquillian framework and the Gradle build system.

Java EE 7 Developer Handbook

Develop professional applications in Java EE 7 with this essential reference guide

Peter A. Pilgrim   [PACKT] enterprise
PUBLISHING

Please check **www.PacktPub.com** for information on our titles

[PACKT] enterprise ❀
PUBLISHING professional expertise distilled

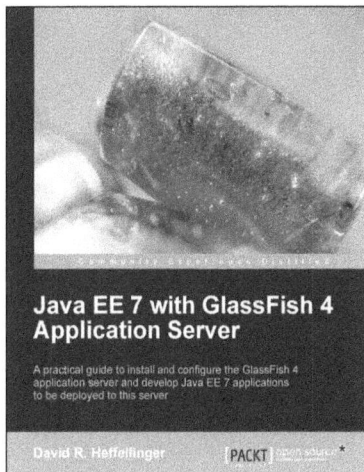

Java EE 7 with GlassFish 4 Application Server

ISBN: 978-1-78217-688-6   Paperback: 348 pages

A practical guide to install and configure the GlassFish 4 application server and develop Java EE 7 applications to be deployed to this server

1. Install and configure GlassFish 4.

2. Covers all major Java EE 7 APIs and includes new additions such as JSON Processing.

3. Packed with clear, step-by-step instructions, practical examples, and straightforward explanations.

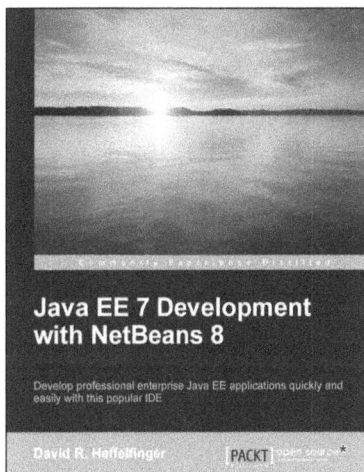

Java EE 7 Development with NetBeans 8

ISBN: 978-1-78398-352-0   Paperback: 364 pages

Develop professional enterprise Java EE applications quickly and easily with this popular IDE

1. Use the features of the popular NetBeans IDE to accelerate your development of Java EE applications.

2. Covers the latest versions of the major Java EE APIs such as JSF 2.2, EJB 3.2, JPA 2.1, CDI 1.1, and JAX-RS 2.0.

3. Walks you through the development of applications utilizing popular JSF component libraries such as PrimeFaces, RichFaces, and ICEfaces.

Please check **www.PacktPub.com** for information on our titles

www.ingramcontent.com/pod-product-compliance
Lightning Source LLC
Chambersburg PA
CBHW080125220326
41598CB00032B/4958